Next-Generation Gamemaking

A Beginner's Guide to GameMaker

Robert Ciesla

apress®

Next-Generation Gamemaking: A Beginner's Guide to GameMaker

Robert Ciesla

Helsinki, Finland

ISBN-13 (pbk): 979-8-8688-1777-9   ISBN-13 (electronic): 979-8-8688-1778-6
https://doi.org/10.1007/979-8-8688-1778-6

Copyright © 2025 by Robert Ciesla

This work is subject to copyright. All rights are reserved by the Publisher, whether the whole or part of the material is concerned, specifically the rights of translation, reprinting, reuse of illustrations, recitation, broadcasting, reproduction on microfilms or in any other physical way, and transmission or information storage and retrieval, electronic adaptation, computer software, or by similar or dissimilar methodology now known or hereafter developed.

Trademarked names, logos, and images may appear in this book. Rather than use a trademark symbol with every occurrence of a trademarked name, logo, or image we use the names, logos, and images only in an editorial fashion and to the benefit of the trademark owner, with no intention of infringement of the trademark.

The use in this publication of trade names, trademarks, service marks, and similar terms, even if they are not identified as such, is not to be taken as an expression of opinion as to whether or not they are subject to proprietary rights.

While the advice and information in this book are believed to be true and accurate at the date of publication, neither the authors nor the editors nor the publisher can accept any legal responsibility for any errors or omissions that may be made. The publisher makes no warranty, express or implied, with respect to the material contained herein.

> Managing Director, Apress Media LLC: Welmoed Spahr
> Acquisitions Editor: Spandana Chatterjee
> Editorial Project Manager: Gryffin Winkler

Cover image designed by photoroyalty on freepik.com

Distributed to the book trade worldwide by Springer Science+Business Media New York, 1 New York Plaza, New York, NY 10004. Phone 1-800-SPRINGER, fax (201) 348-4505, e-mail orders-ny@springer-sbm.com, or visit www.springeronline.com. Apress Media, LLC is a Delaware LLC and the sole member (owner) is Springer Science + Business Media Finance Inc (SSBM Finance Inc). SSBM Finance Inc is a **Delaware** corporation.

For information on translations, please e-mail booktranslations@springernature.com; for reprint, paperback, or audio rights, please e-mail bookpermissions@springernature.com.

Apress titles may be purchased in bulk for academic, corporate, or promotional use. eBook versions and licenses are also available for most titles. For more information, reference our Print and eBook Bulk Sales web page at http://www.apress.com/bulk-sales.

Any source code or other supplementary material referenced by the author in this book is available to readers on GitHub. For more detailed information, please visit https://www.apress.com/gp/services/source-code.

If disposing of this product, please recycle the paper

This book is dedicated to Dr. Markus Hendrik "Mark" Overmars (b. 1958), the originator of a wonderful piece of software called GameMaker.

Table of Contents

About the Author ....**xvii**

About the Technical Reviewer ....**xix**

Acknowledgments ....**xxi**

Introduction ....**xxiii**

Chapter 1: A Quarter Century of GameMaker 1

    A Concise History of GameMaker 1

    Why Make Games Anyway? 2

    GameMaker Platforms and Licenses 3

    Getting GameMaker 4

    GameMaker System Requirements 5

    Setting Up GameMaker for Linux 5

    Creating a New Project 6

    The GameMaker Integrated Development Environment (IDE) 8

    Run, Stop, and Clean 9

    GML Visual/Drag-and-Drop vs. GML 10

    Feather, at Your Service 11

    GameMaker Asset Types 11

    On the Gameloop, Frames, and Step 12

    GameMaker's Objects, Instances, and Events 13

    Basic Object Parameters 15

    On Rooms and Layers 18

    Adding Assets with Right-Click 20

    A Few Words on Optimization 21

TABLE OF CONTENTS

    Compiled vs. Interpreted Code 21

    In Closing 24

Chapter 2: Game Logic with GML 27

    On the Ecstasy of Variables 27

    Variable Operators 29

    Comparison and Conditional Operators 30

    Not So Fast! Variable Naming Rules 31

    The Wonders of Macros 32

    Commenting Code 32

    Enumeration 32

    On the Necessity of Loops 33

    While 33

    Repeat 34

    Do/Until 35

    For 35

    Taking a Break 36

    The Switch Case 38

    Variable Scope 40

    On Inheritance 41

    On Object-Oriented Programming (OOP) 42

    Arrays: For Your Inventories and Mazes 44

    One-Dimensional Arrays (1D) 44

    Push and Pop: Adding and Removing Items Quickly 45

    Multidimensional Arrays 46

    Going 3D with Arrays 47

    Unleashing the Awesome Power of GML Data Structures 48

    DS Grids 48

    Changing Regions Quickly 50

    DS Lists: The Mightier Arrays 51

    DS Maps—and a Primer on JSON 52

A Few Words on JSON 53
DS Stacks 56
DS Queues 57
DS Priority Queues 59
Structs 61
Struct Constructor Methods 62
Structs and Inheritance 63
In Closing 66

Chapter 3: Core GameMaker Visual Functions 67

Importing Visuals into GameMaker 68
Drawing with the Image Editor 69
On Image Formats 71
Raster vs. Vector Images 72
Texture Pages and Groups 72
The Dreaded Texture Swap 74
Surfaces 75
Behold, the Application Surface 76
Drawing Depth 76
Views and Cameras 77
On Alpha 78
GameMaker Blend Modes 78
Going Primitive: Drawing Lines and Rectangles 79
Frenzy with Circular Shapes 82
GML Ellipses—with Alarms 84
Triangles 86
Primitives and Vertex Formats 87
Fonts in GameMaker 89
Aligning Your Text 90
Font Settings 92
On SDF 92

vii

TABLE OF CONTENTS

GameMaker Scripts 94
The Return Keyword and Gauging Distances 95
Documentation Inside Scripts 97
More on Undefined 98
More on "Not a Number" (NaN) 99
Infinity and GML 100
On Sprites and Collision Masks 101
Draw_Sprite 102
Common Sprite Attributes 102
On Texture Filtering 103
A Few Words on GML Visual/Drag-and-Drop 103
PNOG: A Drag-and-Drop (DnD) Game Prototype 105
Space Heck: Our First GML Game Prototype 109
Events for obj_Player 111
obj_Bullet 113
obj_Controller 113
obj_Enemy 115
obj_Starfield 116
On the GameMaker Drawing Pipeline 117
In Closing 119

Chapter 4: Audio, More on Keyboards, and Particles 121
2D vs 3D Audio in GameMaker 122
Importing Audio into Your Projects 122
Audio Target Options 124
Volume 125
Sound Mixer 125
Audio Groups 126
OGG Conversion 126
Basic GML Audio Properties 126
Audio_play_sound 127

TABLE OF CONTENTS

The Whole Spiel on audio_play_sound 128

Sound Instances 129

Pausing Audio 129

Master Volume and Audio Configuration 130

Changing Pitch 131

On the Keyboard Buffer 132

More on Game Input: keyboard_check and Friends 132

Catching Letters with Ord 133

Typing in Names in GML 134

Remapping Keys in GML 134

Clearing Keyboard Strokes 135

Stunning Wizardry with Particles 136

Simple Particle Effects 137

Custom Particles in GameMaker 138

Going Beyond the Basic Shapes 142

Creating Fire with Custom Particles 143

Creating New Particles 145

Emitters and Their Regions 145

On-Demand Particles: part_emitter_burst 146

Particles from the Create Event: part_emitter_stream 147

Quick and Easy Particles: part_particles_create 148

Collisions with Particles 148

Particle Collision Demo 149

obj_Controller 149

obj_Catcher 150

obj_Ufo 151

Adding Particles into Space Heck (Version 0.2) 152

obj_Controller 152

obj_Enemy 154

obj_Player 154

TABLE OF CONTENTS

obj_Bullet 155
Particle Memory Management 155
Clearing On-Screen Particles 157
Counting Particles 157
Stopping and Hiding Particles 158
IDE Particle Systems 159
Particles Recap 160
In Closing 162

Chapter 5: Cameras, Layers, and Tilesets 163
Views in the IDE 164
Setting Up a Camera in GML 166
Layers 167
Dynamic Layers in GML 169
Layer Properties in GML 170
Zooming In and Out 171
Inside obj_Zoomcam 172
Effect Layers 174
Effect Layers in GML 175
Single-Layer Mode 176
Retrieving Effects Parameters 176
Clearing Effects 177
Tilesets and Tile Layers 177
Tile Animation 178
Auto-tiling in GameMaker 179
Tileset Management in GML 180
Tilesets in Action 181
Tilesets and Collisions with Invisible Objects 182
Tilesets and Collisions with tilemap_get_at_pixel 182
Tilemap Collisions Demonstration Project 183
Working with Instance IDs 184

More on happy_tile_collision 186

A Peek Inside obj_UAP 186

Changing the Mouse Cursor 187

Introducing Tank Merriment Version 0.1 187

Inside Tank Merriment 189

The Tank for Player One: obj_Player1 190

Duplicating Objects: The Tank for Player Two 193

Pausing a Game with GML 193

Slowing Down Tanks 194

Collision Masks and GML Collisions 194

lengthdir_x and lengthdir_y 197

On Angles: Degrees and Radians 198

Solid Objects and Collisions 199

Robots in a Maze 199

Spawning Robots 200

Unleashing Bonus Items 201

Particle Fences 201

Views and Cameras in Tank Merriment 202

Layers in Tank Merriment 203

The Bottom Line on Cameras, Layers, and Tilesets 204

In Closing 204

Chapter 6: Spatial Audio, Motion Planning, and Paths 207

Setting Up a 3D Audio System 207

Demonstrating Dynamic 3D Audio 209

A Primer on Motion Planning and Pathfinding 212

Simple Motion Planning in GML 213

The Beauty of Paths 215

Dynamic Paths 216

On path_add_point and path_set_kind 217

Orbiter Paths: Fun with IDE-Created Paths 218

TABLE OF CONTENTS

More on Dynamic Paths in GML 220
obj_Arrow in GML Paths 222
Path Functions at a Glance 222
An Introduction to A-Star 223
Wobbly Legs: A Demonstration of A-Star 224
obj_Controller 225
obj_Fiend 227
Drawing Grids and Paths 229
In Closing 230

Chapter 7: Physics in GameMaker 231

On Box2D and Rigid-Body Physics 231
On Newton's Laws of Motion 232
Object Physics Settings 233
Object Physics Settings 235
The Fundamental Forces in GameMaker Physics 236
A Simple Physics Demonstration 238
Physics Properties in GML 240
Happy Physics: A Demonstration in Three Rooms 241
Compromised Soccer with Ragdolls 245
Wobbly Pyramids with Particle Groups 247
Simple Fixtures: A Demonstration 250
Musings on Distance Joints 252
Reflecting on Rope Joints 253
Meditations on Weld Joints 254
Ruminations on Wheel Joints 256
Prismatic Joints 258
Physics Space Combat: Frolicking with Galactic Worms 260
On Targeting 261
Spitting Bullets Using a Custom Script 261
Moving Ships in Space 263

On Selection Rectangles 264

More Joints: Meet Gear and Pulley 265

Gear and Pulley Joints: A Demonstration 265

Changing Mass and Inertia During the Gameloop 268

Adjusting Physics Precision 269

Good Practices in Physics-Based Projects 269

On Collision Categories and Parenting in Physics 270

Collision Groups vs. Collision Categories 271

Ad Hoc Physics Objects 272

Fixture Manipulation 274

Mixing Regular and Physics-Based Objects 275

In Closing 275

Chapter 8: Sequences, Audio Effects, and Gamepads 277

A Primer on Sequences 277

Making a Very Simple Sequence 279

Broadcast Messages 280

Simple Sequences: A Demonstration with Penguins 281

More on Persistent Objects 284

Menu Moments: A Demonstration 285

Real-Time Audio Effects 287

Audio Effects: A Presentation 289

AudioEffectType.Reverb1 290

AudioEffectType.Delay 291

AudioEffectType.LPF2 291

AudioEffectType.HPF2 291

AudioEffectType.Bitcrusher 292

AudioEffectType.Tremolo 292

AudioEffectType.PeakEQ 293

Mixing Digital Audio 293

On Digital Dynamics and Compressors 295

TABLE OF CONTENTS

AudioEffectType.Compressor 296
Gamepads in GameMaker 298
The Three Pillars of GameMaker Gamepads 298
Twin Stick Fun with Gamepads 299
Detecting Gamepads in Async System 301
On Analog Input and Vibration 302
GML for Gamepads 303
Pausing Games with Select 305
Retrieving a GUID and Controller Description 305
Implementing Local Co-Op with Gamepads 306
In Closing 310

Chapter 9: Debugging and Sharing Your Game 313

Keeping It Clean 314
The Opera GX Browser (GX.games) 314
Building for Windows 316
Setting Up Visual Studio for Windows and YYC 317
Building for Linux 318
Building for macOS 320
Back to Mac 322
Building for iOS (iPhone and iPad) 322
Troubleshooting Undetected Devices 323
Building for Browsers (HTML5) 324
Building for Android 327
Connecting an Android Phone to Windows 330
Connecting an Android Phone to macOS 331
Wrapping Up Android Shenanigans 331
Deploying for PS4, PS5, and Nintendo Switch 332
Deploying for Xbox One and Series X/S 334
A Primer on Debugging in GameMaker 334
GameMaker Debugger Basics 341

TABLE OF CONTENTS

Keeping an Eye on RAM and FPS 343

Watching Your Variables 343

Breakpoints 344

Implementing Touch-Screen Controls 344

In Closing 347

Chapter 10: Assorted Superior Techniques 349

Platformer Prototype 349

obj_Player 351

The Step Event of obj_Player 351

On instance_place 355

Making Levels for Platformers 355

GameMaker Blend Modes 356

Using Blend Modes in GML 357

Wacky Blend Modes 358

Two More Fascinating Blend Modes 359

Optimizing Blend Modes 361

Surface Tomfoolery 361

obj_SurfaceController 363

Drawing Surfaces 365

Tiled Backgrounds with Surfaces 366

Secrets of the Application Surface 367

More on GameMaker's Drawing Pipeline 368

The Application Surface and GML 369

The Application Surface and Your GUI 369

Resizing Your Surfaces 370

Taking Screenshots with Surfaces 370

Surfaces Summarized 371

On User Events 372

Step Begin vs. Step vs. End Step 373

Outside View and Intersect View 373

xv

TABLE OF CONTENTS

Animation Events 374

Path Ended 375

Saving and Loading Settings 375

On Vector Graphics in GameMaker 381

Flash and SWF in GameMaker 383

Checkpoints with Buffers 384

Free Audiovisual Resources for Your Games 386

Importing Sprite Sheets 387

More on Texture Group Settings 389

Default vs. Dynamic Texture Groups 392

Basic Video Playback in GameMaker 394

On AI Assets 395

In Closing 399

Making Games in a Putamen Nucis 400

Afterword 402

Index 405

About the Author

 **Robert Ciesla** is an author from Helsinki, Finland. He has a BA in Journalism, an MA in Intercultural Encounters, and a keen interest for writing urban fiction and cinematography. Robert is the author of seven nonfiction books. His official website is www.robertciesla.com.

About the Technical Reviewer

Simon Jackson is a longtime software engineer and architect with many years of game development experience, as well as an author of several game development titles. He loves to both create game projects as well as lend a hand to help educate others, whether it's via a blog, vlog, user group, or major speaking event.

His primary focus at the moment is with the Reality Toolkit project, which is aimed at building a cross-platform Mixed Reality framework to enable both VR and AR developers to build efficient solutions in Unity and then build/distribute them to as many platforms as possible. He is also a board member of the MonoGame foundation, aiming to secure and promote open source game development for all developers.

Acknowledgments

Thank you to the Association of Finnish Nonfiction Writers for their support in the production of this book.

Introduction

Playing games can be an exciting experience for many people. Making them is several orders of magnitude more so. This book will focus on one of the finest tools available for indie developers: the legendary *GameMaker*. Even teams of one can learn to create competitive products with this software, and *Next-Generation Gamemaking* is all about empowering them. This book does not feature every single function supported by GameMaker nor does it shed light on the rather infrequent use of the software for 3D games. The focus here is on the basic building blocks for making simple 2D games. This, I feel, is the best approach for any beginner getting to grips with GameMaker. A game does not have to be complicated or manifest in 3D to be enjoyable (think *Tetris*, *Flappy Bird*, or *Plants vs. Zombies*).

This book is intended to be read while simultaneously examining the provided projects for each chapter, found from the following link:

- **https://github.com/Apress/Next-Generation-Gamemaking**

The first chapter of this book is an introduction to GameMaker, featuring a brief history of the software, an overview of its *integrated development environment (IDE)*, and some of its workflow basics. Chapter 2 focuses on *GameMaker Language (GML)*, a highly flexible scripting language providing the software with an unparalleled set of audiovisual functions for 2D games. We'll learn all about variables, loops, and data structures found in this powerful language fine-tuned for game development.

The third chapter of this book will have us explore GameMaker's basic visual functions. We'll be drawing exciting lines and fantastic rectangles—all the while enjoying succulent sprites (i.e., pixel art). Chapter 4 is a close look at some more visual delicacy in the form of particles, a must-have type of eye candy in modern games. Chapter 5 tells the important tale of camerawork in GameMaker and introduces a two-player game prototype. At that point, reading the book, you will hopefully have an understanding of how to put GML to basic use.

But the fun doesn't stop there. In Chapter 6, we have a trio of fascinating topics, namely, spatial audio, motion planning, and paths. Chapter 7 focuses on GameMaker's implementation of the Box2D physics library again with numerous example projects

INTRODUCTION

to help demonstrate its abilities. Chapter 8 takes a gander at topics such as sequences and real-time audio effects with a strong emphasis on the latter, sometimes overlooked technique. We also learn how to implement basic gamepad support. Chapter 9 is about the deployment process and how to deliver your games for the numerous platforms supported by GameMaker. The book ends with Chapter 10, a thorough look at techniques like surfaces and blend modes. The last chapter also features a prototype of a platformer game.

A generation is typically defined as spanning between 20 and 30 years. In November of 2024, GameMaker turned 25 years. The software is still here, in use by zoomers, some boomers, and probably even a few jaded representatives of generation X. Many individuals have doubtless found GameMaker a sheer joy to use, and many more will probably join their ranks in the future.

This book is for those who have been curious about GameMaker for a while without taking the plunge and actually installing it. It is intended to give the reader insight on this software enough for them to eventually create games shaped by their own vision. Step by step, little by little, any motivated individual can make the transition from gamer to developer. *Next-Generation Gamemaking* will hopefully aid in this process.

Sincerely,
—Robert

CHAPTER 1

A Quarter Century of GameMaker

This chapter is an introduction to the spellbinding world of GameMaker. We'll cover some background of the software as well as some of its main features. Also, we'll learn how to acquire and set up GameMaker on your personal battlestation.

In November of 1999, a Dutch computer scientist *Dr. Markus Hendrik "Mark" Overmars (b. 1958)* set a bit of a digital revolution in action. It was during those times of wretched boybands and the unfounded Y2K panic when the first ever edition of the GameMaker software was released. Twenty-five years later, this software is still in active development, having been used to produce quite a few commercially viable titles.

GameMaker combines ease of use with some powerful technologies. The system deploys to most popular gaming platforms, including Windows, PlayStation 5, and Nintendo Switch. Its programming language, *GameMaker Language (GML)*, is powerful, flexible, and elegant. Some popular titles made with GameMaker include *Undertale, Hotline Miami, Spelunky,* and *Gunpoint.* Despite some serious competition, it's rather obvious GameMaker is a solid contender for the ultimate 2D games making software.

A Concise History of GameMaker

The first ever version of GameMaker from 1999 was actually a quaint piece of software called *Animo.* This was primarily intended as an animation tool, but it did offer some scripting capabilities for simple gamemaking. Animo was rebranded as GameMaker at the turn of the millennium. Several versions of GameMaker were released free of charge until version 5.1 in 2003. After this, Dr. Overmars began offering both free (or "Lite") and paid (or "Pro") versions of the software, the latter having a better feature set. Version 6.0 from 2004 introduced rudimentary support for 3D games and improved game physics.

CHAPTER 1   A QUARTER CENTURY OF GAMEMAKER

In 2007, Dr. Overmars partnered with *YoYo Games*. This British company took over the development of the product soon after with Dr. Overmars acting as director. GameMaker 7.0 was released in 2007, bringing with it ornate particle effects and support for custom extensions (in the form of dynamic-link libraries, i.e., DLLs). In 2009, the first version of GameMaker for macOS, based on version 7, saw daylight for some fanfare.

The first GameMaker to introduce limited exporting to the HTML5 platform turned out to be version 8.0 from 2009. This iteration also featured an upgraded script editor and object collisions. This version was a big step from the previous one, but it suffered from a number of performance issues and bugs. Then in 2011, the seminal GameMaker 8.1 was released to great acclaim. New features included the addition of layer mechanics in the room editor, bug fixes, advanced data structures, enhanced HTML5 exports, and better file handling. Sufficiently quirky hobbyists might still enjoy working with version 8.1, thanks to its decent feature set for basic Windows-based 2D game development.

The year 2012 saw the release of *GameMaker: Studio,* which provided better overall features and support for more export platforms. Its user interface, unfortunately, was still largely based on the older versions of the software. GameMaker was acquired by Playtech, an online gambling software company, together with YoYo Games in 2015.

In 2017, the first version of *GameMaker: Studio 2* was made public. Its biggest change was in a completely redesigned and far more modern user interface. In 2020, version 2.3 of GameMaker: Studio 2 came out. This version introduced Sequences, which represent a dynamic animation system great for making cut scenes (think good old Adobe Flash).

In early 2021, *Opera*, a Norwegian technology company, purchased YoYo Games. As a result, their gamer-oriented web browser *Opera GX* became affiliated with GameMaker. All titles made with the software could then be deployed on Opera's *GX.games* online gaming platform as browser games. In 2022, the software title was officially shortened to *GameMaker*.

Why Make Games Anyway?

Playing games of all types can be a riveting form of entertainment. But creating them is a far more satisfying activity. The global video game industry is expected to reach a revenue of $257 billion by 2028.[1] While a financial incentive is certainly there (mostly in

---

[1] https://www.forbesmiddleeast.com/innovation/consumer-tech/global-revenue-from-video-games-forecast-to-reach-%24257b-by-2028

the case of larger game studios), dilettantes and hobbyists of all ages can draw a whole assortment of skills from the art of gamemaking. Programming is a great way to improve your critical thinking skills, problem-solving, and mental fortitude. The audiovisual aspects of gamemaking are naturally great for reaching new levels of artistic self-expression, if the coder so desires. Also, while mathematics is sometimes an overlooked aspect in 2D gamemaking, it's still there, in particular when it comes to algebra.

GameMaker Platforms and Licenses

As of 2025, GameMaker supports deployment for 14 software ecosystems (see Table 1-1).

Table 1-1. *The four categories of software ecosystems supported in GameMaker*

Desktop	Mobile	Consoles	Web
Microsoft Windows	Android	PlayStation 4	HTML5
macOS	Android TV	PlayStation 5	
Linux	Amazon Fire	Nintendo Switch	
	tvOS	Xbox One	
	iOS	Xbox Series X and S	

The *Universal Windows Platform (UWP)* is a framework created by Microsoft which lets developers create a single application that can run in a variety of devices within the Windows ecosystem (e.g., desktop PCs, Xbox consoles, tablets, smart-phones, and mixed-reality headsets). Although once supported, UWP is being phased out of GameMaker.

Do notice the difference between deployment and development. In 2025, development on GameMaker is only possible on a computer running Windows, macOS, or Linux.

Now, there are three tiers of GameMaker licenses (see Table 1-2).

Table 1-2. *The three tiers of GameMaker licenses*

License	Free	Professional	Enterprise
Cost	None	97.50 EUR (one-time purchase)	67.99 EUR monthly or 679.99 EUR yearly
Type	Noncommercial	Commercial	Commercial
GX.games	Supported	Supported	Supported
Desktop	Supported	Supported	Supported
Web	Supported	Supported	Supported
Mobile	Supported	Supported	Supported
Consoles			Supported
Source code access			Supported

Source code access refers to an advanced feature where developers gain access to some of the GameMaker code itself; this is generally not necessary for smaller projects. The free edition of the software is perfectly fine for learning purposes; it does not impose any strict restrictions.

Getting GameMaker

The best way to get started with GameMaker is simply to navigate to the official YoYo Games website and visit the page with the download links (`https://gamemaker.io/en/download`). Next, choose the right type of installer for your current operating system (i.e., Windows, macOS, or Linux). Execute the installer and follow the instructions it presents. You can also download GameMaker from Valve Software's Steam store[2] (as of 2025, Steam only offers the software for Windows and macOS).

---

[2] `https://store.steampowered.com/app/1670460/GameMaker`

GameMaker System Requirements

GameMaker has the following minimum system requirements on the product's Steam store page (see Table 1-3).

Table 1-3. GameMaker minimum system requirements

Operating system	Windows	macOS
OS version	Windows 7	macOS 10.14 Mojave
CPU	Dual-core	Dual-core
RAM (memory)	2 GB	2 GB
Graphics	OpenGL 4-compliant GPU	OpenGL 4-compliant GPU
DirectX	Version 11	n/a
Hard drive space	3 GB	3 GB

While a computer with the above system specs may indeed be able to run GameMaker, it is recommended you have at least 8 GB of RAM at your disposal for a much more snappy experience.

Setting Up GameMaker for Linux

Getting GameMaker running in Linux requires both Ubuntu (version 24 and up) and a rather Herculean setup process. Begin the process by installing Steam. Navigate to Terminal and input *sudo snap install steam*. Press enter. This should start the installation process for Steam.

Now, open Terminal and enter *sudo apt-get update* to refresh the repository records. Next we need to install all of the software packages found in Table 1-4.

Table 1-4. The software packages required by the Linux version of GameMaker

libssl-dev	build-essential	openssh-server	clang
libxrandr-dev	libxxf86vm-dev	libopenal-dev	libgl1-mesa-dev
zlib1g-dev	libglu1-mesa-dev	libcurl4-openssl-dev	ffmpeg
libfuse2	curl	nproc	pulseaudio

You may enter *sudo apt-get install* followed by an individual package name (e.g., ffmpeg) for each software package you may be missing. You can also install all of these essential packages using a single command by entering the following into Terminal and pressing enter:

sudo apt-get install build-essential openssh-server clang libxrandr-dev libxxf86vm-dev libopenal-dev libgl1-mesa-dev zlib1g-dev libglu1-mesa-dev libcurl4-openssl-dev ffmpeg libfuse2 curl nproc pulseaudio

We still need to install a few more components.

Steam runtime libraries: First, type *sudo mkdir /opt/steam-runtime* in Terminal and press enter.

Next enter the following into Terminal and press enter:

curl `https://repo.steampowered.com/steamrt-images-scout/snapshots/latest-steam-client-general-availability/com.valvesoftware.SteamRuntime.Sdk-amd64,i386-scout-sysroot.tar.gz`

Linux deploy: You'll need to run two separate commands to download and install this software package, respectively. Type each command into the Terminal and press enter.

To download: wget `https://github.com/linuxdeploy/linuxdeploy/releases/download/continuous/linuxdeploy-x86_64.AppImage`

To install: *sudo install -m 0755 linuxdeploy-x86_64.AppImage /usr/local/bin/linuxdeploy*

AppImage build tools: AppImage is a format for binary software distribution. We need it for the Steam runtime libraries.

To download: wget `https://github.com/AppImage/AppImageKit/releases/download/continuous/appimagetool-x86_64.AppImage`

To install: *sudo install -m 0755 appimagetool-x86_64.AppImage /usr/local/bin/appimagetool*

Creating a New Project

Let us now go through the simple procedure of creating a brand-new project in GameMaker. After firing up the software, you'll notice three icons labeled *New, Open,* and *Import.* To start working on a blank project, please select New. To resume work on a previously created project, you would click Open and navigate to the correct file

CHAPTER 1   A QUARTER CENTURY OF GAMEMAKER

on your device's folder system. In case you have projects made with an older version of GameMaker (i.e., version 1.4), you can bring them over to a current version of the software by choosing Import.

You also get to select between a few game templates as starting points or a completely blank project. Also on offer are a Live Wallpaper and a Game Strip which are apps intended to run on the Opera GX browser (see Figure 1-1).

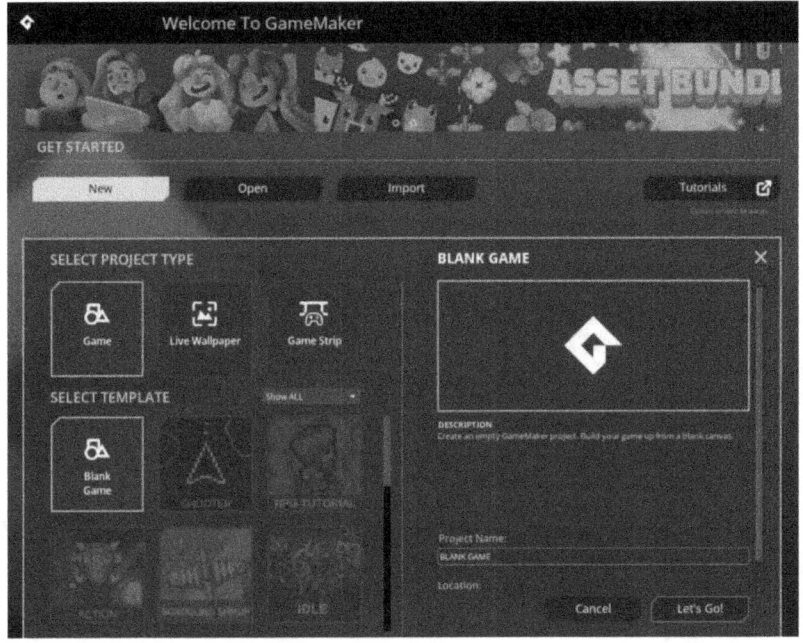

Figure 1-1. *The GameMaker starting screen*

After clicking *Blank Game,* you can enter a name for your project. Finally, a button titled *Let's Go!* takes you to the main GameMaker project view for your brand-new game.

You will be asked whether you want to make a project in GML Code or GML Visual (i.e., Drag-and-Drop) after adding events in your new blank project.

CHAPTER 1   A QUARTER CENTURY OF GAMEMAKER

The GameMaker Integrated Development Environment (IDE)

One of GameMaker's strengths is in its robust IDE, the primary interface where developers create and manage their games using the engine. It's with this tool we create our maps, levels, and objects and do our coding in. Audiovisual assets made with external software can be brought in easily, although a basic graphics editor is also built into the IDE. The asset browser in GameMaker is quite intuitive, and you can organize your assets with it effortlessly.

The GameMaker IDE is divided into the following sections:

- **Workspace:** This is the main area where you design and code your game. It uses a highly flexible tab-based approach. Opened resources (e.g., objects, sprites, and rooms) appear as draggable panels. You can also pan and zoom freely on the workspace at your leisure.

- **Asset browser:** Shows all the assets (sprites, objects, sounds, etc.) in your project and lets you freely organize them into groups (e.g., level 1 foes, level 2 obstacles, etc.) To open an asset for editing, just double left click on it.

- **Toolbar, a.k.a. run/stop/clean:** There are quick access buttons for executing, stopping, cleaning the asset cache, and debugging your game. These probably represent the most commonly used parts of the GameMaker IDE's toolbar.

- **Code editor:** A robust text editor with which you write GML. Becomes active when accessing an object's events (in GML Code mode only, not in GML Visual) or writing external script/function files.

- **Room editor:** This is where you create your game's levels (i.e., rooms) and add instances of objects such as foes, walls, and bonus items into different layers. You can do this simply by dragging objects from the asset browser into the room view. You also set several properties in the room editor such as room size and physics settings. An object inspector element sits beneath the layer view.

While the available preferences in the IDE are rather numerous and thus perhaps daunting at first, the default settings work perfectly for many projects.

See Figure 1-2 for a view of the GameMaker IDE.

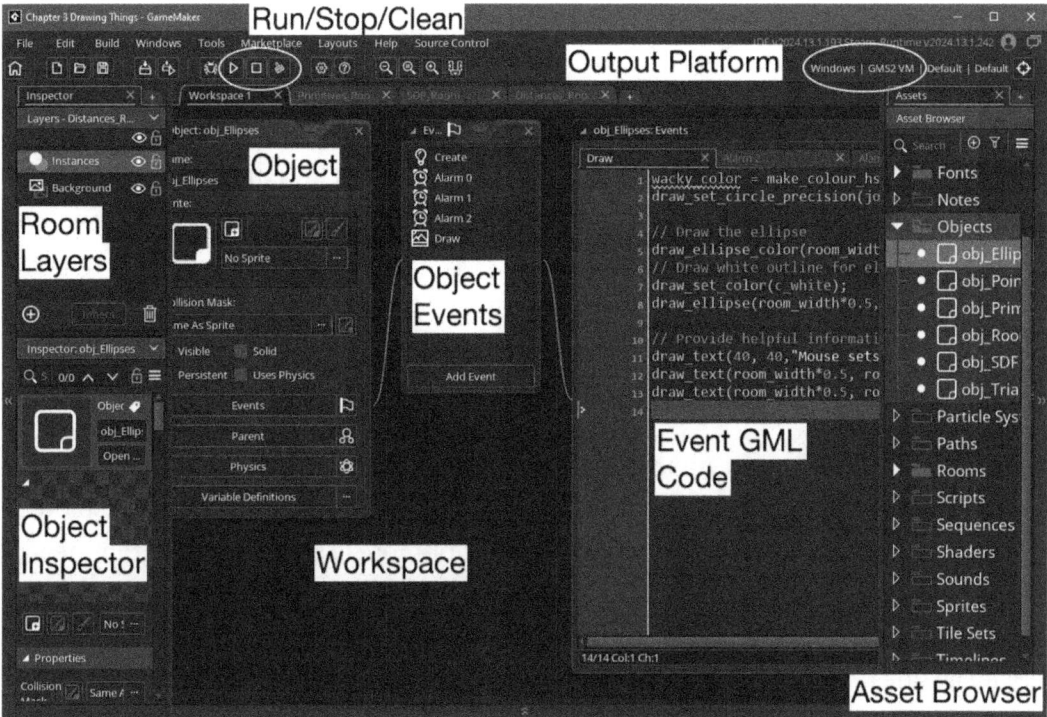

Figure 1-2. The GameMaker IDE with labeled sections. Output Platform specifies the ecosystem you are creating the current project for (this one in set to Windows)

Run, Stop, and Clean

There's a group of important buttons on top of the GameMaker IDE. The first one is labeled *Debug,* which refers to a tool for locating problems in your projects (we'll discuss debugging in depth in Chapter 9). The next icon, shaped like a classic play button, is labeled *Run.* This will compile and execute your project letting you see it in action. Next up is a rectangular icon labeled *Stop,* which will simply tell GameMaker to stop running your game.

Finally we have a button labeled *Clean*. GameMaker creates and maintains an *asset cache* on your game development computer to help speed up compile time. This temporary storage consists of all the various resource assets used by your projects, including its sprites (visuals) and audio files. Sometimes this cache gets a tad wonky. If you see strange behavior in your games, in particular when it comes to graphics, try cleaning the asset cache. This cache will then be rebuilt from scratch, which might take a few moments, but it just might fix your issue(s).

You can also run your game projects by simply pressing F5 on your keyboard. Be careful: this key is seated dangerously close to F6, which in GameMaker starts the debugging process!

GML Visual/Drag-and-Drop vs. GML

GameMaker offers two main approaches to programming your games. GML Visual, also known as *Drag-and-Drop (DnD)*, is a rather simplistic system geared toward absolute beginners, while *GameMaker Language (GML)* is for more experienced programmers who enjoy more control and features. Actually, you may find DnD becomes quite cumbersome very quickly; GML Code is in general far easier to create and read. For your very first game prototype, DnD may still be worth your time. However, most examples in this book will be presented in GML due to its numerous strengths.

GML is usually incorporated straight into your game objects' events, but it can also be typed into the *creation code* of your room/map. The latter approach is reserved for more basic things such as setting up a level and not when controlling actual game events.

In April of 2024, GameMaker got a fantastic new feature, called the *Code Editor 2*. It is recommended you switch it on by going into *File* ➤ *Preferences* ➤ *Code Editor 2* and click *enable*. With this approach, you get all of your object events on one page, making game development on the engine much more efficient.

Feather, at Your Service

Feather is an optional tool in GameMaker which provides advanced code-editing features. These include automatic code completion and improved syntax checking. With Feather enabled, hovering over sprites, functions, colors, or other special values reveals their details. Feather includes *asset refactoring,* which automatically updates all references in your project's code when you rename an asset in the asset browser, preventing broken references. Feather also adds *Quick fixes.* When it detects an issue in your code, it provides an icon next to the error or warning. Clicking this icon brings up Quick fix suggestions, which allow you to apply an automatic fix. All of these features can streamline your development considerably. However, it's worth noting that on some lower-end computers, Feather might slow down your workflow somewhat.

You can enable and disable Feather inside the GameMaker IDE by navigating to *File ➤ Preferences ➤ Feather Settings* and toggling *Enable Feather.*

GameMaker Asset Types

The core assets in every GameMaker project consist of 11 main categories (see Table 1-5). For more simple games, you may not use all of the asset types below, but as your projects grow, you will learn how to make the best use of them.

Table 1-5. The 11 core asset categories in GameMaker projects

Fonts	Typefaces used by your games (e.g., comic sans or papyrus)	**Scripts**	GML Code not included inside objects
Objects	Dynamic on-screen actors (e.g., the player, enemies, bonus items)	**Tilesets**	A collection of background tiles created together in one sprite
Rooms	Game maps and screen areas related to presentation (e.g., levels, title screens)	**Sequences**	Cutscenes and user interface animations with keyframes (think Adobe Flash/Animate and **OpenToonz by DWANGO Co.**)
Sounds	Game sound effects and music	**Shaders**	Advanced visual effects
Sprites	Actual graphics including title screens and game characters stored as bitmaps (e.g., as JPG or PNG)	**Particle systems**	Dynamic visual effects like fire, smoke, and explosions. Particles can be visually impressive while remaining computationally efficient
Paths	Premade movement paths for on-screen objects		

Again, while glancing at all these asset types can be seem daunting for the beginner, an exceptionally simple game would require exactly one room and one object. You need not dwell on the intricacies of shaders, particle systems, or even paths to make a fully functional video game in GameMaker.

On the Gameloop, Frames, and Step

Before we go any deeper into GameMaker and GML, there's a few concepts we should get acquainted with. Firstly, there's the indomitable *gameloop*. This refers to an on-going repetition of events which is only terminated once the player has had enough and closes the game (or the program crashes). Inside the gameloop, there are typically numerous other looped sequences, such as the title screen or perhaps a pause mode. Every time a game presents you with something, it is operating from a subloop inside the main gameloop.

As is the case with most programming languages, all GML scripts are executed one command at a time, from top to bottom. The order in which we code things is therefore paramount, some simple data definitions notwithstanding.

There's a setting called *game frames per second*, which has a default setting of 60. Each of these frames is also known as a *step*, and they refer to the number of times game events are executed per second. Typically, 60 frames/steps per second guarantees a good gaming experience, although some projects may need less. Please be aware that a game running on, say, 30 steps per second is less demanding on a computer than 60 steps. However, even most low-end devices built after 2015 or so are perfectly capable of running GameMaker games at the recommended 60 steps per second (unless a game is very poorly optimized). If a game is resource-intensive, setting the room speed to, say, 120 might actually slow things down as the FPS drops due to the increased processing demand. Adjust this value according to your game's requirements.

You can adjust *game frames* per second in **Quick Access ➤ Game Options ➤ Main ➤ General**. For most projects, leaving this at 60 works just fine.

GameMaker's Objects, Instances, and Events

At the heart of GameMaker are *objects* and all the various *events* they contain. We will now take a quick glance at these elements; they will be explored far more deeply later in the book.

An *object* in GameMaker parlance is quite like a blueprint for any kind of game actor; it may be a collectable bonus item, an enemy space ship, or an invisible controller object tracking a human player's actions. An *instance* is a working "product" made with said blueprints. We can make several instances out of a single object. For example, in a riveting game set in the world of retail we could have objects called *Customer, Product,* and *Salesperson*. We could summon numerous instances from each object, as needed, so we would probably have dozens of products and one or two salespeople and/or customer. Yet we would not have to create every single instance from scratch ourselves; instead, we would have GameMaker simply use the "blueprints" that we created (see Figure 1-3).

CHAPTER 1 A QUARTER CENTURY OF GAMEMAKER

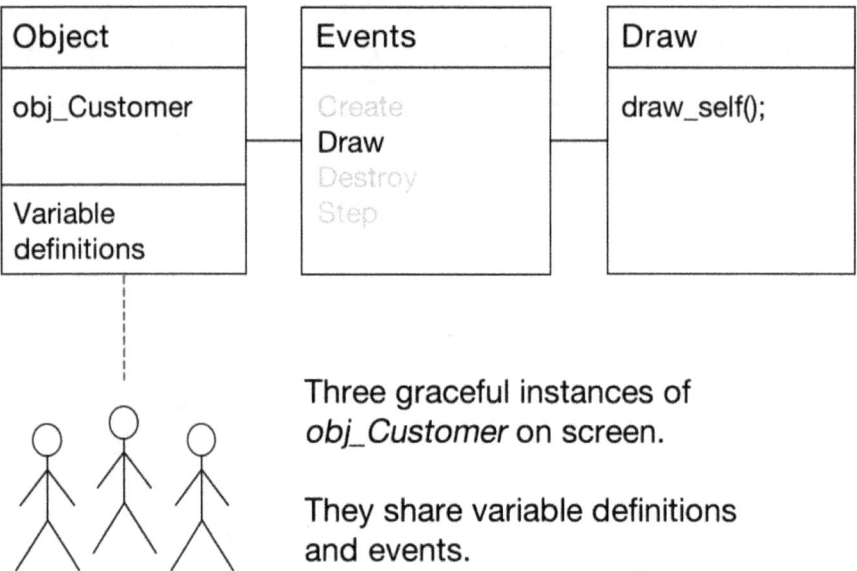

Figure 1-3. *The basic layout of object organization in GameMaker. There are dozens of events for objects in GameMaker, many of which will be discussed later in the book*

Events in GameMaker refer to the internal workings of objects. In Drag-and-Drop, events are presented in a visual form. In GML mode, you'll see plain text under each event. Now, there are several dozen different event categories available in GameMaker. We shall only go through some of the more basic events in this chapter, saving most of the rest for later (see Table 1-6).

Table 1-6. *The most common object events in GameMaker*

Event	Description
Create	Summoned once at the creation of an instance; manages their initial settings.
Draw	This event should contain GML exclusively related to creating visuals, such as drawing sprites and primitive shapes (e.g., rectangles and circles). Heavy calculations do not belong in this event.
Step	Actions executed every single step in the gameloop, such as updates to object position and variable tracking, belong in the Step event. Actions related to drawing should not typically be entered here!
Collision	Activated when one instance collides with some other specified instance.
Destroy	Summoned when the instance is destroyed; this is a good event for triggering explosions both visually and aurally. Can also be used to destroy unneeded data structures.
Draw GUI	Exclusively used for drawing on the *graphical user interface (GUI)*, i.e., the player's view, which often contains things like score and level information.

Again, all instances representing the same object have the same properties, including events. Keep in mind an object does not need every type of event. For that riveting retail game, the Customer object would probably contain most of the events listed in Table 1-6. A lowly Product instance, on the other hand, might contain only a Destroy event as it could simply play some uplifting chime and update score when a customer walks over it to collect it.

It is actually a good practice to have as few events in your GameMaker objects as possible. Also, some developers use specific naming conventions for your objects, mainly by adding "obj" or "obj_" in the beginning of their names (e.g., *objCustomer, obj_Product*). This can help in organizing your assets, but sometimes you may just want to live dangerously and forfeit this tradition.

Basic Object Parameters

There are four checkboxes for every object in the GameMaker IDE, namely, *visible, solid, persistent,* and *uses physics.* These options correspond to specific parameters, which are outlined next.

- **Solid:** If checked/set to true, instances of the object are treated as obstacles. Other instances will not be able to pass through them when they are using specific movement functions.

- **Visible:** If unchecked/set to false, instances of this object will not be drawn on-screen. Useful for control objects that don't display anything and other instances which start their existence as invisible.

- **Persistent:** If checked/set to true, instances of the object will exist throughout the game and retain all of their properties even when rooms/levels changed. Instances of persistent objects need to be manually destroyed to become inactive.

- **Uses physics:** Checking this box enables GameMaker's physics simulation for the object in question. This topic will be discussed in depth in Chapter 7.

The checkboxes in the IDE aside, all of the aforementioned properties can be dynamically set with GML inside object events as needed (e.g., solid = true, visible = false, persistent = true, phy_active = false). See Figure 1-4 for a close-up of the above parameters in the GameMaker user interface.

CHAPTER 1 A QUARTER CENTURY OF GAMEMAKER

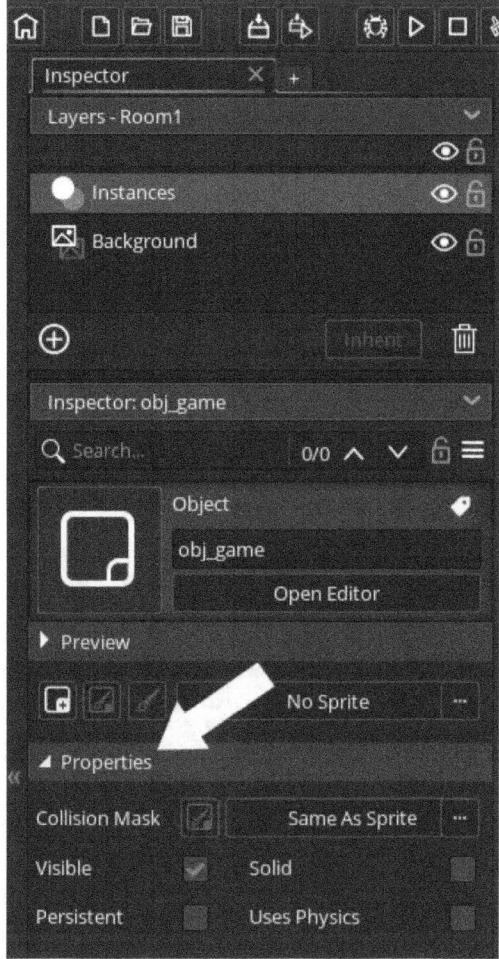

Figure 1-4. *The Properties section in the Inspector showing the four options available individually for every object (i.e., Visible, Solid, Persistent, and Uses Physics)*

All GameMaker objects have numerous built-in variables besides the ones discussed above. The rest will be introduced later in the book.

17

CHAPTER 1   A QUARTER CENTURY OF GAMEMAKER

On Rooms and Layers

Let us now discuss another central concept in GameMaker: the room. This is the stage on which we make things happen. Now, a project will always need at least one room. A typical game actually has multiple rooms for various purposes, ranging from hosting title screens to representing different levels.

The room system in GameMaker is highly flexible. For one, developers get to decide whether to use a few massive rooms or to opt for a larger number of smaller spaces. Room sizes are easily adjustable as every room has a setting for width and height in pixels right inside the GameMaker IDE.

Although the rooms in a GameMaker project don't have to be in any specific order for us to access any one of them at will, they can be reordered using the *Room Manager*. This feature is activated by pressing on the little house (or arrow) icon next to a room resource in the asset browser (see Figure 1-5).

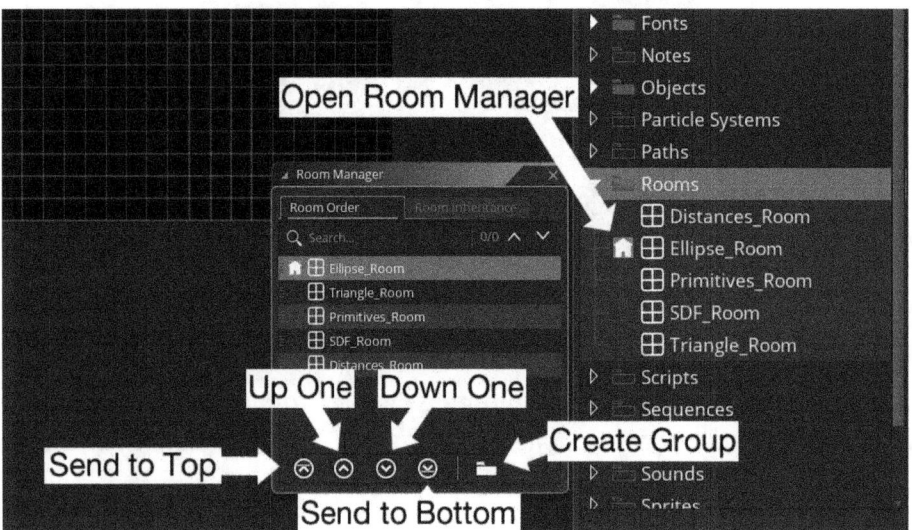

Figure 1-5. *The Room Manager in GameMaker*

The Room Manager has four buttons on the bottom of its window for reordering your rooms. The room at the top of this list is the first one the players experience (it is also denoted with a house icon). You can create groups of rooms, too, which is handy for larger projects.

Now, there are two checkboxes in the section called Room Settings: *Persistent* and *Clear Display Buffer*. The former "freezes" the events in a specific room so if a player is to leave said room and return later, things will be exactly the same as before their departure. If Clear Display Buffer is ticked, some undesirable visual artifacts (e.g., motion trails), which might surface under some scenarios, should get fixed. This feature is useful if you have (partial) transparency in your backgrounds and experience aforementioned visual disturbances; otherwise, it's best to switch it off as it comes with a minor performance hit.

> Rooms are accessed in-game by calling specific GML functions, such as *room_goto_next* or *room_goto_previous*.

Layers are a part of every room in GameMaker. They are basically depth-ordered elements used for storing different types of assets. Layers can be easily reordered in the IDE to change their depth if needed. There are seven types of layers in GameMaker, and they are as follows:

- **Background:** Stores background graphics (e.g., a sprite of a mountain range) or a simple solid color.
- **Instance:** Used for all types of object instances, e.g., the player and their enemies.
- **Tile:** A dedicated layer for a *tileset*, which is a type of resource used for some highly effective background graphics work discussed later in the book.
- **Path:** Used for previewing and editing movement paths inside a room instead of within the confines of their own dedicated editor; a path is a type of (optional) resource discussed later.
- **Asset:** Stores sprites and sequences (the latter will be discussed later in the book, too).
- **Effects:** These layer types offer a selection of built-in visual effects (i.e., shaders) such as "old film," pixelation, and screen shake. Applies the effect to all layers that are beneath the depth of this type of layer.
- **UI (user interface):** Used for displaying score and other pertinent information. Will always stay on top of all the other layers.

CHAPTER 1   A QUARTER CENTURY OF GAMEMAKER

Layers are added into rooms by clicking the plus symbol and then selecting a layer type (see Figure 1-6).

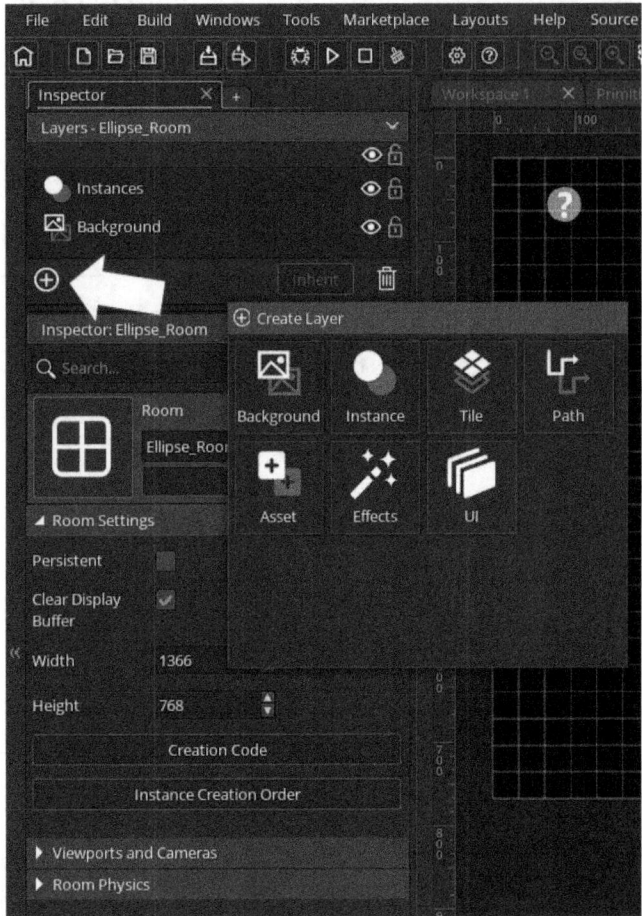

Figure 1-6. The layer creation screen in the GameMaker IDE

You can have multiple layers in your rooms, but for the sake of optimization, it's best to stick to as few as your game actually needs.

Adding Assets with Right-Click

You may agree GameMaker has a rather intuitive and slick user interface. It pretty much has icons for everything. In addition, a gentle but confident tap of the right mouse button will often come to your aid, too. New assets of all kinds can be created by right-clicking the asset browser and by selecting the asset type (e.g., *Create* ➤ *Object* or *Create* ➤ *Sprite*). Also, new layers can be created inside a room by first right-clicking the layer inspector and then choosing what type of layer to add. As mentioned before, resources in the asset browser are opened into their respective editors by double left clicking on them.

A Few Words on Optimization

If there's one concept you should always keep in mind as a game developer from the beginning of a project, it's *optimization.* The four major resources found in a modern electronic device are the *central processing unit (CPU), random access memory (RAM), graphics processing unit (GPU),* and, to a lesser degree, storage space. A poorly optimized game will sap the CPU, RAM, and GPU out of their precious energy. As a programmer, one of your jobs is to make sure your products will not have excessive system requirements or cause computers to crash. Like you probably know, a computer has finite resources it can work with. We do not have devices with infinite processing power quite yet; many systems will struggle to play the latest games. Also, the average gamer typically has a limited budget to work with when assembling their gaming battlestation; not everyone will invest in a high-end PC.

There are numerous factors we must take into account when optimizing our games. We will take a good look at them later in the book. For now, just keep in mind you should strive to minimize the amount of assets in your projects; this goes for the on-screen instances, background graphics, special effects (e.g., shaders and particles), and audio files. The less your game needs to process, the smoother it will run.

Compiled vs. Interpreted Code

Digital devices cannot directly read any typed-in computer language. They operate on a level of *machine code* (i.e., ones and zeroes) which is pretty much not readable by humans. GML is a so-called *high-level programming language.* This basically means it is well understood by most human beings, once they learn its basic syntax and functions. Other such languages include Python, Java, and JavaScript. Very experienced programmers tend to levitate toward *assembly language* (sometimes called *assembler*), which is a *low-level programming language.* Each CPU architecture (e.g., ×86 on Intel/

AMD CPUs) has its own version of assembly language. Assembler is very close to the "heart" of a digital device and thus fast, but it's quite challenging to work with. In the glorious 1980s and 1990s, many more ambitious commercial games (e.g., flight simulators) were written on some variety of assembly language for the processing speed it offered. As a language specifically geared for game development, GML comes loaded with powerful high-level audiovisual functions out of the box, but it can also be used for general-purpose programming tasks. See Figure 1-7 for the basic levels of programming abstraction.

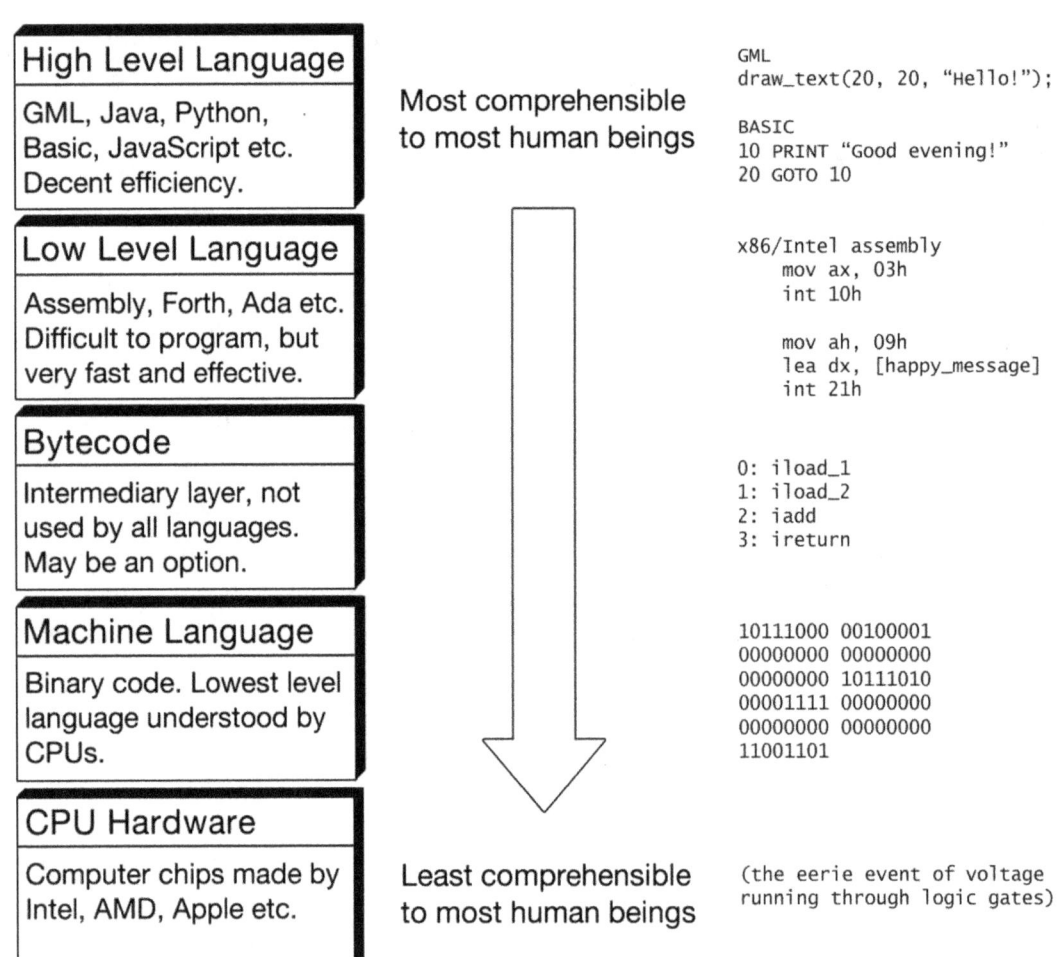

Figure 1-7. *The basic levels of programming abstraction*

Now, there are basically two ways of converting code into machine language: *compiling* or *interpreting*. With compiled software, the entire source code of a programming project is translated into machine code, creating an executable app in the process (e.g., HappyGame.exe). On the other hand, **interpreted software is** executed **line by line** in real time by a piece of software called an *interpreter,* without ever creating a separate executable app. Compiled software often executes its audiovisual marvels faster, but is slower to develop for; compiling software every time you change something does take a while. Interpreted software takes a bigger toll on a device's resources and is computationally less efficient but usually has a much faster loading time in a development environment.

GameMaker offers both interpreted and compiled output. These are shown in the platform output options as *GMS2 VM* and *GMS2 YYC*. The *VM* in these options stands for *virtual machine* while *YYC* stands for *YoYo Compiler.* The GameMaker interpreted mode, VM, uses *bytecode,* which is an intermediate representation of a program, between high-level GML and machine code. It consists of low-level instructions known as *opcodes.* YYC is a so-called *Ahead-of-Time (AOT)* compiler, which for the most part forfeits bytecode. AOT first compiles projects into C++, a highly efficient language, which is then compiled into machine code for execution.

Compared to interpreted mode, YYC in GameMaker is also more strict on the use of syntax. **YYC enforces** better coding practices; this lead to unexpected issues if your GML Code relies on the VM's syntax leniency. Tracking these issues can also be more of a challenge in YYC due to the somewhat vague nature of some of its error messages.

Now, compiling a GameMaker project can have a dramatic positive effect to the amount of resources and effects you get to leverage in your games. However, it is recommended you develop in the interpreted environment, only switching to YYC/compiled closer to your game's deadline. Also, when you output in YYC, you need to have additional *software development kits (SDKs)* installed on your computer. This is something which will be discussed in depth later in the book. See Table 1-7 for a rundown on the main differences of interpreted and compiled output targets in GameMaker.

Table 1-7. The main differences of interpreted and compiled output targets in GameMaker

Platform output	GMS2 VM (virtual machine)	GMS2 YYC (YoYo Compiler)
Approach	Interpreted	Compiled (via C++)
Main strength(s)	Fast launching for near-instant testing	Computational efficiency, lower memory (RAM) impact, optimized game physics
Syntax	Loose	Strict
Best suited for	Testing and development, releasing smaller projects	Prerelease testing, release-ready, and optimized executables

In GameMaker parlance, a software interpreter is actually called a *runner*.

In Closing

In this introductory chapter, we discussed the following topics:

- GameMaker's minimum system requirements and how to acquire the software
- The four main buttons in the GameMaker IDE: debug, run, stop, and clean
- The basics of the GameMaker rooms and layers
- The main categories of GameMaker assets (objects, sprites, particles, rooms, etc.)
- Objects, instances, and events

- The gameloop and frame/step
- The key differences between interpreted and compiled projects
- The basic levels of programming abstraction (high vs. low level, etc.)

In Chapter 2, we shall begin submerging ourselves in the fine art of GameMaker Language (GML) in earnest. We'll learn about concepts like variables and the many exciting data structures available in this superb programming language.

CHAPTER 2

Game Logic with GML

The gamemaking experience in GameMaker Language (GML) can be roughly split between two layers: basic game logic based on universal programming principles and specialized audiovisual functions provided by GameMaker. In this chapter, we shall examine GML's basic structures and syntax in depth, before boldly entering the realm of GameMaker's visual functions in the chapter to follow.

Before we start game building, we need to understand the core components of GML logic. And there is no better topic to begin with than the variable.

The examples in this chapter are only intended to demonstrate how basic GML logic operates. You can try them out by creating a new blank project, creating an object in the GameMaker IDE, putting the code in its Create event, and placing said object in a room. However, it should suffice you take a look and understand what is happening.

On the Ecstasy of Variables

Data structures called *variables* are a key concept in any programming language, including GML (naturally, GameMaker's Drag-and-Drop mode also manipulates variables). This is where a touch of algebra comes in. A variable is an abstract storage location in a device's memory paired with a symbolic name. We can freely assign any name to any variable. Variables are used to store things like an object's vertical coordinates on screen—or some character's favorite vegetable. It is through variables that we can access game actors and manipulate a game's proceedings.

Variables come in different *data types*; some of these types are used to store alphanumerical strings while others work with different kinds of numbers. Table 2-1 showcases the five basic variable data types in GML.

Table 2-1. Examples of the five basic variable data types in GML

Data type	Description	Example definitions in GML
Real number	Any type of number, positive or negative, with optional decimal point	`Score=0; temperature=-30; Happiness=100.1;`
String	Any alphanumerical string of characters, including nonnegative numbers (number strings are not used for arithmetic operations)	`full_name="Richard Schnippelschnappel"; favorite_food="Surströmming"; postal_code="P12345";`
Boolean	Two-state variable; either true or false	`player_alive=true; enemy_alive=false;`
Array	A collection of variables, can be either numbers or strings	`great_names=["Leopold", "Dimples"]; lucky_numbers=[1, 2, 3.1, -4];`
Struct	A collection of different types of variables	`happyStruct = { a : 99, b : -3.3, c : "Good evening! I like you!" };`

Unlike many other programming languages (such as C and Java), GML will try to automatically assign the proper data type for your variables based on the type of information you feed into them (e.g., *name="Pete"* will be interpreted as a string). Also, there are ways of converting information between different data types; this is something we'll look into later in the book.

CHAPTER 2 GAME LOGIC WITH GML

> Semicolons (;) act as a kind of "period" at the end of each command statement in many programming languages. It is not absolutely necessary in GML to put a semicolon after each statement, but many programmers do it out of habit. If you do this, know that it is okay.

Variable Operators

We can't do much with static variables. Luckily, GML offers a great assortment of *variable operators*. With these, we can manipulate the contents of our variables in real time, whenever we feel like it. Let's begin with some basic arithmetic, shall we?

```
Health = Health + 1;
Health++;
```

The above two lines of GML do the same thing: they add one (1) to a variable called Health. Now, let's play with bigger values next.

```
Health += 20;
Happiness -= 1000;
```

The above lines use *compound operators* (+= and -=) to add twenty (20) to Health and subtract 1000 from Happiness. These types of operators are very handy for potentially heavy-handed arithmetic manipulation of variables with single lines of code.

There are two other main types of compound operators in GML: one for multiplying (*=) and one for division (/=). Let's see them in action.

```
Health *= 2;
Happiness /= 2;
Happiness *=0.5;
```

The first line doubles the value of Health, while the second one divides Happiness in half. The third line actually repeats the second action, only this time with a multiplication operator.

29

Comparison and Conditional Operators

Performing arithmetic on variables is great, but we do need to check their contents often, too. And for that, we have a *conditional operator* called *if*, and its good friend, the *else* keyword. We will work with it in conjunction with the *comparison operators* listed in Table 2-2.

Table 2-2. *The six basic comparison operators in GML*

==	Equal to	!=	Is not equal to
>	Greater than	>=	Greater or equal than
<	Smaller than	<=	Smaller or equal than

Let's go through a couple of simple examples of conditional logic in GML. In the following little listing, we set a Boolean variable called *happy* to true as soon as *gold* reaches a value of over 300.

```
if gold > 300 happy=true; else happy=false;
```

Next, we'll take a gander on how to use the else keyword with the following example:

```
if x != 0 {
if x>=30 y += 20; else y -= 20;
} else z++;
```

In the above incidental listing, we first check if variable x is not zero (0). If this state is met we then check if x is 30 or greater and if so, we add twenty (20) to variable y. If x is under 30, we reduce y by twenty (20). If x was zero (0) the whole time, we add one (1) to variable z, skipping the section in the curly brackets entirely.

Curly brackets denote a *code block* in GML (and many other programming languages), inside of which we can add more than one statement.

Now, let's do something a bit different. We'll leverage combinatory operators (OR and AND) for a slightly more complicated statement.

```
if gold>50 or silver>100 || copper>200 {
show_message("A jolly message!");
} else show_message("Go acquire more currency!");
```

The above statements read as follows: we check if gold is above 50 or silver is over 100 or copper is above 200. If just one of these conditions is met, the program displays a jolly message. In GML, we can use both the keyword *or* and the symbol || for the same purpose (that's two vertical bars).

As for the fabulous AND operator? Let's see it in action:

```
if gold>100 and silver>200 && copper>500 {
message_display("You have enough coins. Cheers!");
} else message_display("Acquire more coins, ye dullard.");
```

The above if statement checks if we have over 100 gold and over 200 silver and over 500 copper. If, and only if, all of these conditions are met do we get a cheerful message. In addition to using the keyword *and*, we can string conditional checks together by using the symbol &&.

Let us next combine these techniques. We'll use both the *and* and *or* keywords in a statement.

```
a=99; b=99; c=99; e=0;
```

```
if a>10 && b<100 || c>100 e=1;
```

Since variable a is well over 10 AND b is under 100, variable c does not have to be over 100 for variable e to be changed into one (1), although we checked for that as well with our or keyword (i.e., ||).

Not So Fast! Variable Naming Rules

Although we can name our variables rather freely, there are a few rules for this. Variables in GML must contain only letters, numbers, and underscores (_), and they cannot begin with numbers or special characters. Also, variables can't contain spaces. To demonstrate, these variables are fine: *Apple, Happy_Apple_Delivery,* and *Nsync_123*. Unworkable variables include things like *123Apple, !!NSYNC,* and *Happy Apple Delivery*.

The Wonders of Macros

Not all variables are dynamic and ever-changing. There is a group of variables that are not to be changed during a gameloop, which are known as *constants*. They are set up at the beginning of a game project, and they will remain static until it's time for those two harrowing words "quit" and "game." In GML, constants often refer to *macros*. You leverage macros basically as a way to make your code more comfortable to modify. Like typical variables, you can call a macro whatever you wish and assign any value to it.

```
#macro SHIP_HORIZONTAL_SPEED 2;
#macro GRAVITY_SETTING 1.5;
```

Above are two definitions of macros in GML. Should we now want to change the effects of gravity in a (fictional) game, we could simply adjust the macro's value instead of going through every line of code which sets the gravity currently (ostensibly) at 1.5.

Commenting Code

Sometimes you just want to make little notes right inside your code, or disable certain parts of it temporarily for testing purposes. Luckily, GML supports *code commenting*. Let's see it in action next.

```
// Hello! This is a comment.
/* Good evening. I am a comment and I span
two rows. Are you impressed? */
/* I am also a comment. */
```

Commented lines are not processed by GML and can contain any type of text and the strangest of characters.

Enumeration

GML allows you to define sets of numbered constants. This process is known as *enumeration*, and it uses the keyword *enum*. Let's say we need to work with a catalog of moods. By enumerating them, we gain handy numeric handles for all of them. The numbering begins at zero. We can also assign custom values to specific items. Enumerations are accessed using the so-called *point method* (e.g., Cars.Ford, People.Jerk).

```
enum Moods {
Happy, // Receives value 0
Irate, // Receives value 1
Jolly = 5, // Receives value 5
Cranky // Receives value 6, thanks to previous value
}
show_message(Moods.Jolly) // Displays "5"
```

On the Necessity of Loops

We'll now get into a very crucial concept for any programming language: loops. Pretty much every time a player glances on the screen, there's some kind of loop in action, whether it's a title screen or the game itself. Things are drawn and keyboards/controllers are listened for events during loops. Basically, continuous things happen during loops. We couldn't have much of a game without them.

Also, loops can tackle tasks best left to automation, such as procedural level generation and iteration of data structures. It's often just not practical to use single manual statements all the way. Loops can greatly simplify repetitive tasks, and they come in many flavors.

While

Firstly, there's an approach called a *while loop*. This approach keeps looping a code block until a specified condition is met (see Listing 2-1).

Listing 2-1. Demonstration of a while loop

```
// This example should be put inside the CREATE-event of an object
// We set a variable for maximum number of loops to 5
sum=0; maximum_loops=5; loops=maximum_loops;

while (var loops>0) {
sum += loops;
    loops--;
}
```

```
show_message("The sum of numbers between 1 and " + string(maximum_loops) +
" is " + string(sum) );
```

In the above little example, we loop four times and keep adding the amount of variable *loops* into variable *sum*. Variable *loops* is reduced by one (1) every loop. This results in a final sum of 10.

The while loop is quite useful for situations when the number of iterations needed to complete tasks is not predetermined.

Now, you may remember us previously discussing the possibility of converting variable data types. In order for the show_message function to display a numerical variable, said data type must be first converted into a string. In GML, we do it simply by wrapping *string( )* around it. This works for every occasion (including with functions like *draw_text*, introduced later in this chapter), not just in conjunction with show_message.

You may have also noticed there's a few plus signs in the previous example listing. This is a part of GameMaker's text-formatting syntax. When displaying messages, the plus sign is simply used to merge segments of text together (e.g., *show_message("Hello!"* + *"How are"* + *"you?")* will display a single sentence).

Repeat

It's now time to feast upon the elegance of the *repeat loop*. Sometimes it's all you need. This comes in handy if you need to go through command statements and know the exact number of iterations needed beforehand. For example, you may want to summon several instances of an object at the same time. But for now, we shall keep things simple.

```
// Let us display the same message twice, for some reason
repeat(2) { show_message("Good day to you!"); }
```

In the following slightly more elaborate example, we add ten (10) random numbers of up to nine (9) in value into variable *sum* and display the result. In this example, we introduce three more keywords: *randomize, floor,* and *random*. First, we summon the randomize function to set the "seed" of random values. Think of it as rerolling some dice to get fresh results each roll. The random function takes a parameter as the upper range for its random values. In this example, it is asked to return numbers between zero (0) and nine (9). *Floor* is a function which rounds down values so we get nice, whole numbers (see Listing 2-2).

Listing 2-2. Demonstration of the floor function

```
sum=0;
randomize();
repeat(10)
{
    sum += floor(random(9));
}
show_message("The sum of ten random numbers: " + string(sum));
```

Do/Until

Next we have the almighty *do/until loop.* This type of loop is executed until a specific condition is met as specified with the until keyword (see Listing 2-3).

Listing 2-3. Demonstration of the do/until loop

```
// Set maximum number of hellos to three for the sake of our sanity
var done=false; var i=0; var maximum_hello=3;
do { // Begin loop
    i++;
  show_message("Hello number " + string(i) + " out of " + string(maximum_
  hello) + "!");
      if i>2 done=true;
} until done==true; // Repeat until variable "done" equals "true"
show_message("Good riddance!");
```

For

Finally, there's the stalwart *for loop.* A true classic among its brethren; it is found pretty much in all programming languages (see Listing 2-4).

Listing 2-4. Demonstration of a for loop.

```
// This example runs in the DRAW or DRAW GUI-event of an object
for (var i=0; i<10; i++) {
draw_text(200, 25*i, "Hello number " + string(i+1));
}
```

This example uses a draw_text function, which is great for displaying text at exact screen coordinates. In the above example, we are setting the horizontal (i.e., x coordinates) to 200 pixels from the left while the vertical coordinates (i.e., y coordinates) are made relative to variable i for a handy automatic line shift.

Taking a Break

Let's next explore a slightly more complicated listing which features more elements. These include the *break keyword* which is used to manually break out of loops. The program in question looks for prime numbers (i.e., numbers only divisible by themselves or the number two). It uses *nested loops,* which refers to a loop inside another one (see Listing 2-5).

Listing 2-5. Demonstration of the break keyword

```
// Try this listing in a CREATE event of an object
// Look for primes up to this number
max_number=15;

for (var num = 2; num <= max_number; num++) {
    prime_number = true;
    // Check divisors for the current number
    for (var divisor = 2; divisor <= sqrt(num); divisor++) {
        if num mod divisor == 0 {
            prime_number = false;  // Not a prime number..
            break; // .. so break out of second loop
        }
    }
    // If a prime number is found, display popup
    if prime_number show_message(string(num) + " is a prime number!");
}
```

The keyword *mod* as used in the above example is a *modulo operator*. It's used to see if a given number is divisible by some other number as it returns a remainder of a division. The modulo operator in GML also uses the symbol %. Also, note the use of a function called *sqrt* which simply returns the square root of the given number.

In GML, we can shorthand **if <variable>==1** with **if <variable>** for more elegant listings. Conversely, we can replace **if <variable>!=1** with **if !<variable>** when we are checking for variables that do not contain specific values.

Having briefly introduced a few math-related functions in our examples, this is a good time to focus some more on these. See Table 2-3 for a rundown on some functions you may need sometime in the future. We will revisit all of them later in the book in the context of actual gamemaking purposes.

Table 2-3. *Some useful GML math functions*

Function	Description	Example
floor	Rounds a number down	value = floor(3.8); // Returns 3
ceil	Rounds a number up	value = ceil(6.1); // Returns 7
sign	Detects whether a number is positive, negative, or neither	sign(75) returns 1, sign(-2) returns -1, sign(0) returns 0
clamp	Maintains a value inside specific limits	happiness = clamp(happiness, 75, 100); // Limits happiness between 75 and 100

round	Rounds numbers up or down to the nearest integer	sum = round(41.2); // Returns 41
		sum = round(52.7); // Returns 53

frac	Returns the fractional part of a number	value = frac(4.2); // Returns 0.2
mean	Returns the average of a set of numbers	sum = mean(3, 4, 4, 5, 5); // Returns 4.20
sqrt	Returns the square root of a given number	result = sqrt(204);

CHAPTER 2   GAME LOGIC WITH GML

The Switch Case

All these wonderful statements just keep coming—say hello to *switch*. This is a versatile one as it allows you to perform multiple different actions depending on a specific value as defined by case keywords. You escape a switch statement with the previously used keyword break. Also, switches can leverage the default keyword in case the input variable does not correlate with any action (see Listing 2-6).

Listing 2-6. A switch case demonstration

```
// Try this out in a CREATE-event and experiment with different values.
score=30; // Set our score
switch (score) {
    case 10:
        show_message("You reached the rank of nincompoop.");
        break;
    case 20:
        show_message("You reached the rank of novice.");
        break;
    case 30: // This is the message for our initial settings
        show_message("You reached the rank of master!");
        break;
    default:
// if variable score is not specified in this example, display message:
        show_message("Your rank is unknown");
        break;
}
```

See Listing 2-7 for a slightly more elaborate example of rolling dice with switch.

Listing 2-7. A different switch case demonstration

```
dice=choose(1,2,3,4,5,6);
switch (dice) {
    case 1:
        show_message("You rolled a one!");
        break;
```

```
    case 2:
        show_message("You rolled a two!");
        break;
    case 3:
        show_message("You rolled a three!");
        break;
    case 4:
        show_message("You rolled a four!");
        break;
    case 5:
        show_message("You rolled a five!");
        break;
    case 6:
        show_message("You rolled a six!");
        break;
    default:
        show_message("Something went wrong."); // This will not be triggered
}
if show_question("Re-roll?")
    {
    game_restart();
    } else game_end();
```

You may notice several new elements in the above example. For one, there's another statement, *choose*. This is handy for selecting values from a small set of numbers in a random fashion. In addition, we have a question dialog (i.e., *show_question*) which is mostly used when testing/debugging programs and doesn't really see other use in GameMaker. Finally, we have two functions which *are* rather frequently used: *game_restart* and *game_end*. The former resets the game completely, while the latter quits a game, putting the player back into their respective operating system.

Variable Scope

Not all variables need to reach everywhere inside your projects. *Variable scope* determines where a variable can be accessed within your game project. There are four main types of variable scopes, which are summarized in Table 2-4.

Table 2-4. *The main types of variable scopes in GameMaker.*

Scope type	Description	Example definition

Script	Variables used as script arguments or return values	`function Foe(`**`speed, health`**`){`
		`...`
		`}`

Instance	Variables that belong to a specific instance and can be accessed by other objects	**`foe`** `= "Dingbat";`
Local	Only works inside a specific function or script. Discarded after the event passes	**`var foe`** `= "Dingbat";`
Global	Variable accessible from anywhere in the game	**`global.`**`level = 4;` **`global.`**`game_name = "Dingbat";`

Let's discuss the difference between instance and local variables. The former (without "var") should be used when you need to access values across multiple instances. Think of the latter more as disposable variables used for iteration (i.e., for loops). Sometimes the difference is a bit of a gray area and it's not a huge deal if you iterate a for loop with an instance variable.

Global variables are useful for storing persistent game-wide data, such as player scores, settings, or game states (e.g., paused/not paused). Also, instead of using multiple global variables, you can use a *global struct* to group relevant data. Here's what a global struct might look like for a player: *global.player = { name: "Zeke", health: 100, energy: 50, inventory: ["Spatula", "Surströmming"] };*

Temporary values like instance coordinates do not generally make great global variables.

On Inheritance

Let's next discuss a very important topic in GML: *inheritance.* This refers to so-called *parent-child relationships* between objects. Children of objects can inherit variables and events from their respective parent object. This basically allows us to reuse code and speed up game development very effectively.

Say we have a generic object for vegetables, we'll imaginatively call it *obj_Vegetable.* In it, we define a Boolean variable *isEdible.* Our obj_Vegetable also has a single Draw event. Let us then define three child objects for obj_Vegetable. Say hello to *obj_Artichoke, obj_Carrot,* and *obj_Turnip.* These three objects, being "children" of the same object, inherit all the variables and events of obj_Vegetable, which is their "parent." This translates to all of them getting a Draw event and the variable called isEdible. Whatever we define in the Draw event of obj_Vegetable happens in all instances derived from the three children.

Child objects get to define their own variables and events, too. However, these do not go "up the chain" back to the parent object. In our example, obj_Turnip adds two Boolean variables called isDelicious and isSuperior. In addition, obj_Turnip has a Step event of its own. See Figure 2-1 for a diagram for this example.

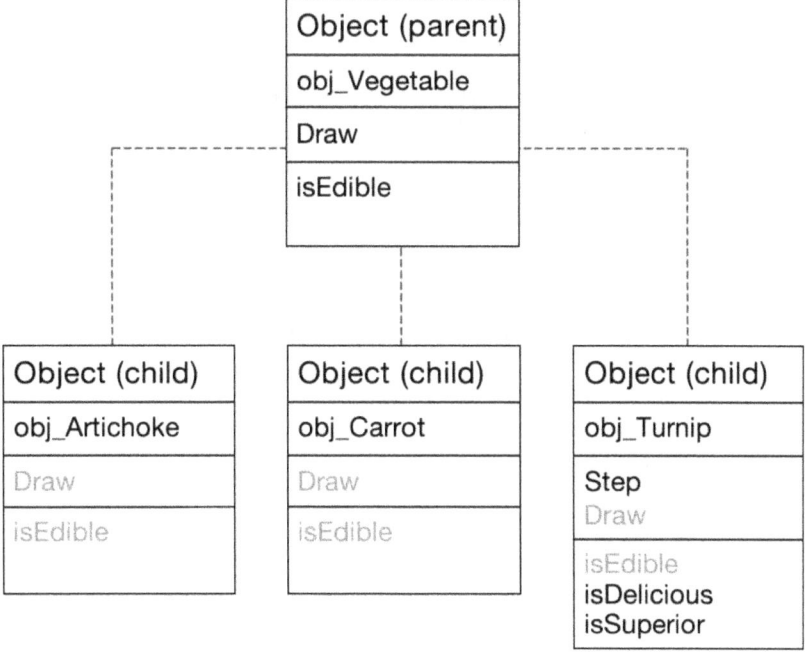

Figure 2-1. *A diagram demonstrating inheritance in GML*

Inheritance in GameMaker is obviously not limited to making family trees of vegetables. We can devise a whole range of inheritance-based hierarchies for our games, including the following:

- **Game characters:** We might define *obj_Character* as a parent object to represent a generic character which is able to run around and collide with obstacles in the game world. Its children include *obj_Player,* a controllable entity, and an *obj_NPC* who just wanders aimlessly.

- **Enemy units:** First we define, say, *obj_Enemy* as the parent object with variables for health and speed to represent a generic enemy blueprint. We then define three children: *obj_Bike, obj_Tank,* and *obj_Jeep,* all with slightly different properties.

- **Static interactive entities:** A parent object by the name of *obj_StaticEntity* could represent doors, windows, and switches through its children (e.g., *obj_Door, obj_Window,* and *obj_Switch*).

We'll be looking into inheritance to a greater extent later in the book as it is a highly useful technique that every developer should get comfortable with.

On Object-Oriented Programming (OOP)

Inheritance in programming was introduced in the *Simula 67* language all the way back in the 1960s.[1] This language set in motion the monumental paradigm known as *object-oriented programming (OOP)*. Object-oriented programming helps developers write well-organized and reusable code, especially when modeling real-world entities. OOP's principles allow developers to create structures that closely resemble real-world objects, their parameters, and their interactions. This is particularly useful in fields like game development and different types of simulations. Popular languages representing the OOP paradigm include *Java, C++,* and *C#.*

---

[1] Simula 67 was developed at the Norwegian Computing Center in Oslo, Norway, by Ole-Johan Dahl (1931–2002) and Kristen Nygaard (1926–2002).

While similar, GML is not actually a fully OOP-based programming language. While inheritance is indeed a major part of OOP, there are other elements such as *encapsulation* and *polymorphism* that are only partially implemented in GML. See Table 2-5 for the well-established so-called *four pillars of OOP*.

Table 2-5. *The "four pillars" of object-oriented programming (OOP)*

Inheritance	A system for allowing one class to inherit properties (e.g., methods and variables) from other classes.
Polymorphism	Using a single function to work with different types of objects, with the correct behavior being chosen automatically based on the object's type. Simple example: an Interact function. Opens passages if used on doors. Alerts enemy if used on hostile units.
Encapsulation	Hides the internal details of how an object works by limiting variable/function access with modifier keywords like *public*, *protected*, and *private*.
Abstraction	The act of exposing only mission-relevant data in a development environment. Improves code readability and security.

Be aware that GML does not support *multiple inheritance*. Instead, an object can only inherit from one other object; in GML, a child can only have one parent.

In most OOP-based languages, there are **classes** and **objects**. In GML, an object functions similarly to a class by defining behavior and properties. Both contexts use the term **instance** when referring to an entity created from a class (OOP) or object (GML).

While GML includes some OOP-like features, it does not fully adhere to the four pillars of OOP. The absence of elements like access modifiers and multiple inheritance disqualifies GML for being called a true object-oriented language. This is not a slight on GameMaker at all, since it represents a specialized niche where it does not need all OOP features to be considered a well-rounded piece of software.

CHAPTER 2   GAME LOGIC WITH GML

Arrays: For Your Inventories and Mazes

Games sometimes call for the storage of larger amounts of information than mere single variables can offer. In this section, we'll tackle constructs like arrays, structs, lists, and maps. We'll also go through many of the basic functions for manipulating these data structures.

One-Dimensional Arrays (1D)

As mentioned previously in this book, arrays are collections of variables. They are extremely handy for building little databases for your game. Variables in arrays may, e.g., represent items, character names, or places. Arrays in GML come in two main varieties: one-dimensional and multidimensional, meaning arrays with two or more dimensions. Let's get into the former variety first with the following little listing (see Listing 2-8).

Listing 2-8. Demonstration of 1D arrays in GML

```
// Create an array of three items with a default value
our_array = array_create(3,"Hello!");
for(var i=0; i<array_length(our_array); i++)
    show_message(our_array[i]);
```

Above we used the function called *array_create* to initialize a new array of three (3) items, each containing the same (optional) friendly greeting. We then iterate this array using our friend the for loop, in which the variable *i* stands for *iteration*, but we could have named it anything (the "i" is a bit of a classic with for loops). We can also create arrays the following way (see Listing 2-9).

Listing 2-9. Demonstration of an array with strings

```
// Create an array of strings
item_names = ["Sword", "Minigun", "Pencil", "Pet Rock"];
// Iterate through all elements in the array and display them
for(var i=0; i<array_length(item_names); i++)
show_message(item_names[i]);
```

In the above example, we first create an array of string variables called *item_names*. This example introduces us to a most useful function, *array_length*, which (like you may have gathered) returns the number of elements inside an array. We simply leveraged this function for iterating our data in order to stay within the bounds of the array in question. Iterating outside of an array's length results in an error.

Arrays start their indexing at zero. In our example, this means Sword is at place 0, Minigun is at place 1, and so on.

How about we remove, say, the pencil from our array and replace it with a spatula? GML contains many useful functions for doing these sorts of things. Let's find out how this is done next.

```
array_delete(item_names, 2, 1); // Delete one (1) item at location 2
array_insert(item_names, 2, "Spatula"); // Add an item at location 2
```

Above are two handy functions for adding and deleting array items. With *array_delete*, we can delete either a single variable or several as specified by the last attribute (in our example it is set to a single item).

Push and Pop: Adding and Removing Items Quickly

How about we simply want to add a single item at the end of an array? Or a whole lot of them? In these cases, we can do this:

```
array_push(item_names, "Lamp");
array_push(item_names, "Chair", "Banana", "Accountant");
```

Should we want to remove an item from an array, we have the pop function for deleting single variables.

```
array_pop(item_names); // This will remove the last item from an array
```

What if we feel like organizing our items in some kind of order? Well, there's a function for that and it's called *array_sort*. In its simplest form, we can use it to put variables in an ascending ("true") or descending ("false") order. This works for both strings (in English) and numbers.

```
// Sort our array in an ascending manner, i.e. from A to Z
array_sort(item_names, true);
```

Multidimensional Arrays

It's time to move on to a more complicated data structure: the multidimensional array. These types of arrays can prove useful for creating tile-based maps in more basic maze games, procedural generation of levels, and for organizing general object data. Let's create a 5 × 5 grid as a two-dimensional array. The upper left coordinate sits at 0,0 while the middle spot is at 2,2 (see Listing 2-10).

Listing 2-10. Demonstration of multidimensional arrays

```
tile_map = [
    ["A", "C", "A", "A", "E"],
    ["A", "B", "A", "A", "A"],
    ["A", "B", "G", "A", "A"],
    ["A", "B", "A", "A", "A"],
    ["A", "A", "A", "A", "A"]
];

tile = tile_map[1][1]; // Get the tile value at row 1, column 1
show_message("Tile at (1, 1): " + string(tile));
tile = tile_map[0][4]; // Get the tile value at row 0, column 4
show_message("Tile at (0, 4): " + string(tile));
// Change the value at row 2, column 2 from "G" to "F"
tile_map[2][2] = "F";
```

Listing 2-11 represents a simple case of storing object data into a multidimensional array.

Listing 2-11. Demonstration of a multidimensional array

```
// Create a 3x3 2D array for storing enemy stats
enemies = [
    [10, 2, "Nitwit"], // Health, damage, name (or whatever we need)
    [20, 4, "Lummox"], // You may have noticed, in GML..
```

```
    [50, 10, "Dolt"] // ..we can store both numbers and strings in the
    same array
];
// Retrieve health of "dolt" into variable enemy_health
enemy_health = enemies[2][0];
show_message("Dolt health: " + string(enemy_health));
```

Going 3D with Arrays

As previously stated, multidimensional arrays in GML are not limited to two dimensions. In GML, a 3D array can be created by nesting 2D arrays within an outer array. But why have more than two dimensions? Some projects, such as voxel-grid-based games (think *Minecraft*), are best developed with this approach; 3D arrays are great for procedurally generated maps where individual grid elements experience a lot of events including frequent creation and/or deletion (see Listing 2-12).

A voxel refers to a *volumetric pixel.* These represent small, cube-shaped units of volume existing in a 3D space.

Listing 2-12. A demonstration of 3D GML arrays

```
// Create a 3x3x3 array
cube = array_create(3); // Create the first dimension
// Initialize our 3D array
for (var i = 0; i < 3; i++) {
    cube[i] = array_create(3); // Create the second dimension
    for (var i2 = 0; i2 < 3; i2++) {
        cube[i][i2] = array_create(3); // Create the third dimension
        for (var i3 = 0; i3 < 3; i3++) {
            // Assign a value to each element based on our iterator variables
            cube[i][i2][i3] = i + i2 + i3;
        }
    }
}
```

```
value = cube[2][2][1]; // Access the element at (2, 2, 1)
show_message("Value at (2, 2, 1): " + string(value));
cube[2][2][1] = 232; // Change the value at (2, 2, 1) to 232
value = cube[2][2][1];
show_message("New value at (2, 2, 1): " + string(value));
```

Unleashing the Awesome Power of GML Data Structures

Besides arrays, GameMaker has a ton of other data structures. In the following section, we'll go through some of the basics of these wonderful data processing tools (see Table 2-6).

Table 2-6. Categories of GML data structures

Data structure	Description	Common use cases
DS grids	Dynamic array-like 2D grid	Maps, visual inventories
DS lists	Dynamic ordered list of elements	Inventories, character dialog
DS maps	Key-value pair storage system	Dictionaries (e.g., localization)
DS stacks	Last-in-first-out (LIFO) data structure	Sequential tasks for undo/redo
DS queues	First-in-first-out (FIFO) data structure	Task queueing (e.g., NPC actions, cutscenes, playing soundtracks, or sound effects sequentially)
DS priority queues	Priority queue; elements are processed based on priority values	Task prioritization, pathfinding for moving objects, leaderboards

DS Grids

DS grids in GML are basically two-dimensional collections of variables. So are they simply 2D arrays? Well, not quite. While they can be used for the same purposes (e.g., inventory systems and maze games), DS grids have more built-in special functions

CHAPTER 2 GAME LOGIC WITH GML

for grid operations, such as setting and retrieving a grid's parameters and advanced iteration functions. Plain old 2D arrays can offer more flexibility if you need to store data in a nongrid format (e.g., storing object data of enemies, as previously discussed). See Table 2-7 for a rundown on the main differences between DS grids and 2D arrays.

Table 2-7. *The main differences between DS lists and 2D arrays*

	DS grids	**2D arrays**
Ideal for	Grid-based games, e.g., maze games Role-playing games (RPGs) Puzzle games Strategy games	Inventory systems Item and opponent databases Game maps
Mixed data types in a single cell	No	Yes
Dimensions	Fixed at 2D	Not limited (nesting allowed)
Available functions	Comprehensive	Basic
Dynamic resizing	Automatic	Manual
Performance	Typically slower	Often better

We shall now examine some basic functions for working with DS grids in GML (see Listing 2-13).

Listing 2-13. Demonstration of DS grids

```
// Create a (happy) 5 x 5 grid filled with zeros
happy_grid = ds_grid_create(5, 5);
// Set the value of the cell at (3, 3) to 1
ds_grid_set(happy_grid, 3, 3, 1);
// Retrieve the value of the cell at (3, 3) into variable jolly_value
jolly_value = ds_grid_get(happy_grid, 3, 3);
// Display jolly_value
show_message(string(jolly_value));
// Destroy the grid
ds_grid_destroy(happy_grid);
```

The above example displays the four basic functions you need for working with DS grids. As you will probably agree, they are rather self-explanatory. It is worth noting you should never forget to summon *ds_grid_destroy* after you're done with a grid to prevent memory leaks and other issues in your games. This is known as *manual memory management* and DS grids need that; the same is not the case for plain arrays.

Changing Regions Quickly

Like previously stated, DS grids have excellent functions for manipulating their contents. We shall investigate some of these next. Now, let's take the 5 × 5 "happy_grid" from the previous example. We'll apply the following function to it:

ds_grid_set_region(happy_grid, 2, 2, 4, 4, 1);

The above function modifies a rectangular region in our grid from its current value zero (0) to one (1), starting from position 2,2 and ending at 4,4 (see Figure 2-2).

	0	1	2	3	4
0	0	0	0	0	0
1	0	0	0	0	0
2	0	0	1	1	1
3	0	0	1	1	1
4	0	0	1	1	1

Figure 2-2. *A 5 × 5 grid demonstrating ds_grid_set_region*

Now, what if we want to change the values of an entire grid to, say, one (1)? We should use *ds_grid_clear,* like so:

```
ds_grid_clear(happy_grid, 1);
```

And should we ever want to randomly move all values around in a grid, we simply need to do this:

```
ds_grid_shuffle(happy_grid);
```

There are many more commands available for working with DS grids in GameMaker. We will take a good look at them later in the book.

DS Lists: The Mightier Arrays

Moving on to the next type of GML data structure, we have the DS lists. These are a versatile and popular tool for storing and manipulating ordered lists of data. A bit like an array, a DS list is more flexible and requires less manual tinkering when adding or removing items. In addition to numbers and strings, these wonderful structures can store things like arrays and even other DS lists.

Listing 2-14 will demonstrate the basics of DS lists. In it, we shall create an inventory, add, and remove items.

Listing 2-14. Demonstration of DS lists

```
// Try this inside a CREATE-event
// Create a new DS List, "inventory"
inventory = ds_list_create();
// Add items
ds_list_add(inventory, "Apple", "Orange", "Surströmming");
// Calculate inventory size and display it
inventory_size = ds_list_size(inventory);
show_message("Inventory size: " + string(inventory_size));
// Display inventory
show_debug_message("Your inventory contains the following items:");
for (i = 0; i < ds_list_size(inventory); i++) {
    item = ds_list_find_value(inventory, i);
    show_message("- " + item);
}
```

CHAPTER 2 GAME LOGIC WITH GML

```
// Remove Surströmming
index = ds_list_find_index(inventory, "Surströmming");
if index != -1 {
    ds_list_delete(inventory, index);
    show_message("Removed item: Surströmming");
} else { // Message for scenario where item was not found (a good practice)
    show_message("Item not found in inventory.");
}

// Check inventory size
inventory_size = ds_list_size(inventory);
show_message("Inventory size: " + string(inventory_size));

// Remove the ds_list from memory
ds_list_destroy(inventory);
```

DS Maps—and a Primer on JSON

In GameMaker, a DS map is a data structure designed for storing key-value pairs. In other words, they associate symbolic identifiers with specific values. This structure is paramount to many programming languages. Now, in listing 2-15, we'll have three keys: name, score, and health, each associated with their specific respective values.

Listing 2-15. Demonstration of DS maps

```
// Create a (happy) ds_map
happy_map = ds_map_create();
// Add key-value pairs
ds_map_add(happy_map, "name", "Jimmy");
ds_map_add(happy_map, "score", 56);
ds_map_add(happy_map, "health", 10);
// Access data
if ds_map_exists(happy_map , "score") {
    score = ds_map_find_value(happy_map, "score");
    show_message("Score: " + string(score));
} else show_message("Score not found!");
// Replace a value
```

```
ds_map_replace(happy_map, "level", 4);
// Serialize to JSON
json_data = json_encode(happy_map);
show_message("JSON data: " + json_data);
// Clean up
ds_map_destroy(happy_map);
```

A Few Words on JSON

JSON, short for *JavaScript Object Notation,* is a lightweight system-agnostic storage format. It works great for online data exchange as well as local file storage. Typically, JSON files are friendly on the human eyes and also rather small in size. The JSON format was specified by programmer *Douglas Crockford* in the early 2000s. He and software architect *Chip Morningstar* sent the first JSON message in April 2001.

Now, when JSON data is *serialized,* it means it has been prepared for transfer between systems. In the context of GML, when JSON data is *deserialized,* this means it is converted for processing inside GameMaker. Luckily, serializing DS maps (and lists) is a rather effortless process with the function known as *json_encode,* as demonstrated in the above listing.

This is what our DS map from this section looks like as a JSON file:

```
{
"name": "Jimmy",
"score": 56,
"health": 10
}
```

Like code blocks in GML, every JSON file begins and ends in those lovely curly brackets. Next, let's modify the listing in the section and make a program that saves a JSON file locally (i.e., on your computer) and loads it into GameMaker, shall we? (See Listing 2-16.)

Listing 2-16. Demonstration of basic file operations in GML

```
// We'll call our file 'happy_savefile'
filename = "happy_savefile";
// Create a ds_map to hold the save data
```

```
save_data = ds_map_create();
    // Add data
    ds_map_add(save_data, "name", "Jimmy");
    ds_map_add(save_data, "score", 56);
    ds_map_add(save_data, "health", 10);
    // Convert the ds_map to a JSON string
    json_string = json_encode(save_data);
    // Save the JSON string to a file
    file = file_text_open_write(filename);
    file_text_write_string(file, json_string);
    file_text_close(file); // Close file after use

    // Destroy map after use
    ds_map_destroy(save_data);
    show_message("Game saved to " + filename);

// Load data from JSON
    // Check if the file exists
    if !file_exists(filename) {
        show_message("Save file not found: " + filename);
        return undefined;
    }
    // Open the file and read the JSON string
    file = file_text_open_read(filename);
    json_string = file_text_read_string(file);
    file_text_close(file); // Close file after use
    // Decode the JSON string into a ds_map
    loaded_data = json_decode(json_string);
    // Read the data
    name = ds_map_find_value(loaded_data, "name");
    score = ds_map_find_value(loaded_data, "score");
    health = ds_map_find_value(loaded_data, "health");
    // Output the data
    show_message("Name: " + name);
    show_message("Score: " + string(score));
```

```
show_message("Health: " + string(health));
// Destroy map after use
ds_map_destroy(loaded_data);
```

- On Windows, GameMaker saves local storage at \
  Users\\<Username>\\AppData\\Local\\<Game Name>. After running
  the above listing, you should find *happy_savefile* in that location.

- On macOS, the storage directory is usually ~/**Library/Application
  Support/<Game Name>**.

- Linux folk should find their local storage at **Home/.
  config/<Game Name>**.

As demonstrated by the previous listing, GameMaker provides us excellent functions for writing and reading files. They are not limited to working with JSON. We can use this for storing game options, high scores, and many other things on a player's computer. Let's recap some of these functions before moving on (see Table 2-8).

Table 2-8. Some common file operation functions in GML

file_exists(filename)	Checks whether a file exists or not.
file = file_text_open_write(filename)	Opens a text file with for writing only. If the file does not exist, it will be created.
file = file_text_write_string(filename)	Write a string to a previously opened text file.
file = file_text_open_read(filename)	Opens a text file for reading only.
file = file_text_read_string(filename)	Reads a string from a text file.
file_text_close(file)	Close the file. Execute after file operations are complete.

DS Stacks

The exciting DS stack is a so-called *last-in-first-out (LIFO)* data structure. You add values to a stack by pushing them and remove values by popping them. The most recently pushed value is the first one to be popped off the stack. Stacks are frequently used for recursive functions (e.g., undo functionality). Let's examine such a program next (see Listing 2-17).

Listing 2-17. Demonstration of DS stacks

```
// Create a stack to store health
health_stack = ds_stack_create();
// Set health to 0
health = 0;
// Push the initial value onto the stack
ds_stack_push(health_stack, [health]);
// Add 99 to health
health += 99;
// Push value into stack
ds_stack_push(health_stack, [health]);
// Show current stack contents
show_message("Stack contents before undo:");
// Create temporary stack
temp_stack = ds_stack_create();

while !ds_stack_empty(health_stack) { // Repeat/loop as long as health_stack is not empty
pos = ds_stack_top(health_stack); // Retrieve top value in health_stack
    show_message("Health: " + string(pos[0]));
    // Pushes the value retrieved from the ds_stack_pop(health_stack)
    // operation onto the temp_stack
    ds_stack_push(temp_stack, ds_stack_pop(health_stack));
}
// Restore the stack from the temporary stack
while !ds_stack_empty(temp_stack) {
    ds_stack_push(health_stack, ds_stack_pop(temp_stack));
}
```

```
// Destroy temporary stack from memory
ds_stack_destroy(temp_stack);
// Perform an "undo"
if !ds_stack_empty(health_stack) {
    last_position = ds_stack_pop(health_stack);
    health = last_position[0];
    show_message("Undo applied, health now " + string(health));
}
// Destroy stack from memory
ds_stack_destroy(health_stack);
```

Table 2-9 features a rundown of the functions used in the above listing.

Table 2-9. *Some basic functions involving DS stacks in GML*

stack_name = ds_stack_create()	Create a stack.
value = ds_stack_pop(stack_name)	Removes a value from the stack and returns it in a variable.
ds_stack_push(stack_name, x, y, z..)	Adds a maximum total of 15 values to the stack.
ds_stack_empty(stack_name)	Check if a stack is empty.
ds_stack_destroy(stack_name)	Remove stack from memory. Always summon this function after a stack is no longer needed.

DS Queues

A DS queue may seem rather similar to a DS stack, but it's actually a first-in first-out (FIFO) data structure. What this means is that the value that is put into a queue first is also the first one to be removed from it. These queues automatically adjust their size as items are added or removed; they are great for sequential processing.

> Instead of "pushing and popping," in the context of queues, values are *enqueued* (added) and *dequeued* (removed).

When making games, we can use queues for practically any kind of event, including playing animation sequences, synchronizing events in multiplayer games, and ordered loading of audiovisual assets.

Now, let's take a glance at a program listing which represents these wonderful queues in action. The listing also demonstrates the making of custom functions using the aptly named function keyword. Implementing these types of custom functions is a good practice and practically mandatory for larger projects. Instead of repeating a segment of code, we can summon a custom function to repeat tasks at will, increasing code efficiency and readability. In Listing 2-18, we create a nice little function called *Show_queue* to display the contents of a DS queue.

Listing 2-18. Demonstration of DS queues

```
// Create a message queue
messageQueue = ds_queue_create();
currentMessage = "";
// Create a custom function for displaying queues
// using the function-keyword. We'll call it Show_queue
function Show_queue() {
    while !ds_queue_empty(messageQueue)   // Display queue contents as long
                                          //                as queue is not empty
    {
      currentMessage = ds_queue_dequeue(messageQueue);
      show_message(currentMessage);
      }
}
// Add a few messages to the queue
ds_queue_enqueue(messageQueue, "Greetings traveller!");
ds_queue_enqueue(messageQueue, "Use surströmming to your advantage.");
ds_queue_enqueue(messageQueue, "Watch out for falling rocks!");
Show_queue();
if show_question("Add and display another message?") {
```

```
    ds_queue_enqueue(messageQueue, "Surströmming is indeed delicious!");
  Show_queue();
}
// Destroy queue when done
ds_queue_destroy(messageQueue);
```

Let us review the functions found in the above listing (see Table 2-10).

Table 2-10. *Some basic functions involving DS queues in GML*

queue_name = ds_queue_create()	Create a queue and assign a variable for it.
ds_queue_enqueue(queue_name, x, y, z..)	Add a value into a queue. Accepts a maximum of 15 values in a single call.
variable = ds_queue_dequeue(queue_name)	Remove a value from a queue and assign it into a variable.
ds_queue_empty(queue_name)	Check if a queue is empty.
ds_queue_destroy(queue_name)	Remove queue from memory. Always summon this method after a queue is no longer needed.

DS Priority Queues

A DS priority queue is a data structure similar to a standard DS queue, but with one major difference: the values in the queue are ordered based on their user-defined priority values (which are always real numbers). This structure is particularly useful for creating information lists where each entry can be ranked according to its relative importance (e.g., leaderboards or object behavioral patterns).

It's time for an example. Listing 2-19 creates a priority queue, adds four items with their corresponding priority values (that we can freely choose), and displays the queue on screen. In this type of data structure, the items are prioritized so that the lower the priority value, the higher the actual priority.

CHAPTER 2   GAME LOGIC WITH GML

Listing 2-19. Demonstration of DS priority queues

```
// Create a priority queue
mission_queue = ds_priority_create();
// Add missions to the priority queue.
// Priorities are assigned with any real numbers.

ds_priority_add(mission_queue, "Do nothing", 4); // Lowest priority
ds_priority_add(mission_queue, "Attack player", 2);
ds_priority_add(mission_queue, "Repair self", 3);
// Highest priority:
ds_priority_add(mission_queue, "Attack player base", 0.1);

// Process tasks in priority order
show_message("Enemy missions in priority order:");
while ds_priority_size(mission_queue) > 0 {
// Retrieve the mission with the highest priority
next_mission = ds_priority_find_min(mission_queue);
// Retrive priority value of mission/queue item and store
// it into "priority_value"
priority_value = ds_priority_find_priority(mission_queue, next_mission);
// Display each mission and its priority value
show_message("Mission: " + next_mission + " (priority: " + string(priority_value) + ")");
// Remove processed mission
ds_priority_delete_min(mission_queue);
}
// Destroy the priority queue
ds_priority_destroy(mission_queue);
```

Table 2-11 provides a rundown for the functions used in the above listing.

Table 2-11. Some functions for working with priority queues in GML

queue_name = ds_priority_create()	Creates a priority queue.
ds_priority_size(queue_name)	Returns a priority queue's length.
priority = ds_priority_find_min(queue_name)	Retrieve the item in a queue with the lowest priority value (i.e., the highest priority)
priority_value = ds_priority_find_priority(queue_name, priority)	Retrieve the numeric priority value of a given item. Works together with ds_priority_find_min.
ds_priority_delete_min(queue_name)	Delete an item with the lowest priority value from the queue.
ds_priority_destroy(queue_name)	Destroys a priority queue. Always execute this when you are done with a queue.

Structs

There's one more exciting data structure left to explore: the *struct*. As previously touched upon in this chapter, a struct is a variable that holds other variables of any type. They have been a part of GameMaker since version 2.3 was released in 2020.

Unlike arrays, structs are unordered. New variables can be effortlessly added into a struct after its initial definition. Accessing struct variables is easy, too. Think of structs as lightweight GameMaker objects. Unlike the traditional object instance approach, structs have no real processing overhead during their lifetime—they are easier on the computer. You can use structs for every type of game actor, such as enemies, bonus items, and player objects.

Listing 2-20 is a simple example of making a struct with two functions. When functions are formulated inside data structures, they are called *methods*.

Listing 2-20. Demonstration of structs with two methods

```
randomize(); // Roll the dice..

Player = { // Create a struct called Player
    name: "Cletus Campbell",
    hitpoints: 10, // Set hitpoints/health to 10
```

CHAPTER 2 GAME LOGIC WITH GML

```
    defence: 2, // Set defence at 2
take_damage: function(amount) { // Create a method for taking damage
hitpoints -= amount;
show_message(name + " takes " + string(amount)+ " points of damage!");
if hitpoints<=0 show_message(name + " has perished!");
},
display_health: function() { // Create a method for displaying hitpoints
        show_message("Current health: "+string(hitpoints));
        }
};
while Player.hitpoints>0 { // Loop as long as hitpoints are over 0
    Player.display_health();
    // Reduce hitpoints by either 3, 5, or 8, reduce defence (2) from
    this value
    Player.take_damage(choose(3,5,8) - Player.defence);
}
delete Player; // Flag struct for deletion/garbage collection
```

The last line in the above listing contains a new keyword: *delete*. This flags a struct that is no longer needed to head into *garbage collection*. This is a background process which frees memory from data structures that are no longer needed. The GameMaker garbage collector should remove unused structs from memory automatically, but it is a good habit to flag them manually for this purpose just in case.

Struct Constructor Methods

The program in Listing 2-21 demonstrates how we can instantiate structs, kind of like we would do with typical GameMaker objects. In this listing, we turn a *struct* called Fruit, into a *constructor*. This allows us to spawn new instances of this struct ad hoc using the keyword *new*.

Listing 2-21. Demonstration of struct instantiation in GML

```
// Define a constructor function for a Fruit-object
 function Fruit(_x, _y, _speed) constructor {
    x = _x;
    y = _y;
    speed = _speed;

    // Method to drop the fruit down using its y-coordinate
    fall_down = function() {
        y += speed;
    };
}

// Create two instances of the Fruit struct
// Both are assigned a random falling speed of 1, 2, or 3 pixels per step
fruit1 = new Fruit(100, 0, choose(1,2,3));
fruit2 = new Fruit(500, 0, choose(1,2,3));
// Execute the fall_down method inside both instances
fruit1.fall_down();
fruit2.fall_down();
```

You will encounter two concepts that at first seem very similar: *function* and *method*. A function is a piece of code that is not tied to any specific object or struct. A method represents a function which is defined and operates within a data structure, such as a struct.

Structs and Inheritance

We can create inheritance-like behavior by combining structs and sharing methods (and properties) between them. Listing 2-22 demonstrates this by first creating a base struct, *Fruit,* and following that up with an inherited struct, *Vegetable.* The latter struct inherits the method *fall_down* from the Fruit struct and can thus leverage it during runtime. In addition, this inheriting struct (Vegetable) includes a new method, *rise_up.*

Listing 2-22. Demonstration of inheritance in structs

```
// CREATE EVENT
randomize();
// Define a constructor function for a Fruit-object
 function Fruit(_x, _y, _speed) constructor {
    x = _x;
    y = _y;
    speed = _speed;
    // Method to drop the fruit down using its y-coordinate
    fall_down = function() {
        y += speed;
        if y>room_height y=0; // Make object wrap around its y-coordinate
        if y<0 y=room_height;
    };
}

// Define an inherited function for the Fruit-object, "Vegetable"
function Vegetable(_x, _y, _speed) : Fruit(_x, _y, _speed) constructor {
    // Method to make the vegetable go up using its y-coordinate
    rise_up = function() {
        y -= speed;
        if y>room_height y=0; // Make object wrap around its y-coordinate
        if y<0 y=room_height;
    };
}

// Create instances of the Fruit and Vegetable structs
// room_width is a constant variable which simply references the width of
the room
// It's always available for all GameMaker projects
fruit = new Fruit(room_width*0.5, room_height, choose(1,2,3));
veggie = new Vegetable(0, 0, choose(1,2,3));
veggie2 = new Vegetable(room_width*0.25, 0, choose(1,2,3));

// DRAW EVENT
draw_text(fruit.x, fruit.y,"Orange");
```

```
draw_text(veggie.x, veggie.y,"Turnip");
draw_text(veggie2.x, veggie2.y,"Turnip");
// Execute methods. Since the Vegetable-struct inherits Fruit,
// it can also run fall_down
fruit.fall_down();
veggie.rise_up();
veggie2.fall_down();
```

Having established structs are somewhat similar to objects, let's discuss their differences in detail (see Table 2-12).

Table 2-12. *The main differences between structs and objects in GML*

	Structs	Objects
Defined in	Code	GameMaker IDE
Events	None	Full set
Best used for	Data storage, simple game actors	Any type of game actor or element
Performance	Fast	Normal
Memory management	Automatic (garbage collection)	Manual

If you're new to GameMaker, structs might feel overwhelming at first. They use things like constructors and methods which can be confusing for beginners. Thankfully, it is not necessary for the beginner to leverage structs as their game objects of choice. However, more advanced programmers will probably do so to varying degrees. Structs are great for situations where you need to manage a lot of data without the need for the full feature sets of GameMaker objects. This approach can greatly increase the speed of more complicated projects. However, objects are a primary candidate for actors who need to interact with the game world via GameMaker events. Collisions, for one, may be harder to implement with structs.

In Closing

This chapter was all about the core elements of programming in GameMaker Language. We discussed the following topics:

- Variable data types (strings, real numbers, Booleans)
- Inheritance (i.e., parent-child relationships between objects)
- Basic GML data structures, i.e., arrays and structs
- Advanced GML data structures: grids, lists, maps, queues, priority queues, and stacks
- Different looping techniques, such as for, do/until, and while

The next chapter is all about the core visual functions in GameMaker. We'll also experiment with two simple game prototypes, namely, *PNOG* and *Space Heck*, putting our budding know-how into action. Some truly exciting merriment awaits!

CHAPTER 3

Core GameMaker Visual Functions

In this chapter, we'll shift our focus onto the fundamental visual functions available in GameMaker. We'll be drawing lines, rectangles, circles, and sprites in all their majesty. There's far more to the visuals of the engine than the admittedly stylish show_message function.

Instead of providing completed game projects, the aim of this book is to demonstrate the basic mechanics for 2D game development in GameMaker. It is ultimately probably more rewarding for the budding developer to use these building blocks as they see fit and unveil their personal visions for games. Having said that, a number of simple projects have been prepared to get up and running on the reader's computer. The two game prototypes presented in this chapter (i.e., PNOG and Space Heck) will be available for download in a file repository. Also, some of the drawing-related examples will be stored online. You are encouraged to download and experiment with these projects. The rest of the shorter code snippets here are intended solely for your perusal and analysis.

This is the link to the file repository for all of the book's sample projects:

https://github.com/Apress/Next-Generation-Gamemaking

Before we get into the meat substitute and potatoes of the various drawing functions in GML, let us cover some of the basic concepts related to GameMaker's highly capable 2D graphics system. All of these will be looked into in more detail in the later chapters of the book.

CHAPTER 3   CORE GAMEMAKER VISUAL FUNCTIONS

Importing Visuals into GameMaker

Bringing assets such as sprites and backgrounds into your projects is a rather simple process. We first navigate on the asset browser on the right side of the IDE. Locate the asset-type labeled sprites and right-click on it. Select Create > Sprite. You will now have a brand-new blank sprite asset at your disposal. Alternatively, you can click Alt+S on your keyboard. A window for the sprite you just created should open (see Figure 3-1).

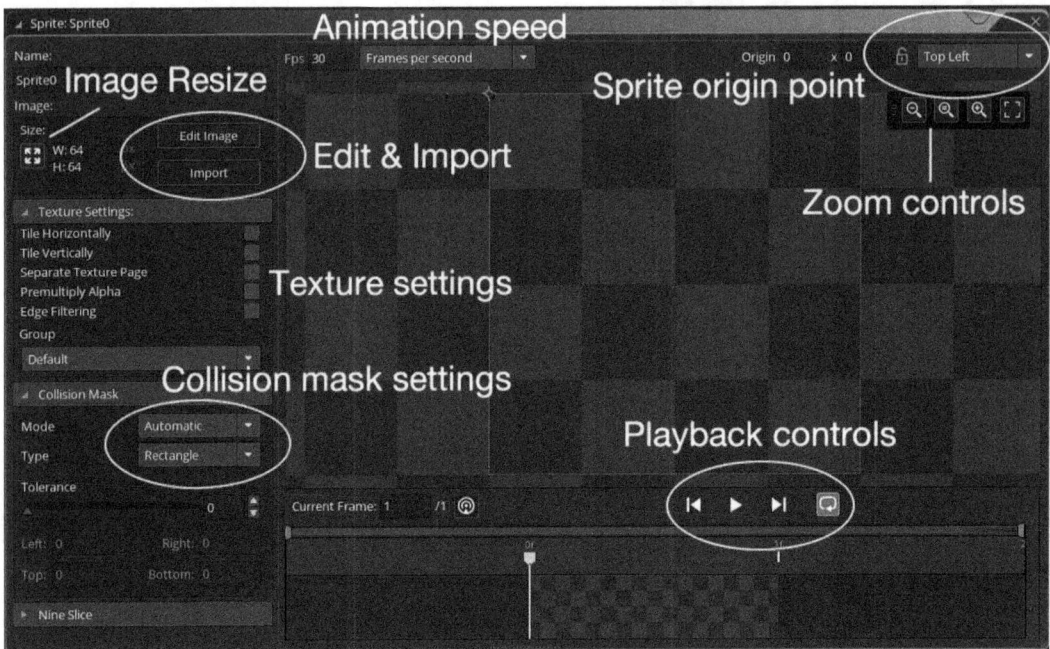

Figure 3-1. *The GameMaker sprite editor*

The sprite editor is split into the following sections:

- **Image resize:** By clicking this icon, a new panel shall open from which you can resize either the image or its container, i.e., the canvas.

- **Edit image and import:** Should you click Edit Image, you are taken to GameMaker's built-in pixel-art editor (i.e., the image editor). Clicking Import will let you choose previously prepared image files from your device to use as the sprite (should you have any available).

CHAPTER 3 CORE GAMEMAKER VISUAL FUNCTIONS

- **Animation speed:** Here you can set the speed of a sprite's animation using either frames per second or frames per game time. Naturally, this setting only has an effect if your sprite has multiple frames. All frames in a sprite are visible on the bottom of this window; you can move the yellow playhead over them to preview them.

- **Playback controls:** If your sprite has multiple frames, you can preview the entire animation by clicking the play button.

- **Collision mask:** This section is used to set the shape and size of a *collision mask* which is basically an invisible area of the sprite that collides within the game world. This topic will be discussed in depth later in the book.

- **Sprite origin point:** This setting, issued in x and y, determines the central reference point (in pixels) for a sprite's position, scaling, and rotation. GameMaker provides numerous presets for origin points on the upper right corner in this window (e.g., top left, middle center, bottom right, etc.). For most purposes, middle center works best.

- **Texture settings:** Here we can adjust numerous settings pertaining to textures, most importantly the *texture group*. This concept will be discussed in detail next. Also, when going for infinitely scrolling horizontal or vertical backgrounds, the two tiling settings under this heading are of paramount importance.

Drawing with the Image Editor

GameMaker's built-in image editor is a decent enough tool for creating sprites out of scratch. Let us now examine the interface as presented in Figure 3-2.

CHAPTER 3   CORE GAMEMAKER VISUAL FUNCTIONS

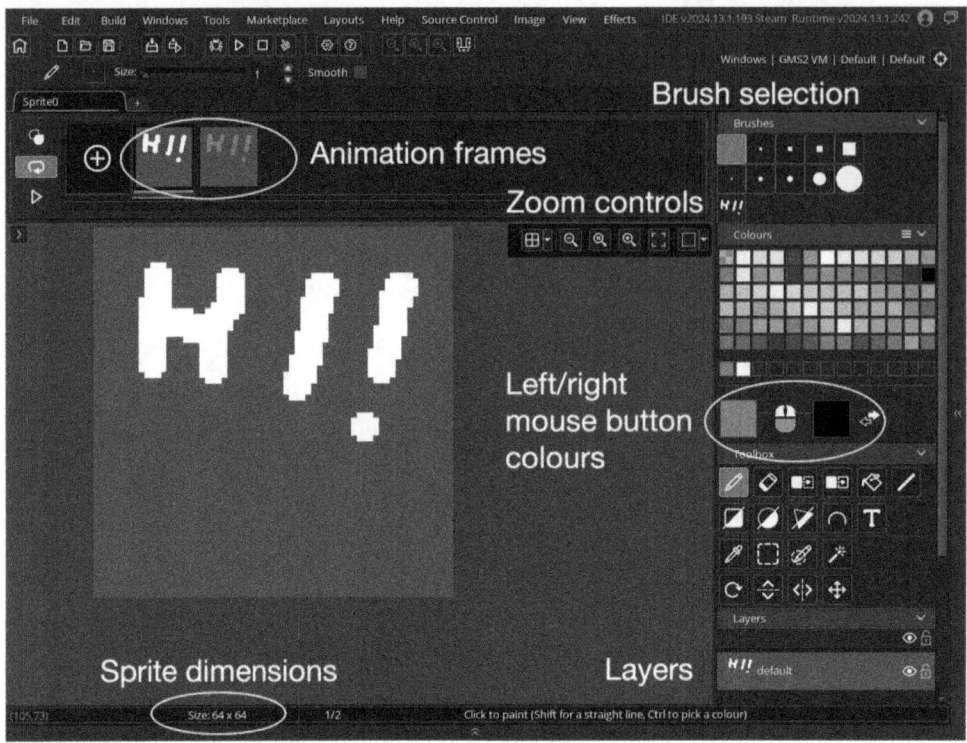

Figure 3-2. The GameMaker image editor

As previously stated, the image editor is accessed by clicking **Edit Image** on the sprite editor shown in Figure 3-1.

The image editor lets you draw anything you want within the boundaries of the canvas size you potentially specified earlier; by default, new GameMaker sprites canvases are 64×64 pixels in size. You create animation by adding frames using the large plus icon in the editor. You can preview animations inside this view, too, by clicking the familiar play icon. There are a number of "brushes" available of varying size and shape. You get to assign different colors for your drawing to both the left and right mouse buttons by clicking with either on parts of the palette. A full set of zoom controls is there, too.

Like rooms, sprites can have multiple layers. These are added using the button titled *Add Layer to All Frames* found on the bottom of the layer section. Sprite layers can be toggled on and off using the eye icon and secured using the lock icon.

On Image Formats

Digital images come in different varieties, ranging from animated gifs to plain old jpegs. Most of us experience these and many other image formats daily on our trips to the internet. GameMaker supports several of these image formats, and they all have a place in it. All remotely modern image editors (e.g., even ancient versions of Photoshop) are capable of producing output in these formats. Let us now go through the four supported (raster-based) image formats you can import visuals into GameMaker in.

- **JPEG:**[1] This is a good general-purpose image format when transparency is not needed. Think title screens, simple backgrounds, or other rectangular elements. JPEGs are a so-called *lossy format*, which means they are reduced in quality when we try to reach a smaller file size. Smaller size results in lower quality JPEGs.

- **PNG:**[2] This is a high-quality image format with full support for transparency. PNGs use an advanced lossless compression, making them fairly small in size while retaining great clarity. This is a go-to format for smaller elements in a game, like animated main characters, their detractors, and potentially some user interface components. With their advanced transparency, PNGs are great for making shapes with beautiful tapered edges.

- **GIF:**[3] Not only good for distributing memes across the internet, some game elements look just fine with this image format. For small animated game actors, you might opt for a gif. While not as colorful as PNGs, GIFs do support simple transparency by having an optional transparent background color; this type of approach is not as smooth as the transparency offered by PNGs. When an animated gif is imported into GameMaker, its animation frames are automatically converted into individual frames within a sprite asset.

---

[1] JPEG stands for *Joint Photographic Experts Group*. JPEGs support 16.7 million colors.
[2] PNG is short for *Portable Network Graphics*. PNGs support 16.7 million colors.
[3] GIF is an abbreviation of *Graphics Interchange Format*. GIFs support up to 256 colors per image.

- **BMP (or "bitmap"):** This is an aging format often providing pictures with fairly large file sizes. BMPs come in many varieties, from grainy black and white images to fully modern versions with 16.7 million colors. However, transparency is poorly implemented in this format. In the age of PNGs, there is not much demand for BMPs, but GameMaker's support for them may occasionally come in handy. For one, highly compressed low-color BMPs can offer a type of interesting retro aesthetics.

Raster vs. Vector Images

All of the previously discussed image formats are so-called *raster formats.* They are made of rows and columns of individual pixels coming in different colors. Raster images are not best suited for upscaling as they become quite blocky rather quickly. However, they are just fine for most 2D games where large amounts of scaling are not needed.

On the other limb, *vector images* scale up wonderfully. This is because instead of individual pixels, vector-based images consist of geometric primitives, i.e., lines and shapes. They basically offer unlimited scalability with little to no loss in image quality. Vector images also tend to be rather small in file size due to not storing every single pixel they are to occupy on the screen. We shall discuss these types of images later in the book.

Sprites created or edited in GameMaker's built-in editor are saved in the PNG format.

Texture Pages and Groups

GameMaker combines sprites, background graphics, and visual user interface elements into bigger resources called texture pages; these are sometimes also referred to as texture atlases. This technique greatly improves graphics processing efficiency for any game with an abundance of 2D visuals. Basically, texture pages are large bitmap files (think JPG, PNG, BMP, etc.). See Figure 3-3 for an example of such a resource.

CHAPTER 3　CORE GAMEMAKER VISUAL FUNCTIONS

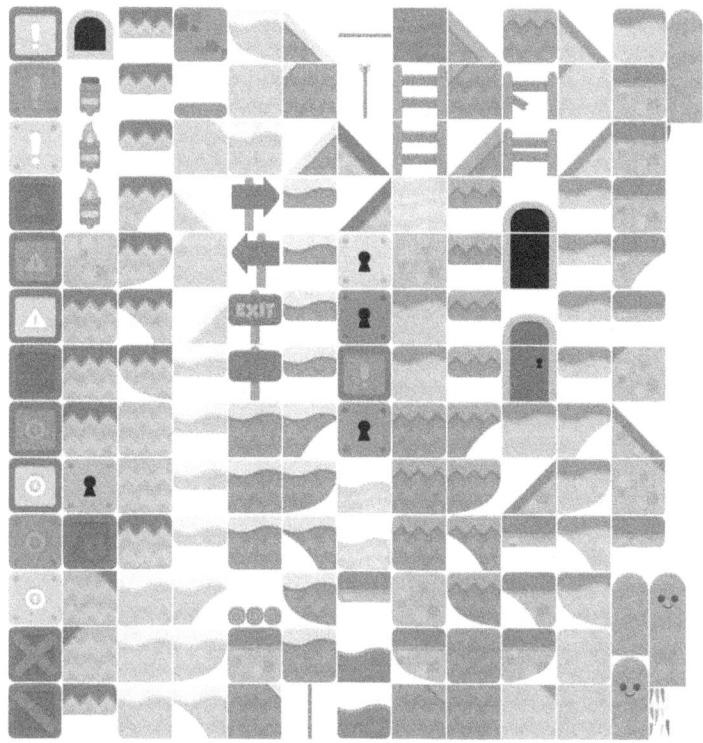

Figure 3-3. *A single texture page/texture atlas showing partial game visuals*

Let's examine a feature called *texture groups* next. While not necessary for most smaller games, grouped textures become increasingly handy as your projects grow in complexity. With this technique, you can summon only those visual assets needed by specific rooms. This is very important for smooth running of your games. The following two steps let you leverage this feature.

We first navigate to *Tools ➤ Texture Groups.* It is here that we create each group simply by clicking *Add New* (see Figure 3-4). You can rename a group by clicking on the text next to *Current Group* and typing in your preferred group name.

Visual assets are added to a texture group by clicking *Add Asset* found on the bottom of the window; a selector window will appear and let you do this for the sprites of your choice.

CHAPTER 3   CORE GAMEMAKER VISUAL FUNCTIONS

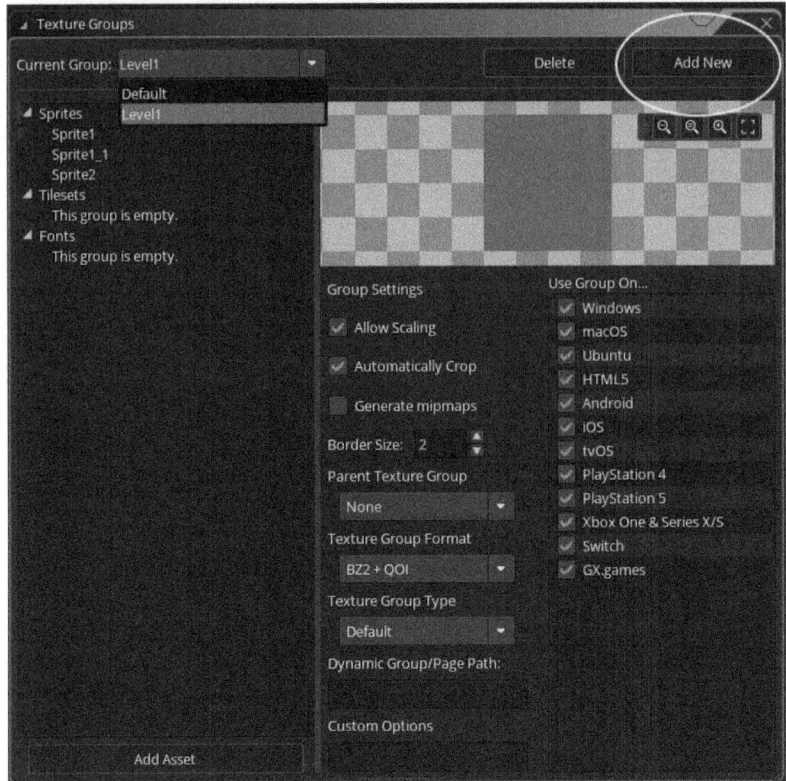

Figure 3-4. *The texture group window in GameMaker*

As you can tell from the previous figure, there are many different settings for texture groups. Not all of them need to be even tweaked for most simple projects. For now, it suffices you are aware of how texture groups are created. The related settings will be discussed in more depth in Chapter 10.

The Dreaded Texture Swap

Larger projects typically have numerous texture pages. Now, a *texture swap* is an incident where GameMaker switches from one texture page to another during runtime because it needs resources from both. This can take a toll on a game's performance, especially on less capable devices. Typically, such a swap introduces a delay ranging from a few measly milliseconds up to a couple of painful seconds. As an intrepid game developer, one of your primary tasks will be to minimize texture swaps. Luckily, there are a handful of techniques for this:

CHAPTER 3 CORE GAMEMAKER VISUAL FUNCTIONS

- **Leverage texture groups:** This technique we just discussed can minimize texture swaps by having each section of the game use only those assets it needs at a specific time. For example, you can have separate texture groups for presentation and others for all the different levels/dungeons in your games.

- **Experiment with texture page sizes:** GameMaker offers several sets of dimensions for your texture pages. These range from a modest 256 × 256 to a whopping 8192 × 8192 pixel. The smaller the page size, the more texture swapping will take place but the less GPU memory will be sacrificed.

- **Use power of two:** Texture pages do not take well to graphical elements with strange dimensions (e.g., 64 × 741 pixels or some other irregular shape). It is often a good idea to break down your larger assets into smaller pieces of, say, 128 × 128 or 64 × 64 pixels, sticking to the rule of *power of two*. This way a texture page is optimally filled with no wasted space. Let's say you have a large sprite with dimensions of 512 × 1024. Instead of using it as a single image, you could split it into smaller tiles of 128 × 128. It would take a total of 32 of these tiles over 4 columns and 8 rows to recreate the image.

- **Monitor the amount of texture swaps in real time:** GameMaker provides a function for detecting texture swaps, namely, the wonderful *draw_get_texture_swaps*. If this function returns a value of at most 10, you're doing fine. Any more than and some optimization is sorely needed.

In 3D games, which are not really GameMaker's forté and are outside of the scope of this book, textures represent the surface color and details wrapped around 3D models.

Surfaces

A *surface* is one of the most powerful visual components in GameMaker. Proper use of surfaces can greatly enhance a game both visually and in computational efficiency. They can be leveraged for effects such as mirror images, water reflections, dynamic lighting, and those sassy screen transitions. These assets are created during a gameloop, as needed, letting you place and process graphics on them off-screen before displaying the end result.

Surfaces are offloaded on the video card (GPU), and they therefore reduce the load on the CPU. However, they are somewhat volatile. A game may suffer from disappearing or warped surfaces during scenarios like sudden screen resolution changes if the developer has not been meticulous enough with optimization.

While surfaces are indeed versatile, care must be taken to not overuse them and/or leave them lingering in memory after they are no longer needed.

Behold, the Application Surface

The *application surface* is a special type of surface automatically created by GameMaker to process the visuals in your game before displaying the final product on-screen. It's primarily used for scaling your game to fit all the various screen resolutions found on different types of devices. The application surface is also wonderful for leveraging full-screen special effects (e.g., shaders) for that extra polish. Think of it as an internal automatic surface where everything is drawn before being displayed on the screen.

By default, the application surface matches the size of your game's view or window. If no view is configured, it matches the room size. GameMaker automatically handles the creation and deletion of the application surface. You can switch it off if you prefer total manual control over your games' visuals. For most projects, this is not necessary. We shall discuss surfaces, including the application surface, in much greater detail in Chapter 10.

Drawing Depth

Drawing enticing things on-screen is not the only important factor in a game's visuals. What is just as relevant is the order in which we do this. For example, we can't usually have much of a game if the backgrounds are drawn over the game actors. Now, every visual element in GameMaker has a depth value. This is a number that runs from −16000 (the top of the heap) to 16000 (the very bottom). Let's say we had background graphics at depth zero (0) and everything else at (1). This would cause the aforementioned problem of clouding a game's proceedings. If we were to reverse this (e.g., setting backgrounds at depth level one and other visuals at zero), we'll get a more playable product where we actually see what's going on.

The drawing depth can be manually set for each object with the property simply called *depth* (e.g., *depth = 0*) in any event (except the Draw event) and thus changed dynamically during the gameloop.

Views and Cameras

A *view* in a video game is simply a rectangular area rendered to the screen. They come in many sizes, from full screen to a more miniaturized variety. A *camera* in this context is an object that defines how a view renders its content. Simple GameMaker projects don't need views at all, but for many types of games, they are essential. For one, this is the case for games that do not display the entire playing area all at once, i.e., games that are "zoomed in" on the player or other entities.

GameMaker uses an *orthographic camera* when rendering 2D content. This refers to a flat view where objects are drawn without any perspective distortion. In this approach, all visual elements are to maintain their size and proportions regardless of their distance from the camera.

There's a robust camera system built right into GameMaker. This means implementing multiview rendering of game visuals is a rather effortless process. Things like minimaps and multiplayer games with many viewing areas on-screen simultaneously are delightfully quick to create.

All the core functionality for view-related operations is found right there in the GameMaker IDE, under the section "Viewports and Cameras." In addition, a ton of related GML functions are available for meticulous control of your in-game camerawork; this is something we shall thoroughly explore later in the book.

On Alpha

Sometimes you may want a greatly reduced opacity for, say, a layer of clouds passing over the game world, or perhaps a body of digital water. The opacity of each individual pixel is defined on the *alpha channel* of an image; think of *alpha* as another word for transparency. GameMaker has the functions and means for changing the alpha value of any visual asset. An alpha of 1.0 means a visual resource is fully visible.

A pixel's color in most digital ecosystems is represented as *RGBA* which stands for *Red, Green, Blue, and Alpha*. For alpha-related functions, GML accepts floating point values between zero (0) and one (1), e.g., 1.0, 0.5, and 0.0, etc.

Many of the drawing functions in GML have an alpha parameter in them. We can also create *alpha blocks* by leveraging a function called *draw_set_alpha,* which will affect subsequent drawing calls. Such a block ends when alpha is set back to 1.0.

```
draw_set_alpha(0.4); // Begin alpha-block
draw_text(20,20, "Hello! I represent alpha at 0.4");
draw_rectangle(200,200, 600,600, true); // So does this rectangle
draw_set_alpha(1); // End alpha-block
draw_text(100,100, "Hi! I represent alpha at 1.0");
```

GameMaker Blend Modes

Again, a feature familiar to anyone with Photoshop experience, a *blend mode* determines how the colors of a source asset are combined with the colors of a destination asset. We can create many exciting types of eye candy with blend modes in GameMaker, such as lights, shadows, smoke, and screen overlays. Blend modes can be applied to pretty much all types of visual assets including sprites, surfaces, text, and primitive shapes (e.g., rectangles and circles). We shall get into detail on how to implement blend modes in GameMaker in Chapter 10.

Excessive use of blend modes can be demanding even for a high-end system. It's best to apply them in your projects with caution.

Going Primitive: Drawing Lines and Rectangles

Let's start drawing things on-screen. A *primitive* is a visual representation of a shape that uses coordinates to define itself. GameMaker has a decent selection of functions for drawing these types of shapes. While these may be challenging to leverage for compelling primary visuals, they can be used for special effects and user interface elements. Some techniques presented in this section are demonstrated with the project file **Chapter 3 Drawing Things.zip.**[4] To access this compressed/zipped project in GameMaker (and others like it), do the following:

1. Download a project file from `https://github.com/Apress/Next-Generation-Gamemaking` and double-click on it to decompress/unzip it into a folder of your choice (e.g., Downloads).

2. Open GameMaker. On Steam, you click *Launch* on the software's library page.

3. Once you reach the GameMaker start page, click *Open* under the heading *GET STARTED.* Navigate to the folder you downloaded the project file (e.g., Downloads/Chapter 3 Drawing Things). Double-click on the project file to load it into GameMaker. These types of files have the file extension *.yyp* (e.g., Chapter 3 Drawing Things.yyp)

Before looking into the more elaborate visuals elements, we shall begin with a classic: the line.

```
// DRAW event
draw_set_color(c_white); draw_line(50, 50, 400, 400);
draw_set_color(c_red); draw_line(150, 50, 400, 400);
wacky_color = make_colour_rgb(100, 150, 255);
draw_set_color(wacky_color); draw_line(20, 400, 400, 400);
```

The previous little listing will draw three lovely lines in white, red, and blue. The function *draw_set_color* is there, like you may have guessed, to set the color of the primitive to follow. GameMaker has a handy built-in palette of 19 color presets (see

---

[4] "Drawing Things" contains demonstrations for ellipses, triangles, vertex primitives, distance gauging, and SDF-based fonts.

Table 3-1), although we can create custom colors using decimals as well. We actually do this on line three in our listing using the function *make_colour_rgb* which sets the red, green, and blue values for a custom color and stores them in variable *wacky_color*.

Table 3-1. The 19 GameMaker color presets

Color name	Decimal value	Color name	Decimal value
c_aqua	16776960	c_green	32768
c_black	0	c_lime	65280
c_olive	32896	c_fuchsia	16711935
c_dkgray	4210752	c_maroon	128
c_gray	8421504	c_red	255
c_ltgray	12632256	c_orange	4235519
c_silver	12632256	c_yellow	65535
c_white	16777215	c_navy	8388608
c_teal	8421376	c_blue	16711680
c_purple	8388736		

Let's next cover another primitive: the stimulating rectangle. In the next simple listing, you'll see three different variations of this shape. Rectangles do not have to be drawn in single color and can turn out quite vibrant. GameMaker offers some great functions for creating multicolored rectangles, in both filled and unfilled forms.

```
// DRAW event
draw_set_color(c_white); draw_rectangle(10, 10, 400, 400, true);
draw_rectangle_color(310, 310, 700, 700, c_aqua, c_blue, c_fuchsia, c_lime, false);
draw_roundrect_ext(400, 400, 600, 600, 50, 50, false);
```

CHAPTER 3　CORE GAMEMAKER VISUAL FUNCTIONS

Table 3-2. *Three types of rectangle functions in GML and their attributes*

draw_rectangle(x1, y1, x2, y2, outline)	Outline specifies whether the rectangle is filled ("false") or not ("true"). Specify color with draw_set_color
draw_rectangle(x1, y1, x2, y2, col1, col2, col3, col4, outline)	col1 = top left color, col2 = top right color, col3 = bottom right color, col4 = bottom left color
draw_roundrect_ext(x1, y1, x2, y2, xrad, yrad, outline)	xrad = the radius of the curve along the x axis, yrad = the radius of the curve along the y axis

The first four attributes in the functions outlined in Table 3-2 represent the beginning and ending pixel coordinates for a rectangle; to begin, draw something at the very left and top of the screen you would enter zero (0) to both x1 and y1. In fact, let's do something like that next with yet another set of rectangles.

```
// DRAW event
hue = clamp(mouse_x * 0.25, 0, 255);
wacky_color = make_colour_hsv(hue, 255, 255);
draw_roundrect_colour_ext(0, 0, mouse_x, mouse_y, 50, 50, c_black, wacky_color, 0);
draw_text(room_width * 0.5, room_height * 0.5, "Hue: " + string(hue));
```

Here a most handy function called *clamp* makes sure the value of variable *hue* stays between 0 (zero) and 255 at all times. In the above listing, we also introduce another function for creating new colors in GameMaker: the awesome *make_colour_hsv*. HSV is short for *hue, saturation,* and *value.* The hue defines the primary color with 0 being red, 40 being yellow, 70 being green, and so on, as per basic digital color theory.

Saturation refers to the chromatic intensity of a color; a saturation setting of zero means black and white color reproduction. The "value" in this context fades the color into black with 255 being least faded. Hue, saturation, and value take a number between 0 and 255 for a total of well over 16.7 million variations.

The listing also introduces yet another function for drawing shapes: *draw_roundrect_colour_ext*. This is exactly like *draw_roundrect_ext* from our previous sample program, except it offers an option for color gradation.

CHAPTER 3 CORE GAMEMAKER VISUAL FUNCTIONS

You may have spotted two new types of built-in variables in the above listing: *mouse_x* and *mouse_y*. These simply return the x and y coordinates of your computer mouse on-screen. They are obviously useful when creating mouse-controlled games, and in our listing they are leveraged for both the size and hue of the rectangle.

In GML, **mouse_x** and **mouse_y** are highly useful built-in read-only variables for detecting the x and y coordinates of your pointing device.

Frenzy with Circular Shapes

It's time to look into two other types of amazing primitive shapes: the circle and the ellipse. The following somewhat more complicated listing demonstrates how circles work in GameMaker. This time we need three events for our program: *Create, Draw,* and *Global Left Pressed* which listens to the player pressing the left mouse button with the cursor being anywhere on the screen.

```
// CREATE
i=0; // Set iterator variable to zero
// Store precision-values in an array
precisions=[4, 8, 16, 24, 32, 64];
// Set initial value into 4, i.e. the first value in the array
jolly_precision=precisions[0];

// DRAW
hue = clamp(mouse_y, 0, 255); // Limit hue to 255
happy_radius = clamp(mouse_x, 30, 600); // Limit radius between 30 and 600
wacky_color = make_colour_hsv(hue, 255, 255);
draw_set_circle_precision(jolly_precision);
// Draw the circle
draw_circle_color(room_width*0.5, room_height*0.5, happy_radius, c_black,
wacky_color, false);
// Provide helpful information
draw_text(40, 40, "Mouse X sets circle radius.\nMouse Y sets hue.\nLeft
mouse button changes circle precision");
```

```
draw_text(room_width*0.5, room_height*0.5, "Radius: " + string(happy_
radius) +
"\nHue: " + string(hue));
draw_text(room_width*0.5, room_height*0.5 + 40, "Precision: " +
string(jolly_precision));

// GLOBAL LEFT PRESSED
// Cycle through the available values stored in array "precisions"
i++;
if i >= array_length(precisions) i=0;
jolly_precision = precisions[i];
```

You might have noticed in some of the draw_text functions there's a two character sequence \n. This simply represents a *line break,* and we can put those in whenever it's convenient. See Table 3-3 for a rundown of some of the functions we used in the previous listing.

Table 3-3. *Three drawing-related functions in GML*

draw_circle(x, y, radius, outline)	Outline specifies whether the circle is filled ("false") or not ("true")
draw_circle_colour(x, y, radius, col1, col2, outline)	col1 = inner color, col2 = outer color
draw_set_circle_precision(precision)	Takes any value between 4 and 64 divisible by 4

We can easily position things in the middle of the room by halving the variables *room_width* and *room_height* and feeding these values into an element's x and y coordinates (as long as said element's origin point is in its middle).

GML Ellipses—with Alarms

The next listing demonstrates both how ellipses and *alarms* work in GM. An alarm is basically a timer represented by a one-dimensional array. It is used as a countdown mechanism to trigger either single or repeated events. Basically, you give a timer a number of steps to wait on before a specific action is executed. Each object in GameMaker can have a maximum of twelve alarms, numbered between 0 (zero) and 11 (eleven). Every alarm has its own event into which we code the action to follow when its timer reaches zero. Alarms are a great tool for timed and/or repeating events in any type of game.

If your project fps is set to 60, a timer with an initial value of 60 represents an event that is to occur every second. In the same scenario, an alarm with an initial value of 120 represents an event for every two seconds and so on.

Now, there are three alarms in the following listing. The initial values for them are set in the Create event. This program displays an ellipse that responds to mouse movement, all the while periodically cycling through its precision settings and changing its hue and saturation.

```
// CREATE
i=0; // Set iterator variable to zero
hue=0; // Set hue to zero
saturation=255; // Set saturation to 255
// Store precision-values in an array
precisions=[4, 8, 16, 24, 32, 64];
// Set initial value into 4, i.e. the first value in array
jolly_precision=precisions[0];
alarm[0]=1; // Set alarm 0 to 1 step/frame
alarm[1]=60; // Set alarm 1 to 60 steps (i.e. one second)
alarm[2]=10; // Set alarm 2 to 10 steps (i.e. a sixth of a second)

// DRAW
wacky_color = make_colour_hsv(hue, saturation, 255);
draw_set_circle_precision(jolly_precision);

// Draw the ellipse
draw_ellipse_color(room_width*0.5, room_height*0.5, mouse_x, mouse_y, c_black, wacky_color, false);
```

```
// Draw white outline for ellipse
draw_set_color(c_white);
draw_ellipse(room_width*0.5, room_height*0.5, mouse_x, mouse_y, true);

// Provide helpful information
draw_text(40, 40,"Mouse sets ellipse shape.\n");
draw_text(room_width*0.5, room_height*0.5, "Hue: " + string(hue) + "\
nSaturation: " + string(saturation));
draw_text(room_width*0.5, room_height*0.5+42, "Precision: " + string(jolly_
precision));

// ALARM 0
hue++;
if hue>255 hue=0;
alarm[0]=1; // Set alarm 0 to 1 step

// ALARM 1
// Cycle through the available values stored in array "precisions"
i++;
if i >= array_length(precisions) i=0;
jolly_precision = precisions[i];
alarm[1]=60; // Set alarm 1 to 60 steps (i.e. one second)

// ALARM 2
saturation--;
if saturation<1 saturation=255;
alarm[2]=10; // Set alarm 2 to 10 steps
```

To repeat an alarm-tied action, we simply need to set the alarm again inside its event. The above program exclusively leverages alarms with repeating events. If we were to trigger an alarm after, say, 12 seconds, we would set it up at 720 (60 steps * 12). See Table 3-4 for a rundown on functions for drawing ellipses in GML.

Table 3-4. Functions for drawing ellipses in GML

draw_ellipse(x1, y1, x2, y2, outline)	Outline specifies whether the ellipse is filled ("false") or not ("true")
draw_ellipse_color(x1, y1, x2, y2, col1, col2, outline)	col1 = inner color, col2 = outer color

Triangles

Next up, we have the time-honored triangle. The two basic functions GML offers for drawing them (i.e., *draw_triangle* and *draw_triangle_colour*) take three sets of variables for their respective three corners as well as a Boolean for outlined/filled triangles.

The following listing leverages both mouse buttons. In it, we can randomize some of the triangle's drawing coordinates with the left mouse button and change its drawing color with the right one.

```
// CREATE
// Set initial coordinates
x1=room_width*0.5; y1=room_height*0.5;
x2=mouse_x;  y2=mouse_y;
x3=room_width*0.25; y3=room_height*0.25;
colors=[c_aqua, c_fuchsia, c_green, c_blue, c_purple]; // Create an array
                                                       for colors
i=0; // Set iterator to zero

// DRAW
x1=room_width*0.5; y1=room_height*0.5;
x2=mouse_x;  y2=mouse_y;

// Set triangle drawing color
draw_set_color(colors[i]);
draw_triangle(x1, y1, x2, y2, x3, y3, false); // Draw the triangle

// Provide helpful information in white
draw_set_color(c_white);
draw_text(40, 40, "Mouse sets triangle shape. Left mouse button randomizes
X3 and Y3 coordinates.\nRight mouse button changes triangle color.");
```

```
draw_text(40, 440,"X1: " + string(x1) + " Y1: " + string(y1));
draw_text(40, 470,"X2: " + string(x2) + " Y2: " + string(y2));
draw_text(40, 500,"X3: " + string(x3) + " Y3: " + string(y3));

// GLOBAL LEFT PRESSED
x3=random(room_width); y3=random(room_height); // Randomize x3 and y3

// GLOBAL RIGHT PRESSED
i++; // Pick the next color in colors-array
if i == array_length(colors) i=0;
```

Table 3-5 displays the format of the two functions used for drawing triangles with GML.

Table 3-5. *The two functions for drawing triangles in GML*

```
draw_triangle(x1, y1, x2, y2, x3, y3, outline)
draw_triangle_colour(x1, y1, x2, y2, x3, y3, col1, col2, col3, outline)
```

Primitives and Vertex Formats

There's much more to primitives than what we've covered so far. There are a number of fabulous functions for creating more elaborate shapes with in GML. We can create almost any shape using vertices; a *vertex* stores the position, color, and other attributes of points in a 2D (or 3D) environment. These vertices can then be used to perform specific calculations to create line-based or filled graphical elements.

There are six types of vertex-based primitives in GML:

- **Point lists** simply display a bunch of pixels at the specified vertices.

- **Line lists** produce individual, unconnected lines. They are great for displaying objects or maps in wireframe.

- **Line strips** produce interconnected lines. They are good for drawing connected paths or curves.

- **Triangle lists** are a set of individual triangles where every three vertices form a triangle.

CHAPTER 3   CORE GAMEMAKER VISUAL FUNCTIONS

- Unlike triangle lists, **triangle strips** recycle vertices, making them computationally more efficient. The sequence of vertices determines how the triangles are connected. Incorrect ordering can lead to distorted shapes.

- In a **triangle fan,** every two vertices connect to the first one to make a triangle. As of June 2025, this primitive type is not natively supported on Windows or Xbox and will run slower on those platforms.

The next listing demonstrates vertex-based primitives. You'll notice two important functions: *draw_primitive_begin* and *draw_primitive_end* between which we put the actual calls for vertices.

```
// CREATE
x1 = 400; y1 = 50; x2 = 600; y2 = 200;
x3 = 150; y3 = 300; x4 = 850; y4 = 500;
x5 = 350; y5 = 550;
selection = 0;
description=["pr_pointlist", "pr_linelist", "pr_linestrip",
"pr_trianglelist", "pr_trianglestrip", "pr_trianglefan"];
primitive_type=[pr_pointlist, pr_linelist, pr_linestrip, pr_trianglelist,
pr_trianglestrip, pr_trianglefan];

// DRAW
draw_set_color(c_white);
draw_text(40, 40, description[selection]+"\nPress left mouse button to
cycle");

draw_primitive_begin(primitive_type[selection])
draw_vertex_color(x1, y1, c_yellow, 0.5);
draw_vertex_color(x2, y2, c_red, 0.6);
draw_vertex_color(x3, y3, c_white, 0.5);
draw_vertex_color(x4, y4, c_aqua, 1);
draw_vertex_color(x4-100, y4+200, c_lime, 1);
draw_vertex_color(x5, y5, c_teal, 1);
draw_primitive_end();
```

```
// GLOBAL LEFT PRESSED
selection++;
if selection>array_length(primitive_type) - 1 selection=0;
```

The function *draw_vertex_color* takes x and y coordinates, color, and a floating point alpha value between 0.0 and 1.0. See Table 3-6 for a rundown on the different types of vertex-based primitives available in GameMaker.

Table 3-6. *The six GML vertex primitives*

pr_pointlist	A set of individual points
pr_linelist	A set of individual line segments, where each pair of vertices defines a line
pr_linestrip	A continuous line connecting each vertex to the next in sequence
pr_trianglelist	A series of individual triangles, where every three vertices define a triangle
pr_trianglestrip	A connected strip of triangles. Each additional vertex creates a new triangle based on the last two vertices
pr_trianglefan	A fan-like arrangement of triangles sharing a common central vertex

Fonts in GameMaker

Leveraging the right fonts can add greatly to a game's presentation. In GameMaker, we are not stuck on one default font for our typesetting needs. We can use any fonts installed on our system in our games. They will be automatically integrated into your projects as textures; the end user does not need to have the same fonts installed.

The next listing demonstrates the basic use of fonts in GameMaker. Before we can execute any font-related functions, we need to have a font resource in a project. We can do this by clicking right mouse button on top of the asset browser and selecting *Create* ➤ *Font*. You can set attributes such as size and style in the screen that follows (see Figure 3-5).

CHAPTER 3   CORE GAMEMAKER VISUAL FUNCTIONS

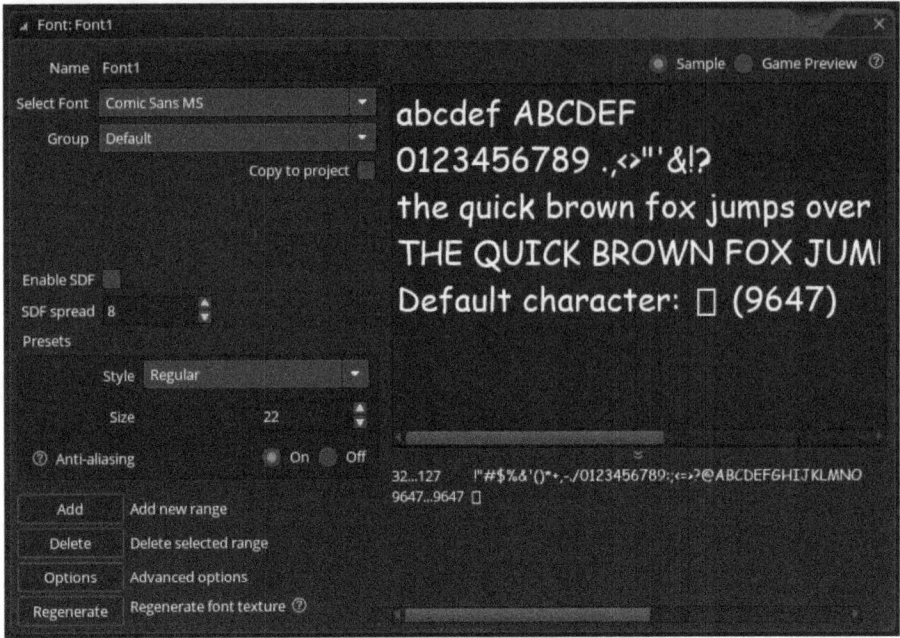

Figure 3-5. *The font configuration screen in GameMaker*

```
// CREATE
font_info = font_get_fontname(Font1);
// DRAW
draw_set_font(Font1);
draw_set_color(c_yellow);
draw_text(100, 100, "Font: " + string(font_info) + "\nSize: " +
string(font_get_size(Font1)));
draw_text_color(100, 300, "Hello there! This is a great font!", c_aqua,
c_white, c_fuchsia, c_lime, 1);
```

Aligning Your Text

In addition to *draw_set_font, draw_text*, and *draw_text_color*, there are a number of other useful text functions in GML. These include *draw_set_halign* and *draw_set_valign*. These functions configure the horizontal and vertical alignment of text, respectively. They define how text is aligned relative to a given position.

CHAPTER 3　CORE GAMEMAKER VISUAL FUNCTIONS

The function draw_set_halign works like this: with option *fa_left*, the text starts at the given coordinates (i.e., x and y) and extends to the right. With *fa_right*, the text starts at the given coordinates and extends to the left. Using *fa_center*, the text is centered at the aforementioned coordinates. The default value for horizontal drawing is *fa_left*. See Figure 3-6 for a visualization of draw_set_halign.

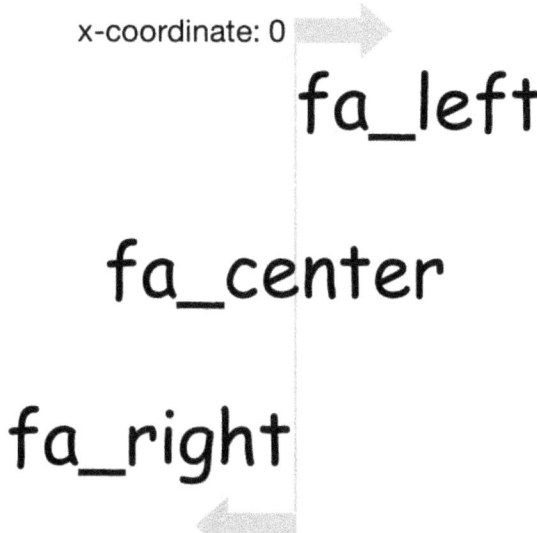

Figure 3-6. *The horizontal positioning of text in GameMaker using draw_set_halign*

As for draw_set_valign, the option *fa_top* (the default) aligns text to the top of the given position, *fa_middle* centers the text vertically around the specified coordinates, and *fa_bottom* aligns it to the bottom.

You should get befittingly acquainted with draw_set_halign as it can make a big difference to your typographical work in GameMaker (see Table 3-7).

Table 3-7. *The two GML functions for setting horizontal and vertical text alignment*

Function	draw_set_halign	draw_set_valign
Attributes	fa_left, fa_center, fa_right	fa_top, fa_middle, fa_bottom

91

You can retrieve values for the attributes presented above using two functions, namely, *draw_get_halign* and *draw_get_valign*, by associating a variable with them, e.g., *horizontal_value = draw_get_halign()* and *cheerful_vertical_value = draw_get_valign()*.

Font Settings

There are a handful of settings for each font inside the GameMaker IDE. At the very top of the screen, you'll notice three settings: *Name, Select Font,* and *Group*. Name simply specifies the title for your font resource inside GameMaker (e.g., Font1) while *Select Font* is the actual typeface (e.g., Comic Sans).

Now, the section labeled *Presets* lets you set the size and style (e.g., italic, bold) for your font. This section also contains a switch for *Antialiasing;* this is a type of smoothing where the edges of a font are rounded out. These settings can be revisited anytime making it easy to try different things.

Games with a modern aesthetic typically benefit from antialiased typefaces. For more retro-style "big pixel" projects, antialiasing is best switched off.

On SDF

You'll notice a switch for a feature called *SDF (signed distance field)* in the font options panel. This is an alternate way of storing your fonts. Instead of traditional texture data, SDF saves the distances of points from the nearest edge of a shape. SDF gives you the highest quality reproduction of fonts at any scale or resolution. You won't need separate assets for each font size. Also, this technology offers better support for effects such as outlines, glows, and drop shadows.

The setting called *SDF spread* is there to control how far from the edges of a shape (or text glyph) the distance field data extends. This value directly impacts how sharp or smooth the rendered shape looks, especially when applying effects like outlines, glows, or soft shadows. A small spread provides high precision near the edges but may lose detail when scaled up. A large spread value sacrifices some edge precision but better supports upscaling SDF typefaces. Smaller projects typically look fine without SDF, but text-heavy games may greatly benefit from this feature.

For the next listing, let's create a font asset called *Font1* using the outstanding typeface known as "Comic Sans" (or "Comic Sans MS") which should always be available on your platform. Make sure the setting "Enable SDF" is checked. We then apply the following parameters into "Font1" inside an object's Create event:

```
// CREATE
font_enable_effects(Font1, true, {
    glowEnable: true, // Enable SDF glow
    glowEnd: 18,
    glowColour: c_aqua, // Set glow color to aqua
    outlineEnable: true, // Enable SDF outline
    outlineDistance: 3,
    outlineColour: c_red, // Set outline color to red
    dropShadowEnable: true, // Enable SDF drop shadow
    dropShadowColour: c_white, // Set shadow color to white
    dropShadowSoftness: 10,
    dropShadowOffsetX: 5,
    dropShadowOffsetY: 5,
    dropShadowAlpha: 1
});
// DRAW
draw_set_font(Font1);
draw_text_ext_color(100, 300, "Wow! What a huge font!", 80, 800, c_aqua, c_white, c_fuchsia, c_lime, 1);
```

The above listing demonstrates how we can leverage effects with SDF. In this example, the struct *font_enable_effects* is configured to use glow, outline, and drop shadow.

We also use a more advanced draw_text function in the Draw event, the incredible *draw_text_ext_color*. This function introduces two new settings between the text itself and the color definitions: *separation* and *maximum width*. The latter defines the maximum width in pixels of the string before a line break. The former value is then referenced for the distance in pixels between text lines.

Veterans of *Adobe Illustrator* take heed: SDF is not a true vector-based approach. It is a texture-based raster technique that maintains some advantages of vector graphics, while working within a raster framework. This means SDF is often computationally more effective than vectors.

CHAPTER 3 CORE GAMEMAKER VISUAL FUNCTIONS

GameMaker Scripts

After the major GameMaker update to version 2.3 in 2020, the term "script" has been replaced with "function." However, in popular GameMaker parlance, scripts are still mentioned. As of June 2025, legacy script functions such as *script_execute* are still supported.

Now, not only can we write code inside objects or the room creation section, we can also execute external script files. Scripts are great for cutting down on redundancy. They can serve any purpose, whether it's something to do with audiovisual assets, game logic, or data structures. You can try this out by right-clicking on the GameMaker asset browser and selecting Create ➤ Script. In the example to follow, we create a script called *Script1*, which looks like this:

```
function Script1(happy_value, multiplier){
    _sum = happy_value * multiplier;
    show_message(string(happy_value) + "x" + string(multiplier) +
    "=" + string(_sum));
}
```

It's a simple script which multiplies *happy_value*, our arbitrary argument for this one, with a second argument called *multiplier*. Next, in the create event of an object, we can summon Script1 as follows:

```
// CREATE
number_one=10; number_two=300; // Define a couple of variables
Script1(number_one, 1); // Run script
// Run script using an older method
script_execute(Script1, number_two, 2);
```

Arguments are values that you pass to scripts or functions for processing. Script files in GML start with the keyword *function*. Also, we don't need to go along with GameMaker's default naming conventions for scripts (i.e., Script1, Script2); we can rename them at our leisure in the asset browser. Please note the name of a script shown in the asset browser does not have to equal the actual handle for a script, e.g., we could have renamed our Script1 file to, say, Jolly_Script, but unless we changed the function name inside the script, we can only ever summon Script1 (i.e., *Jolly_Script(number_one, 1)* would produce an error).

The Return Keyword and Gauging Distances

We can retrieve values from scripts and other data structures using a keyword called *return*. We do this and much more in the example to follow, which visualizes the distance between two points in 2D space. First, we define a script like this:

```
function check_distance(x1, y1, x2, y2, range) {
// Calculate the distance between two points using the Pythagorean theorem
    dx = x2 - x1;
    dy = y2 - y1;
    distance = sqrt(dx * dx + dy * dy);
    // Check if the distance is within the specified range
    if distance <= range return true else return false;
}
```

The script contains an implementation of the Pythagorean theorem, which states that the area of the square whose side is the hypotenuse is equal to the sum of the areas of the squares on the other two sides. In this script, we use a square root function (i.e., sqrt).

The Boolean values *true* and *false* are equivalent with one (1) and zero (0) and can be used interchangeably in GML, i.e., if a script returns "true" it returns one (1).

Next we have these events for the example:

```
// CREATE
// Set initial coordinates for points A and B
pointA_x = 250; pointA_y = 250;
pointB_x = mouse_x; pointB_y = mouse_y;
range = 300;

// DRAW
pointB_x = mouse_x; pointB_y = mouse_y;
// Draw a smooth dark gray circle around Point A
draw_set_color(c_dkgray); draw_set_circle_precision(64);
draw_circle(pointA_x, pointA_y, range, false);
```

```
// Draw point A
draw_set_color(c_white);
draw_circle(pointA_x, pointA_y, 5, false);
draw_text(pointA_x + 10, pointA_y - 10, "Point A");

// Draw point B
draw_circle(pointB_x, pointB_y, 5, false);
draw_text(pointB_x + 10, pointB_y - 10, "Point B");

// Draw a line connecting the two points
draw_line(pointA_x, pointA_y, pointB_x, pointB_y);

// Execute the check_distance-script
in_range = check_distance(pointA_x, pointA_y, pointB_x, pointB_y, range);

// Display the result
// Here we shorten "if in_range == 1" with "if in_range"
if in_range draw_text(pointA_x, pointA_y+30, "Points are within range!");
 else draw_text(pointA_x, pointA_y+30, "Points are NOT within range.");

// GLOBAL LEFT PRESSED
pointA_x=mouse_x; pointA_y=mouse_y;
```

All of this may seem somewhat complicated, but thankfully, there's a more elegant way to gauge distances between points in GameMaker. Say hello to the wonderful function called *point_distance*. Let's demonstrate this with the little listing below:

```
// CREATE
pointA_x=300; pointA_y=300; distance=0; diameter=280;
pointB_x=mouse_x; pointB_y=mouse_y;

// DRAW
pointB_x=mouse_x; pointB_y=mouse_y;

// Draw circle
draw_set_circle_precision(64);
draw_set_color(c_dkgray); draw_circle(pointA_x, pointA_y, diameter, false);
draw_set_color(c_white);
draw_circle(pointA_x, pointA_y, 10, false); draw_circle(pointB_x, pointB_y,
10, false);
```

```
// Draw a line connecting the two points
draw_line(pointA_x, pointA_y, pointB_x, pointB_y);
// Calculate distance using point_distance
distance = point_distance(pointA_x, pointA_y, pointB_x, pointB_y);

// Display the result and distance in pixels
if distance <= diameter draw_text(pointA_x, pointA_y+30, "Points are within range!");
 else draw_text(pointA_x, pointA_y+30, "Points are NOT within range.");
draw_text(40, 40, "Distance: " + string(distance));
```

GML's point_distance lets us calculate distances in pixels between any objects in a 2D space. It can even be used as a type of circular collision detection.

Documentation Inside Scripts

GameMaker provides great facilities for documentation inside scripts used to describe the purpose, parameters, and the return value of a script/function. This information is shown as *tooltips* when hovering over with one's mouse in the code editor. The feature is particularly useful when multiple developers are working together. Below is a simple example of a documentation comment.

```
/// @description Checks if a number is positive
/// @param {real} number The number to check
/// @return {bool} Returns "true" if the number is positive, otherwise returns "false"
function is_positive(number) {
    if number > 0  {
        return true;
    } else return false;
}
// CREATE
show_message(is_positive(3)); // Returns true i.e. one (1)
show_message(is_positive(-3)); // Returns false i.e. zero (0)
```

You'll notice the three main elements of a documentation comment are *@description*, *@param*, and *@return*. The first of these is a free (and hopefully useful) description of the script/method. Any parameters for the script are described using the keyword @param. The keyword @return describes the possible return value of the script; these two sections take the descriptors listed in Table 3-8.

Table 3-8. *Descriptors for the arguments @param and @return in GML documentation comments*

@param, @return	{real}: A number, integer or floating-point.
	{bool}: A Boolean value (i.e., true/1 or false/0).
	{string}: A text string.
	{array}: An array.
	{struct}: A struct.
	{instance}: An instance of an object.
	{void}: Function does not return a value.
	{undefined}: Return value does not have a specific type.

More on Undefined

The return type known as *{undefined}* tells other developers (or yourself) that the type of the return value is flexible or as of yet unknown. It can therefore work as a placeholder. Also, if a script/function is to return different types of values depending on the input or condition, it's the best choice. It should be used only when necessary in order to keep things as clear as possible. The following listing demonstrates the undefined scenario with a simple script which is able to return both numbers and strings.

```
/// @description Returns a value based on the input condition
/// @param {bool} condition A boolean condition determines the return type
/// @return {undefined} The return value depends on the condition

function get_value(condition) {
    if condition
        return 123; // If condition is true (or 1) return a number
    else return "Game over!"; // If condition is false (or 0) return
                                a string
```

```
}
// CREATE
result1 = get_value(true);   // Store the results in two variables
result2 = get_value(false);
// Use the results elsewhere in the object
if is_real(result1) {
    // Add number to score-variable
    score += result1;
}
if is_string(result2) {
    // Display string
    show_message(result2 + " Score: " + string(result1));
}
```

Documentation commentary for scripts is purely optional in GameMaker. However, it is a highly recommended practice if you are working as part of a team and/or you want to future-proof your projects.

In the listing above, we leveraged two functions for checking the types of variables, namely, *is_real* and *is_string*. These and other such functions in GML are summarized in Table 3-9.

Table 3-9. Some functions for variable identification in GML

Function	Checks for	Function	Checks for
is_real(x)	Any type of numbers	is_struct(x)	Structs
is_string(x)	Strings of text	is_undefined(x)	Undefined values
is_bool(x)	Boolean variables	is_nan(x)	Values that are not a number
is_array(x)	Arrays	is_infinity(x)	Infinity (positive or negative)

More on "Not a Number" (NaN)

Performing invalid mathematical operations, such as dividing zero with zero, might result in an error known as *not a number* or *NaN*. Taking the square root of a negative number (i.e., sqrt(-5)) will also produce this result. A NaN can take place for some on-the-fly calculations, and they usually introduce unpredictable behavior in any game. NaNs should be caught in your code early, and the function called *is_nan* is just the ticket. By using this function, you can identify and handle NaNs before they cause problems.

If you plan to perform division on a variable, it's best not to initialize or assign it with a zero. Doing those things can lead to a division-by-zero error, which will probably crash your game.

Infinity and GML

There's another rascal skulking in the innards of GML: infinity. This can understandably cause problems as processing infinities is not really within the grasp of our computing devices. Dividing values by zero will get us there, as will going over the bounds of maximum and minimum values in GML (which will result in positive and negative infinities, respectively). Thankfully, we can check for these scenarios too in GameMaker with a function called *is_infinity*. The next listing demonstrates the use of *is_nan* and *is_infinity*.

```
jolly_value = -10 / 0; // Returns negative infinity
//jolly_value = 10 / 0; // Returns infinity
//jolly_value = 0 / 0; // Returns NaN
//jolly_value = 10 / 1; // Returns 10

if is_nan(jolly_value) {
    show_message("NaN detected!");
} else if is_infinity(jolly_value) show_message("The end result is infinite! (" + string(jolly_value)+")"); else show_message("The value is neither NaN nor infinite!");
```

The largest numeric value GML supports is 1.7976931348623157e+308. That's a rather substantial number with 308 zeros after it. Conversely, negative infinity in GML begins under −1.7976931348623157e+308. This is in line with *the IEEE[5] Standard for Floating-Point Arithmetic (IEEE 754)* introduced in 1985.

On Sprites and Collision Masks

We shall now elaborate on the enchanting world of *sprites* in GameMaker. Sprites, like you may remember, are visual representations of 2D game objects and GML has excellent functions for working with them. A sprite can either be a single static image or consist of multiple frames for animations.

A closely related element, a *collision mask,* is an invisible area associated with a sprite which detects collisions between objects. They come in different shapes and vary in computational intensity; a simple rectangular collision mask drains far less resources than a precise, sprite-matched one. In larger projects, collisions tend to be the most problematic area of game optimization as many issues often arise. These include objects getting stuck somewhere in the game world or dramatic, unintended slowdowns. There are numerous methods of implementing collisions, all of which we will explore in the later chapters of the book. For simple projects, a plain Collision event provided in the GameMaker IDE will usually do.

Now, the easiest way to use sprites is done by assigning one to an object in the GameMaker IDE. As previously mentioned, there are also several functions for sprite control available in GML, the simplest being *draw_self()*. This draws a sprite without any manipulation of its properties and sometimes it's all you need. Also, if you create a Draw event for an object and leave it empty or without any drawing functions, its sprites will not get drawn; you'll need to have at least *draw_self* in there.

Please remember to keep all drawing-related functions only in the various Draw events of objects. Maintain game logic separate inside other events, such as Step and the Alarm system.

---

[5] IEEE stands for the Institute of Electrical and Electronics Engineers.

Draw_Sprite

You may often have the need to simply draw visuals and move them around a tad. For this, there's a function called *draw_sprite*. We can summon sprites and other visuals with it from within any instance. The syntax for this function is as follows: draw_sprite(sprite_index, image_index, x, y); we populate the attribute *sprite_index* with the image file we want for our object; this can be done with a few clicks inside the GameMaker IDE or programmatically in GML (e.g., by putting *sprite_index = happy_lad* inside an object's event).

Do note that displayed sprites themselves are not instances per se. Say we have an object called *obj_Restless_Vegetable.* One of its on-screen instances has a collision mask and some game logic as it wanders around the screen. We could use *draw_sprite* to summon, say, rotating accountants around these vegetable instances. However, none of those accountants could collide or interact with the game world; they would remain purely cosmetic. For collisions and other types of interaction, we would need actual objects orbiting our restless vegetables instead.

Common Sprite Attributes

Sprite work in GameMaker is very dynamic. We can examine and manipulate our sprites during gameloops with ease. We can recolor, rotate, alter the transparency, and resize sprites whenever we feel like it. Let us now discuss some of the most commonly accessed sprite-related attributes available in GML. There are a handful more and we shall go in depth with those later in the book (see Table 3-10).

Table 3-10. Some commonly accessed sprite-related attributes in GML

Attribute	Target
sprite_index	The current sprite file for an instance. Returns −1 if none is assigned.
image_index	The subimages (i.e., animation frames) of sprites.
image_angle	A sprite's image rotation between 0 and 360.
image_alpha	A sprite's alpha value (i.e., opacity) between 0.0 and 1.0.
image_xscale	The horizontal scale of a sprite (1.0 represents the original scale).
image_yscale	The vertical scale of a sprite (1.0 represents the original scale).
sprite_width	Returns the horizontal size of a sprite in pixels. Dependent on image_xscale.
sprite_height	Returns the vertical size of a sprite in pixels. Dependent on image_yscale.

On Texture Filtering

There's a setting in GameMaker called *Interpolate colors between pixels.* This refers to a type of *texture filtering*. With this setting on, adjacent pixels are blended into each other using linear interpolation, creating a less jagged look for your visuals. Typically, games with a more modern aesthetic benefit from this feature. However, some games will look considerably worse with texture filtering switched on; think more retroish titles which need that crisp, sharp edge to their graphics (i.e., the pixel art look). There is also a minor hit on performance when texture filtering is switched on.

You can control texture filtering in GameMaker either from the IDE (Game Options ➤ Platform (e.g., Windows) ➤ Graphics) or in real time using the GML function *gpu_set_texfilter(true/false)*.

A Few Words on GML Visual/Drag-and-Drop

We shall now explore the wonders of the GameMaker's Drag-and-Drop environment (DnD) also known as *GML Visual*. As previously mentioned in the book, this is a more serpentine and clumsy approach to making games in GameMaker. The best thing about DnD is you can switch to GML at any moment.

CHAPTER 3   CORE GAMEMAKER VISUAL FUNCTIONS

- Right-click on an object in the IDE and select **Convert to GML.** This will generate the equivalent GML code for your Drag-and-Drop actions.

- If you insist, you can convert your code into Drag-and-Drop, as long as it's simple enough for DnD to understand it by right-clicking an object and choosing **Convert to Drag-and-Drop.**

The DnD interface itself is intuitive. Upon creating a new project, you will see dozens of square icons under *Toolbox*. These represent object behaviors and the most important ones are probably the conditional structures and loops (e.g., *if* and *while*), instance variable manipulators, instance collisions, and movement. While complicated behaviors are there in the toolbox (such as some advanced data structures), you probably won't use them for the type of projects feasible with the DnD approach. Luckily, there's a text-based search option for the behaviors as well as a list of those recently used (see Figure 3-7).

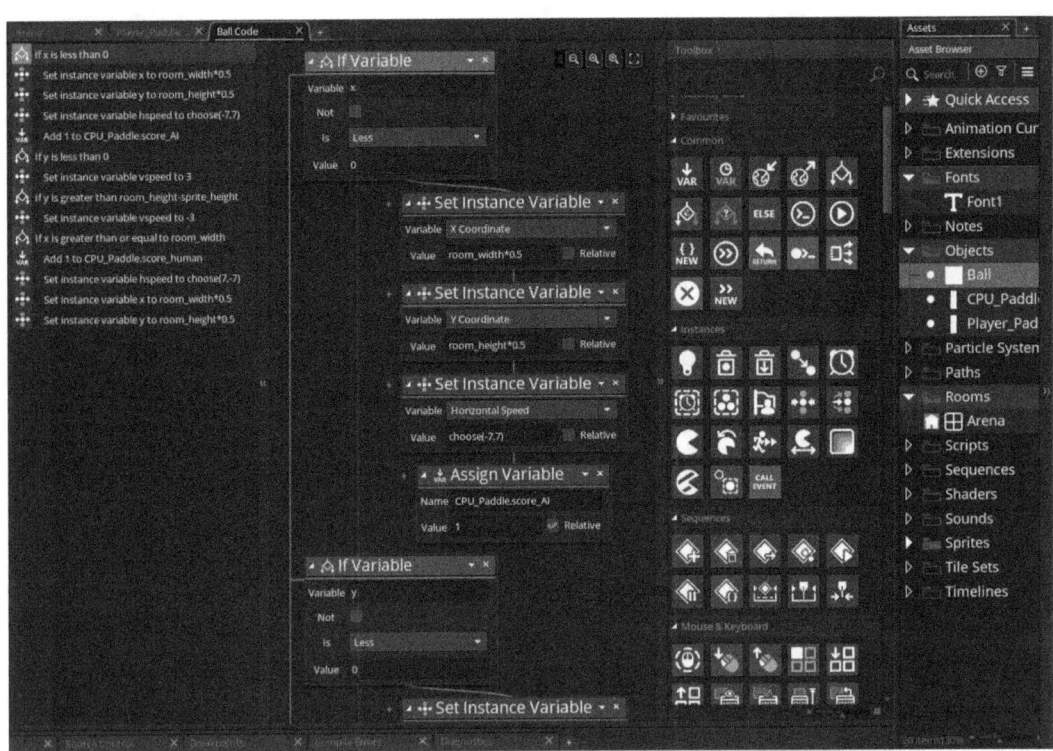

Figure 3-7. *A view of the Drag-and-Drop environment in GameMaker*

All the usual GameMaker events will be grouped on the left side of the screen in DnD. Also, the excellent *asset browser* is still there on the right side of the IDE. It is there we create our objects and other assets by right-clicking and choosing the type of resource we need.

Now, in DnD, we are to string behaviors together. As with GML, they are executed from top to bottom. Adding a behavior at the top of another one prioritizes it over the lower one. However, when using conditional logic in DnD, we attach behaviors to the right side of an if block. If we were to add them to the bottom of if blocks, any conditional checks would simply not get processed.

PNOG: A Drag-and-Drop (DnD) Game Prototype

This and other projects discussed in this book are found here:

`https://github.com/Apress/Next-Generation-Gamemaking`

We'll next explore a simple game project made with DnD. You will find the project files in the online storage area created for this book. PNOG is a take on *Pong,* a game from Atari dating back to 1972. The objective is simply to bounce back a ball with your paddle. Players score every time the ball passes by an opponent. PNOG is controlled with the mouse and it goes on until the player presses the Escape key.

This project features the following resources:

- **Three objects:** Player_Paddle, CPU_Paddle, Ball
- **Two sprites:** Paddle, Ball_
- **One font:** Font1 (Verdana, size 24 with antialiasing)
- **One room:** Arena (1366 × 768 pixels)

This prototype demonstrates the following game mechanics:

- Simple AI and collisions
- Score tracking, drawing primitives, and the Draw GUI event

We will now examine the behaviors implemented into the three objects in this prototype. You'll notice we can use point notation with DnD, too, in order to set or retrieve values (e.g., *CPU_Paddle.score_AI, CPU_Paddle.score_human*) (see Table 3-11).

Table 3-11. *Behaviors for object Ball in PNOG*

Event	Behaviors
Create	**Set instance variable** hspeed to choose (-7, 7)

Step	**If** x is less than 0
	    Set instance variable x to room_width*0.5
	    Set instance variable y to room_height*0.5
	    Set instance variable hspeed to choose (-7, 7)
	    Add 1 to CPU_Paddle.score_AI
	If y is less than 0
	    Set instance variable vspeed to 3
	If y is greater than room_height-sprite_height
	    Set instance variable vspeed to -3
	If x is greater than or equal to room_width
	    Add 1 to CPU_Paddle.score_human
	    Set instance variable x to room_width*0.5
	    Set instance variable y to room_height*0.5
	    Set instance variable hspeed to choose (-7, 7)

Collision with CPU_Paddle	**Show effect** at other.x, other.y **Set instance variable** hspeed to choose (-5, -6, -7, -10) **Set instance variable** vspeed to choose (0, 1, 1.5, -1, -1.5)
Collision with Player_Paddle	**Show effect** at other.x, other.y **Set instance variable** hspeed to choose (5, 6, 7, 10) **Set instance variable** vspeed to choose (0, 1, 1.5, -1, -1.5)

Next we have the AI-controlled paddle object, CPU_Paddle. In addition to representing your opponent, this object handles drawing the background gradient and also displays game-related information in its Draw GUI event.

In order to "humanize" the AI paddle and make it move somewhat erratically, we will introduce some arbitrary movement. For this, we leverage one alarm in the object with a delay of 20, 30, or 40 steps chosen at random. With the default frame rate of 60 in GameMaker, these translate to 0.33, 0.5, and 0.67 seconds, respectively, and it is after these intervals when the AI paddle may move up or down on its vertical axis. However, if the ball object is within a range of half of the size of the room to the AI paddle (i.e., within 683 pixels), your opponent will always start to home on to the ball instead (see Table 3-12).

Table 3-12. Behaviors for object CPU_Paddle in PNOG

Event	Behaviors
Create	**Set alarm 0** to choose(20, 30, 40) **Set window state** to full screen **Set** score_human to 0 **Set** score_AI to 0

Step	**If vk_escape is pressed** Exit game
	If y is greater than room_height - sprite_height
	    Set instance variable y to room_height - sprite_height
	If y is less than 0
	    Set instance variable y to 0
	If Ball.x is greater than room_width*0.5
	    If Ball.y is less than y
	    Set instance variable vspeed to -3
	    else
	    If Ball.y is greater than y
	    Set instance variable vspeed to 3

Alarm 0	**Set instance variable** vspeed to choose(0, 0, 3, -3) **Set alarm 0** to choose(20, 30, 40)

(continued)

CHAPTER 3　CORE GAMEMAKER VISUAL FUNCTIONS

Table 3-12. (*continued*)

Event	Behaviors
Draw	**Set** drawing alpha channel to 0.9 **Draw line** room_width*0.5, 0 to room_width*0.5, room_height **Draw gradient rectangle** from 0,0 to room_width, room_height **Draw transformed sprite** Ball_ frame 0 with scale 1 **Draw transformed sprite** Paddle frame 0 with scale 1 **Draw transformed sprite** Paddle frame 0 with scale 1 **Set** drawing alpha channel to 1 **Draw self**
Draw GUI	**Set Font** Font1 **Draw Transformed** "Human: " ... **Set Text Alignment** to fa_center and fa_top **Draw Transformed** "Welcome to PNOG!" ...

Finally, we have the following events and behavior for the human player's paddle. This is the least complicated object of the three; the only thing it does is follow the player's mouse on the vertical axis (see Table 3-13).

Table 3-13. *Behaviors for object Player_Paddle in PNOG*

Event	Behaviors
Step	**If** mouse_y is greater than to Player_Paddle.y 　**Set instance variable** vspeed to 3 **If** mouse_y is less than to Player_Paddle.y 　**Set instance variable** vspeed to -3

See Figure 3-8 for what the end result of this project looks like.

108

CHAPTER 3   CORE GAMEMAKER VISUAL FUNCTIONS

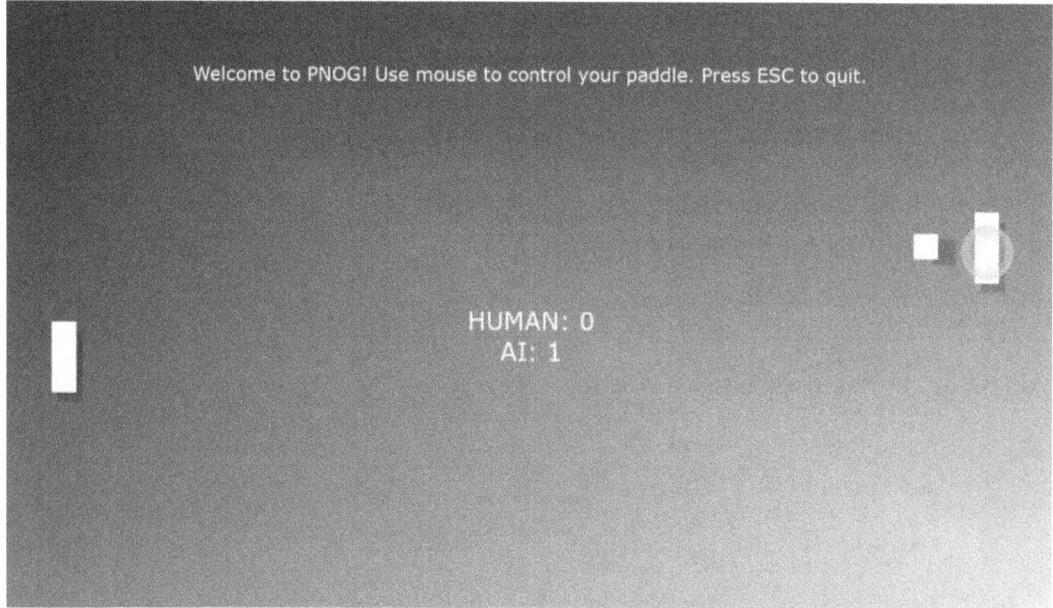

Figure 3-8. *A screenshot from PNOG*

It can be comfortably argued that GameMaker's Drag-and-Drop (DnD) is indeed a tad clunky. Even making a simple project like PNOG is a bit of a grind. Time spent on working in DnD is far better used on getting to grips with GML proper.

Space Heck: Our First GML Game Prototype

Again, this and other projects discussed in this book are found here:

`https://github.com/Apress/Next-Generation-Gamemaking`

It is now time to explore our first game project made with pure GML. This section shows how to implement basic shooting game mechanics in GameMaker. We'll call our first shoot 'em up prototype "Space Heck." It's a simple endless blaster with the player piloting a triangular ship on the bottom of the screen. Enemies fall down from the top of the screen for your shooting pleasure. A collision between your ship and an enemy unit results in the game ending. The goal is to destroy as many enemy units as possible and survive for as long as you can. You may wish to download a barebones version of this project and type the code into it to bring it to life (i.e., Chapter 3 Space Heck Barebones).

CHAPTER 3   CORE GAMEMAKER VISUAL FUNCTIONS

This version of the project has the rooms, the visual assets, and objects (including events). However, all of the GML will be missing aside from *obj_Starfield* (i.e., the background visuals) and *obj_Controller*.

In case you don't feel like typing GML into the bare bones Space Heck project, a completed file is on the repository, too. Just look for a file called **Chapter 3 Space Heck.**

This project features the following resources:

- **Six objects:** obj_Player, obj_Bullet, obj_enemy, obj_Controller, and obj_Starfield
- **Three sprites:** Happy_lad (enemy), Laser, and Ship
- **Two fonts:** SmallFont (Verdana 16) and BigFont (Verdana 28)
- **Two rooms:** SpaceHeck and GameOver (both 1366 × 768 pixels)

Version 0.1 of this game demonstrates the following mechanics:

- Creation of new instances using *instance_create_depth* and destroying them using *instance_destroy*
- Progress/score tracking using *score* and instance number tracking using the function *instance_number*
- Simple keyboard controls (A and D to fly left and right, S to shoot, ESC to quit game)
- Texture filtering, full-screen mode, and mouse cursor removal
- *draw_sprite*, *draw_set_halign*, and *image_xscale*
- Basic instance collisions using Collision events
- Instance horizontal and vertical speed (*hspeed* and *vspeed*) as well as *friction*
- Drawing circular primitives both with and without arrays
- The Draw GUI and Outside Room events

See Figure 3-9 for a screenshot of the first version of Space Heck.

CHAPTER 3 CORE GAMEMAKER VISUAL FUNCTIONS

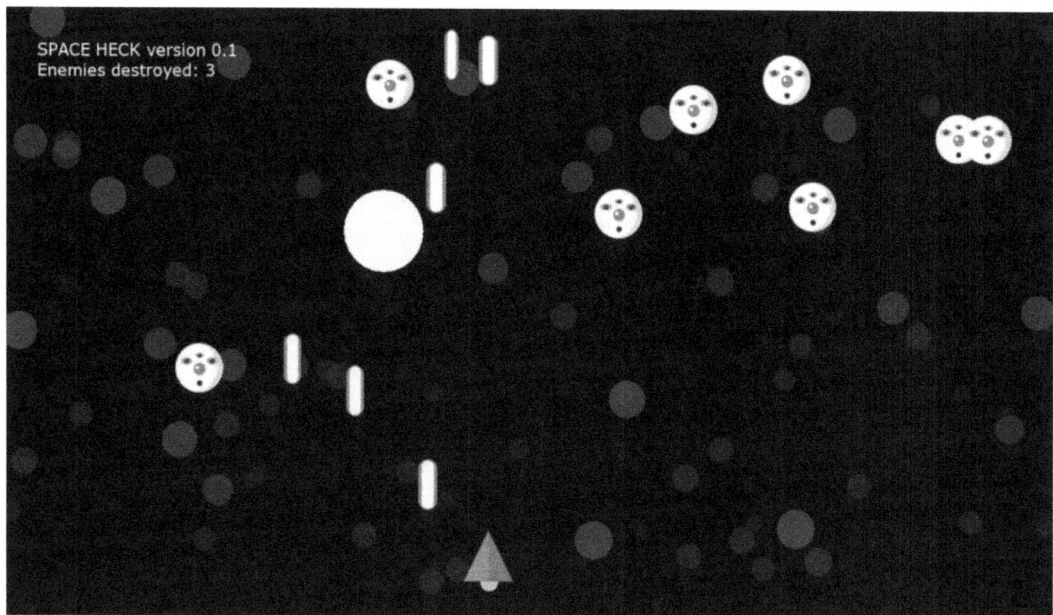

Figure 3-9. *A screenshot of Space Heck version 0.1*

Let's examine the contents of Space Heck's objects next, shall we?

Events for obj_Player

We introduce a new object property right away in the Create event: *friction*. Like its name suggests, it represents a resisting force in the game world. Using subtle amounts of friction in conjunction with hspeed and/or vspeed can add a touch of realism to the movements of any GameMaker game actors. Be careful: anything close to 1.0 can stop an actor in its tracks.

```
// CREATE
x=room_width*0.5; y=room_height*0.9;
// Set instance friction to 0.07. Any more and it might move too slow
friction=0.07; score=0;
// STEP
// Limit x to sprite_width and room_width minus sprite_width
x = clamp(x, sprite_width, room_width-sprite_width);
// Limit horizontal speed to between -8 and 8 pixels per step
hspeed = clamp(hspeed, -8, 8);
```

CHAPTER 3 CORE GAMEMAKER VISUAL FUNCTIONS

```
// Set hspeed to zero if x is less that sprite_width OR
// x is greater than room width minus sprite_width
if x<sprite_width || x>room_width-sprite_width hspeed=0;

// DRAW
draw_set_color(choose(c_yellow,c_orange,c_red));
// Draw a circular exhaust flame
draw_circle(x, y+sprite_height*0.5, random_range(10, 20), false);
// Draw ship sprite
draw_sprite(sprite_index,0,x,y);
```

The controls for the space ship are as follows: A key to move left, D key to move right, and S key to fire laser. These are all implemented using GameMaker's Key Down events. In our prototype, movement for obj_Player is created by altering the horizontal speed variable (hspeed).

```
// KEY 'A' PRESSED
hspeed -= 1;
// KEY 'D' PRESSED
hspeed += 1;
// KEY 'S' PRESSED
// Create bullets at depth 1
instance_create_depth(x,y-10, 1, obj_Bullet);
// COLLISION WITH obj_Enemy
room_goto(GameOver);
```

You'll notice inside obj_Player there's a function for spawning new instances, called *instance_create_depth*. Like the name implies, it does so at a specific depth value. This is a rather essential function for any game. In this prototype, we spawn player bullets at depth one (1), which goes beneath the player's ship which flies at depth zero (0). This makes the bullets fly from underneath the ship at all times for a distinctive cosmetic result.

Finally, we have a collision event between the player (obj_Player) and the enemy (obj_Enemy). Should this unfortunate scenario unfold, we go straight to a different room called *GameOver* using a fantastic function known as *room_goto*.

obj_Bullet

We can add nice little visual touches to our games simply by adjusting sprite properties. In this object, we make the lasers wobble by adjusting *image_xscale.* This is more efficient than animating the sprite using multiple frames/subimages.

As previously stated in the book, GameMaker's objects can access variables inside other objects, as long as these variables are not defined using the keyword *var.* The last line of the Collision event of obj_Bullet features this line: *other.exploding = true.* In collisions, we can reference the object we're colliding with using the keyword *other.*

```
// CREATE
vspeed = -choose(7, 8, 9); // Choose upward vertical speed
// STEP
image_xscale = choose(1, 0.8, 1.1); // Make bullet wobble
// COLLISION WITH obj_Enemy
instance_destroy(); // Destroy bullet
other.exploding = true; // Set "exploding" to true in collided enemy
```

obj_Controller

Here we have a so-called controller object in which we do three important things: we enable full-screen view, hide the mouse cursor, and switch texture filtering on (as previously discussed in this chapter). We also use this object to summon enemies on-screen using GameMaker's amazing alarm system.

The function *window_set_cursor* lets you select from a number of preset cursor types for your pointing pleasure. The most relevant settings are *cr_none* to hide the cursor completely and *cr_default,* which brings back the regular system cursor, should we ever so desire.

```
// CREATE
alarm[0]=10 + random(40); depth=2;
window_set_fullscreen(true); // Enter fullscreen mode
window_set_cursor(cr_none); // Hide mouse cursor
gpu_set_texfilter(true); // Enable texture filtering for smoother visuals
```

CHAPTER 3　CORE GAMEMAKER VISUAL FUNCTIONS

```
// ALARM 0
// Create a new foe at depth 1 as long as there are less than 30 on-screen
if instance_number(obj_Enemy) < 30
instance_create_depth(random(room_width),0,1,obj_Enemy);
alarm[0]=10 + random(40);
```

A handy function called *instance_number* is used in Alarm 0 to track how many enemy instances are currently on-screen. As long as this value stays below 30, we create a new enemy every time Alarm 0 reaches zero.

```
// DRAW GUI
draw_set_color(c_white); draw_set_font(SmallFont);
draw_set_halign(fa_left); // Set horizontal text alignment to left
draw_text(40, 40, "SPACE HECK version 0.1\nEnemies destroyed: " +
string(score));

// Display Game Over -text
if room==GameOver {
    draw_set_color(c_yellow); draw_set_font(BigFont);
    draw_set_halign(fa_center); // Set  horizontal text alignment to center
    draw_text(room_width*0.5,room_height*0.5,"GAME OVER\nPRESS ESC TO QUIT
    OR SPACE TO RESTART");
}
// KEY 'ESC' PRESSED
game_end();
// KEY 'SPACE' PRESSED
if room==GameOver game_restart();
```

This object also has a previously discussed Draw GUI event which is used to display the game's name and version as well as the number of enemies destroyed. Draw GUI becomes more relevant in later versions of Space Heck after we implement views. A nonscrolling game might as well use a regular Draw event set at a low enough depth value to display this information.

The variable *score* as used in our listings is actually a built-in global variable which doesn't need a manual definition. There are vicious rumors these types of variables will be removed from future versions of GameMaker.

---

obj_Enemy

In the Step event for each enemy, we monitor a Boolean variable called *exploding*. If this is set to True, we decrease another variable, *explosion_size,* which controls the radius of an exploding enemy. Once explosion_size reaches zero, we add one (1) to variable *score* and destroy the instance using *instance_destroy*.

```
// STEP
if exploding { // If exploding
    explosion_size-=2; // decrease explosion radius
    vspeed=-vspeed;
 if explosion_size<=0 { // If radius zero or less, destroy instance
    score++;
    instance_destroy();
}
}
// DRAW
// If not exploding draw sprite. Else create flashing circle
if !exploding draw_self(); else {
    draw_set_color(choose(c_yellow, c_orange,c _red));
    draw_circle(x, y, explosion_size, false);
}
```

For an actual explosion, we use the Draw event and summon a nice flashing circle for each exploding enemy. This only occurs when *exploding* is True. If it is not True, we display the instance's sprite with function *draw_self.*

```
// OUTSIDE ROOM
y=0; x=random(room_width);
```

There's a great event called *Outside Room* in GameMaker which is there to monitor if any instances are crossing a room's borders; it is available from *Events > Other > Outside Room* in the GameMaker IDE. In this version of our little prototype game, the enemies can only ever cross the bottom border of the screen. If this happens, they are put back up on the screen by setting their *y* to zero (0) as well as randomizing their horizontal position with *random(room_width).*

CHAPTER 3　CORE GAMEMAKER VISUAL FUNCTIONS

obj_Starfield

Now it is time for some sweet eye candy. The object *obj_Starfield* creates a field of circular stars moving on multiple levels for a classic parallax effect. The starfield array contains three properties: *x, y,* and *speed*.

```
// CREATE
num_stars = 90; // Set number of stars
starfield = array_create(num_stars); // Create a new array, starfield
randomize(); depth=2; // Set depth as the lowest in the game
for (var i = 0; i < num_stars; i++) {
    starfield[i] = {
        x: random(room_width),
        y: random(room_height),
        speed: random_range(1,5)
    };
}
// STEP
for (var i = 0; i < num_stars; i++) {
    star = starfield[i];
    star.y += star.speed;
    if star.y > room_height {
        star.y = 0;
        star.x = random(room_width);
    }
}
```

In the Step event, we simply move the stars in the array vertically with their respective speed value. Once a star hits the bottom edge of the screen, its *y* is set to zero (0) and its horizontal position *x* is randomized within the boundaries of the room's maximum width. Lastly, we have the Draw event:

```
// DRAW
for (var i = 0; i < num_stars; i++) {
    star = starfield[i];
    size = star.speed * 5; // Make size correlate with speed
```

```
        alpha = star.speed * 0.12; // Also make alpha correlate with speed
        draw_set_alpha(alpha);
        draw_set_color(make_colour_rgb(25*star.speed*0.1, 215*star.speed*0.1,
        230*star.speed*0.1));
        draw_circle(star.x, star.y, size, false);
}
draw_set_alpha(1);
```

The size and transparency of each star are set based on its speed, creating a sense of depth. Faster/closer stars are larger and more opaque, while slower stars appear smaller and more transparent. The color of the stars is also based on the speed variable, with the slower stars drawn in a darker hue; the color is defined using a function called *make_colour_rgb* which was discussed previously in this chapter. We close the Draw event of obj_Starfield with *draw_set_alpha(1)* which returns the alpha level to normal; this is always a good idea after we tinker with transparency.

On the GameMaker Drawing Pipeline

Before ending this chapter, let us cover the basics of the GameMaker drawing pipeline. You'll probably have noticed there are quite a few events for drawing (see Figure 3-10).

CHAPTER 3   CORE GAMEMAKER VISUAL FUNCTIONS

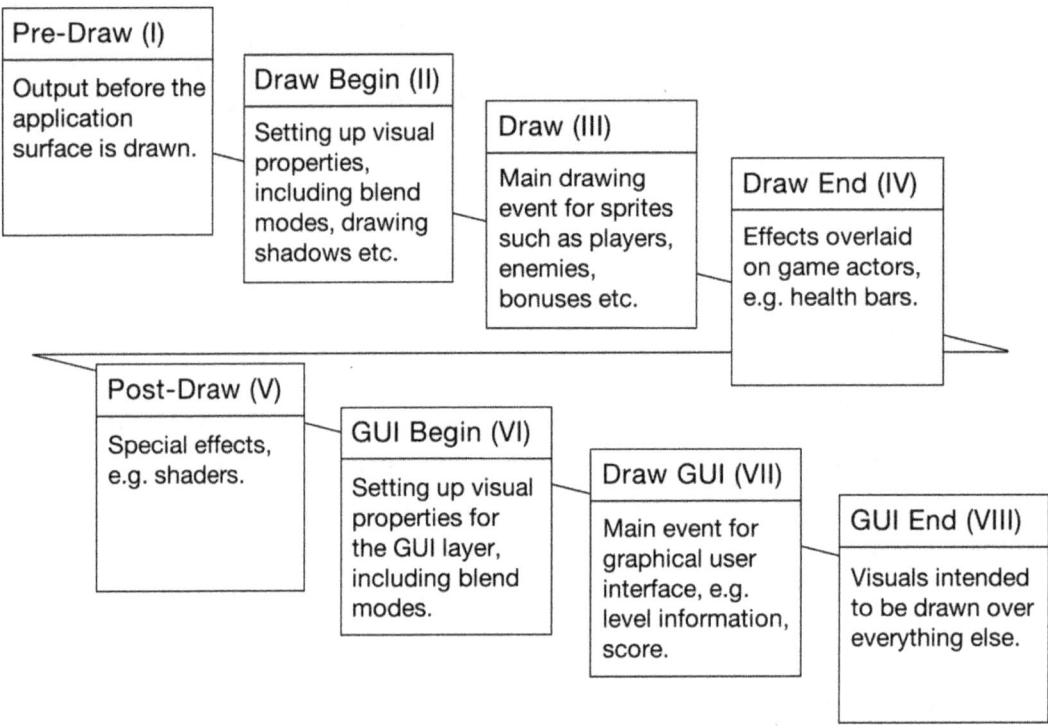

Figure 3-10. The eight Draw events in GameMaker in the order of execution (from top left to bottom right). GUI is short for graphical user interface

Although all of them deal with drawing things on the screen, the events in the above diagram are there to serve different purposes. Some of these are best used to optimize your game's performance. For the beginner, the biggest takeaway from this is you should use the plain Draw event (III) inside objects to display your game's primary visuals. You will also benefit from using the Draw GUI event (VII), which is often there to display the user interface (e.g., score and level information). All of the Draw GUI events always draw on the topmost layers in any game and remain independent of screen moving/scrolling.

We shall be discussing these events in Figure 3-10 later in the book, but for now, it suffices to state most simple games only need the Draw and Draw GUI events for their visuals.

In Closing

This chapter was centered on GameMaker's core visual functions in GML as well as the basics of the Drag-and-Drop approach to gamemaking. The following topics were discussed:

- Texture pages and the dreaded texture swap
- Drawing primitives (draw_rectangle, draw_circle, draw_line, etc.) including vertex-based primitives (point lists, line lists, line strips, etc.)
- GameMaker typography, including signed distance fields (SDF) and their various effects
- Basic sprite properties (image_index, image_xscale, image_alpha, etc.) and how to access some of them
- Functions for creating and destroying instances (instance_create_depth, instance_destroy)
- Functions for enabling full-screen applications, hiding the mouse cursor, and enabling texture filtering (window_set_fullscreen, window_set_cursor, gpu_set_texfilter)

This chapter featured two simple game prototypes: versions 0.1 of *PNOG* and *Space Heck*. In the chapters to come, we'll be adding plenty of new features into the latter project, while also introducing other prototypes.

Chapter 4 will focus on audio, advanced keyboard input, and visual effects including those lovely custom particles.

CHAPTER 4

Audio, More on Keyboards, and Particles

It is now time to enhance our gamemaking with an ample dose of fanciful audio as we unlock this assuredly important aspect of video games. We shall also explore the fascinating world of keyboard control in more depth, moving beyond simple keyboard events. Finally, this chapter will also have us applying momentous visual effects into our creations in the form of particles.

Let us begin our exploration of the audio pipeline in GameMaker. The system is quite powerful and its basics are not that difficult to master. GameMaker offers the tools to provide some convincing audio immersion, too, in the form of flexible real-time effects. However, this chapter will focus on the mere basics of GameMaker audio. More advanced topics, such as the aforementioned real-time effects, will be examined later in the book.

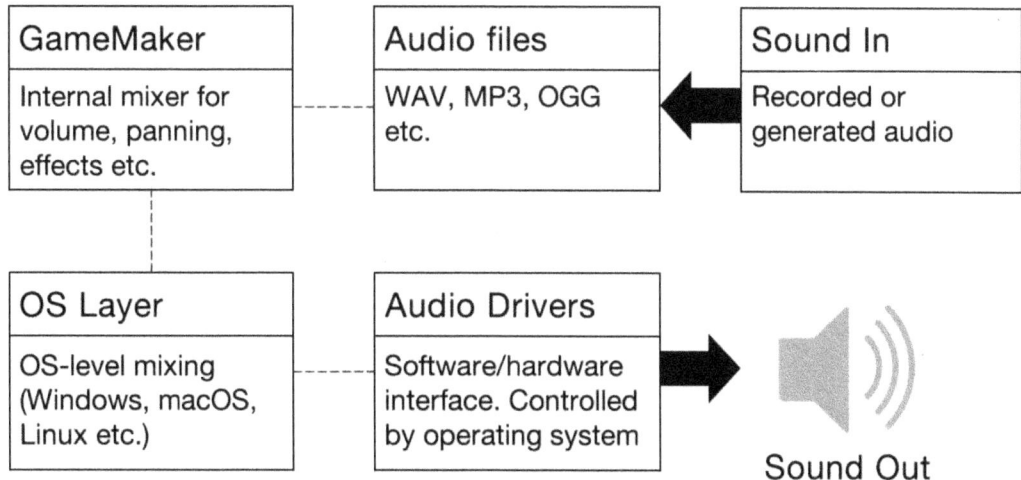

Figure 4-1. *A simplified diagram representing the GameMaker audio pipeline*

CHAPTER 4   AUDIO, MORE ON KEYBOARDS, AND PARTICLES

GameMaker is interfaced with the audio layer provided by the operating system (see Figure 4-1). The audio hardware in any device runs on driver software, which is also maintained by the operating system. GameMaker has a separate internal sound mixer for adjusting the volume, stereo image, pitch, and other properties of audio in its projects.

2D vs 3D Audio in GameMaker

GameMaker supports both traditional digital sound delivery (referred to as 2D audio) and spatial audio (known as 3D audio). This chapter will focus on the former; the latter will be discussed in Chapter 8. See Table 4-1 for a comparison of these two approaches.

Table 4-1. Comparison of GameMaker 2D and 3D audio approaches

	2D audio	3D audio
Used for	Sound effects in 2D games, music, ambient sounds	2D games with a spatial component, 3D games
Panning	Left and right channel (stereo)	Directional
Volume management	Manual control	Based on distances between objects
Performance overhead	Low	Medium
Implementation	Straightforward with dedicated functions	Uses a system of listeners and emitters

Let's next get to grips with the audio asset pipeline in GameMaker, shall we?

Importing Audio into Your Projects

To add an audio resource into GameMaker projects, you simply navigate to the asset browser and right-click and choose *Create* ➤ *Sound*. A new window should open with multiple settings for your sound (see Figure 4-2).

CHAPTER 4   AUDIO, MORE ON KEYBOARDS, AND PARTICLES

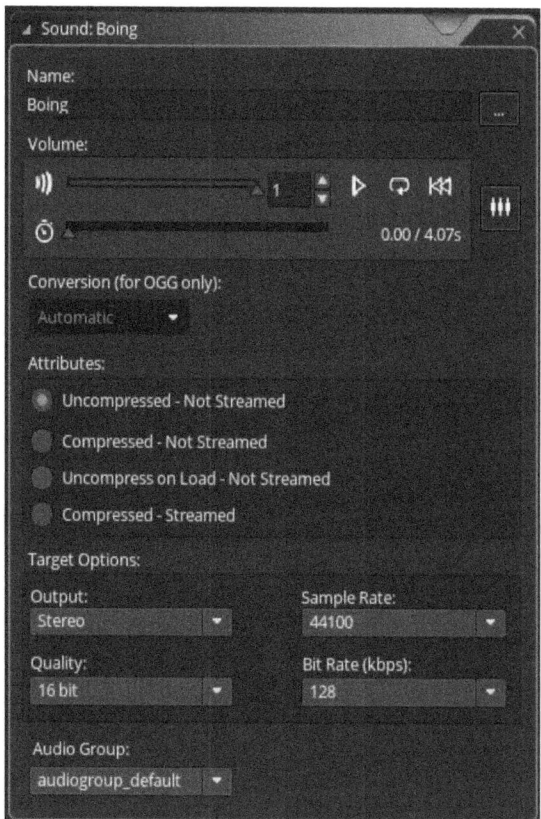

Figure 4-2. *A GameMaker audio resource dialog*

At the top of this window, we have a text box for *Name,* which lets us set the resource handle. Next to this section, we have a button with three dots that opens a file explorer for you to add the audio file with. For audio, GameMaker supports WAV, WMA, MP3, and OGG file formats.

The section called Attributes contains the following four properties:

- **Uncompressed: Not streamed**
- **Compressed: Not streamed**
- **Uncompress on load: Not streamed**
- **Compressed: Streamed**

These settings govern how the audio files are stored and used in your projects. Each has their own pros and cons when it comes to optimizing audio file size and RAM usage. The two compressed options will (re)compress an audio file into *Ogg Vorbis .OGG* format for *all* platforms. These types of sounds take less space to store, but will cause a slight hit on the CPU.

A *streamed* type of sound will be played in real time from storage (e.g., hard drive) rather than loaded into memory. Streaming audio is a good choice for music and background ambience, but it might prove resource-intensive when used with sound effects. *Uncompress on load* will place all the sounds into device memory for faster playback but this will eat up some RAM.

A generally good approach is to use compressed audio for music/ambience and uncompressed audio for sound effects.

A lossy/compressed file format discards parts of the original audio's frequencies in order to cut down on file size. *Ogg Vorbis* represents a high-quality, open source lossy audio format initially released in 2000 and developed by the *Xiph.Org Foundation*.

Nonlossy/uncompressed audio maintains all of the details of their source files; these types of formats include the *Waveform Audio File Format (WAV)* and *Audio Interchange File Format (AIFF)*. Uncompressed audio files are great when it comes to overall fidelity, but they are usually rather massive in file size.

Audio Target Options

The section labeled *Target options* is used to set various attributes for each audio file.

- **Output:** Includes options for *Stereo, Mono,* and *3D*. Stereo delivers audio files with two channels (i.e., left and right) while mono has just one channel. The 3D option marks an audio file to be used with *positional audio*. As previously discussed, this is an advanced approach which lets us create distance-based audio effects. 3D audio resources in GameMaker should be created out of mono audio files.

- **Sample rate:** This option lets you select sample rates between 5512 Hz and 48000 Hz. For most purposes, 44100 Hz is the best choice. For a bit of retro flavor, you may want to experiment with lower sample rates.

- **Quality:** With this option, you have the choice between 8-bit and 16-bit audio. The latter (default) setting is far superior in quality and is recommended for basically all projects.

- **Bit rate (kbps)** gives you the choice between 8 and 512. The optimal choice again is the default at 128.

Sample rate refers to the number of times digital audio is sampled per second. The higher the sample rate, the more accurate the digital representation of the original sound is. However, higher sample rates also result in larger files. 44.1 kHz is a bit of a gold standard, first established by the *compact disc (CD)* in the 1980s; very few modern commercial games present us with audio in a lower sample rate.

Bitrate represents the amount of data processed per second in a compressed audio file such as MP3 and OGG. Higher bitrates produce higher quality audio, but use slightly more storage.

Volume

This section is for setting the volume/gain for your sounds. This value is used as the asset-level volume/gain for this particular resource. For example, if the slider is set to 0.7, the gain for all instances of this sound in the game will also be 0.7. If, after making this setting, we set an instance-level gain to 0.5, the final volume level for that particular instance would be 0.35.

Sound Mixer

Next to the volume controls, we have an icon for the *Sound Group Mixer*. This feature is basically only there for you to check how the different audio resources in your game sound together. It can be handy for detecting volume-related discrepancies or frequency clashes, but it cannot be used to create new resources.

CHAPTER 4 AUDIO, MORE ON KEYBOARDS, AND PARTICLES

Audio Groups

Like textures (as discussed in the previous chapter), audio assets in GameMaker can be grouped by purpose, such as on a level-by-level basis. After assigning an audio file to a group, you can use specific audio group functions to modify it and to load or unload it from RAM. Audio groups can be defined in *Tools* ➤ *Audio Groups*.

OGG Conversion

This setting is only available if your original imported audio file is in OGG format. There are two options for this setting: *Automatic* and *Required*. With the Automatic option, your OGG sound file will be simply copied into your game project. This may cause issues if the attributes of the source file and the sound asset are mismatched as it pertains to stereo vs. mono and other properties. The Required option guarantees that the source audio file is always converted by GameMaker into a brand-new OGG file using the attributes specified in the Sound Editor.

You may benefit from cleaning the asset cache (by clicking Clean in the GameMaker IDE) after making changes to an audio asset to make sure the changes really took hold.

Basic GML Audio Properties

Every audio asset in GameMaker has a handful of basic properties. The most crucial ones are *gain (volume)*, *pitch*, and *offset*.

- The default value for **gain** is adjusted with the "Volume" slider in the GameMaker Sound Editor and is initially set to one (1).
- The default value for **pitch** is one (1). A value of less than 1 will lower the pitch and greater than 1 will raise the pitch. Pitch has a lower limit of −8 octaves and a higher limit of 8 octaves for uncompressed audio. Compressed sounds have a upper limit of +4 octaves.
- The default **offset** is set to zero (0).

126

Audio_play_sound

If there's one function for audio in GameMaker you should get acquainted with, it's *audio_play_sound*. It accepts numerous parameters, but you only need three to use this amazing function. These are in order of application: *resource name, sound priority,* and *looping*. Let's say we want to play a funny sound effect over some wacky theme music. First, we would need two audio resources. Let's call them *Theme1* and *Boing*. Like with other resources in GameMaker, we could right-click the *asset browser* and click *Create audio* to add these two hypothetical audio files into a project. Then we would simply put something like this into an object's Create event:

```
audio_play_sound(Boing, 1, false); audio_play_sound(Theme1, 1, true);
```

This would play a sound effect once (e.g., *Boing*) and repeat *Theme1* indefinitely, until this sound was stopped inside the game or the player shut the program down.

Let's next examine how we can stop sounds inside GameMaker. Say Theme1 is still playing. There are two ways to stop it: we can summon *audio_stop_sound(Theme1)* or we can execute *audio_stop_all()* to stop every single audio resource from playing.

Let's exert more control on our audio. It's a good practice to check if an audio resource is already playing before summoning it, like we do in the following line:

```
if !audio_is_playing(Theme1) audio_play_sound(Theme1, 1, false);
```

You'll notice a function called *audio_is_playing* being leveraged above, paired with a not operator (i.e., !). Often your games do not benefit from multiple instances of the same audio resources playing and the aforementioned function comes in quite handy.

But what about volume adjustments? For that, we have an effective function called *audio_sound_gain*. It can either be applied immediately or it can fade a sound's volume slowly over time. The following example starts playing Theme1 at zero (0) volume, fading it to full volume (1) within six seconds (i.e., 6000 milliseconds).

```
audio_play_sound(Theme1, 1, true);
audio_sound_gain(Theme1, 0, 0);
audio_sound_gain(Theme1, 1, 6000);
```

See Table 4-2 for a recap on the core GML audio functions.

Table 4-2. *The five basic functions for manipulating audio in GML*

audio_play_sound(resource, priority, looped)	Plays an audio resource, optionally looping it.
audio_stop_sound(resource)	Stops a specific sound from playing.
audio_stop_all()	Stops all audio from playing.
audio_is_playing(resource)	Returns "true" if specified sound is playing.
audio_sound_gain(resource, volume, time)	Changes a sound's volume either immediately (0) or over time in milliseconds (>0).

The Whole Spiel on audio_play_sound

While audio_play_sound works fine with just the first three parameters (i.e., audio resource name, sound priority, and looping), it does accept four more. These are as follows (entered in the following order):

- **Gain:** The volume level of the sound at hand. Set between 0.0 (silent) and 1.0 which refers to the full original volume of the sound resource. Going over 1.0 may boost the audio of a sound but also introduce unwanted distortion.

- **Offset:** Sets the playback starting point offset in seconds. Setting this to 0 (zero) plays back an audio resource from its very beginning.

- **Pitch:** Sets the pitch multiplier of an audio resource. A value of 1 leaves it untouched. A value of 2 would double the pitch of a sound.

- **Listener mask:** Determines which "audio listeners" can detect the sound when working with positional audio (this topic is discussed in Chapter 8).

Adding small variations to audio pitch is a good approach when playing repeating sound effects. This is something we will introduce in Space Heck version 0.2, discussed later in this chapter.

Again, this is what the function call at hand looks like; the optional parameters are marked with square brackets:

```
audio_play_sound(soundid, priority, loops, [gain], [offset], [pitch], [listener_mask])
```

Sound Instances

There's a way we can control specific instances of a sound independently of a sound resource which is great for busier games. Let's next create a new instance of a sound and return its ID:

```
wackySound = audio_play_sound(Boing, 1, false).
```

We can now use a sound instance ID (i.e., wackySound) in functions to handle the audio properties of audio within instances, like this:

```
// Stop audio playback at the instance-level
if audio_is_playing(wackySound) audio_stop_sound(wackySound);
```

This way we can control individual sound instances without affecting others. For example, you could have multiple "Boing" sounds all playing at once each with its own volume or playback state.

Pausing Audio

Basic functions aside, GameMaker provides dozens more for all your audio-related needs. Sometimes we simply need to pause all audio playback in our games. We can achieve this with an elegant function called *audio_pause_all*. Audio resources can also be individually paused; this is done with *audio_pause_sound*, which takes the resource handle to be paused as its only parameter. See Table 4-3 for a rundown on pause-related audio functions in GML.

Table 4-3. *Pause-related audio functions in GML*

audio_pause_all	Pauses playback for all sounds.
audio_pause_sound(resource)	Pauses playback for a specific sound.
audio_is_paused(resource)	Returns "true" if audio resource is paused.
audio_resume_all	Resumes playback for all sounds.
audio_resume_sound(resource)	Resumes playback for a specific sound.

The next simple listing demonstrates how we can pause and unpause audio in GameMaker:

```
// CREATE
audio_play_sound(Theme1,1,true);

// KEY PRESSED "SPACE"
if !audio_is_paused(Theme1) audio_pause_sound(Theme1);  else
audio_resume_sound(Theme1);
```

Master Volume and Audio Configuration

Muting and setting volume individual aside, we can control the volume of entire audio mixes in your games. For this, we have an astonishing function called *audio_master_gain*. To halve the volume of all sounds in a game, we would simply apply the following: *audio_master_gain(0.5);* to bring the volume to its full splendour, we can replace the 0.5 with 1.

Just like with visual resources, using too many audio files at the same time takes a toll on a device. To gauge this, we have a function called *audio_channel_num*. If the number of simultaneous sounds exceeds this value, those with a lower priority (as configured in audio_play_sound) are muted in favor of sounds with a higher priority. Setting *audio_channel_num* to zero (0) disables audio playback completely (see Table 4-4).

Table 4-4. *Volume-related audio functions in GML*

audio_master_gain(gain)	Sets the value for global volume (i.e., all sounds and music, range is between 0.0 and 1.0).
audio_channel_num(channels)	Sets the number of available audio channels. The default value (128) is good for most types of games.
audio_system_is_available	Returns "true" if the audio system has been initialized.
audio_system_is_initialised	Returns whether the audio system is initialized on the HTML5 platform. Used in browser games only.

There are also ways to discover whether an audio system is available in the first place. This is done with the aptly named function *audio_system_is_available*. For HTML5/browser projects, there is a special function called *audio_system_is_initialised*.

Changing Pitch

As previously stated, *pitch* is one of the core attributes of audio in GameMaker. We can change and fetch pitch settings with a couple of excellent functions in GML: *audio_sound_pitch* and *audio_sound_get_pitch*. Let's demonstrate these two in a little listing next.

```
// CREATE EVENT
audio_channel_num(1); // Set maximum audio channels to one
// Play audio
jolly_track = audio_play_sound(Theme1,1,true);
gain=1;
audio_master_gain(gain); // Set master gain to 1 (full)

// STEP
if keyboard_check_pressed(vk_up) { // Check for up arrow key
    gain+=0.1;
    audio_master_gain(gain);
}
if keyboard_check_pressed(vk_down) { // Check for down arrow key
```

```
        gain-=0.1;
        audio_master_gain(gain);
}
gain=clamp(gain,0.1,1); // Limit gain between 0.1 and 1
if keyboard_check_pressed(vk_space) { // Check for space key
// Toggle between 1 and 0.75 pitch
        if audio_sound_get_pitch(jolly_track)!=0.75 audio_sound_pitch
        (jolly_track, 0.75);
                else audio_sound_pitch(jolly_track, 1);
}
// DRAW
draw_text(20,20,"Master Volume: " + string(gain)+"\nPress UP and DOWN ARROW
to change gain\nPress SPACE to toggle pitch value");
```

That about covers the basics of audio in GameMaker, and we shall leave these matters for now. It is time to expand our knowledge on the riveting topic of keyboard controls!

On the Keyboard Buffer

The *keyboard buffer* is basically a queue that stores keyboard events as soon as they occur. These events are then processed by a program in the order they were received. This ensures that no key presses are missed. This has been a common feature of digital keyboard controls since the early days of home computing.

GameMaker leverages your operating system's (i.e., Windows, macOS, Linux) robust input handling mechanisms to manage keyboard events. GameMaker reads keyboard events from the OS buffer during each game step/frame which are then stored in GameMaker's own internal keyboard buffer.

More on Game Input: keyboard_check and Friends

The previous listing (i.e., a demonstration of audio pitch control) also showed how we can read the keyboard straight from the Step event instead of using dedicated key-related events, using a delightful function called *keyboard_check_pressed*. These types of functions use a number of constants, most commonly used of which are listed in Table 4-5.

Table 4-5. Some common constants for keyboard input functions in GML

vk_up	Up arrow	vk_space	Space bar
vk_down	Down arrow	vk_lalt	Left Alt
vk_left	Left arrow	vk_ralt	Right Alt
vk_right	Right arrow	vk_alt	Either Alt
vk_enter	Enter	vk_lcontrol	Left Control (CTRL)
vk_escape	Escape	vk_rcontrol	Right Control (CTRL)
vk_anykey	Any key	vk_control	Either Control

Now, there are a number of functions for keyboard input in GML (see Table 4-6) as we can check for slightly different actions.

Table 4-6. The four main keyboard functions in GML

keyboard_check_pressed(key)	Registers a single complete press of a key (down and up).
keyboard_check_released(key)	Checks whether a key has been let go of or not.
keyboard_check(key)	Registers constant pressing of keys each and every step.
keyboard_check_direct(key)	Checks keys directly on a hardware-level (Windows only).

The function *keyboard_check_direct* bypasses the operating system's keyboard buffer making it slightly more responsive. It's best used for games that benefit from very low-latency input, such as fast-paced fighting games or platformers.

Catching Letters with Ord

In addition to the keys referenced in Table 4-5, we can also read single characters in GML. This is done using the function *ord*. It can be leveraged in conjunction with the functions from Table 4-6 as follows:

```
if keyboard_check(ord("A")) show_message("You pressed A!");
if keyboard_check_pressed(ord("1")) show_message("You pressed 1!");
```

The syntax for the Ord function only supports capitalized letters and numbers between 0 and 9.

Typing in Names in GML

Sometimes you want your audience to type in things into your games, such as their character's name or perhaps their favorite gill-bearing vertebrate animal. For this, we can leverage a vivacious built-in variable called *keyboard_string*. The following little listing demonstrates how a player can enter their name using this technique.

```
// STEP EVENT
if string_length(keyboard_string) > 10
    keyboard_string = string_copy(keyboard_string, 1, 10);
    Name = keyboard_string;
    if keyboard_check_pressed(vk_enter) show_message("Your name is "
    + string(Name));

// DRAW EVENT
draw_text(20, 20, "Enter your name and press Enter.\nYou are limited to 10
characters: " + string(keyboard_string));
```

In the above listing, the name of the player is first captured with *keyboard_string* and then stored into variable *Name*. We also use a function called *string_copy* to remove those characters that are over the limit of ten (10) by copying them back into *keyboard_string*.

Remapping Keys in GML

Imagine a scenario where you coded your game to use the arrow keys for control, but you also wish to implement the popular WASD approach into it as well (i.e., pressing W for up, A for left, etc.). For this and any similar scenarios, there's a handy function in GameMaker. It's called *keyboard_set_map*, and it lets you map one key to another; any input from either key will result in the same action(s).

The following listing demonstrates how keys are remapped in GML. In it, we have a custom script/function called *WASD,* which switches keyboard mapping on. Pressing the space bar will achieve this. To disable keyboard mapping, we summon a function called *keyboard_unset_map.*

```
// CREATE
global.wasd_enabled=false; // Create a global variable and set it to false by default

function WASD() { global.wasd_enabled=true;
keyboard_set_map(ord("W"), vk_up); keyboard_set_map(ord("A"), vk_left);
keyboard_set_map(ord("S"), vk_down); keyboard_set_map(ord("D"), vk_right);
}
// STEP
if keyboard_check_pressed(vk_up) show_message("You pressed up or W!");
if keyboard_check_pressed(vk_left) show_message("You pressed left or A!");
if keyboard_check_pressed(vk_down) show_message("You pressed down or S!");
if keyboard_check_pressed(vk_right) show_message("You pressed right or D!");

if keyboard_check_pressed(vk_space) {
   if !global.wasd_enabled WASD(); else {
        keyboard_unset_map(); // Reset keyboard map
     global.wasd_enabled=false;
      }
}

// DRAW
draw_text(20, 20, "Press SPACE to toggle WASD. When enabled, W is the same as arrow key up etc.");
if global.wasd_enabled draw_text(20, 20, "\nWASD enabled!");
```

Clearing Keyboard Strokes

Sometimes you just need to clear all the captured strokes associated with specific keys. For this task, there's a function called *keyboard_clear.* For example, if we wanted to clear any strokes associated with the up arrow key, we would type in *keyboard_clear(vk_up).*

CHAPTER 4   AUDIO, MORE ON KEYBOARDS, AND PARTICLES

This function may come in handy in, say, a menu as you might want to clear the input after a selection is made to prevent the same key press from being processed multiple times. Or perhaps you might want to clear a jump key after the player has jumped to prevent double action. Repeated keystrokes tend to be common during cutscenes and scene transitions, too, so they should be taken into account.

There's also a more robust function for clearing buffers from all keyboard controls and mouse buttons called *io_clear*. Use keyboard_clear when you wish to reset a specific key and io_clear when you need to clear the entire keyboard and/or mouse. Consider this example:

```
// STEP
if transition_timer < transition_duration {
    // Increment the transition timer
    transition_timer++;
    // Clear all input states during the transition
    io_clear();
} else {
    // Transition is complete, move to the target room
    room_goto(apress_office);
}
```

That's it for keyboards for now. We shall engage in techniques for some impressive visual effects.

Stunning Wizardry with Particles

We shall now indulge in some serious eye candy found in practically every modern 2D or 3D game. Say hello to particles! As previously mentioned in the book, particles are a type of on-demand dynamic visual effect with a fairly small performance footprint. They are great for representing fire, smoke, electricity, and other visuals consisting of many animated components in any type of game. Particles can be put in motion in GameMaker by either using some built-in "simple effects" or by creating one's own custom particles.

It is generally a good idea to make our own particles in GameMaker instead relying on the previously mentioned simple effects. This allows for maximum control of your game's visuals and tends to look a lot better. We shall discuss both approaches next, starting with the more basic simple effects.

Simple Particle Effects

For the budding developer, GameMaker offers some rudimentary particle-based effects that are really quite easy to implement. We actually dabbled with these in our first prototype of PNOG back in the previous chapter; a simple effect was invoked every time the ball collided with a bat. There are two GML functions for summoning these effects: *effect_create_below* and *effect_create_above*. Both of these take the same parameters; the difference is in their depth value (50 for *effect_create_below* vs. −15000 for *effect_create_above*). Now, the parameters for simple effects are type, x, y, size, and color. See Table 4-7 for all the available effect types.

Table 4-7. Simple GML visual effect types

ef_cloud	ef_rain
ef_ellipse	ef_ring
ef_explosion	ef_smoke
ef_firework	ef_smokeup
ef_flare	ef_snow
ef_spark	ef_star

The size of these simple effects is assigned with a number between 0 and 2, with 0 being the smallest. The following listing demonstrates GameMaker simple effects (some of which are modest, some of which are perfectly usable). All of the following takes place inside the object *obj_Simple*.

This project is called *Simple Particles*, and it's available for download at the file repository for this book here:

https://github.com/Apress/Next-Generation-Gamemaking

```
// CREATE
// Create an array for the effects
jolly_effect=[ef_cloud, ef_flare, ef_firework, ef_explosion, ef_ellipse,
ef_smoke, ef_smokeup, ef_spark, ef_ring, ef_star, ef_snow, ef_rain];

// Create a second array for the names of the effects.
jolly_effect_names = [
```

CHAPTER 4   AUDIO, MORE ON KEYBOARDS, AND PARTICLES

```
    "ef_cloud", "ef_flare", "ef_firework", "ef_explosion", "ef_ellipse",
    "ef_smoke", "ef_smokeup",  "ef_spark", "ef_ring", "ef_star", "ef_snow",
    "ef_rain"
];

i=0; // Define an iterator
alarm[0]=9;

// STEP
if keyboard_check_pressed(vk_space) {
    if i<array_length(jolly_effect)-1 i++; else i=0;
}
if keyboard_check_pressed(vk_escape) game_end();

// ALARM 0
effect_create_above(jolly_effect[i], random(room_width), random(room_
height), choose(0, 1, 2),
choose(c_lime, c_aqua, c_purple, c_ltgray, c_yellow, c_orange));
alarm[0]=9;

// DRAW
draw_text(20, 20, "Press SPACE to cycle through built-in GameMaker
particle-effects.\nPress ESC to quit.");
draw_text(20, 500,"Currently drawing with the function 'effect_create_
above': "+string(jolly_effect_names[i]));
```

We can destroy all on-screen simple effects with a function called *effect_clear()*.

Custom Particles in GameMaker

We shall now go far more in-depth with this wonderful category of assets, starting with the very basics. First off, the particle pipeline consists of three components in GameMaker (and many other gamemaking software):

- **Particle systems:** A particle system is a container that holds particles and emitters.

- **Particle definitions:** Each particle is defined with their own colors, alpha (i.e., opacity), size, gravitational effects, and duration. You never have control over an individual particle as they function randomly within their predefined ranges of parameters.

- **Particle emitters:** Emitters are on-screen areas where particles are to appear. They vary in size and shape.

Unlike instances with sprites, particles cannot collide with anything per se. They are purely a cosmetic effect most of the time. This lack of collision masks makes them computationally effective. As long as a particle is simple enough, we can have several hundred of them on-screen without much of a slowdown. However, unmanaged particle systems can take quite a bit of memory (RAM). Going completely overboard with particles may cause memory leaks and eventually crash your game.

On HTML5/browser and mobile platforms, some particles may occasionally act strangely. These platforms often lack the resources to deal with unusually large quantities of particle data.

Now, a custom particle in GML has a number of attributes assigned to it. Some are purely optional, but for more professional results, quite a few need to be usually leveraged. See Table 4-8 for a rundown on these functions and their attributes.

Table 4-8. *The most commonly used particle definition functions in GameMaker*

Function	Attributes	Function	Attributes
part_type_shape	index, shape	part_type_alpha2	index, alpha1, alpha2
part_type_size	index, size_min, size_max, size_incr, size_wiggle	part_type_alpha3	index, alpha1, alpha2, alpha3
part_type_scale	index, xscale, yscale	part_type_blend	index, additive (true or false)
part_type_speed	index, speed_min, speed_max, speed_incr, speed_wiggle	part_type_life	index, life_min, life_max
part_type_direction	index, dir_min, dir_max, dir_incr, dir_wiggle	part_type_death	index, death_number, death_type (i.e., particle type)
part_type_gravity	index, amount, direction (between 0 and 360 degrees)	part_type_colour1	index, color1
part_type_orientation	index, ang_min, ang_max, ang_incr, ang_wiggle, ang_relative	part_type_colour2	index, color1, color2
part_type_alpha1	index, alpha (i.e., opacity)	part_type_colour3	index, color1, color2, color3

Let's now discuss some of the particle functions from Table 4-8 in detail. The parameter *index* in all of them always takes the name of a particle resource you're working on.

Now, GameMaker comes with 14 built-in shapes for your custom particles. They do the job for most common tasks, including basic explosions, fire, sparks, and many types of sci-fi effects. You also have the option of using custom sprites for particle shapes. Let us tackle the shape-related definitions on particles (see Table 4-9).

Table 4-9. The 14 built-in shapes available for part_type_shape

part_type_shape	Parameters: index, shape. The available shapes are listed below
pt_shape_pixel	pt_shape_sphere
pt_shape_disk	pt_shape_flare
pt_shape_square	pt_shape_spark
pt_shape_line	pt_shape_explosion
pt_shape_star	pt_shape_cloud
pt_shape_circle	pt_shape_smoke
pt_shape_ring	pt_shape_snow

The particle shapes in GameMaker can be transformed quite dramatically. We can, say, quadruple a pixel particle (pt_shape_pixel) by combining it with another function, part_type_size. We can also make particles change in size over time–or perform some exciting wiggling.

part_type_size	Parameters: index, size_min, size_max, size_incr, size_wiggle

Size_min refers to minimum allowed size and *size_max* to maximum. *Size_incr* refers to how much the size is to grow each step; keep this value low unless you want stupendous amounts of particle growth. The parameter *size_wiggle* is all about how much size is added or subtracted from the particles per step.

part_type_scale	Parameters: index, xscale, yscale

Sets the scale of a particle type. An xscale or yscale of two (2) doubles the respective factor. This is a great function for more static resizing of particles. However, with some shapes, higher values of scaling may result in overtly pixelated particles.

part_type_speed	Parameters: index, speed_min, speed_max, speed_incr, speed_wiggle

Sets the movement speed of the particle upon creation. Can also be used to make the particle change its speed over its lifetime using *speed_incr*. The minimum and maximum speed values' default is to move one (1) pixel per step. *Speed_wiggle* determines how much speed is added or subtracted from the particles per step.

part_type_gravity	Parameters: index, grav_amount, grav_direction

This setting simulates directional gravity. Grav_direction follows the standard GameMaker directions of 0° being right, 90° being up, 180° being left, and 270° being down. As with many parameters in GML, be careful with *grav_amount;* it can quickly get out of control. It's best to stay far under 0.5 for most purposes.

part_type_direction	Parameters: index, dir_min, dir_max, dir_incr, dir_wiggle

This setting sets the direction of the particle based on the previously mentioned GameMaker directions (0° being right, etc.). For this, it takes a minimum and maximum direction value. Again, we can "wiggle" this parameter if we so choose.

part_type_colour1	Parameters: index, color

Sets the color of a particle type. Accepts GameMaker color presets (e.g., c_aqua, c_orange). Part_type_colour2 and part_type_colour3 are variations of this function, which set a two- and three-color timed gradient, respectively.

Going Beyond the Basic Shapes

We're not limited to the shapes offered by the easy effects or the presets (e.g., pt_shape_flare) for our particles in GML. GameMaker's particle architecture allows us to create entirely new shapes using sprites of our choosing. This is done using the function *part_type_sprite* as discussed next.

part_type_sprite(index, sprite, animate, stretch, random)

The *index* in the above function simply refers to the particle index (e.g., pt_snowflake). *Sprite* is the slot for the sprite_index parameter (e.g., happy_dude) for the particle-to-be. The next parameter, *animate*, decides whether the particle is animated as defined in the sprite. If *stretch* is set to true, the animation will be time-stretched to last the lifespan of the particle. When the last parameter, *random*, is set to true, a random image from the sprite will be chosen for the particles.

Creating Fire with Custom Particles

Let's get busy with actual particle work. We shall now construct proper particle-based fire, a popular effect found in many types of games. There will be three types of particles in this system: fire, embers, and smoke. Fire and embers will spawn independently of each other. The smoke shall only arise from "dead" fire particles, i.e., fire particles that have outlived the maximum number of steps allotted to them. We create our particles in the Create event and spawn them in the Draw event. Also, we leverage a most handy function, *part_system_depth,* to set our particle system's depth at –100. The object in question goes by the name of *obj_Fire*.

This project is called *Particle_Fun*, and it's available for download at the file repository for this book here:

```
https://github.com/Apress/Next-Generation-Gamemaking
// CREATE
window_set_cursor(cr_none); window_set_fullscreen(true); gpu_set_texfilter(true);
wacky_system = part_system_create(); // Create a new particle system
part_system_depth(wacky_system, -100); // Set particle system depth to -100

// SMOKE PARTICLE
pt_smoke = part_type_create();
part_type_shape(pt_smoke, pt_shape_cloud);
part_type_color2(pt_smoke, c_gray, c_black);
part_type_life(pt_smoke, 50, 80);
part_type_size(pt_smoke, 0.8, 1.5, 0, 0);
part_type_speed(pt_smoke, 0.1, 1, 0.05, 0);
part_type_direction(pt_smoke, 70, 110, 1, 2);
part_type_gravity(pt_smoke, 0.01, 90);
```

CHAPTER 4   AUDIO, MORE ON KEYBOARDS, AND PARTICLES

```
part_type_alpha2(pt_smoke, 0.2, 0.1);
part_type_blend(pt_smoke, true);

// FIRE PARTICLE
pt_fire = part_type_create();
part_type_shape(pt_fire, pt_shape_flare);
part_type_life(pt_fire, 10, 40);
part_type_size(pt_fire, 0.1, 1.0, 0.01, 0.1);
part_type_speed(pt_fire, 0.2, 0.4, 0.2, 0);
part_type_direction(pt_fire, 80, 100, 0.1, 0.1);
part_type_color3(pt_fire, c_yellow, c_orange, c_red);
part_type_alpha3(pt_fire, 0.6, 0.5, 0.4);
part_type_blend(pt_fire, true);
part_type_death(pt_fire, 1, pt_smoke); // Summon smoke when fire
particle "dies"

// EMBER PARTICLE
pt_ember = part_type_create();
part_type_shape(pt_ember, pt_shape_pixel);
part_type_color3(pt_ember, c_yellow, c_orange, c_red);
part_type_alpha3(pt_ember, 1, 0.6, 0.6);
part_type_life(pt_ember, 80, 260);
part_type_size(pt_ember, 0.2, 0.6, 0, 1);
part_type_direction(pt_ember, 75, 105, 0.25, 0.5);
part_type_speed(pt_ember, 0.05, 0.1, 0.025, 0);
part_type_blend(pt_ember, true);

happy_emitter = part_emitter_create(wacky_system); // Create an emitter

// STEP
if keyboard_check_pressed(vk_escape) game_end();

// DRAW
draw_rectangle_color(0, 0, room_width,room_height,c_black,c_blue,c_dkgrey,c_purple,false);
part_emitter_region(wacky_system, happy_emitter, mouse_x-15, mouse_x+15, mouse_y, mouse_y, ps_shape_ellipse, ps_distr_invgaussian);
draw_sprite(sprite_index, -1, mouse_x, mouse_y+5);
```

```
part_emitter_burst(wacky_system, happy_emitter, pt_fire, 2); // Fire
part_emitter_burst(wacky_system, happy_emitter, pt_ember, 4); // Embers
draw_text(20, 20, "Use mouse to move emitter. Press ESC to quit.");
```

Creating New Particles

There are a number of important elements to consider in the above listing. First of all, let's examine the Create event. There we have the statement *wacky_system = part_system_create()* which is how we create a particle system (called, yes, *wacky_system*). This is how a custom particle architecture is initialized in GML.

Next we have the particle definitions, and as previously stated, there are three of them in this example: *pt_smoke, pt_fire,* and *pt_ember*. Each of these definitions begins with *(particle name) = part_type_create()*. Underneath each definition, we are to store the various functions related to our particle; their order doesn't usually matter. However, since we are to summon *pt_smoke* in one of the functions of *pt_fire*, this particle must be defined first. You see, in the fire particle, we have the following line: *part_type_death(pt_fire, 1, pt_smoke)*. This purely optional function produces a single smoke particle after the lifespan of a fire particle is extinguished (pun somewhat intended).

The last statement in the Create event of obj_Fire, *happy_emitter = part_emitter_create(wacky_system),* simply manufactures an emitter called *happy_emitter* inside our particle system (i.e., wacky_system).

Emitters and Their Regions

The Draw event in our example contains the function *part_emitter_region*. This important piece of code defines the on-screen region for the particles to be emitted. Let's go through this function and its eight (8) parameters:

```
part_emitter_region(system, emitter, x_min, x_max, y_min, y_max, region_shape, distribution)
```

The area of the emitter is defined by four variables: *x_min, x_max, y_min, and y_max*. *Region_shape* accepts four (4) types of settings, which are discussed in Table 4-10.

Table 4-10. *The four types of region shapes for particle emitters in GameMaker*

ps_shape_rectangle	A rectangular box-like shape.
ps_shape_diamond	A diamond shape with the points at 50% width and 50% height.
ps_shape_ellipse	An ellipse with the width and height set by the minimum and maximum values. Best for explosions.
ps_shape_line	A single line. Its starting point is the left and top values and the end point is the right and bottom values.

Finally, we have the *distribution* variable, which accepts one of the distribution curves listed in Table 4-11.

Table 4-11. *The three types of distribution curves for particle emitters in GameMaker*

ps_distr_linear	A distribution where all particles have an equal chance of appearing anywhere inside the defined area.
ps_distr_gaussian	A Gaussian distribution where more particles are generated in the center rather than the edges of the area.
ps_distr_invgaussian	An inverse Gaussian distribution where more particles are generated at the edges than the center of the area.

On-Demand Particles: part_emitter_burst

Rounding off our listing is the awesome function known as *part_emitter_burst*. This one leverages an area of screen estate as set by an emitter. Basically, *part_emitter_burst* is there to generate a specific number of particles inside a single step/frame. It's typically used for effects such as explosions and sparks. Its parameters are rather self-explanatory.

```
part_emitter_burst(wacky_system, happy_emitter, pt_fire, 2)
```

The line above creates a burst of two (2) particles of the variety pt_fire using our particle system *wacky_system* and its associated emitter *happy_emitter*.

It can be easy to overdo particles. Eventually, this can take a toll on a device's resources. In the above listing, we create a perfectly presentable fire with a mere two particles per step; hundreds of them are generally not needed.

Particles from the Create Event: part_emitter_stream

A *particle stream* can be described as a method for creating continuous flow of particles. Instead of summoning particles in every step/frame of a game, we can sometimes choose to make a single stream in the Create event of an object. Think of particle streams as running faucets. The following example demonstrates particle streams and brings a kind of a plasma effect on your screen.

```
// CREATE
window_set_cursor(cr_none); window_set_fullscreen(true); gpu_set_texfilter(true);

// Create a new particle system
wacky_system = part_system_create();
// Set particle system depth to -100
part_system_depth(wacky_system, -100);

// PLASMA PARTICLE
pt_plasma = part_type_create();
part_type_shape(pt_plasma, pt_shape_sphere);
part_type_color3(pt_plasma, c_aqua, c_blue, c_purple);
part_type_alpha3(pt_plasma, 0.1, 0.1, 0.1);
part_type_life(pt_plasma, 44, 64);
part_type_size(pt_plasma, 2, 2, 0, 0.2);
part_type_orientation(pt_plasma,0,359,4,0,1);
part_type_blend(pt_plasma, true);

happy_emitter = part_emitter_create(wacky_system); // Create an emitter
part_emitter_stream(wacky_system, happy_emitter, pt_plasma, 3); // Create a stream
```

CHAPTER 4   AUDIO, MORE ON KEYBOARDS, AND PARTICLES

```
// STEP
if keyboard_check_pressed(vk_escape) game_end();

// DRAW
draw_rectangle_color(0,0,room_width,room_height,c_black,c_green,c_dkgrey,c_maroon,false);
part_emitter_region(wacky_system, happy_emitter, mouse_x-5, mouse_x+5, mouse_y, mouse_y, ps_shape_ellipse, ps_distr_invgaussian);
draw_text(20, 20, "Use mouse to move emitter. Press ESC to quit.");
```

Quick and Easy Particles: part_particles_create

Sometimes you won't need to full power of an emitter-based particle system with its regions in your projects. To quickly create some custom particles at specific points of the screen, you can use the following function:

```
part_particles_create(index, x, y, particle_type, number)
```

For this function to work, you need to have a particle system available which goes into *index*. This can be a global system, too (e.g., global.wacky_system). You then specify the x and y coordinates for your particle. In addition, you need some complete particle definitions created with part_type_create (e.g., pt_smoke, pt_fire). Finally, you enter the number of the aforementioned particles you want to summon.

We also have *part_particles_create_colour*, which takes the following parameters:

```
part_particles_create_colour(index, x, y, particle_type, colour, number)
```

This function simply takes an extra parameter, color, which accepts any of the GML color presets (e.g., c_aqua, c_lime) to change the hue of particles.

Collisions with Particles

While particles do not have collision masks, we can use sprite-based collisions with them. This is done by assigning a sprite with its associated collision mask into an object that has a particle emitter. Naturally, the collision mask should roughly be the size of the particle emitter in question. This is a great technique for creating all types of sci-fi-ish laser projectiles and other dynamic visual elements that have a degree of desirable irregularity to them.

Particle Collision Demo

The following project explores collisions with particles. The user controls a yellow ball (i.e., the catcher) with their mouse, which is a regular sprite-based object. Colliding with a "Ufo" adds to the collision counter tracked with variable *score*. Also, hovering the catcher close to Ufos will slowly invert their vertical speed.

This demo features the following resources:

- **Three objects:** *obj_Catcher, obj_Controller, and obj_Ufo*
- **One sprite:** *Ball*
- **One room:** *HappyRoom* (1366 × 768 pixels)

This program demonstrates the following mechanics:

- Collisions between emitter-based objects and regular objects
- Randomized sets of parameters in particle emitters (i.e., different shapes and colors)
- Global particle systems and emitters
- Addressing objects using the with keyword

This project is called *Particle Collision Demo*, and it's available for download at the file repository for this book here:

https://github.com/Apress/Next-Generation-Gamemaking

obj_Controller

```
// CREATE
window_set_cursor(cr_none); window_set_fullscreen(true); gpu_set_texfilter(true);
alarm[0]=choose(30,60); score=0;
global.wacky_system = part_system_create(); // Create a global particle system
part_system_depth(global.wacky_system, -100); // Set particle system depth to -100
global.happy_emitter = part_emitter_create(global.wacky_system); // Create a global emitter
```

We first create a global particle system with a corresponding global emitter. This type of **particle system** exists independently of any specific instance or object. It can be accessed from anywhere in your game. This makes it ideal for effects that need to be summoned from multiple objects. Globally managed particles will often also improve your games' performance. Next we create an Alarm event and one for Draw, as follows:

```
// ALARM 0
instance_create_depth(random(room_width), 0, -11, obj_Ufo); // Spawn a Ufo
alarm[0]=choose(30,60);
```

```
// DRAW
draw_rectangle_color(0, 0, room_width, room_height, c_black, c_blue, c_dkgrey, c_maroon, false);
draw_text(20, 20, "PARTICLE COLLISION DEMO. Use mouse to move catcher. Press ESC to quit.\nCollisions: " + string(score));
```

obj_Catcher

```
// CREATE
// Make an EXPLOSION PARTICLE
pt_explo = part_type_create();
part_type_shape(pt_explo, pt_shape_explosion);
part_type_color3(pt_explo, c_yellow,c_orange,c_red);
part_type_life(pt_explo, 10, 40);
part_type_speed(pt_explo,4,5,0.1,0);
part_type_direction(pt_explo,250,290,0,0.2);
part_type_size(pt_explo, 1, 2, 0.1, 0.1);
part_type_orientation(pt_explo,0,359,4,0,1);
part_type_alpha3(pt_explo, 0.7, 0.3,0.2);
part_type_blend(pt_explo, true);
depth=-15000;
```

The Step event observes the distance between the Catcher and each particle-based obj_Ufo. If it is under 150 pixels, the obj_Ufo in question will start to reverse its vertical speed. We can access all active instances of obj_Ufo simply by leveraging the keyword *with*. Think of this keyword as a shift in perspective. After it's evoked, we are looking

CHAPTER 4 AUDIO, MORE ON KEYBOARDS, AND PARTICLES

from the viewpoint of the specified object's instances. Coordinates and any other variables are all examined from this vantage point in the code block to follow. Also, as we stick to good programming habits, we check for the existence of obj_Catcher before accessing data on it.

```
// STEP
x=mouse_x; y=mouse_y;
with(obj_Ufo) {
    if instance_exists(obj_Catcher) && point_distance(x, y, obj_Catcher.x,
    obj_Catcher.y)<150 {
    if vspeed>-4 vspeed-=0.4;
        }
}

// COLLISION WITH obj_Ufo
instance_destroy(other); score++;
part_emitter_region(global.wacky_system, global.happy_emitter, other.x,
other.x, other.y, other.y, ps_shape_ellipse, ps_distr_invgaussian);
part_emitter_burst(global.wacky_system, global.happy_emitter, pt_
explo, 11);
```

obj_Ufo

With this object, its particle appearance is altered every time it spawns. We do this by recreating the particle for each instance and feeding the shape and color attributes randomly chosen values as it pertains to part_type_shape and part_type_color2.

```
// CREATE
// Make a PLASMA PARTICLE
pt_plasma = part_type_create();
part_type_shape(pt_plasma, choose(pt_shape_sphere, pt_shape_spark,
pt_shape_flare));
part_type_color2(pt_plasma, c_white,choose(c_yellow,c_blue,c_purple,
c_aqua,c_red,c_lime));
part_type_life(pt_plasma, 4, 30);
part_type_size(pt_plasma, 1, 1, 0, 0.1);
```

CHAPTER 4   AUDIO, MORE ON KEYBOARDS, AND PARTICLES

```
part_type_orientation(pt_plasma,0,359,4,0,1);
part_type_alpha2(pt_plasma, 0.05,0.2);
part_type_blend(pt_plasma, true);
vspeed=choose(7,8);

// STEP
if keyboard_check_pressed(vk_escape) game_end();
if y>room_height || y<0 instance_destroy();

// DRAW
part_emitter_region(global.wacky_system, global.happy_emitter, x, x, y, y,
ps_shape_ellipse, ps_distr_invgaussian);
part_emitter_burst(global.wacky_system, global.happy_emitter, pt_
plasma, 6);
```

Adding Particles into Space Heck (Version 0.2)

It's time we upgrade the currently rather old-fashioned explosions in version 0.1 of Space Heck with the power of particles. First, we shall update the Create event in obj_Controller, adding a global particle system and definitions for three global particles: *global.pt_explosion, global.pt_zap,* and *global.pt_exhaust*. Also, we add an enigmatic new event called *Game End*. All will be explained later in this chapter.

This project is called *SpaceHeck02,* and it's available for download at the file repository for this book here:

https://github.com/Apress/Next-Generation-Gamemaking

obj_Controller

```
// CREATE
alarm[0]=10 + random(40); depth=2;
window_set_fullscreen(true); // Enter fullscreen mode
window_set_cursor(cr_none); // Hide mouse cursor
gpu_set_texfilter(true); // Enable texture filtering for smoother visuals

global.wacky_system = part_system_create(); // Create a global
particle system
```

CHAPTER 4 AUDIO, MORE ON KEYBOARDS, AND PARTICLES

```
part_system_depth(global.wacky_system, 0); // Set particle system
depth to 0
global.happy_emitter = part_emitter_create(global.wacky_system);
// Create a global emitter

global.pt_explosion = part_type_create();
part_type_shape(global.pt_explosion, pt_shape_flare);
part_type_size(global.pt_explosion, 1, 1, 0, 0);
part_type_color3(global.pt_explosion, c_yellow, c_red, c_aqua);
part_type_alpha3(global.pt_explosion, 1, 0.5, 0);
part_type_life(global.pt_explosion, 30, 50);
part_type_speed(global.pt_explosion, 1, 4, 0, 0);
part_type_direction(global.pt_explosion, 0, 360, 0, 0);
part_type_blend(global.pt_explosion, true);

global.pt_zap = part_type_create();
part_type_shape(global.pt_zap, pt_shape_sphere);
part_type_size(global.pt_zap, 0.5, 0.5, 0, 0);
part_type_color3(global.pt_zap, c_red, c_purple, c_aqua);
part_type_alpha3(global.pt_zap, 0.8, 0.5, 0.1);
part_type_life(global.pt_zap, 10, 30);
part_type_speed(global.pt_zap, 1, 4, 0, 0);
part_type_direction(global.pt_zap, 270, 270, 0, 0);
part_type_blend(global.pt_zap, true);

global.pt_exhaust = part_type_create();
part_type_shape(global.pt_exhaust, pt_shape_flare);
part_type_size(global.pt_exhaust, 0.5, 0.5, 0, 0);
part_type_color3(global.pt_exhaust, c_silver, c_dkgray, c_aqua);
part_type_alpha3(global.pt_exhaust, 0.15, 0.2, 0.1);
part_type_life(global.pt_exhaust, 10, 40);
part_type_speed(global.pt_exhaust, 1, 4, 0, 0);
part_type_direction(global.pt_exhaust, 270, 270, 0, 0);
part_type_blend(global.pt_exhaust, true);

// GAME END
part_system_destroy(global.wacky_system);
```

CHAPTER 4   AUDIO, MORE ON KEYBOARDS, AND PARTICLES

obj_Enemy

Next, we update obj_Enemy with a couple of things. Let's add a Destroy event with the following contents:

```
// DESTROY
score++;
audio_play_sound(explosion, 1, false,1,0,0.9+random(0.2));
```

We just added a thunderous explosion sound every time a foe is neutralized. We also leveraged the audio function's pitch property for slight variation every time the audio is played; this is a good idea for reducing listener's ear fatigue with repeating sound effects. Next we'll update the Draw event with the following:

```
// DRAW
// If not exploding draw sprite. Else create particles & destroy instance
if !exploding draw_self(); else {
    part_emitter_region(global.wacky_system, global.happy_emitter, x, x, y,
    y, ps_shape_ellipse, ps_distr_invgaussian);
    part_emitter_burst(global.wacky_system, global.happy_emitter, global.
    pt_explosion, 20);
    instance_destroy(); // Activate our new Destroy-event
}
```

Also, in version 0.2 of Space Heck, obj_Enemy does not need a Step event, so we can safely delete it. It is always a good practice to delete unneeded events. In addition, we can delete the following line from this object's Create event: *explosion_size=sprite_width;*

obj_Player

It's time to focus on the player's ship, obj_Player, and its Draw event. Here we add some exhaust fumes for our spaceship for that extra "je ne sais quoi." We do this by applying some particles, again emitting them using our global particle system.

```
// DRAW
draw_set_color(choose(c_yellow,c_orange,c_red));
// Draw a circular exhaust fume
draw_circle(x,y+sprite_height*0.5,random_range(10,20),false);
```

```
// Summon particles
part_emitter_region(global.wacky_system, global.happy_emitter, x, x,
y+sprite_height*0.5, y+sprite_height*0.5, ps_shape_line, ps_distr_
invgaussian);
part_emitter_burst(global.wacky_system, global.happy_emitter, global.pt_
exhaust, 2);
// Draw ship sprite
draw_sprite(sprite_index, 0, x, y);
```

obj_Bullet

Let's add a sound effect each time a laser projectile is created; we'll use a resource called *snd_Laser*.

```
// CREATE
vspeed = -choose(7, 8, 9); // Choose upward vertical speed
audio_play_sound(snd_Laser,1,false,1,0,0.9+random(0.2));
```

Finally, for the player's laser fire in obj_Bullet, we add some nice particles with an inverted Gaussian distribution pattern in its Draw event like this:

```
// DRAW
part_emitter_region(global.wacky_system, global.happy_emitter, x, x, y, y,
ps_shape_ellipse, ps_distr_invgaussian);
part_emitter_burst(global.wacky_system, global.happy_emitter, global.pt_
zap, 3);
draw_self(); // Draw bullet-sprite over the particles
```

Particle Memory Management

Having a few dozen unmanaged particles is nary a cause for concern. However, more complicated projects need some form of memory management for their particles and emitters. You can best remove your particle systems in an event known as Game End (found by clicking Events ▶ Other in the GameMaker IDE).

The Game End event is only triggered once when the game app stops running. The instance of an object that has this event has to be active when the game is exited. Not only is this a great event for managing memory leaks, it serves well as a go-to event for saving data related to your game.

Now, GameMaker has a trio of elegant functions for freeing particles from RAM. These are *part_type_destroy*, *part_emitter_destroy*, and *part_system_destroy* for destroying individual particle definitions, emitters, and entire particle systems, respectively. See Table 4-12 for how these functions would work in the context of the particle work featured in this chapter.

Table 4-12. GML functions for destroying particles, emitters, and particle systems

part_type_destroy(index)	part_type_destroy(global.pt_explosion);
part_emitter_destroy(system, emitter)	part_emitter_destroy(global.wacky_system, global.happy_emitter);
part_system_destroy(system)	part_system_destroy(global.wacky_system);

The function part_system_destroy will remove a complete particle system from memory (i.e., RAM), including all associated emitters; any of these associated emitters do not need to be destroyed manually after executing said function. However, you'll probably come across situations in your game where certain emitters can be removed, but their associated particle system is to be preserved for future use. This is when part_emitter_destroy comes in handy.

All parts of the particle system eat up a little bit of memory. Systems and emitters aside, individual particle definitions can also be freed from RAM using a simple function called part_type_destroy. Removing particle definitions may be a good idea when a specific type of particle is no longer needed. For example, an introductory level might feature particular types of particles which are never leveraged in the game to follow and can thus be destroyed at the end of said level. Particles can naturally be redefined/resurrected at any point in a GameMaker project, should the need arise using the standard GML functions (i.e., part_type_create and its associated functions). What matters is only keeping the types of particles defined (and thus eating up RAM) that are actually needed at a specific point in time.

Always optimize your particles. Old and low-end devices are still out there.

Unlike particle systems, emitters and particle definitions are best removed in the Room End event of an active controller object. You can find this event from the Other category of GameMaker events in the software's IDE.

Clearing On-Screen Particles

Sometimes you just need to wipe all the particles on-screen without deleting any related data structures. For these scenarios, *part_particles_clear* is the function you need. It takes a single argument for a particle system and removes all visible particles for said system.

A function called *part_system_clear* is also there to remove all emitters belonging to a specific system. Be cautious: this function will cause errors if your code relies on specific emitters which then get suddenly deleted. Actually, you can use a function called *part_emitter_exists* (at all times) to avoid any such errors, like this:

```
// Make sure a specific emitter exists..
if part_emitter_exists(global.wacky_system, global.happy_emitter) {
// .. before using said emitter
part_emitter_burst(global.wacky_system, global.happy_emitter, pt_smoke, 2);
}
```

Counting Particles

One great way of optimizing your particle work is to keep count of visible particles. You can increase the performance of your particle-heavy games somewhat by limiting how many are spawned. The function *part_particles_count* will observe how many particles are currently spawned by a specific particle system. We can use this function to control when new particles are to be created on-screen, like this:

```
// Count particles for system global.wacky_system and
// spawn them ONLY if the total amount of spawned particles is under 90
if part_particles_count(global.wacky_system) < 90 {
part_emitter_burst(global.wacky_system, global.happy_emitter, global.pt_zap, 3);
}
```

Stopping and Hiding Particles

By default, particle systems in GameMaker are updated automatically every step/frame of the game. This can be computationally costly if you have numerous emitters pushing out heavy loads of particles. If you want to optimize your particle pipeline, you can disable automatic updates using a function called *part_system_automatic_update*. To disable these automatic updates, we would do this:

`part_system_automatic_update(global.wacky_system, false);`

That would stop all particles in their tracks. To execute a manual refresh on the particle system, we would use the following function at specific intervals:

`part_system_update(global.wacky_system);`

The above function could be inserted into an Alarm event to be executed every, say, two steps/frames instead of every single step which is the case in the automatic update. With a lot of particles, this approach can indeed reduce pressure on a device's hardware.

If you're using basic effects generated by the effect_create_above or effect_create_ below functions, you can use the values 0 (for effects created below) or 1 (for effects created above) as the particle system index. This allows you to enable or disable the automatic update for these effects as well.

There's another fabulous function for high-level particle control: *part_system_ automatic_draw*. If we want to pause drawing of particles for the sake of, say, a pause mode, we can do this by summoning the following piece of code:

`part_system_automatic_draw(global.wacky_system, false);`

To then manually draw a single step/frame of particles, we do this in the Draw event of an object:

`part_system_drawit(global.wacky_system);`

The last two functions also work great for pausing the rendering of particle systems that are currently not needed. Part_system_automatic_draw is a nice function for special effects, too, such as strobing particles. Please remember that part_system_drawit does not work inside the Alarm events; it needs a drawing-related event pipeline.

CHAPTER 4   AUDIO, MORE ON KEYBOARDS, AND PARTICLES

IDE Particle Systems

There is a way to implement particles in GameMaker from within the IDE by applying just a few mouse clicks. While not as dynamic as manually evoked particles, this approach gives you a live preview of the particle systems being created. These can be easily resized, too, by dragging on their edges. You can make a new IDE-based particle system by clicking Create ➤ Particle System on the asset browser. Doing this will take you to the particle editor screen. See Figure 4-3 for a partial view of the IDE particle editor.

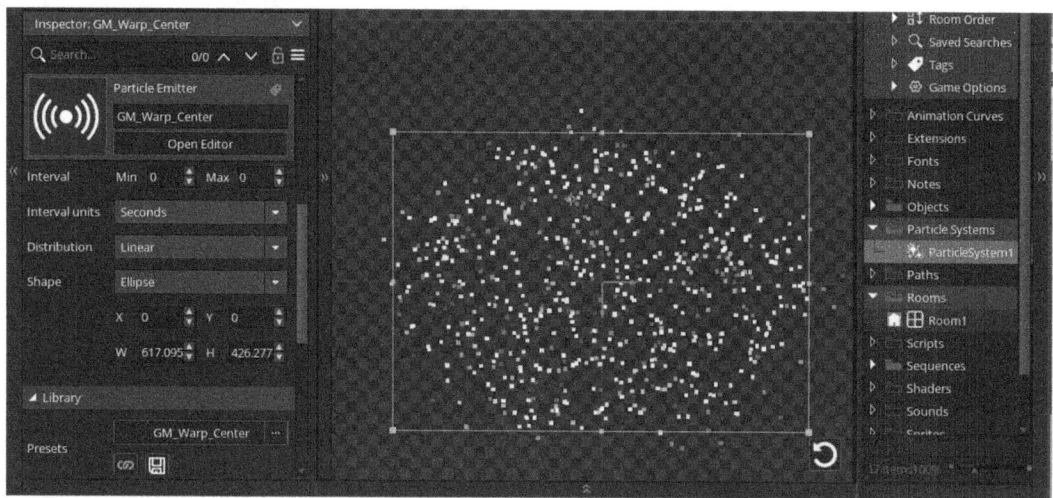

Figure 4-3. *A partial view of the IDE particle system editor in GameMaker*

All of the previously discussed parameters (e.g., color, life, and scale) are found in the left side of the IDE particle editor. A section called *Subparticles* lets you effortlessly spawn different types of particles during the "death" of the main particle (a technique discussed earlier in this chapter).

Particle systems created this way are to be placed on asset layers inside rooms. They are most useful for creating static environmental particle effects, such as fire, smoke, and other phenomena you might want to cosmetically enhance your levels with.

The particle system creator offers a small set of presets in its library section; you can add your own by clicking *Save as Preset* (i.e., the disk icon).

The canvas of the particle editor screen also has a most handy button labeled *Copy GML to clipboard*. Clicking it copies the currently edited particle data (i.e., system, emitter, and particle) in GML Code into your operating system's clipboard. You can then paste it into a script or object of your choosing; on Windows, you would use the familiar key combination of Ctrl and V to do this. For Mac users this translates to the combination of cmd and V (see Figure 4-4).

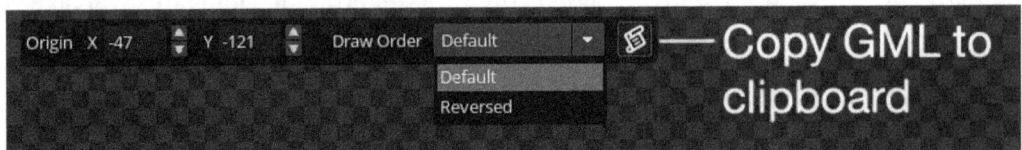

Figure 4-4. *The upper window in the particle editor screen*

You can also set the origin points for these particle systems from the above window being similar to the sprite origin point as previously discussed. The *Draw Order* section in the window decides whether newer particles are drawn over older ones or vice versa.

Particles Recap

Before finishing this chapter, let's remind ourselves on how to setup and use particles in GML. First comes the creation of a particle system. This can either be a local (bound to a specific object) or a global system (usable from within any object). We pair this with an emitter. Here we make a simple local system that is to only work inside some specific object:

```
// CREATE
merry_system = part_system_create();
lonely_emitter = part_emitter_create(merry_system);
```

Then, we define our particle in the Create event. Let's make something quite simple.

```
happy_flare = part_type_create();
// Use a flare shape
part_type_shape(happy_flare, pt_shape_sphere);
// Give it a yellow-aqua gradient
part_type_colour2(happy_flare, c_yellow, c_aqua);
// Set blending to full (1)
```

```
part_type_blend(happy_flare, 1);
// Set minimum and maximum lifespan in steps/frames
part_type_life(happy_flare, 40, 150);

// DRAW
// Make the emitter follow your mouse around the screen
part_emitter_region(merry_system, lonely_emitter, mouse_x, mouse_x,
mouse_y, mouse_y, ps_shape_ellipse, ps_distr_invgaussian);
part_emitter_burst(merry_system, lonely_emitter, happy_flare, 5);
```

And that's GameMaker's particles in the shell of a nut. There are a few other functions related to this topic which we did not cover in this chapter. They shall be tackled in later chapters of the book.

Cherish and enjoy your particles. They can be quite visually enticing, but you should keep optimization in mind when working with them. Especially in larger projects, don't forget to manage your particle systems' memory usage by, say, pairing a Game End event with a *part_system_destroy*. Also, make sure to remove unneeded emitters in real time whenever possible using *part_emitter_destroy*.

Let's finish off this chapter with a visualization of the GML particle pipeline (see Figure 4-5).

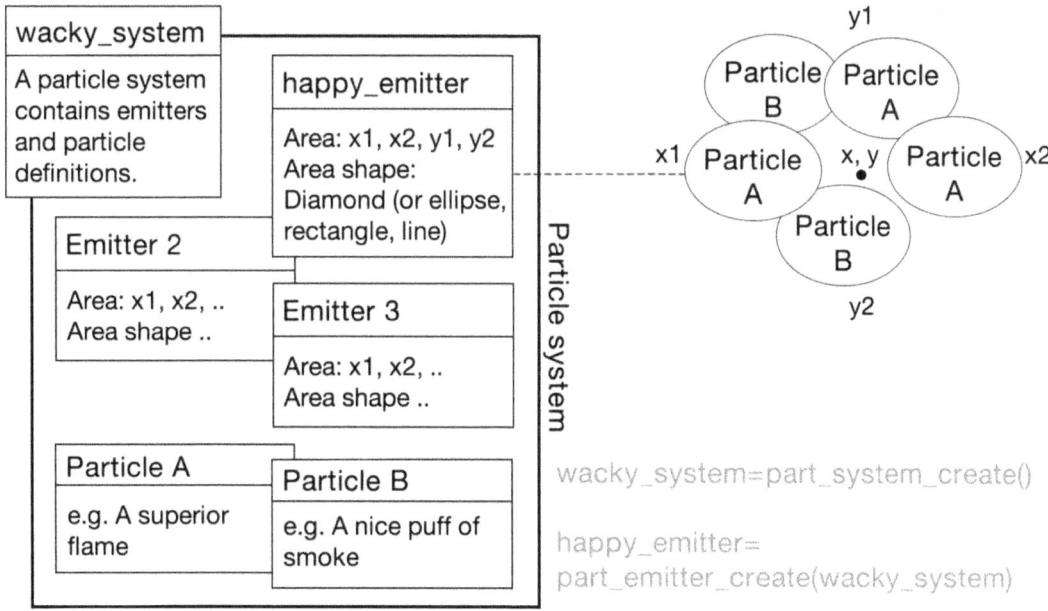

Figure 4-5. *A visualization of the particle pipeline in GML*

CHAPTER 4   AUDIO, MORE ON KEYBOARDS, AND PARTICLES

In Closing

This chapter focused on implementing audio and particles into our GameMaker projects. We discussed the following topics:

- GML audio functions, including the mighty audio_play_sound and audio_is_playing
- Keyboard functions (keyboard_check_pressed, etc.)
- Particle systems, emitters, and particle definitions
- Particle memory management (part_type_destroy, part_emitter_destroy, part_system_destroy, etc.)

Chapter 5 will be all about cameras, views, and motion planning (a.k.a. obstacle avoidance). There's an exciting game prototype for two players coming up, too.

CHAPTER 5

Cameras, Layers, and Tilesets

In this chapter, we will learn how to implement camera systems in GameMaker, using both the software's GUI and GameMaker Language. Cameras are one of GameMaker's most powerful features. They let us create beautiful scrolling and zooming, while doing wonders for simultaneous two-player games, too. We'll also explore the different types of room layers GameMaker offers us—and take a good look at tilesets. Much merriment awaits!

All of the projects mentioned in this chapter (i.e., JollyTilemaps and Tank Merriment, etc.) are available from the following link:

https://github.com/Apress/Next-Generation-Gamemaking

As previously mentioned in the book, the camera system in GameMaker is both powerful and flexible. It is also somewhat simple to set up, but before we do that, we should go through the three closely related components.

- Like you probably know by now, a **room** is the current game world/level with a width and a height set in pixels. New rooms are made by right-clicking the asset browser and selecting *Create Room*. Double-clicking on a room will open the room editor where you get to specify its dimensions and camera-related settings.

- The **viewport** is the area of the screen where the game is displayed to the player. It is defined by its width and height in pixels. Viewports are independent of the room's size. If you don't check *Viewports and cameras* ➤ *Enable viewports* in the IDE, GameMaker will automatically display the entire room scaled to fit the game window. You can think of viewport as virtual screens.

- The **camera** determines which part of the room is visible within a viewport. It has properties like position, size, zoom, and angle. You can make a camera follow any object from within the GameMaker IDE; usually, you would want this object to be the player. You can also have multiple cameras for scenarios such as simultaneous two-player games displayed at the same time. Basic camerawork in GameMaker can be done fully from the IDE. For more dynamic approaches, such as real-time zooming, we must leverage GML.

Views in the IDE

The simplest way of setting up a camera system in GameMaker is done inside the IDE. First, double-click on a room inside the asset browser. Next locate the inspector on the left side of the IDE and navigate to the section labeled *Room Settings*. Click on the section underneath it called *Viewports and cameras*. Make sure the box *Enable Viewports* is checked. You'll see there are eight viewports in the settings below. By clicking Viewport 0, i.e., the first one, we get access to a number of settings: *Camera Properties, Viewport Properties,* and *Object Following* (see Figure 5-1).

CHAPTER 5   CAMERAS, LAYERS, AND TILESETS

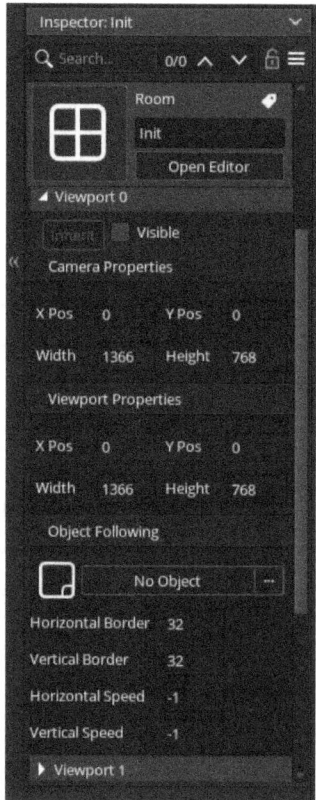

Figure 5-1. *Settings for views in the GameMaker IDE*

Now, we enable a view by clicking *Visible*. Again, a camera controls what part of the room is visible, while the viewport controls where that visible area is shown on the screen. By default, the coordinates for both of these settings are set on the top-left corner of the screen. The section labeled *Object Following* offers the option having a camera center on a specific game actor, such as a player's craft. The horizontal and vertical borders represent an invisible area around the object which "push" the screen around. Small borders let the followed object reach the very edge of a screen before any scrolling occurs. Large borders (i.e., settings greater than the width and height of the view) make the object stick to the center of the screen.

Finally, we can set both the horizontal and vertical speed for scrolling in pixels per step/frame. The default settings of –1 tell GameMaker the followed object is to be tracked at the very speed of the object, which is usually a good choice. A setting of zero will not move the camera at all; this works in case you want to disable either horizontal

CHAPTER 5 CAMERAS, LAYERS, AND TILESETS

or vertical scrolling completely. In case you want to have a kind of a laggy tracking of an object, you can experiment with horizontal and vertical speeds that are slower than the speed of the followed object.

Setting Up a Camera in GML

Let's say we want to create a camera with a size of 640 × 360 pixels and make it follow the player, i.e., obj_Player. The GML for this task would look like something this:

```
// CREATE
fun_camera = camera_create(); // Create a camera
view_camera[0] = fun_camera;  // Assign the camera to viewport 0
camera_set_view_size(fun_camera, 640, 360); // Set camera size
camera_set_view_speed(fun_camera, 10, 10);  // Set camera movement speed
// STEP
if instance_exists(obj_Player) {
var p_x = obj_Player.x; // Store player x-position into p_x
var p_y = obj_Player.y; // Store player y-position into p_y
// Center camera on player
camera_set_view_pos(fun_camera, p_x - 320, p_y - 180);
}
// DESTROY
camera_destroy(fun_camera); // Destroy the camera
```

Let's break down the GML functions used in the previous listing (see Table 5-1).

Table 5-1. *Some basic camera-related functions in GML*

camera_name = camera_create()	Create a new camera. You need to manually assign it using *view_camera*.
view_camera[viewport_index]	Assign camera to viewport. For example, view_camera[0] = camera_name.
camera_set_view_speed(camera, hspeed, vspeed)	Sets the horizontal and vertical speeds at which the camera moves or follows an object.
camera_set_view_pos(camera, x, y)	Set the position of a camera inside a room. Can be used for following objects around.
camera_destroy(camera)	Destroy a camera. Always summon this function when a camera is no longer needed.

GameMaker cameras are room-specific, so you'll need to recreate them when switching rooms.

We shall now leave camerawork in GameMaker for a while to explore an important (and related) concept: layers.

Layers

As discussed all the way back in Chapter 1, GameMaker offers seven types of layers for your rooms each with their specific purposes. You can have several kinds of layers in each room. As a refresher, they are as follows:

- **Instance layer:** This type of layer accepts any type of object, i.e., your game actors. Instances on the same layer are drawn in the order they were created or based on their internally defined depth value.

- **Tile layer:** This layer is for tilemaps. Tiles are a handy approach for building computationally effective scenery in games; this will be one of the core topics of this chapter.

- **Asset layer:** Meant for cosmetic elements such as sprites and particle systems. Not every part of a game's scenery needs to be an object's instance.

- **Effect layer:** GameMaker has a number of simple real-time visual effects which go into this category of layer. These can be either created from the GameMaker IDE or dynamically during the gameloop. The output of an effect layer is applied on all layers beneath it.

- **Background layer:** This simplest type of layer presents us with a background image/sprite. It can be made to scroll horizontally and/or vertically at various speeds.

- **Path:** Used for previewing and editing movement paths inside a room.

- **UI (user interface):** Used for displaying score and other pertinent information. Will always stay on top of all the other layers.

Layers offer plenty of flexibility into your game projects. They are rendered in the order they appear in the layer list from top to bottom. This makes it effortless to manage the drawing order of larger sets of objects and backgrounds. You can toggle the visibility of layers inside the GameMaker IDE, or lock them to prevent accidental edits. You can also group layers together in "folders" for better organization; this can be very useful for larger projects.

To access the layer inspector, double-click on a room in the asset browser.

New layers are easily added into rooms using the GameMaker IDE (see Figure 5-2). You can also reorder layers in the inspector element simply by dragging and dropping. Layers can also be created and manipulated in real time using GML, which is something we'll look into next.

CHAPTER 5　CAMERAS, LAYERS, AND TILESETS

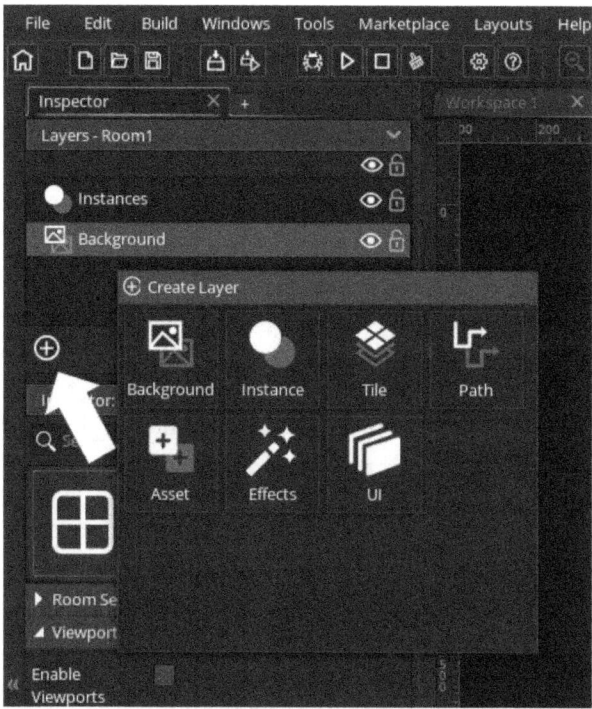

Figure 5-2. *Layers are added in the IDE by clicking the plus symbol in the inspector and choosing a type of layer on the window to the right*

Dynamic Layers in GML

For many more straightforward projects, the layer inspector element in the GameMaker IDE offers enough features for layer management. But sometimes you need the extra flexibility offered by GML for these tasks. Let us look into a pair of excellent functions: *layer_create* and *layer_destroy*.

To create a new layer during the gameloop, we can simply do this:

new_happy_layer = **layer_create**(-100);

This creates a new layer at depth value of −100. If we were to remove this layer from a room, we would do this:

layer_destroy(new_happy_layer);

The previous two commands create temporary layers which do not persist between different rooms. Now, if we were to spawn instances of, say, obj_Tomato onto *new_happy_layer*, we would execute the following statement:

```
instance_create_layer(0, 0, "new_happy_layer", obj_Tomato);
```

There's a handy function for adding a background graphic into a layer, too. With *layer_background_create*, we can add a bitmap graphic (i.e., a sprite) into a layer. We can then further modify this layer with a handful of functions. The following statement adds a sprite-based background (spr_Clouds) into new_happy_layer with 50% alpha:

```
var background1 = layer_background_create(new_happy_layer, spr_Clouds);
// Set the background's alpha (transparency) to 50%
layer_background_alpha(background1, 0.5);
```

Please be aware that in order to manipulate some of the dynamic layer's properties (such as alpha), you need to assign and use a handle for a layer. In the above example, the handle is called *background1*.

Unlike in the IDE's room editor, you are not limited to specific asset types for each layer created with GML. Assets of different varieties can be added to the same dynamic layer. You can have a background and instances all on the same layer.

The functions *layer_create* and *layer_destroy* only work with layers created during the gameloop. Layers created in the IDE's room editor cannot be removed with *layer_destroy*.

Layer Properties in GML

Opacity aside, we can control many properties of our dynamically created layers from within the gameloop. See Table 5-2 for a rundown on some of these functions.

Table 5-2. *Some useful properties for dynamic layers in GML*

layer_hspeed(layer, speed)	Set layer horizontal scrolling speed.
layer_vspeed(layer, speed)	Set layer vertical scrolling speed.
layer_background_htiled(handle, true)	Set layer's horizontal repetition. Use with a handle.
layer_background_vtiled(handle, true)	Set layer's vertical repetition. Use with a handle.
layer_background_speed(handle, value)	Set the animation speed of a sprite assigned to a background layer. Use with a handle.
layer_x(layer, x_position)	Layer horizontal position in pixels.
layer_y(layer, y_position)	Layer vertical position in pixels.

Zooming In and Out

Let us return to GameMaker cinematography. We are not limited to following objects or maintaining a static shot. Live zooming is a classic technique which can add a lot of chutzpah to any game. A project called *ZoomDemo* is there to show you how to get from close-up to wide shot in your games. This simple project, which also leverages dynamic layers, has the following elements:

- Three layers:
- A background layer populated with an assortment of static game characters
- A dynamically created and vertically scrolling layer (i.e., *brick_layer*)
- A layer for instances which includes a single object, i.e., *obj_Zoomcam*
- A GameMaker camera (i.e., fiesty_cam) that zooms in and out while keeping the view centered

This project is completely set up in GML and contains only a single object called *obj_Zoomcam*. The project creates a constant pulsating zoom. You can exit this demonstration by pressing the Escape key.

CHAPTER 5   CAMERAS, LAYERS, AND TILESETS

Inside obj_Zoomcam

Let us now take a peek under the hood of ZoomDemo. The Create event for *obj_Zoomcam* contains variable definitions. We also create a camera called *feisty_cam*.

```
// CREATE
window_set_fullscreen(true);
zoom = 1; // Zoom level
zoom_min = 0.985; zoom_max = 1.015;
zoom_speed = 0.00015; // Zooming speed
zoom_direction = 0; // 0 = zoom in, 1 = zoom out

feisty_cam = camera_create(); // Create camera
camera_set_view_pos(feisty_cam, 0, 0); // Set position at top left (0,0)
// Set view size in pixels
camera_set_view_size(feisty_cam, room_width, room_height);
// Assign this camera to view 0
view_set_camera(0, feisty_cam);
// Enable view 0
view_visible[0] = true; view_enabled = true;
```

The Create event also contains the GML for setting up a layer called *brick_layer* for an infinitely scrolling backdrop. It is assigned a depth value of 15000, which represents a very low depth in GameMaker.

```
// Create new dynamic layer for the room and put it at the bottom
brick_layer = layer_create(15000);
// Assign a handle/ID for the layer
var handle1 = layer_background_create(brick_layer, Sprite2);
// Make background horizontally and vertically tiled (infinite)
layer_background_htiled(handle1,true);
layer_background_vtiled(handle1,true);
// Make layer scroll vertically three pixels down per step/frame
layer_vspeed(brick_layer, 3);
```

As for the Step event, it looks like this:

```
// STEP
// Zoom in or out
if silly_zoom_direction == 0 zoom += zoom_speed; else zoom -= zoom_speed;

if zoom >= zoom_max silly_zoom_direction = 1;
if zoom <= zoom_min silly_zoom_direction = 0;
zoom = clamp(zoom, zoom_min, zoom_max);
```

Our example uses a controller variable called *silly_zoom_direction* when deciding what to do with the camera. A value of zero (0) zooms in while a value of one (1) zooms out.

```
// Get current camera properties
var _x = camera_get_view_x(feisty_cam);
var _y = camera_get_view_y(feisty_cam);
var _w = camera_get_view_width(feisty_cam);
var _h = camera_get_view_height(feisty_cam);

// Apply zoom (centered on camera's current position)
var _new_w = _w / zoom;
var _new_h = _h / zoom;

// Adjust position to keep zoom centered
var _new_x = _x + (_w - _new_w) * 0.5;
var _new_y = _y + (_h - _new_h) * 0.5;
```

The above properties are used to center the camera when zooming in or out. Like you might guess, *_x* and *_y* represent the current camera position (0 and 0 being the top-left corner). The *_w* and *_h* represent the original camera width and height before zoom. The variables *_new_w* and *_new_h* track the updated camera width and height after the zoom; *_new_x* and *_new_y* are there to record the adjusted camera position to keep the zoom centered.

```
// Update camera
camera_set_view_size(feisty_cam, _new_w, _new_h);
camera_set_view_pos(feisty_cam, _new_x, _new_y);
```

Effect Layers

A conservative use of effect layers can add a touch of polish into your games. Upon creating a new effect layer from the IDE and clicking on it, we can see a fairly large number of effects listed under the heading called *Effect type*. All of these effects have different parameters easily adjusted from the IDE.

You may or may not find a use for all of GameMaker's built-in effects; some of the more useful effects are discussed in Table 5-3.

Table 5-3. Some useful visual effects for GameMaker's effect layers

Vignette	Darkens edges creating focus on the center of the screen.
Screen shake	Shakes the screen. Great for emphasizing explosions and creating earthquakes.
RGB noise	Generates colored noise with optional animation. Great for a "film grain" type of look.
Pixelate	Creates a pixelated old school look reminiscent of video games of the 1970s and early 1980s.
Colorize	Changes all visuals to match the given hue and saturation.
Color balance	Lets you adjust the highlights, midtones, and shadows (dark tones) of your visuals.
Desaturate	Reduces the saturation levels of your visuals. Great for turning color graphics into black and white.
Tint	Colorizes a screen using red, green, and blue components (RGB)
Zoom blur	Creates a zoomed-in motion blur filter.

One great thing about GameMaker's visual effects is they can be applied on any layer from the IDE and not just on dedicated effect layers. This is done by first clicking on a layer in an open room and then navigating to a section called *Filters & Effects* underneath the inspector element. A section labeled *Effect type* provides a list of available effects for a specific layer.

Now, the GameMaker IDE aside, we can create effect layers from within our gameloop as well. To do this, we summon three functions: *fx_create, fx_set_parameter,* and *layer_set_fx*. All effects have their unique parameters. Let's say we want to create a layer with a nice purple colorization effect. We would go about it in the following fashion in an object's Create event:

```
// Create a new layer at depth -15000
layer_create(-15000,"EffectLayer");
var _jolly_fx = fx_create("_filter_colourise");
fx_set_parameter(_jolly_fx, "g_TintCol", [0.6, 0, 0.6]); // Set RGB
fx_set_parameter(_jolly_fx, "g_Intensity", 1); // Set intensity
layer_set_fx("EffectLayer", _jolly_fx);
```

All effects found in the GameMaker IDE have their corresponding handles and parameters in GML. In the above listing, the colorization effect is referenced with *_filter_colourise*.

Effect Layers in GML

Let us next go through the parameters associated with the effects listed in Table 5-3. You'll need this information when you create effect layers dynamically during the gameloop (see Table 5-4).

Table 5-4. Some useful effect names and their parameters for layers in GML

Effect	Handle	Parameters
Vignette	_filter_vignette	g_VignetteEdges, g_VignetteSharpness
Screen shake	_filter_screenshake	g_Magnitude, g_ShakeSpeed
RGB noise	_filter_rgbnoise	g_RGBNoiseIntensity, g_RGBNoiseAnimation, g_RGBNoiseColour
Pixelate	_filter_pixelate	g_CellSize
Colorize	_filter_colourise	g_Intensity, g_TintCol
Color balance	_filter_colour_balance	g_ColourBalanceShadows, g_ColourBalanceMidtones, g_ColourBalanceHighlights
Desaturate	_filter_greyscale	g_Intensity
Tint	_filter_tintfilter	g_TintCol
Zoom blur	_filter_zoom_blur	g_ZoomBlurCenter, g_ZoomBlurIntensity, g_ZoomBlurFocusRadius

Single-Layer Mode

There are quite a few useful functions for manipulating your effect layers in GML. One of the most useful ones is *single-layer mode*. When enabled, your effect(s) are processed only on one specific layer, instead of every other layer beneath it. Imagine a scenario where you want to colorize, say, all turnip objects, and leave all other objects alone. This of course means all of your turnips need to be created on a specific layer. After you've done that, you can enable some effects for said turnip layer and summon something like this:

```
colour_effect = fx_create("_filter_colourise");
fx_set_single_layer(colour_effect, true);
layer_set_fx("Turnip_Layer", colour_effect);
```

Like you can probably tell from the code snippet above, *fx_set_single_layer* takes the effect name and a Boolean (true/false) for its operation.

Retrieving Effects Parameters

In addition to setting parameters, we can also fetch information about them. For that, we have this quartet of wonderful functions: *fx_get_parameter, fx_get_parameters, fx_get_name,* and *fx_get_parameter_names*. Let us add the following to the previous listing to test these functions out:

```
// Get the effect name
var effectName = fx_get_name(_jolly_fx);
show_message("Effect Name: " + string(effectName));
// Get all parameter names
var parameterNames = fx_get_parameter_names(_jolly_fx);
show_message("Parameter Names: " + string(parameterNames));
// Get all parameters and their values
var parameters = fx_get_parameters(_jolly_fx);
show_message("Effect Parameters: " + string(parameters));
// Get the value of a specific parameter
var tintColor = fx_get_parameter(_jolly_fx, "g_TintCol");
show_message("Tint Colour: " + string(tintColor));
```

The output from the complete listing should be as following:

Effect Name: _filter_colourise

Parameter Names: ["g_Intensity", "g_TintCol"]

Effect Parameters: { g Intensity: 1, g_TintCol: [0.60,0,0.60] }

Tint Colour: [0.60,0,0.60]

Clearing Effects

Most of the time an effect is not needed to stick around forever. When we are done with our zoomed blurs or whatever else, we can remove them by using the following simple bit of GML:

layer_clear_fx("Name_of_Layer");

The layer itself will remain after clearing effects. Also, the layer will be visible unless you specifically hide it.

Next we shall begin an exploration of tilesets, another highly useful type of visual asset.

Tilesets and Tile Layers

As previously mentioned in the book, *tilesets* are a handy and effective type of resource for building backgrounds. They are basically collections of reusable images that you place in a rectangular grid-like fashion into your rooms' backgrounds. You can have multiple layers of tiles (e.g., ground, road, pavement, etc.) on top of each other. Although similar to a texture atlas, as discussed in Chapter 3, a tileset is its own specific type of visual resource focused on background graphics. For one, because of their extremely flexible nature, tiles are an enormously low-impact way to implement detailed visuals into your rooms. Instead of gigantic backgrounds made with massive sprites, recycling tiles eats a lot less memory from a device's resource pool.

Now, the most basic process for using tilesets in GameMaker is as follows:

1. A visual representation of the tiles-to-be are prepared as a single bitmap file (e.g., PNG). All tiles should have a square aspect ratio (e.g., each tile is 16×16 or 32×32 pixels).

2. The aforementioned file is imported into GameMaker by right-clicking in the asset browser and selecting *Create* ➤ *Tile Set*.

3. A properties window opens inside the IDE. Most crucially, the width and height of the tiles need to match the intended tile size from step one. You may also assign a specific tileset into a specific texture group from this window.

4. We next create a tileset layer in the room of your choice. Select *Create New Tile Layer* from a room's inspector element. You are now told to choose a tileset to be used on this layer; click *No Tile Set* and navigate to the tileset you created and configured in the previous steps.

5. Finally, you have a selection of fresh tiles available for you to paint a room with on the right side of the IDE. Click on tiles in the inspector element to choose them and press left mouse button inside the tile layer to bring them into your room; right mouse button removes a tile.

The above five steps describe the basic workflow of tilesets in GameMaker, but there's so much more to them. We'll delve into the more advanced techniques for tile work next.

Tile Animation

We can create simple animations for our tiles in GameMaker, too. This is wonderful for some grass swaying in the wind or perhaps for a windmill rotating its sails. The tool for tile-based animations is accessed in the asset browser simply by clicking on a tileset and then clicking *Tile Animation*. You can now create animations by clicking *Add Animation*. There is a small selector graphic for the number of frames you want for your animations, ranging between 2 and 256 frames. To add animation cells, you simply click on the tileset itself on the left side of the animation tool.

Tile-based animations are implemented in the room view of your project. You are to first click on the tile layer the animation(s) rests on. Then you should navigate to the side panel called *Libraries* found on the right side of the screen. You can now pick the animation you want from the section called *Animations Library*. Animations are "painted" into rooms the same way you would add regular tiles.

Tile-based animations are only previewed in the room editor if you click the Play Animation button in the IDE next to the zoom controls.

Auto-tiling in GameMaker

A feature called *Auto-tiling* in GameMaker automatically selects the appropriate tile based on its neighboring tiles. This feature, known as *bitmasking,* is there to quickly implement environments like terrain, walls, or mazes, where tiles must connect in a natural fashion. This obviously reduces the need for manual tile work.

GameMaker supports two widely used auto-tiling techniques: *16-tile* and *47-tile* auto-tiling. They are described as follows:

- **The 16-tile system** leverages a four-bit mask to determine tile placement based on the presence of adjacent tiles in the four main directions of up, down, left, and right. This system is ideal for simpler dungeon/maze designs.

- **The 47-tile system** expands on the 16-tile system by including diagonal connections, resulting in 47 total tile variations. This system is better suited for more complex environments, such as cities and elaborate caverns.

Both systems are designed to save time and effort, letting developers focus on making cohesive tile-based maps with minimal fuss. They are wonderful for making those large, sprawling cities and dungeons for role-playing games. GameMaker aside, auto-tiling is a common feature found in several well-known gamemaking tools.

To set up a new auto-tile system, make sure you have a suitable sprite resource available. You'll need a bitmap image with all the necessary variations for either 16-piece or 47-piece auto-tiling. When such a resource has been imported into GameMaker as a tileset, just click on it and select *Auto Tiling* from the ensuing properties window. Then click on one of the plus signs next to the numbers 47 or 16 (see Figure 5-3).

CHAPTER 5   CAMERAS, LAYERS, AND TILESETS

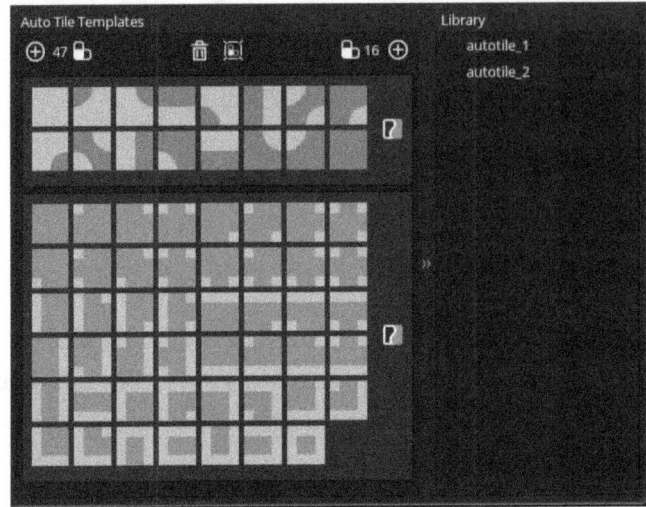

Figure 5-3. *A partial view of GameMaker's auto-tiling settings window*

You now get to create your auto-tiling system by first clicking on an auto-tile shape followed by a click on a tile. The darker grey area represents a "filled" area (e.g., unpassable terrain).

Now, the behavior of an auto-tile near room edges is determined by the *open or closed edges* button (represented by the icon to the center right of each template in Figure 5-2). By default, when an auto-tile is placed along a room's edge, it assumes the area outside the room is empty. This results in tiles that create an "edge." However, if you enable this button, the auto-tile will treat the outside area as if it were filled with tiles and choose tiles that blend seamlessly and eliminate said edge effect.

Tileset Management in GML

There are a number of functions for managing your tiles in GML. In the following code listing, the first one (i.e., *layer_tilemap_get_id*) retrieves the unique handle/ID of a tileset so we gain access to it. After this bit of data is stored (in this case in *tilehandle1*), we can do a number of manipulations on this tile layer.

```
var tilehandle1 = layer_tilemap_get_id("Grasslayer");
if tilehandle1 != -1 { // Make sure tilehandle1 exists (is not -1)
    var tile_index = tilemap_get(tilehandle1, 5, 5);
    if tile_index == 3 { // Tile index 3 represents a tree stump
```

```
        show_message("There's a darn stump at 5, 5!");
        // Change the tile at position (5, 5) to tile index 1
        // which might represent, say, a turnip
        tilemap_set(tilehandle1, 5, 5, 1);
    }
    // Actually, let's wipe the entire layer clean
    tilemap_clear(tilehandle1);

    // Let's then fill a 10 x 10 area with tile index 0 (grass)

    tilemap_set_region(tilehandle1, 0, 0, 10, 10, 0);
}
```

Let's break down the five main functions for manipulating tilesets in GML (see Table 5-5).

Table 5-5. *Some useful functions for manipulating tilesets in GML*

handle = layer_tilemap_get_id(layer_name)	Get tile layer handle/ID
index = tilemap_get(handle, x, y)	Get tile index at position x, y
tilemap_set(handle, x, y, index)	Change tile index at position x, y
tilemap_clear(handle)	Clear a tile layer completely
tilemap_set_region(handle, x1, y1, x2, y2, tile_index)	Change a rectangular region of tiles into tile_index

Like you can tell by now, tiles in GameMaker are not static and can be altered dynamically during the gameloop. This makes them a great type of asset to work with. In fact, for your games' backgrounds, you should always implement tilesets, at least in the case of more elaborate maps.

Tilesets in Action

A small project file has been prepared for you to demonstrate tilesets. *JollyTilemaps* contains the following features:

CHAPTER 5   CAMERAS, LAYERS, AND TILESETS

- Four layers of tilesets (i.e., Stuff, PlantsTrees, Shadows, and Grass)
- A camera system set up from the GameMaker IDE
- A blur effect added inside the IDE on the Shadows layer for some sweet softening of shadows

In JollyTilemaps, you can enjoy a little grassy landscape[1] that you can scroll through with your mouse. Pressing 1, 2, and 3 toggles the visibility of the first three tileset layers on and off. Left mouse button will toggle texture filtering; it's obvious pixel art usually looks much better without it. The project has a handy custom function, *toggle_layer*, which takes a single parameter as a layer name.

Tilesets and Collisions with Invisible Objects

There are a number of ways to integrate collisions into rooms that use tilemaps. If there is only a handful of scenery to collide with, you can use so-called *invisible objects*. These are objects that usually have a single color sprite assigned to them which gives them a collision mask. The visibility of these objects is then disabled by unchecking the box *Visible* from the GameMaker IDE (or by including *visible=false;* in such an object's Create event). These objects can nonetheless be made to collide with other game actors in the usual way, i.e., through Collision events or functions like place_free, as previously discussed.

Objects set to invisible will remain visible in the GameMaker editor for easy level design. They are quite flexible; instead of placing numerous invisible objects next to each other, you can stretch a single invisible object in the GameMaker IDE to fill larger spaces for collisions.

Tilesets and Collisions with tilemap_get_at_pixel

Another way to handle collisions with tilemaps is to use a function called *tilemap_get_at_pixel*. Let's say we have a player object called *obj_Player*. We have placed all tiles to be collided with into a single layer called *Stuff*. By inserting the following code into the Step

---

[1] The graphics for JollyTilemaps were graciously donated by Cainos, a creator on itch.io.

event of obj_Player, this object would then collide with all tiles inside Stuff, aside from tile number zero (i.e., the top-left tile in the tileset) which we assume is empty.

```
// Define the tilemap layer for collisions
var collision_layer = layer_tilemap_get_id("Stuff");
// Check the tile at the object's position
var tile = tilemap_get_at_pixel(collision_layer, x, y);

// Handle the collision
if tile != 0 { // If index zero is not an empty tile
  speed=-speed*2; // Make object bounce away at twice its speed
}
```

Tilemap Collisions Demonstration Project

A project file called *TilemapCollisions* is there to demonstrate how the aforementioned simple collisions are implemented. It has the following features:

- Three layers of tilesets[2] (i.e., JollyLayer, WackyLayer, and BottomLayer) and a single layer for instances.

- A camera system set up from the GameMaker IDE.

- Two different types of collision checks against tilesets. The left side of the room demonstrates collisions using so-called invisible objects while the right side leverages a function known as *tilemap_get_at_pixel*. Any active invisible barriers will be highlighted in red.

The project presents us a single room of 800 × 768 pixels. A camera follows *obj_UAP*, a lovely little UAP[3] indeed, controlled by the player with their mouse. Holding down the left mouse button accelerates the craft toward the yellow cursor. Pressing the Escape key will end the program.

As previously stated, the left side of the room demonstrates collisions with invisible objects called *obj_Invisible* in our project and the right side of the room is dedicated to purely tile-based collisions enabled by the function *tilemap_get_at_pixel*.

---

[2] The tiles for TilemapCollisions were created by Sethbb, a creator found on itch.io
[3] UAP stands for *unidentified aerial phenomena*. This is what cool people call UFOs these days.

CHAPTER 5   CAMERAS, LAYERS, AND TILESETS

Now, to somewhat optimize invisible objects, we can deactivate all of the ones that are not in the immediate vicinity of the player. This should work fine at least for all simple maps with no obstacle-minding NPC's wandering around the scenery. For this, there are two handy functions: *instance_activate_object* and *instance_deactivate_object*. This approach is leveraged in our project inside the Step event of *obj_Controller*. We cannot execute instance activations from within the instance itself. This is because we cannot readily reactivate an instance while it's deactivated/dormant; it needs an outside actor for that.

Working with Instance IDs

As first mentioned all the way back in the first chapter, instances are the actual implementations of objects in GameMaker. There is one important property we shall now discuss: the *instance ID*. Each individual instance carries one to differentiate it from all the others, and sometimes we need to work on this level of instance IDs.

In TilemapCollisions, we have a global ds_list (a data structure discussed in Chapter 2) called *global.mask_list* which is defined in the Create event of obj_Controller. This list is used in a custom script *deact* to retrieve the instance IDs of our invisible barrier objects (i.e., obj_Invisible).

As discussed in the previous chapter, the keyword *with* will open a code block for all instances of a specific object type. We use this technique once in our project, in an Alarm event inside obj_Controller. It's where we store all instances of obj_Invisible into our DS list. Sometimes it's best to introduce a small delay before executing such an action, just to make sure all the instances truly have been spawned before working on them—hence the use of an alarm.

Now, our custom function *deact* is found in the script file *festive_scripts* and it takes two parameters: an instance type and distance in pixels. Let's explore this function in detail next.

```
function deact(inst, dist) {
// Iterate through global.mask_list
    for (var i = 0; i < ds_list_size(global.mask_list); i++) {
        // Define a temporary variable for ds_list values, id_finder
        var id_finder = ds_list_find_value(global.mask_list, i);
        // Store distance between a member of global.mask and obj_UAP
```

CHAPTER 5   CAMERAS, LAYERS, AND TILESETS

```
    var distance = point_distance(id_finder.x, id_finder.y, obj_UAP.x,
    obj_UAP.y);
    // Activate or deactivate an instance based on the distance
    if distance > dist instance_deactivate_object(id_finder);
    if distance < dist instance_activate_object(id_finder);
    }
}
```

In the above listing, we define a variable (i.e., id_finder) which is fed the output of a function called *ds_list_find_value*. This in turn will return the value contained at specified positions in a DS list; in our script, this index is iterated with the time-honored *i* in a for loop. The actual implementation of the deact function is found in the Step event of obj_Controller and it looks like this:

```
deact(obj_Invisible, 150);
```

As per the function definition, the above use of the deact function will make all instances of obj_Invisible deactivate as soon as their distance from obj_UAP reaches over 150 pixels and reactivate when it's under 150 pixels. Once again, our old friend point_distance is called into action.

The project also displays the number of currently active instances on the right side of the screen. This is done by examining a built-in property called *instance_count*. This count includes all running instances, not just our barrier objects. Finally, we make sure to remove the ds_list with the following statement in the Game End event:

```
ds_list_destroy(global.mask_list);
```

Switching instances on and off may in some cases be a good idea as it can reduce the toll on a device's resources and make things run smoother. This very much depends on the project. In our little example, any such optimization is unnecessary, but it's a good idea to be aware of these techniques.

Deactivating an instance in GameMaker pauses all of its processing and events.

As mentioned before, the right side of the room in TilemapCollisions is used for tileset-based collisions using *tilemap_get_at_pixel*. We basically define everything on the tileset assigned to the layer called *JollyLayer* as an obstacle, except for index number

185

zero (0), a tile which contains no visuals. Checking for collisions this way is achieved by using another custom function called *happy_tile_collision* which is found inside festive_scripts.

More on happy_tile_collision

The function *happy_tile_collision* takes two parameters: layer name and collision radius. In our example, the radius is set to 18 pixels; this value needs some experimentation when used with different tile sizes. The GML inside happy_tile_collision detects for collisions on both a square area around an instance as well as the diagonals. The function is executed from within the Step event of the object we want to collide with the tileset; in the case of our example, that means *obj_UAP*. As is often the case, the tileset in TilemapCollision represent an isometric approach at a slight angle. The tile-based collisions in our project take place with a 75% less of a radius for the top and top diagonals (e.g., *var tile_up = tilemap_get_at_pixel(collision_layer, x, y - collision_radius*0.25)* whereas the reduction of radius does not take place for left, right, and downward collisions).

A Peek Inside obj_UAP

In TilemapCollisions, the previously discussed function (i.e., happy_tile_collision) is summoned inside the player-controlled craft. This is what the Step event of obj_UAP looks like:

```
// STEP
if mouse_check_button(mb_left) {
if x<mouse_x hspeed+=0.1;
if x>mouse_x hspeed-=0.1;
if y<mouse_y vspeed+=0.1;
if y>mouse_y vspeed-=0.1;
    effect_create_below(ef_flare,x,y,0,c_maroon);
}
hspeed=clamp(hspeed,-2,2);
vspeed=clamp(vspeed,-2,2);
happy_tile_collision("JollyLayer", 18);
```

In the first code block, we check if the left mouse button is pressed using the function *mouse_check_button.* If this is true, the horizontal and vertical speeds (i.e., hspeed and vspeed) for this craft will be set based on the location of the mouse cursor and the craft coordinates. A little visual effect is also summoned at the end of the code block.

You may remember our old chum *clamp* from previous chapters in the book; this function is used to limit the values of variables. For obj_UAP, it's used to keep hspeed and vspeed inside a range between −2 and 2. Finally, we execute the custom script happy_tile_collision targeting a layer called *JollyLayer* with a radius of 18 pixels.

Changing the Mouse Cursor

The TilemapCollisions project also introduces us to another handy property for our pointing devices: the gallant *cursor_sprite.* You'll find it in the Create event of obj_Controller, and it's there to change the mouse cursor to a sprite resource (in this case, a yellow pointer by the name of *spr_Cursor*). Please note cursor_sprite won't hide the default system cursor, which must be still removed with the statement *window_set_cursor(cr_none).*

Introducing Tank Merriment Version 0.1

It is time to introduce another exciting game prototype. Say hello to *Tank Merriment,* a simultaneous two-player game where the competitors are to blast each other's tanks to oblivion. This somewhat complicated example will not be reproduced in the book in its entirety. Instead, we shall start with an overview and explore some of the game's mechanics in further detail. The code in the project file is fully commented for your learning pleasure. As always, you are encouraged to explore and tinker with the project file in GameMaker to see all the objects and events in action.

Now, Tank Merriment demonstrates the following features:

- Split screen view using the GameMaker camera system
- Keyboard controls
- Bonus items for ammunition and health
- Score keeping and a title screen
- Simple NPCs in the form of wandering robots

CHAPTER 5   CAMERAS, LAYERS, AND TILESETS

On the GML side of things, Tank Merriment features the following techniques:

- Dynamic layers
- Particle effects
- A custom script file (i.e., superior_scripts) which offers shorthanded (e.g., *iex* which refers to *instance_exists*) and other versions of common GML functions

As is the case with many a two-player video game, the objective of Tank Merriment is to humble your opponent. In this top-down game both players commandeer a tank with a limited supply of ammunition. The battle takes place in a maze-like arena where you also have to worry about rogue robots skulking the perimeter. One must keep an eye on red energy zones, too, which will slow down a tank if run over.

Player one uses the familiar WASD control method, while player two controls their tank with the arrow keys. Firing is done by holding down either the F or the Enter key, respectively (see Figure 5-4). Pressing Escape toggles pause mode also offering the option of pressing Q to quit back to the title screen. The M key toggles music on and off.

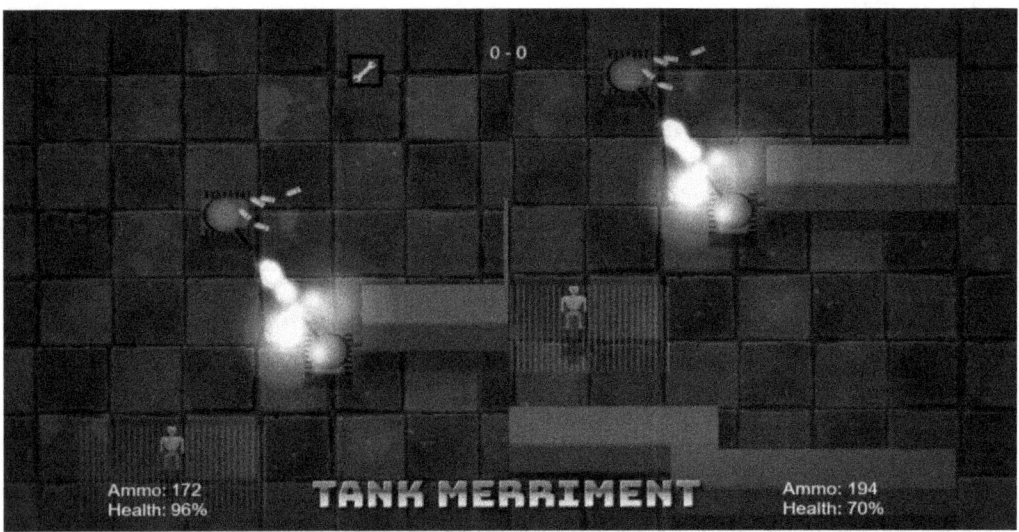

Figure 5-4. *A screenshot of Tank Merriment. Player two is taking a beating while a robotic NPC watches from the sidelines. A bonus item is visible in player one's viewport*

Both tanks have a health rating which dwindles as enemy projectiles make contact. At 25% health, a tank slows down considerably and is set ablaze with a particle-based fire effect. Each enemy projectile that hits a tank reduces one percent of health. Players can replenish their ammunition and repair their tanks by collecting bonus items which spawn on the arena at random positions.

Shells are automatically aimed at the enemy tank; each turret is constantly pointed at the direction of the enemy. This doubles as a handy way to keep an eye on the position of your opponent. The robot NPC in the arena are destroyed either by shooting them or by colliding with them, which reduces a tank's health rating by 5%.

Tank Merriment is loosely based on *Combat*,[4] a popular video game from the late 1970s.

Inside Tank Merriment

Let us now examine some of the GML found in the prototype. First off, a script file called *superior_scripts* contains a number of useful functions. They're basically there to demonstrate how you can make your game development more comfortable. Let us examine two of them, namely, *pburst* and *gburst*.

```
// Particle burst
function pburst(system, emitter, part, radius, number) {
    if number == undefined number=5; if radius == undefined radius=5;
    part_emitter_region(system, emitter, other.x-radius, other.x+radius,
    other.y-radius,other.y+radius, ps_shape_ellipse,1);
    part_emitter_burst(system, emitter, part, number);
}

// Global particle burst using global.Sname & global.emitter1
function gburst(part, radius, number) {
    if number == undefined number=5; if radius == undefined radius=5;
    part_emitter_region(global.Sname, global.emitter1, other.x-radius,
    other.x+radius, other.y-radius, other.y+radius, ps_shape_ellipse,1);
```

---

[4] Combat is a top-down shooting game developed and published by Atari as a launch title for their 1977 console, the Atari 2600. The game was created by Ron Milner, Joe Decuir, Steve Mayer, and Larry Wagner.

CHAPTER 5   CAMERAS, LAYERS, AND TILESETS

```
    part_emitter_burst(global.Sname, global.emitter1, part, number);
}
```

The function *pburst* takes five parameters: particle system, particle emitter, particle type, emitter radius, and the number of particles to spawn.

The function *gburst* expects a global particle system has been declared with the name of *global.Sname*. A global emitter is also needed, called *global.emitter1*. In the case of this project, we define these global structures in the Create event of *obj_Game*.

The Tank for Player One: obj_Player1

The Create event of obj_Player1 looks like this in its entirety:

```
// CREATE
ammo1=200; health1=100; speed_limit=5; fire_delay=0; fire_delay_max=3;
happy_direction=point_direction(x,y,obj_Player2.x, obj_Player2.y);
friction=0.3;
```

We here have a bunch of custom variables for the tank. Variable *ammo1* governs how much ammunition player one receives from the get go; we opted for a hefty 200 rounds. A variable called *health1* is used to gauge the player's condition. Every hit from an enemy projectile reduces this reading, as does running over a pesky robot. Variable *speed_limit* is the maximum allowed top speed for our tanks, set here at a nice five (5) pixels per step. Friction is a built-in property which sets an object's resistance to movement in a room; as discussed previously in the book, this variable is typically best set below 0.5 or you might get a rather immobile object.

The variable called *happy_direction* is assigned an initial value fetched using the function point_direction; this will be discussed later in more detail.

Now, the Step event of obj_Player1 handles keyboard controls and collisions for player one's armored vehicle. The controls are implemented as follows in the first eight lines in this event:

```
// STEP
if keyboard_check(ord("D")) {
    hspeed=speed_limit; vspeed=0; image_angle=90; }
if keyboard_check(ord("A")) {
    hspeed=-speed_limit; vspeed=0; image_angle=90; }
```

```
if keyboard_check(ord("S")) {
    vspeed=speed_limit; hspeed=0; image_angle=0; }
if keyboard_check(ord("W")) {
    vspeed=-speed_limit; hspeed=0; image_angle=0; }
```

The above simply reads the keys W, A, S, and D to set the horizontal and vertical speeds (i.e., hspeed and vspeed) with the tank's maximum allowed velocity as defined by the variable *speed_limit*. We also set a property called *image_angle* to 90 when moving left or right, rotating a sprite by this amount in degrees.

Next we have the Draw event from *obj_Player1*. In here, we leverage a handy custom function found inside *superior_scripts* called *shadow* which draws a transparent shadow image of a sprite. For its two parameters, *shadow* takes vertical distance in pixels and a Boolean (i.e., true/false) for horizontal image flipping. Also we use the succinct function *iex* also found inside *superior_scripts* which is shorthand for *instance_exists*.

```
// DRAW
// Hide shadow if solid objects appear 10 pixels lower (e.g. obj_Obstacle)
if place_free(x,y+10) shadow(10, false);
draw_self(); image_speed=speed*0.1;

if iex(obj_Player2)
draw_sprite_ext(spr_Tank_Turret,-1,x,y,1,1,happy_direction,c_aqua,1);
else draw_sprite_ext(spr_Tank_Turret,-1,x,y,1,1,image_angle,c_aqua,1);

if health1<25 gburst(global.smoke);
```

The above GML also demonstrates the built-in extended sprite function, *draw_sprite_ext*, which takes many more parameters compared to its more basic implementation called *draw_sprite*. For more basic applications, you will do just fine without draw_sprite_ext, but sometimes it fits the bill perfectly for that extra panache. Let's break this function down in Table 5-6.

Table 5-6. *A breakdown of the function draw_sprite_ext in GML*

Property	Access variable	Description
Sprite	sprite_index	Sprite resource name (e.g., spr_Tank).
Subimage	image_index	Takes a number starting from zero (0).
x coordinate	x	-
y coordinate	y	-
x scale	image_xscale	Image width. A value of 1 means original width. A negative value reverses the sprite horizontally.
y scale	image_yscale	Image height. A value of 1 means original height. A negative value reverses the sprite vertically.
Rotation	image_angle	Sprite angle between 0 and 360 degrees. 0 is right, 90 is up, 180 is left, and 270 is down.
Color	image_blend	Takes GML color constants (e.g., c_aqua, c_red, etc.). Entering c_white or −1 means sprite is not to be colorized.
Alpha	image_alpha	Opacity between 0.0 (invisible) and 1.0 (fully visible).

Getting back to obj_Player1 in Tank Merriment, the variables *fire_delay* and *fire_delay_max* (as defined in the Create event) work in tandem for launching projectiles. As player one holds down the F key, fire_delay is increased by one (1) every step. When fire_delay reaches the value defined in fire_delay_max, set at 3, a projectile is launched and fire_delay reset back to zero. This allows for some impressive rapid fire salvos.

Finally, we have *happy_direction*. This variable, which controls the direction of the turret sprite, is updated in the Step event of obj_Player1 as follows:

```
if iex(obj_Player2)
happy_direction=point_direction(x, y, obj_Player2.x, obj_Player2.y);
```

The GML function *point_direction* is leveraged here to point to the position of obj_Player2, or the other player's tank. This is a most useful function and one you'll doubtless use in your future gamemaking efforts time and again.

CHAPTER 5 CAMERAS, LAYERS, AND TILESETS

Duplicating Objects: The Tank for Player Two

The other tank in Tank Merriment was created by first simply duplicating obj_Player1 inside the GameMaker asset browser. This is a great way to speed up game development when you have objects for roughly the same purpose; there is often no need to reinvent circular things.

We can clone objects in the GameMaker IDE by right-clicking on an object inside the asset browser and selecting *Duplicate.* This will result in an exact carbon copy of a specific object.

After duplicating obj_Player1 and renaming the ensuing clone as obj_Player2, a number of alterations were made to its events. First off, a bunch of variables inside this object were renamed. The control keys were also changed from WASD to the arrow keys for obvious reasons.

Pausing a Game with GML

There are many ways we can pause a game's proceedings with GML. Pressing the Escape key during gameplay pauses Tank Merriment, showing us one simple method for doing so. This is executed in the Step event of *obj_Game:*

```
// STEP
if keyboard_check_pressed(vk_escape) {
    if !audio_is_playing(GameBegin) audio_play_sound(GameBegin,1,false);
    paused=!paused;
    if paused instance_deactivate_all(true); else instance_activate_all();
}
 if paused && keyboard_check_pressed(ord("Q")) room_goto(TitleScreen);
```

Basically, we have defined a Boolean variable called *paused* inside obj_Game. Pressing Escape flips it from "true" to "false" and vice versa. If paused is set to "true," we summon a function known as *instance_deactivate_all* which pauses the execution of all instances. This function is issued with a single parameter, which here happens to be

193

"true" in order to keep the issuing object (i.e., obj_Game) active; a value of "false" would tell this object to deactivate itself, too. Also, if the player presses the Q key while paused is set to "true," the game switches to the room called *TitleScreen*.

Slowing Down Tanks

Tank Merriment has a bunch of animated red areas which slow down a tank passing over them. These are some very simple objects called *obj_Slower*, and they have the following three events:

```
// CREATE
depth=199; image_speed=0.5; image_alpha=0.5;
// Collision with obj_Player1
other.speed_limit=2;
// Collision with obj_Player2
other.speed_limit=2;
```

The Create event sets the drawing depth to 199 which makes these objects get drawn beneath your tanks. Next both the animation speed of the associated sprite and its transparency (i.e., alpha) are halved. Finally, we have two classic Collision events, one for each human player. When either player runs over an obj_Slower, their *speed_limit* is downgraded to two (2) pixels per step. Both tanks have this variable defined inside them to limit the tank's top speed. It is being addressed with the keyword *other* from obj_Slower. This keyword comes very handy for Collision events in general.

Collision Masks and GML Collisions

Tank Merriment uses three types of collisions in the form of classic Collision events, a function called *place_free*, and another one known as *place_meeting*.

Now, *place_free* is used to check if a given position is free of any instances. If no collisions are detected at the specified coordinates, the function returns true. Otherwise, it returns false. The rather similar function *place_meeting* looks for specific types of instances at specified coordinates.

Let's review these three types of collision mechanisms in GameMaker (see Table 5-7).

Table 5-7. *The main differences between place_meeting, place_free, and Collision events in GameMaker*

Function	place_meeting	place_free	Collision event
Syntax	place_meeting(x, y, object)	place_free(x, y)	-
Performance hit	Low	Low	Potentially costly
Precision	Potentially low	Potentially low	High
Use case	Interactions with specific objects	Movement (e.g., detecting walls)	Complex collisions

While flexible, IDE-based Collision events in GameMaker can indeed be computationally costly. It all depends on how many of them are currently on-screen as well as on the type of collision masks used. Hundreds of large sprites with precise masks can bring at least a lower-end system to its knees quickly. There are six basic collision shapes for event-based collisions in GameMaker. Care should be taken when choosing masks for your sprites; always weigh the precision of a mask against its computational cost.

- **Rectangle:** Least power-hungry. Best used with, you guessed it, rectangular sprites. However, this mask does not rotate with the object. It remains aligned with the x and y axes of the room regardless of the object's rotation.

- **Diamond:** This special shape with a low performance hit is perfect for those diamond-shaped gem sprites. Think of this as a long-lost relative of the rectangle shape.

- **Ellipse:** Useful for circular or oval-shaped objects, but more demanding on system resources. Consider using the rectangle or diamond shapes for smaller elliptical sprites.

- **Precise:** Compared to the basic rectangle shape, *precise* is both more accurate and resource-intensive. But sometimes you just need to cover all the protrusions and extremities of your creations and for that you need this type of collision mask.

CHAPTER 5   CAMERAS, LAYERS, AND TILESETS

- **Precise per frame:** The most demanding collision mask. This option creates precise masks for each and every subimage (i.e., animation cell) of a sprite. Use with caution.

- **Rectangle with rotation:** This type of collision mask rotates with the object's image_angle property. While not as efficient as the standard rectangle mask, it stresses a system less than precise or precise per frame masks.

In a simple game like Tank Merriment, you can have a perfectly functional game with rectangular collision masks pretty much for every type of object.

Collision masks are accessed by double-clicking on a sprite resource in GameMaker's asset browser. Each sprite has a setting for them in the left side of its respective window (aptly titled *Collision Mask*).

See Figure 5-5 for the window for adjusting sprite collision masks.

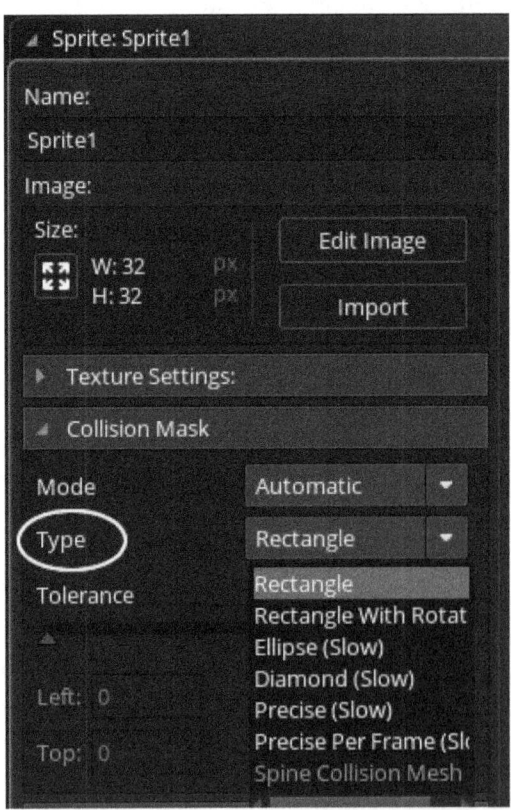

Figure 5-5. *The sprite collision mask controls in the GameMaker IDE*

CHAPTER 5　CAMERAS, LAYERS, AND TILESETS

All preset shapes aside, the GameMaker IDE also offers a manual mode for your collision masks. This basically means you get to adjust the size of one of the basic collision masks. Also, if your sprites have transparent parts, such as shadows, you can remove them from collisions by adjusting a setting called *Tolerance*.

lengthdir_x and lengthdir_y

In GML, *lengthdir_x* and *lengthdir_y* are two functions used to calculate the x and y components of a vector, which is based on a given length and direction. We can use these two functions for launching projectiles from the edge of an object, which is exactly how they are leveraged in Tank Merriment (see Figure 5-6).

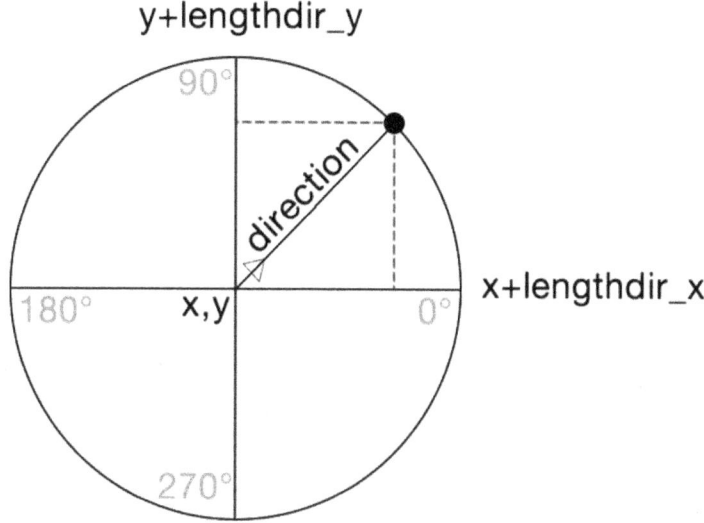

Figure 5-6. A visualization of lengthdir_x and lengthdir_y

These functions are used in the Step events of obj_Player1 and obj_Player2, like so:

```
var _xx = x + lengthdir_x(32, happy_direction);
var _yy = y + lengthdir_y(32, happy_direction);
```

When firing your cannon, the current position of a tank is combined with the appropriate lengthdir function (i.e., x with lengthdir_x) with a distance of 32 pixels and stored into a temporary variable (i.e., _xx). These temporary variables are then fed into an instance_create_depth function (not shown) as the starting coordinates for projectiles. This way we see our bullets getting launched from the turret's business end, instead of from the middle of the tank.

The lengthdir_x and lengthdir_y are great for making objects orbit around other objects, too.

In Tank Merriment, we also use the aforementioned approach to spawn those lovely brass shells (i.e., obj_Shell) for a purely cosmetic effect. These objects even contain a Collision event for bouncing against the walls. This may or may not be a computationally effective approach as we should minimize collisions in general, but for a smaller project like this, there should not be any dramatic slowdown.

On Angles: Degrees and Radians

Degrees and *radians* are two different types of units of measurement for angles. Degrees are a human-friendly unit where a full circle is divided into 360 equal parts. GameMaker takes degrees for most of its angle-related functions (e.g., image_angle, point_direction, lengthdir_x, lengthdir_y, etc.)

Now, a radian measures angles based on the relationship between a circle's radius and its circumference (i.e., the distance around the circle). Radians are used in mathematics, physics, and programming because they simplify many formulas, especially those involving trigonometric functions (e.g., sine, cosine, tan).

In GameMaker, too, radians are sometimes a better unit when calculating things. Actually, radians are used "under the hood" for a lot of functions in GML. However, sometimes you cannot resist transforming the odd degree into a radian or vice versa. There's two functions for this: *degtorad* and *radtodeg*. The following listing demonstrates a simple conversion from degrees to radians.

```
degrees = 180;
radians = degtorad(degrees);
show_message("180 degress is " + string(radians) + " radians");
```

In GML, you do not explicitly define a radian as a type, like you would an array or some other type of variable or data structure. In GameMaker, simple floating-point

CHAPTER 5 CAMERAS, LAYERS, AND TILESETS

numbers (e.g., 0.0001 or 0.025) represent radians when used in the context of angles. Because GML has a built-in constant for pi, you can leverage that when working with radians for extra precise and efficiently derived values (see Table 5-8).

Table 5-8. Degree to radian conversion using π (pi) for precision

Degrees	Radians using pi	Radians	Degrees	Radians using pi	Radians
0	0	0.000	180	π	~3.141
45	π/4	~0.785	270	3 * π/2	~4.712
90	π/2	~1.570	360	2 * π	~6.283

Solid Objects and Collisions

Objects in GameMaker can be marked as *solid* either by using a checkbox in the object editor or by typing in the property in GML (i.e., *solid = true*). The place_free function checks for collisions with solid instances—nonsolid instances do not block movement, only solid ones do. Therefore, in Tank Merriment, we have flagged both of our wall objects as solid, namely, *obj_Obstacle* and *obj_Obstacle2*.

Notice the use of a manual sprite collision mask in *spr_obstacle*, the sprite associated with all instances of obj_Obstacle. This mask does not cover the shadow and the lower part of the wall as we do not want any collisions there.

The maze in Tank Merriment was created simply by dragging a number of obstacle objects into the main gameplay room (i.e., BattleRoom1). Feel free to create your own, perhaps superiorish maze in the GameMaker IDE.

Robots in a Maze

An object called *obj_Robot* represents the blueprint for the wondering cyborgs found inside the main arena of Tank Merriment. They represent a potentially hazardous random element for both of our intrepid tank commanders. Let us peek inside the Create and Step events of these fiends next:

CHAPTER 5   CAMERAS, LAYERS, AND TILESETS

```
// CREATE
speed_limit=2;
hspeed=choose(0, speed_limit, -speed_limit);
if hspeed==0 vspeed=choose(speed_limit, -speed_limit);
// STEP
// Collisions with solid obstacles
if !place_free(x+hspeed,y) || !place_free(x-hspeed,y) || !place_free(x,y+vspeed) ||
    !place_free(x,y-vspeed) {
speed = -speed_limit;
}
image_speed=speed*0.2;
if x>room_width or x<0 or y>room_height or y<0 speed=-speed;
```

The Create event includes the definition of a custom variable called *speed_limit*. This is given a value of two (2). Also, the robot is given a random direction for movement using the built-in properties *hspeed* and *vspeed* for horizontal and vertical speeds, respectively.

In the Step event, the robots are instructed to collide with objects marked as solid, which in this context refers to all instances of *obj_Obstacle* and *obj_Obstacle2*. This is done using the function called *place_free*. The object (i.e., obj_Robot) checks if its next position, based on its current hspeed and vspeed, results in a collision. If a horizontal or vertical collision is detected, the object reverses its direction by setting its speed property to speed_limit (i.e., negative speed_limit).

Spawning Robots

Tank Merriment uses a teleporter-based spawning mechanic to introduce the previously discussed mechanical brutes. There's two instances of a simple type of object called *obj_Teleporter* in BattleRoom1. These periodically create instances of obj_Robot on top of themselves. The only two events inside each obj_Teleporter are presented next:

```
// CREATE
alarm[0]=500; depth=101;
// ALARM 0
if instance_number(obj_Robot)<5 instance_create_depth(x,y,99,obj_Robot);
alarm[0]=500;
```

CHAPTER 5　CAMERAS, LAYERS, AND TILESETS

The Create event reads as follows: set alarm-delay zero (0) to 500 steps (i.e., about 8.3 seconds). Set teleporter drawing depth to 101. Alarm event zero states that if the number of active instances for obj_Robot is less than five, create a new such instance at the teleporter's coordinates (at depth 99). Also reset the alarm timer to 500 steps.

Unleashing Bonus Items

Different bonus items are a bit of a staple in many 2D games. In Tank Merriment, we spawn two types of items on the battlefield: a wrench to fix your tank or a bunch of bullets to replenish ammunition. This is done inside alarm zero (0) within *obj_Game,* a controller object which is also used to set up the camera system in this project.

```
// Alarm 0
if instance_number(obj_Bonus)<5
instance_create_depth(random(room_width),random(room_height),99,obj_Bonus);
alarm[0]=960;
```

The statements above read as follows: as long as there are less than five instances of obj_Bonus, spawn one at a random location in our room at depth value 99. This is done every 960 steps, which translates to every 16 seconds. As for what type of item is spawned, it's decided inside each instance of *obj_Bonus*.

Particle Fences

The arena of combat in Tank Merriment (i.e., BattleRoom1) is surrounded with some fetching particle-based barriers. These stop the players' tanks in their tracks. No collision trickery is needed; these barriers are simply placed around the room's edges. Both tanks are confined inside the room at all times in their respective Step events. The particle fences are drawn inside the Draw event of obj_Game using the region definition *ps_shape_line* for a nicely even type of particle distribution. See Figure 5-7 for a screenshot of Tank Merriment with a particle fence on display.

CHAPTER 5   CAMERAS, LAYERS, AND TILESETS

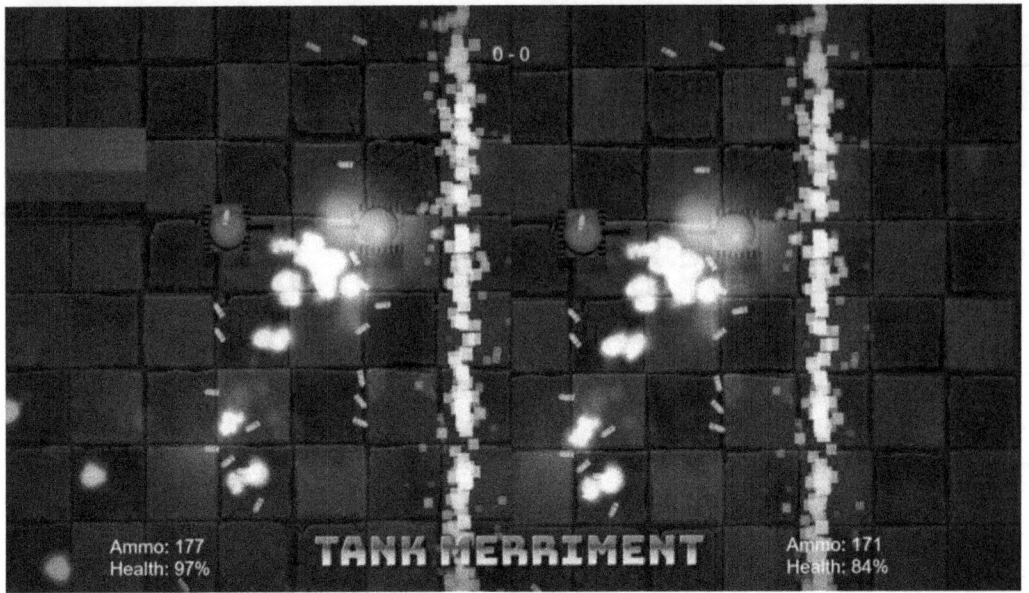

Figure 5-7. *A screenshot from Tank Merriment showing a (cosmetic) particle fence*

Views and Cameras in Tank Merriment

The views for this project are defined in the Create event of object *obj_Game*. Unless we have ticked the checkbox *Enable Viewports* in the room inspector element, we must enable views manually with the following line of GML:

```
view_enabled = true; // Enable viewports
```

Next we enable two views and configure their respective viewports. The x coordinate of viewport 0 is set at 0 and the x coordinate of viewport 1 is at the half point of the screen.

```
view_visible[0] = true; view_visible[1] = true; // Enable views 0 and 1

// Configure viewport 0 (Player 1)
view_xport[0] = 0; // X position of viewport 0
view_yport[0] = 0; // Y position of viewport 0
view_wport[0] = room_width*0.5; // Width of viewport 0
view_hport[0] = room_height*0.5; // Height of viewport 0
```

```
// Configure viewport 1 (Player 2)
view_xport[1] = room_width*0.5; // X position of viewport 1
view_yport[1] = 0; // Y position of viewport 1
view_wport[1] = room_width*0.5; // Width of viewport 1
view_hport[1] = room_height*0.5; // Height of viewport 1
```

We next create two cameras, one for each player, and assign them a view.

```
// Create Player 1 Camera
camera1 = camera_create(); view_camera[0] = camera1;
// Create Player 2 Camera
camera2 = camera_create(); view_camera[1] = camera2;
```

Finally, we set the view size for both cameras at 25% of the room size in width and 50% of the room size in height.

```
// Configure cameras
camera_set_view_size(camera1, room_width*0.25, room_height*0.5);
camera_set_view_size(camera2, room_width*0.25, room_height*0.5);
```

Layers in Tank Merriment

Our project has two layers per room, a background layer and an instance layer. This simple approach is good enough for the prototype in question and for most simple games in general. However, there is one instance where we do use dynamic layers. This approach is found inside an object called *obj_HappyLayer* which is placed on the title screen:

```
// Create new dynamic layer for the room
happy_layer = layer_create(-1000);
// Assign a handle for the layer
var handle1 = layer_background_create(happy_layer, spr_Background);
// Set the background's alpha (transparency) to 10%
layer_background_alpha(handle1, 0.1);
// Make background horizontally tiled (infinite)
layer_background_htiled(handle1,true);
// Make layer move horizontally by two pixel per step/frame
layer_hspeed(happy_layer, 2);
```

CHAPTER 5 CAMERAS, LAYERS, AND TILESETS

The above listing creates an infinitely horizontally scrolling checkered pattern as per the sprite it's based on.

The Bottom Line on Cameras, Layers, and Tilesets

Using GameMaker's room editor (IDE) for setting up cameras is a fine approach for most types of games. You can create many varieties of screen setups effortlessly using this approach without typing a single line of code. The simplest way to use cameras in GameMaker is to enable "Viewports and Cameras," set a viewport size (e.g., 960×540), and choose a player object to follow.

The numerous camera functions provided by GML only become necessary when you need things like dynamic zoom and more complicated movements. You must then get to grips with a number of functions, including camera_set_view_size, camera_get_view_width, and camera_set_view_speed.

Layers offer a ton of flexibility for organizing your games' visuals and depth levels. As is the case with cameras, the GameMaker IDE gives you most of the tools you need for working with these elements. Learning how and when to add different types of layers should suffice for most projects. GML only comes into play when you need finer control.

Tilesets are a highly efficient way of implementing background visuals into your games. A tileset is created from a single sprite image containing multiple tiles of fixed sizes (e.g., 16×16 or 32×32, etc.) This technique has a low impact on a device's resources so tilesets are ideal for larger rooms/levels. Object instances (such as the player) can be made to collide with tilesets, too, as demonstrated by the project TilemapCollisions presented in this chapter.

In Closing

In this chapter, we introduced Tank Merriment version 0.1 in all its majesty and also discussed the following topics:

- Basic GML camera functions including dynamic zooming, as demonstrated with ZoomDemo
- Both IDE-based and dynamic layers in GameMaker

- Tilesets with two example projects: JollyTilemaps and TilemapCollisions
- How to find and store instance IDs
- Collision masks and collisions with place_free and place_meeting
- Solid vs. nonsolid objects

The next chapter will focus on positional audio, motion planning, and other most intriguing topics. Remain alert!

CHAPTER 6

Spatial Audio, Motion Planning, and Paths

We first touched on GameMaker's audio functions in Chapter 4. Now it is time to expand our knowledge on this topic by getting into spatial audio, which is also known as "3D" audio. In addition, we'll take a serious look at motion planning in GML. This includes intelligent pathfinding for your game actors in the form of a mighty algorithm called A* (A-star).

Let us remind ourselves about the main differences of traditional (or 2D) audio and spatial (or 3D) audio in GameMaker. The former performs the same regardless of the player object's position. The latter uses a system of audio emitters and a listener.[1] A 2D audio system is for more simple games and sounds that don't respond to any object's position (e.g., GUI sounds or background music). A 3D audio system is for more immersive, dynamic sound design with features such as distance-based changes to volume and pitch.

As always, all of the projects mentioned in this chapter are available from the following link:

https://github.com/Apress/Next-Generation-Gamemaking

Setting Up a 3D Audio System

The most basic 3D audio system in GameMaker takes exactly one listener and one emitter. Six specific functions are needed for such a system as well as an audio resource (e.g., snd_Fire) flagged as "3D" inside the IDE. The following code snippet goes inside a Create event of a single object and provides rudimentary spatial audio in GML:

---

[1] A "listener" is usually an object representing the player.

```
// Create emitter
tinder_emitter = audio_emitter_create();
audio_emitter_position(tinder_emitter, 400, 100, 0); // Place at 400, 100
// Start fading out at 100px, go silent at 400px
audio_emitter_falloff(tinder_emitter, 100, 400, 1);
// Place the listener left to the emitter
audio_listener_position(150, 100, 0);
audio_listener_orientation(0, 1, 0, 0, 0, 1);
// Play a mono sound through emitter (e.g. a looping fire)
audio_play_sound_on(tinder_emitter, snd_Fire, true, 1);
```

In our example, we set the listener left to the emitter, making the sound mostly come out of the right speaker on a standard stereophonic playback system.

The first function in the code above, *audio_emitter_create*, takes no parameters and is rather straightforward to understand. We then set the position of *tinder_emitter* at 400 (x) and 100 (y) using the standard GameMaker coordinate system using a lovely function called *audio_emitter_position*. The third parameter for this function represents the z axis of this element. As we are not working on a 3D game project, we set this to zero.

Next we have *audio_emitter_falloff* which takes four parameters, namely, emitter index/name, start of falloff (in pixels), start of silence (in pixels), and the falloff factor. The last parameter determines **how quickly** a sound fades between the start of the falloff and the beginning of silence. A value of one (1) works best for most scenarios.

Moving on to the listener components, we first have a function called *audio_listener_position*. It takes three parameters: x, y, and z. The other listener function, *audio_listener_orientation*, is a bit more complicated. Still, let us bravely approach this one and find out what it does. Basically, audio_listener_orientation controls **how your listener object "hears" sounds in 3D space** in GameMaker. It defines which direction is "forward" and which way is "up" for audio positioning. This function uses two vectors. The first three parameters of this function define the direction the listener is facing, i.e., the at vector. The last three define the "up" direction for the listener's orientation, i.e., the up vector.

A vector is a series of numbers that describe direction and magnitude in space.

The statement *audio_listener_orientation(0, 1, 0, 0, 0, 1)* makes us face upward on the y axis and the z axis is pointing forward. In the virtual world, we're now looking straight up and our forehead is pointing forward. This works best for top-down 2D projects in GameMaker.

Finally, we have the function called *audio_play_sound_on* which is a variation of audio_play_sound mentioned previously in the book. It simply takes an extra parameter which is the emitter ID (in this case *tinder_emitter*).

Emitter and listener positions do not have to be static. Their coordinates are usually altered dynamically during the gameloop as game events dictate. This is something we shall look into next with a little project file specifically prepared for this purpose.

In addition to 3D audio, GameMaker offers some excellent real-time audio effects. This topic will be explored in Chapter 8.

Demonstrating Dynamic 3D Audio

The project file *Immersive_Audio_Demo* gives us four emitters: *obj_Emitter* for a fountain sound, *obj_Emitter2* for some fireplace audio, *obj_EmitterMoving* with birdsong, and *obj_EmitterDoppler* with some relaxing tank sounds. The first two of these emitters are static and stay put. Like its name proclaims, obj_EmitterMoving is a more mobile entity. This is also the case with obj_EmitterDoppler, which is there to demonstrate the Doppler effect; this will be discussed later in detail.

You will notice all four emitters have a function by the name of *audio_falloff_set_model* in their respective Create events. This function sets **how the volume of 3D sounds is to fade** over distance. There are a handful of different models for this. See Table 6-1 for a rundown on some of the more useful ones.

CHAPTER 6　SPATIAL AUDIO, MOTION PLANNING, AND PATHS

Table 6-1. *Some useful volume attenuation models in GameMaker 3D audio*

audio_falloff_exponent_distance	Volume drops exponentially as distance increases. Best used for 3D games. Audio might distort at close distance to emitters.
audio_falloff_exponent_distance_clamped	Volume drops exponentially as distance increases, but gain is limited and won't get distorted.
audio_falloff_exponent_distance_scaled	Similar to exponent but with additional scaling control. More realistic than linear models for most real-world sounds.
audio_falloff_inverse_distance	Smooth, natural-sounding attenuation that's great for background ambience (wind, rain). May distort.
audio_falloff_linear_distance_clamped	For predictable, linear volume reduction over distance. Great for 2D games.
audio_falloff_inverse_distance_clamped	An even safer version of the previous model.
audio_falloff_none	This model keeps the emitter volume at a constant level without any falloff. Good for background music.

Each emitter in Immersive_Audio_Demo has a variable called *radius* in their respective Create events. This is used to define the falloff factor for each emitter. It is also used for visualizing the audible area using *draw_circle* we have in their Draw events (see Figure 6-1).

CHAPTER 6   SPATIAL AUDIO, MOTION PLANNING, AND PATHS

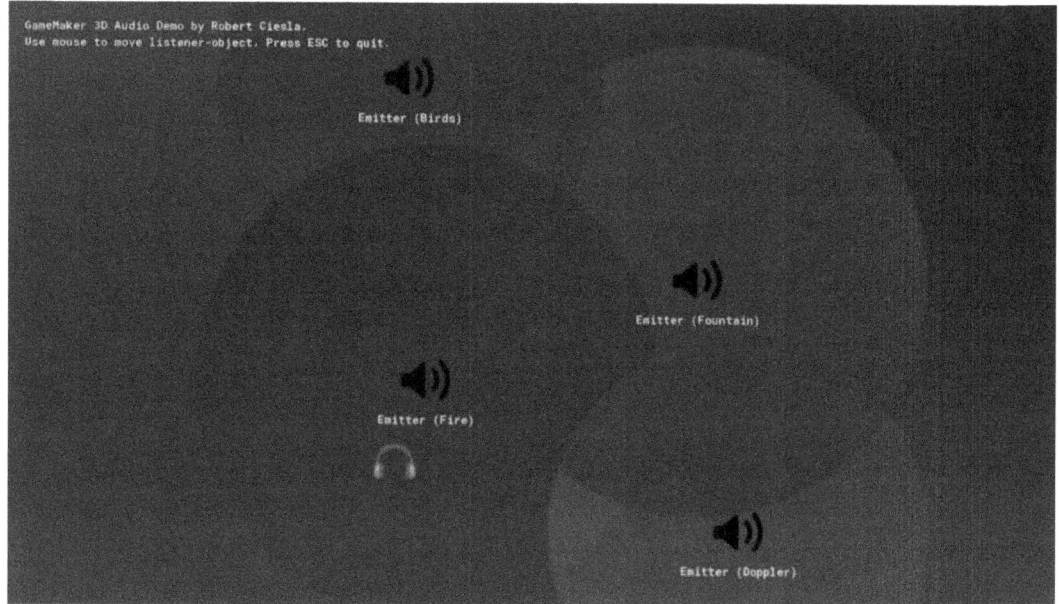

Figure 6-1. *A screenshot of the immersive audio demo with its four spatial sound sources*

The user's listener object is represented by the red headphones.

Pulling obj_DopplerEmiter into focus, like its name states, it features the Doppler effect.[2] This refers to the change in pitch when a sound source and a listener are moving relative to each other. We've all probably experienced the Doppler effect in real life. Take a passing car for example: the engine sounds higher in pitch as it's approaching and lower after it's passed you by. GameMaker offers this cool effect with minimal setup. Basically, it takes a single statement. In the demo project, this is all it takes in the Step event of obj_DopplerEmitter:

```
audio_emitter_velocity(fantastic_emitter, hspeed*15, vspeed, 0);
```

As you can tell, this function takes only three parameters, namely, emitter name and its x, y, and z. In the demo project, the horizontal speed is multiplied by 15 to get a clearly audible Doppler effect as the velocity of the object is quite slow.

---

[2] The Doppler effect is named after the Austrian physicist Christian Doppler (1803-1853) who discovered the phenomenon in 1842. It also applies to waves of light.

211

Now, the quite appropriately labeled listener object, *obj_Listener,* tracks your mouse movements. They are then transferred into the x and y parameters of the function *audio_listener_position*. In essence, obj_Listener represents a simple player object in a game.

You may notice all of the emitter IDs share the same name of *tinder_emitter*. They are all nonetheless unique elements stored in each individual object.

Please remember: stereo sound files will not work as 3D audio in GameMaker. Keep your audio files mono and the option "3D" switched on in the IDE's sound properties when working with spatial audio.

As with particles, we should delete our audio emitters after they are no longer needed. In our demo project, this is done in a Game End event using the function `audio_emitter_free`.

We shall leave audio in GameMaker for now and move on to another topic: say hello to motion planning.

A Primer on Motion Planning and Pathfinding

Whenever we are engaged in determining the movement paths of game actors inside a game world, we are doing *motion planning*. This can come in basic forms such as having an actor choose a random direction at specific intervals or have it home in on specific coordinates without taking any obstacles into account. A more advanced type of motion planning uses a technique called *collision avoidance* in which a game actor steers around obstacles by its own volition.

Pathfinding refers to the process of calculating an optimal path from one point to another. There are many ways to do this, including the fabled *A* (A-star)* as discussed later in this chapter. Game actors engaged in pathfinding avoid obstacles and are indeed somewhat intelligent in discovering the shortest path toward a point of interest. Pathfinding is considered a subset of motion planning.

GameMaker offers a multitude of functions for motion planning. We shall start with the more simple approaches, moving into advanced techniques later in this chapter.

Simple Motion Planning in GML

Let us get acquainted with some basic motion planning functions in GameMaker. First, we have *mp_linear_step* which takes four parameters, namely, x, y, speed, and collisions on (true) or off (false). The following statement has an instance following mouse coordinates without being able to collide with any other instances:

mp_linear_step(mouse_x, mouse_y, 3, false)

Putting the above statement into an object's Step event will evoke basic chasing action for said object at a speed of three (3) pixels per step/frame. Setting this function's last parameter to "true" would only make it get stuck with an obstacle. This can be useful for some scenarios (think of homing missiles flying above a landscape), but often we need something a tad more elaborate.

A closely related function, *mp_linear_step_object,* is also there to offer collisions with specific objects and ignore the rest. It replaces the last parameter of mp_linear_step with a reference to an object (e.g., obj_Wall) which will register collisions.

Now, let's say we have an object that is to advance toward the player's mouse while avoiding all other objects. GML offers a fantastic function for this purpose: meet *mp_potential_step.*

```
if mp_potential_step(mouse_x, mouse_y, 5, true) {
instance_destroy();
}
```

When inserted into a Step event of an object, the above code snippet makes said object chase mouse coordinates at the speed of five pixels per step/frame (and getting destroyed upon impact). It also avoids all other obstacles/objects on its path; mp_potential_step is a nifty little function indeed and perfect for more simple games. The last parameter decides whether the object instance is to avoid all other objects (true) or merely the ones tagged as solid (false).

We can configure how mp_potential_step works its magic using another function called *mp_potential_settings.* This function has four parameters: maximum rotation (maxrot), rotstep (rotation step), ahead, and onspot. Their default values usually work fine for many projects, but it's good to know they can be changed if necessary; usually, it's best to do so in the Create event of an object.

Now, the "ahead" parameter determines how far ahead it looks for obstacles with a default of three steps. A lower value means the object will react later to obstacles while a higher value makes it start turning earlier. If there's an obstacle straight ahead, the function checks alternative angles to the left and right in increments set by "rotstep," which has a default value of 10 degrees. Smaller rotstep values allow more precise path adjustments but require slightly more processing power.

The "maxrot" parameter controls how sharply the object can turn each step with a default of 30 degrees. This limits how much the object's direction can change at once. Higher maxrot values let objects make quicker turns but can result in jerky movements. Lower values create smoother paths but may cause detours or even a complete inability to reach the target.

Finally, the parameter referred to as "onspot" determines what happens when no valid moves are available. When true (default), the object will rotate in place as specified by maxrot. When false, it stops completely. Setting onspot to false works well for vehicle-like objects but reduces the chance of finding a path around obstacles.

We also have the function called *mp_potential_step_object* which is similar to mp_potential_step. However, this one takes an object type as its fourth parameter (akin to mp_linear_step_object). This will set the types of instances the function is to steer around; other categories of objects will simply be ignored.

Let us recap the aforementioned functions once more (see Table 6-2).

Table 6-2. Functions for simple motion planning in GML

`mp_linear_step(x, y, speed, checkall)`	Moves the instance in a straight line at a specific speed toward x and y.
`mp_linear_step_object(x, y, speed, object)`	Moves the instance in a straight line at a specific speed toward x and y colliding with the specified object type.
`mp_potential_step(x, y, speed, checkall)`	Avoids obstacles by navigating around them. The Boolean "checkall" specifies whether to only collide with "solid" objects or not.
`mp_potential_step_object(x, y, speed, object)`	Avoids obstacles specified in "object" by navigating around them.
`mp_potential_settings(maxrot, rotstep, ahead, onspot)`	Configures how mp_potential_step behaves.

The Beauty of Paths

Motion planning in GameMaker doesn't have to be simple. The software offers some potentially very intricate movement patterns for your game objects in the form of *paths*. They can be created in the IDE (see Figure 6-2) or dynamically during the gameloop.

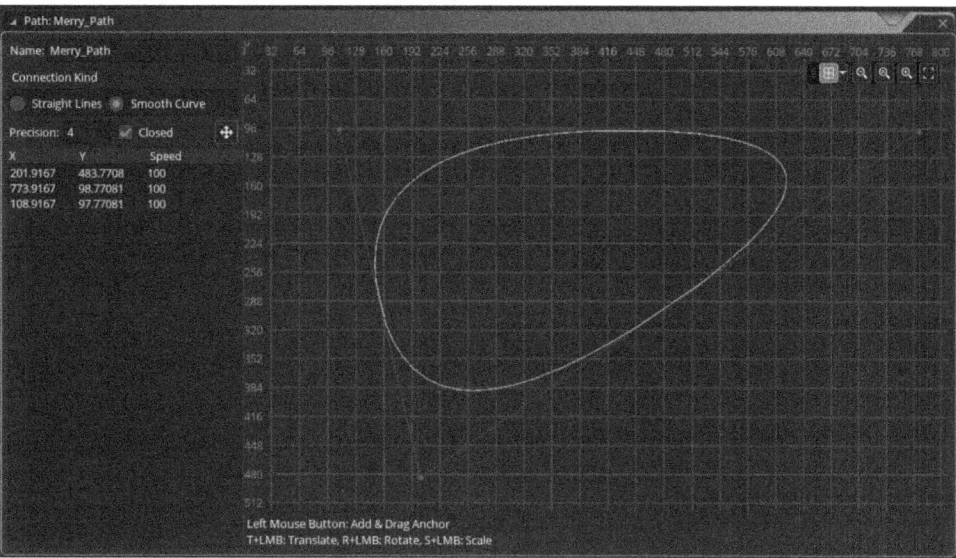

Figure 6-2. *The GameMaker path editor in the IDE showing a smooth, closed path*

When drawing paths in the IDE-based editor, you are dealing with the following attributes:

- **Connection kind:** You can either make paths with straight lines or smooth curves. The former are easier to compute. If you plan to have numerous objects with paths on-screen, it's best to prefer straight lines whenever possible.

- **Precision:** This setting adjusts the precision of the path. The default setting of four (4) is usually enough. Higher values can be detrimental to performance.

- **Closed:** This checkbox lets you create closed paths (as demonstrated in Figure 6-2).

Notice the button with arrows in the path interface labeled *Shift Path*. In case you are preparing absolute paths (i.e., paths that run on specific, static room coordinates), said feature may come in handy. By clicking the aforementioned icon, you can move your path into any of the four basic directions by a desired number of pixels.

To create a new path in the GameMaker's IDE, right-click on the asset browser and select *Create > Path*. The path editor (as seen in Figure 6-2) will open. You then get to add points to this path by clicking on the grid. These points can be repositioned at your will, too, by holding down the left mouse button on them and dragging them across the aforementioned grid. The path editor also has some other useful features such as *translate* (left mouse and T key) which lets your move the entire path around, *rotate* (left mouse and R key), and *scale* (left mouse and S key).

Dynamic Paths

Now, to use and create paths dynamically in GML, we have a wide assortment of functions. Let's begin with *path_add* and *path_add_point*.

```
// Create a new path
our_path = path_add();
// Add two points to the path
path_add_point(our_path, 200, 200, 100); // path index, x, y, speed
path_add_point(our_path, 500, 300, 100);
```

In the above snippet, we create a path called *our_path* and assign two points of travel into it. To assign this path an object instance, we would do the following inside the Create event of the object in question:

```
// Start path movement
path_start(our_path, 3, path_action_reverse, false);
```

Paths in GameMaker have seven primary properties, which are discussed in Table 6-3. Three of them need to be issued for path_start to work. These are in order of appearance *path_index, path_speed,* and *path_endaction*. The final parameter in path_start, a Boolean, specifies whether the function is to use room coordinates (true) or to use coordinates relative to a path's starting position (false).

Table 6-3. *The main path properties in GML*

path_index	Path name, e.g., our_path.
path_speed	The speed for instance on a particular path in pixels per step/frame. Negative values make the instance traverse the path backwards.
path_endaction	The action to take after an instance has finished traversing a path. These are discussed in detail in Table 6-4.
path_position	Sets the position of an instance along a path. Takes values between 0.0 and 1.0.
path_scale	Sets the path scale with the original size being 1.0. A scale of 0.5 would halve it.
path_positionprevious	Sets the position of an instance along its current path in the previous step. Useful for detecting direction changes, smoothing movement, or rewinding.
path_orientation	Sets the path's rotation in degrees. The default is zero (0).

Again, the values for path_endaction are discussed here in Table 6-4:

Table 6-4. *End actions for paths in GML*

path_action_stop	Stop the instance at the end of the path.
path_action_restart	Continue from starting position.
path_action_continue	Start the path again from its final position.
path_action_reverse	Traverse the path in reverse.

On path_add_point and path_set_kind

The first three parameters for this function are path_index, x, and y. The fourth one, which governs speed, is actually a multiplier parameter meaning 100 translates to 100% of the speed of the path. To slow a leg of a path made with this function to, say, a quarter, we would add a point with a speed value of 25.

We can also set the path to closed during the gameloop using *path_set_kind*. Giving this method a zero (0) makes a path straight (the default) while a one (1) makes a path smooth.

CHAPTER 6   SPATIAL AUDIO, MOTION PLANNING, AND PATHS

Orbiter Paths: Fun with IDE-Created Paths

Let us next examine a zany little demo project. *Orbiter Paths* has a kiwi fruit traversing on five different paths, which were all created inside the GameMaker IDE. Four of these paths are of the closed variety. Said kiwi fruit is also orbited by a lovely strawberry at all times. The project shows us how to retrieve a few fundamental path-related properties (see Figure 6-3).

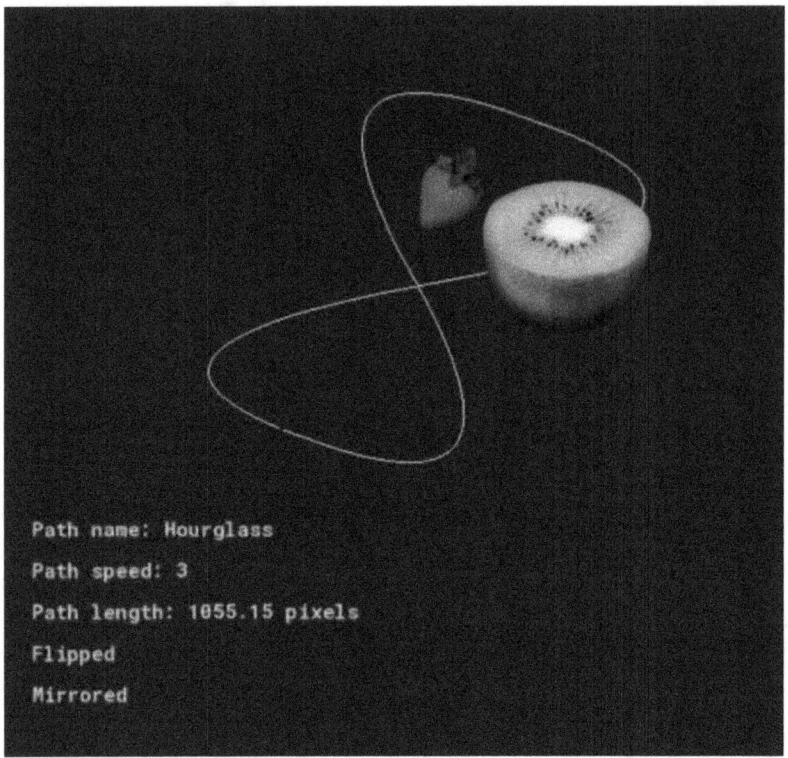

Figure 6-3. *The hourglass path from Orbiter Paths. The bottom of the screen displays some pertinent information*

Now, Orbiter Paths has just two objects: *obj_Kiwi* and *obj_Orbiter*. In the former's Create event, we define an array called *path_selection* that contains references to all of the project's five paths (i.e., triangle, wobble, lightning, hourglass, and Xpath). The data in this array is reordered randomly using a function called *array_shuffle*. As soon as a path has been fully traversed by obj_Kiwi, we fetch the next path from this array. This is gauged using the path property *path_position*. This function operates with values between 0.0 (the beginning of a path) and 1.0 (the end of the path).

218

The orbiting in Orbiter Paths for obj_Orbiter is created using the trusty duo of *lengthdir_x* and *lengthdir_y*. We also leverage *radtodeg*, a function previously discussed in the book, for converting radians to degrees.

The demonstration displays three path-related parameters, namely, path name/index, speed, and length in pixels. When displaying the path index using *path_get_name* and a path's length using *path_get_length*, we need to convert these values into strings using the function *string(value)*. All paths in our project are removed from RAM in a Game End event using *path_delete*.

The project has keyboard controls for moving the path left and right by 150 pixels using a function called *path_shift*. We also get to flip the path vertically using *path_flip* and mirror the path using, you guessed it, *path_mirror*. All of these controls are assigned for the arrow keys on your keyboard in our project. The functions they demonstrate will doubtless be useful for many scenarios in your games. See Table 6-5 for a rundown.

Table 6-5. Some useful functions for path manipulation

path_shift(path_index, xshift, yshift)	Moves a path around the room specified by xshift and yshift.
path_mirror(path_index)	Flips path horizontally.
path_flip(path_index)	Flips path vertically.
path_get_name(path_index)	Return the name of the path resource.
path_get_length(path_index)	Returns the exact length of a path in pixels.

When altering most path parameters, you must restart the path afterwards. In Orbiter Paths, we have a custom function inside obj_Kiwi that simplifies this process called *restart_path*.

CHAPTER 6 SPATIAL AUDIO, MOTION PLANNING, AND PATHS

More on Dynamic Paths in GML

Let's explore on-demand creation of paths. Another little project, *GML Paths*, demonstrates *path_add_point, path_rotate,* and other related functions. It has just two types of objects, *obj_Player* and *obj_Arrow*, working in a single room. Said arrows are fired automatically from the tomato and traverse a randomly generated path. The path can be rotated using classic WASD controls. This creates a new path which can also be achieved by pressing the space bar. By pressing the T key a path is transformed from smooth to simple and vice versa. See Figure 6-4 for what GML Paths looks like in action.

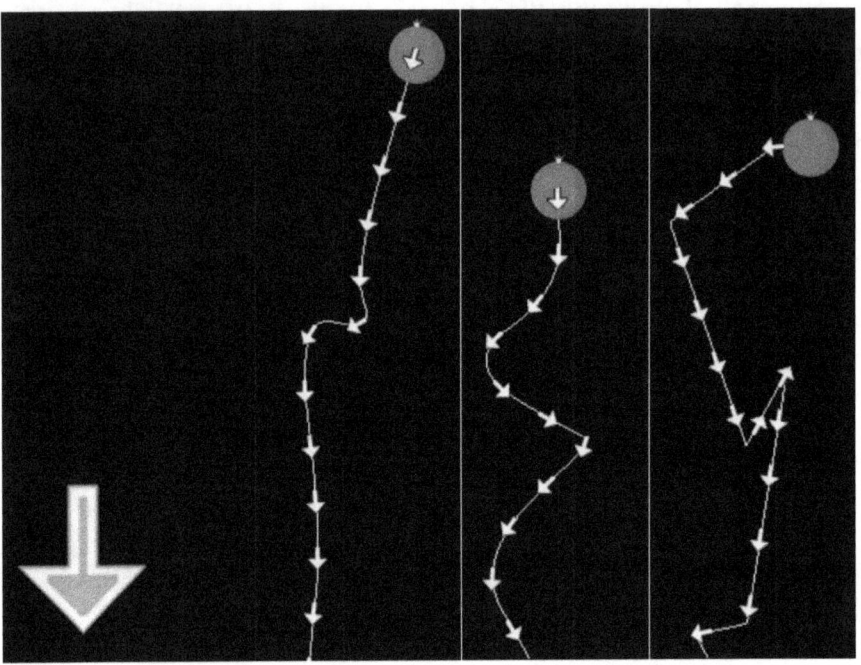

Figure 6-4. *Three different paths generated with GML Paths, a demonstration*

The project has two custom functions, *clear_arrows* and *make_happy_path* inside "*Tomato_scripts*," which look like this:

```
function clear_arrows() {
    // If any arrows exist, delete them
    if instance_number(obj_Arrow)>0 with(obj_Arrow) instance_destroy();
}
function make_happy_path(range, smooth) {
```

```
clear_arrows();
happy_path = path_add(); segments = 10;

for (var i = 0; i < segments; i++) {
    var jitter_x = random_range(-range, range);
    var jitter_y = random_range(-range, range);
    path_add_point(happy_path, x + (i * 60) + jitter_x,
    y + jitter_y, 100); }

path_rotate(happy_path, angle);
path_set_closed(happy_path, false);
path_set_kind(happy_path, smooth);
path_set_precision(happy_path, 8);
}
```

The script called *make_happy_path* creates randomized paths pointing in the direction stored in variable *angle* which is managed inside obj_Player. This variable is fed into a function called *path_rotate*. We also make the path to "open" (i.e., nonlooping) by issuing *path_set_closed* a false for its value. For *path_set_kind*, we input the value of variable *smooth*, a Boolean, which is defined inside the Create event of obj_Player. Finally, we make the paths extra precise by entering an eight (8) into *path_set_precision*.

The other custom function, *clear_arrows*, simply removes any instances of obj_Arrow to maintain some clarity in the proceedings.

Now, the for loop creates a path of ten segments as defined by the variable labeled *segments*. A random deviation is introduced into this otherwise straight path with variables *jitter_x* and *jitter_y*; these two leverage another great built-in function called *random_range*. The statement *x + (i * 60)* inside the loop spaces the path points 60 pixels apart.

The function *random_range* takes minimum and maximum values for its two parameters, e.g., *random_range(1,100)*.

---

obj_Arrow in GML Paths

The object instances traversing the path in our demonstration are quite simple. First, we have the Create event, which looks like this:

```
if path_exists(obj_Player.happy_path)
    path_start(obj_Player.happy_path, 2.5, path_action_stop, false);
```

The path_start function starts each arrow on the path labeled *happy_path* defined inside obj_Player at a speed of 2.5 pixels per step/frame. It is issued with the path-ending action *path_action_stop;* these were discussed in Table 6-4. The final parameter in the function (i.e., false) sets the path's position relative to each instance instead of being absolute/fixed (i.e., true).

The Step event of obj_Arrow is also quite straightforward. It has the following two statements:

```
if path_position >= 1 instance_destroy();
image_angle = direction;
```

In the project, we destroy all instances of obj_Arrow as soon they reach the end of happy_path. The second statement simply rotates the instance's sprite toward its direction. This works for sprites that point to the right as done in the example. If a sprite was, say, facing up, you could use *image_angle = direction - 90* for the same effect.

Path Functions at a Glance

Let us gaze upon the basic path-related functions in GameMaker once more. See Table 6-6 for a rundown.

Table 6-6. Common path functions in GML

path_name = path_add()	Creates a new path. Takes path name as its only parameter.
path_add_point(path_name, x, y, speed)	Adds points to a specified path. Speed is relative (i.e., 100 represents the original speed, 50 is half, etc.).
path_start(path_name, speed, end_action, smooth)	Starts an instance on a specified path. Speed is set in pixels per step/frame.
path_get_x(path_name, position)	Gets the x coordinate of an instance on a path; works between 0.0 and 1.0.
path_get_y(path_name, position)	Gets the y coordinate of an instance on a path; works between 0.0 and 1.0.
path_get_number(path_name)	Returns the number of points inside a path.
path_rotate(path_name, angle)	Rotates a path in degrees.
path_set_kind(path_name, smooth)	True for smooth path, false for simple.
path_set_closed(path_name, closed)	True for closed path, false for open.
path_exists(path_name)	Returns true if path exists.
path_delete(path_name)	Deletes a path.
path_end()	Ends an instance's traversal of a path. Often summoned inside an object's event.

An Introduction to A-Star

A-star (i.e., A*) is a popular grid-based pathfinding algorithm[3] created to discover the shortest path from a starting point to a goal tile while avoiding obstacles. Imagine trying to find the quickest route to a library. A* checks all streets going toward the library first. If a road happens to be blocked by a traffic jam, it tries the next best option that does not include a long detour.

---

[3] The A*/*A-star* algorithm was developed in the late 1960s by a team of researchers at *Stanford Research Institute (SRI)*. It was introduced in a paper by Nils Nilsson, Peter Hart, and Bertram Raphael called "A Formal Basis for the Heuristic Determination of Minimum Cost Paths" (1968).

CHAPTER 6   SPATIAL AUDIO, MOTION PLANNING, AND PATHS

The A-star technique consists of three main components called *ground-cost, heuristic-cost,* and *F-cost,* which are discussed next.

- **The ground-cost (G)** is the total movement cost from the start position to the current position. The cost is added to with each step based on movement direction. Moving horizontally or vertically adds 10 units. Moving diagonally adds 14 units.

- **The heuristic-cost (H)** represents **an estimate** of how far the current position is from the goal zone. It **does not** consider obstacles. The h-cost is basically an educated guess made by the algorithm. Heuristics in general refer to kinds of "rules of thumbs" or common sense; they are not limited to computer science. Not touching a cactus represents a typical heuristic decision (the spikes might be soft but it's more likely they are not).

- **The final-cost (F)** determines the optimal path proper. It is the sum of G and H. The A-star algorithm picks the F-cost with the lowest value. F-cost balances certainty (G) and potential (H) to efficiently find the shortest path.

GameMaker implements this classic algorithm for some of its functions for motion planning, namely, the functions starting with *mp_grid,* including *mp_grid_create, mp_grid_destroy,* and *mp_grid_add_instances.* We shall next discuss them in the context of another demo project.

A-star is actually based on an older technique, called *Dijkstra's algorithm.* This is a more thorough (and slower) approach for pathfinding dating back to 1956. It was created by Dutch computer scientist *Edsger W. Dijkstra (1930–2002).*

Wobbly Legs: A Demonstration of A-Star

The project file *A_Star_Demo* is there to show you how pathfinding based on A-star is implemented within GameMaker. This project presents us with a top-down maze with a player character, *obj_Player,* and seven enemy units by the type of *obj_Fiend.* An object called *obj_Controller* creates a grid for motion planning which has two types of obstacles defined in it, namely, *obj_Block* and the destructible *obj_Block2.*

CHAPTER 6   SPATIAL AUDIO, MOTION PLANNING, AND PATHS

The projects demonstrates the following techniques:

- Paths and grids for movement
- Instance IDs and collisions
- Keyboard control with WASD

Pressing R will restart the demonstration and the Escape key shuts it down. Hitting the space bar will toggle the drawing of paths for all instances of obj_Fiend (see Figure 6-5).

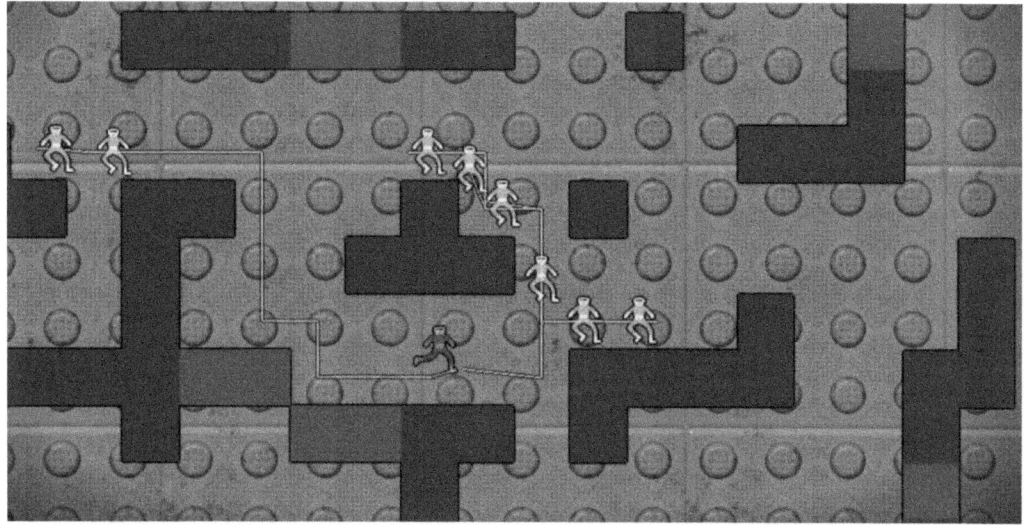

Figure 6-5. *A screenshot from Wobbly Legs, showing the green protagonist and eight antagonists with their A* paths visible as yellow lines. The red blocks are destructible*

obj_Controller

The first statement in the Create event of obj_Controller summons *full screen,* a custom function found in *our_scripts* inside the project. It is there to hide the mouse cursor, enable texture filtering, and enable a full-screen view.

Next we define a variable for the tile size used with our grid. This is set at 64 × 64 pixels. The function *mp_grid_create* is there to offer us a grid for path-based movement; with it, we create a global grid called *global.our_grid*. Like you may remember, global data structures can be accessed from any instance(s).

225

CHAPTER 6   SPATIAL AUDIO, MOTION PLANNING, AND PATHS

We define some obstacles for our grid using a function called *mp_grid_add_instances*. This duty befalls obj_Block and obj_Block2. Instances of these objects will be avoided by all game actors that are running on the A-star algorithm.

The maze in our project was simply created inside the GameMaker IDE in *Room1*.

There is a single Alarm event inside obj_Controller, which is there to define paths for all instances of obj_Fiend every half a second (or 30 steps/frames). This is an action which does not need to occur every single step/frame of gameplay. It is a good way to optimize these types of projects, especially if we have dozens of such instances active on-screen. Let us peek at this Alarm event next.

```
// ALARM 0
with (obj_Fiend)
{
    // Delete old path-variable if one exists using instance ID
    if variable_instance_exists(id, "path")
    {
        if path_exists(path) path_delete(path);
    }
```

We use the keyword *with* in the aforementioned alarm to influence all spawned instances of obj_Fiend. First, we check each instance (referenced using its ID) for a variable named *path*. If one is found, we check whether this variable is a valid path resource using *path_exists*. If this is the case, it is deleted to make way for a new one with a logically named function called *path_delete*.

The Alarm event continues with us creating a brand-new path:

```
// Create new path
path = path_add();
```

We now come across an exciting function called *mp_grid_path*. This is used to issue paths to instances traversing a grid. In this case, we are telling the grid stored in global. our_grid to approach the player's coordinates. The last parameter in mp_grid_path decides whether diagonal movements are accepted; in this project, they are not (hence the "false"). The function called *path_start* also needs to be executed to make the fiends actually move.

226

```
// Check if pathfinding succeeds before starting
if mp_grid_path(global.our_grid, path, x, y, obj_Player.x, obj_
Player.y, false)
{
path_start(path, 2, path_action_stop, true); // Start path for fiend
}
    else path_delete(path); // Delete unused path
}
alarm[0]=30;
```

obj_Fiend

The Create event of obj_Fiend contains the definitions for an empty path, aptly called *path,* and a number of variables. We also set the two-frame animation for our fiends with the image_speed property to a nice and slow 0.1.

You'll notice a Boolean called *ready.* An alarm is raised for 60 steps/frames (which translates to one second in our project) only after which this variable is set to *true.* We have this delay to make sure all the instances have spawned in the room before we start processing them; such a mechanism is often a good practice.

```
// CREATE
path=-1; collision_size = sprite_width * 0.4;
push_force = 0.002; // How hard objects push apart
ready=false; image_speed=0.1;
alarm[0]=60; // Create a delay of one second before processing
```

Now, the Step event of obj_Fiend is quite busy and warrants a good look. Basically, the GML here makes an obj_Fiend follow a path while avoiding collisions with other instances of the same type. If a collision is detected, the fiends in question are pushed away from each other to find the nearest safe/free spot on the path for both. The last thing we want in most maze games is overlapping game actors. Let's analyze this Step event from top the bottom next, shall we?

```
// STEP
if ready {
var old_x = x, old_y = y, collided=false;
```

CHAPTER 6   SPATIAL AUDIO, MOTION PLANNING, AND PATHS

```
x = path_get_x(path, path_position);
y = path_get_y(path, path_position);
```

The above statements save an obj_Fiend's current position into old_x and old_y in case of collisions. Coordinates (i.e., x and y) are updated here to the next position along the path.

Next, each instance of obj_Fiend is to loop through all other currently spawned instances of obj_Fiend. This is done using the keyword *with*. The instance IDs are accessed with the intuitive keyword *id* as well as *other.id*, which refers to the other interacting instance in question. We calculate the distance between an instance of obj_Fiend and the other such instance with our chum point_distance. Then we calculate a value for minimum distance and store it into *min_dist*.

```
with (obj_Fiend) if id != other.id {
    var dist = point_distance(x, y, other.x, other.y);
    var min_dist = (other.collision_size + collision_size) * 0.5;
```

If distance (dist) gets smaller than the minimum allowed distance (min_dist), we register a collision. The closer the colliding instances are, the greater the force used to push them apart; variable *push_force* (as defined in the Create event) is leveraged here as a multiplier. This calculation is then stored into variable *push_amount*.

```
    if dist < min_dist { // Collision occurs
        collided = true; // Set flag
        var push_dir = point_direction(other.x, other.y, x, y);
        var push_amount = (min_dist - dist) * push_force;
        x += lengthdir_x(push_amount, push_dir);
        y += lengthdir_y(push_amount, push_dir);
        other.x -= lengthdir_x(push_amount, push_dir);
        other.y -= lengthdir_y(push_amount, push_dir);
    }
}
```

Next we have a collision for instances on a path. The instances are to repel each other like magnets when colliding. If stuck, an instance is instantly moved to the nearest valid path point. For this, we leverage four functions: *path_get_x, path_get_y, point_distance,* and *position_meeting*. The for loop to follow monitors **100 points** (in 1% increments) of an instance's path. This provides enough precision without being too computationally heavy.

```
if collided {
    var nearest_pos = 0, nearest_dist = infinity;
    for (var i = 0; i <= 100; i++) {
        var test_pos = i * 0.01;
        var test_x = path_get_x(path, test_pos);
        var test_y = path_get_y(path, test_pos);
        var test_dist = point_distance(x, y, test_x, test_y);
```

We next introduce *position_meeting* into this event. The function is used here with the x and y coordinates fetched using the functions *path_get_x* and *path_get_y* in the previous passage.

```
if test_dist < nearest_dist && !position_meeting(test_x, test_y, obj_Fiend) {
            nearest_dist = test_dist;
            nearest_pos = test_pos;
        }
    }
    path_position = nearest_pos;
    x = path_get_x(path, path_position);
    y = path_get_y(path, path_position);
    }
}
```

Drawing Grids and Paths

GameMaker gives us two built-in means of visualizing our motion planning. First, we have a function called mp_grid_draw which can be used to draw an active grid where green refers to free areas and red to obstacles. This is a pretty heavy function, and its calculations do take a toll on device's resource pool. It must only be executed from a Draw event. Also, it can sometimes be unreliable with displaying obstacles. Nonetheless, when it works, mp_grid_draw can be a decent addition to your problem-solving arsenal.

Paths can be visualized, too, and this is done with *draw_path*. This function takes four parameters: the path name, x, y, and an "absolute" Boolean that determines whether to use screen coordinates (true) or the path's native coordinates (false). This function is demonstrated in the Wobbly Legs project as previously discussed in this chapter. You can even change a path's color with draw_set_color to suit your taste; it also responds to draw_set_alpha in case you wish to introduce some transparency into your workflow. Basically, draw_path is an invaluable debugging tool especially for larger projects with many paths.

In Closing

In this chapter, we introduced some new projects including Wobbly Legs, a demonstration of grid-based motion planning, and discussed the following topics:

- The basics of spatial/3D audio in GameMaker (i.e., listeners and emitters)
- Simple motion planning with GML (e.g., mp_linear_step and mp_potential_step)
- Paths, their main functions (path_add, path_exists, path_create, etc.), and some of their fundamental properties (e.g., path_position and path_index)
- GameMaker pathfinding using A* (A-star) in the form of mp_grids

A touch of universe-imitating physics can add a considerable amount of realism into your games. The next chapter will be dedicated to GameMaker's superior(ish) physics simulation. This stimulating chapter will be all about force, friction, density, and gravity.

CHAPTER 7

Physics in GameMaker

Many 2D games work quite well without attempting to capture the nuances of realistic Newtonian physics. However, for those developers that yearn for them, GameMaker includes a flexible and powerful physics engine. While it has its limitations, it is still perfectly able to deliver games with that extra touch of realism only simulated physics can provide. This chapter will have us explore this fascinating facet of game development with GameMaker.

Let us begin by discussing some of the primary features, components, and capabilities of GameMaker's physics engine, which is based on the Box2D library. Later on in this chapter, we'll delve into the core physics-related functions of GML; several demonstration projects will also be introduced.

The projects mentioned in this chapter are available from the following link:

https://github.com/Apress/Next-Generation-Gamemaking

On Box2D and Rigid-Body Physics

The physics engine in GameMaker is provided by an open source software library called *Box2D*[1] which represents a so-called *rigid-body physics simulation*. This refers to simulating physics with objects that do not get deformed or changed as a result of events such as collisions. A far more resource-intensive alternative is known as *soft-body physics;* in this approach, objects are substantially altered during the course of the physics simulation (e.g., crashing cars).

Box2D is not really designed to provide physics for large-scale projects. And like its name states, it does not offer support for 3D games. Sometimes objects using Box2D may display odd behavior in particular when it comes to angular velocities, i.e., rotation.

---

[1] Box2D was created by Erin Catto and is developed in the powerful C-language. The first iteration of the solution was released in 2006 as "Box2D Lite." Box2D went open source the next year.

However, the system does leverage advanced techniques like continuous physics and joints. The former refers to fast-moving objects passing through other objects and still detecting a collision successfully. With joints, we can connect physics-based objects to create things like ropes and ragdolls.

In addition, the good folks at *Google* have produced an extension to Box2D called *LiquidFun*[2] which lets us simulate aspects of soft-body mechanics in the form of physics-based particles. LiquidFun is supported in GameMaker and lets us create all kinds of liquids, from exotic viscous materials to something resembling plain old water. This technology is something we shall look into in this very chapter.

Soft-body particles provided by LiquidFun and the standard particles discussed previously in the book are two very different types of entities. For one, the latter do not have collision masks.

Despite its limitations, when used correctly, Box2D is a lightweight and highly effective solution for 2D video game physics. GameMaker aside, many other game development systems use this fine system for their physics, including *Clickteam Fusion* and *Unity*. Box2D has been an integral part in many a successful game (no, we shall not mention *Angry Birds*).

On Newton's Laws of Motion

Newton's laws of motion refer to three statements by famed British physicist Sir Isaac Newton (1643-1727). He formulated them in his magnum opus, Philosophiæ Naturalis Principia Mathematica (Mathematical Principles of Natural Philosophy), published first in 1687.[3] These principles specify the motion of physical objects under the influence of external forces and form the foundation for many modern physics simulations, including those in Box2D and thus in GameMaker as well. These laws are outlined next with their corresponding implementations in the Box2D physics system:

---

[2] LiquidFun was first announced in December 2013.
[3] The first edition of Principia, as the work is colloquially known, was written in Latin. An English translation by Andrew Motte was published by his brother Benjamin Motte in 1729.

1. **Newton's first law: law of inertia:** An object remains at rest or in uniform motion unless acted upon by an external force. Objects in Box2D maintain their linear (directional) or angular (rotational) velocity unless acted upon by forces like friction, gravity, or collisions.

2. **Newton's second law (F = ma):** The force acting on an object is equal to the mass of the object multiplied by its acceleration. This law quantifies how forces cause motion. Box2D uses the formula F = ma to calculate how forces affect the motion of physics bodies. Forces, such as simulated gravity and user-executed impulses, create acceleration which changes a body's velocity over time.

3. **Newton's third law: action-reaction (FAB = -FBA):** For every action, there is an equal and opposite reaction. Forces always occur in pairs. Collisions in Box2D very much respect the action-reaction principle. When two bodies collide, equal and opposite forces are applied to both. Momentum is retained, unless it's modified by Box2D properties like restitution (bounciness) or friction.

Also, Newton was the first to accurately describe the concept of *universal gravitation*.[4] This refers to the gravity we experience every day in which everything pulls everything else closer. The heavier an object, the stronger its gravitational effect. These effects also depend on proximity; they are increased the closer the objects are seated.

In GameMaker, we can set a global gravity direction, which can be made to approximate the downward pull of gravity on Earth and thus implement a simplified version of universal gravitation. More realistic implementations of Newtonian gravity are technically possible in GML but need quite a bit of work.

Object Physics Settings

In GameMaker, we must first assign resources to represent physics-based objects. The inspector element in the GameMaker IDE has a checkbox for *Uses Physics* for each object. This is something we should obviously tick first for each object we want to

---

[4] Every mass attracts every other mass with a force proportional to the product of their masses and inversely proportional to the square of the distance between them.

CHAPTER 7 PHYSICS IN GAMEMAKER

include in the physics simulation. We are then going to assign these objects collision masks. There are three types of these physics-related masks: box, circle, and convex. The last of these refers to a custom shape which you yourself design within specific constraints. Convex shapes are to curve outward while their middle part remains thicker than their edges (see Figure 7-1).

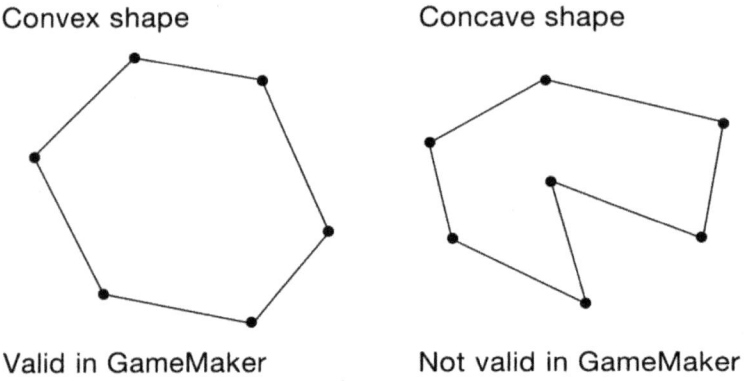

Figure 7-1. *The difference between convex and concave shapes*

Once we have a physics-capable object or two, we must enable the physics simulation within a room; it is switched off by default in each new project. This can be done in the IDE by first clicking on a room to open its properties. Then we navigate to *Room Physics* in the inspector element on the left and click *Enable Physics.* There are three parameters in this section of the IDE: *gravity x, gravity y,* and *pixels to meters.* The two gravity settings govern a room's gravitational pull on the horizontal and vertical axes, respectively. By default, they are set to provide a weak downwards pull. Setting both x and y gravity to zero would result in a rather floaty experience (think the *International Space Station*).

Interestingly, Box2D operates internally in meters instead of pixels. The higher the setting labeled *pixels to meters*, the slower things are updated by the physics system. Setting this value at 1.0 or above would result in a very slow simulation indeed. Typically, values between 0.08 and 0.2 work best.

We can also enable physics in a room by using the function *physics_world_create*. It takes one parameter, namely, the value for a pixel-to-meter scale. For example, *physics_world_create(1/32)* would create a physics-based room where 32 pixels represent one meter.

Object Physics Settings

All objects inside a physics system share a number of attributes that will be discussed next. These can be either set from inside the IDE or dynamically using GML.

- **Density:** This parameter determines an object's mass relative to its size. Depictions of high-density objects (say, small pieces of lead) are heavy and resist movement, while low-density objects (like plastic containers and some Finnish authors) are easy to move around. The physics engine automatically calculates mass based on the given density value and the surface area of the collision shape which influences how the object responds to applied forces and collisions.

- **Restitution:** This parameter basically determines how bouncy an object is during collisions. High restitution makes objects spring apart vigorously, while low restitution results in milder impacts. The actual bounce behavior also depends on other forces like gravity and friction.

- **Collision group:** By default, all objects are set to group one (1), meaning they always collide even without Collision events. Objects put in group zero (0) only collide if you've issued a Collision event (even just an empty one). Objects with negative group numbers never collide.

- **Linear damping:** This setting represents the friction when an object is traveling before colliding with other objects.

- **Angular damping:** This setting controls the rotational friction of objects.

- **Friction:** Higher friction settings make objects lose momentum faster during collisions, while lower friction creates more slippery surfaces that maintain movement longer.

We also have checkboxes for three options: *Sensor, Start Awake,* and *Kinematic.*

- **Sensor:** Ticking this box will make an object ignore all forces of physics. It will then function as a kind of a trigger for events in the physics simulation once you add Collision events for it (think of zones for damaging or healing the player, etc.).

- **Start awake:** This setting, when unchecked, will set an object as inactive inside the physics system. It will not do anything unless collided with. Although often not necessary, this setting can counter slowdown under some scenarios.

- **Kinematic:** Kinematic objects allow controlled movement while ignoring external forces like gravity. This is perfect for moving platforms or elevators that need precise manual positioning using GML with parameters like *phy_speed_x* and *phy_speed_y*.

The Fundamental Forces in GameMaker Physics

Collisions and gravity aside, there are other types of forces working their magic in GameMaker's physics world. We can summon them all using GML.

- **Impulse:** An impulse is there to provide a sudden, fading burst of movement. It's mostly used for things like firing projectiles or jumping in platform games.

- **Angular impulse:** Provides an uptick in rotational speed (i.e., spinning) of an object in the physics world.

- **Force:** A *force* in GameMaker has a continuous effect on objects. It's great for making movement for things like cars or trains. It's also wonderful for creating artificial wind and simulating underwater movements.

- **Torque:** Determines how likely an object is to continue rotating around its axis after a force is applied as well as the rate at which its rotation will decelerate.

To summon these mighty forces, we have a handful of functions at our disposal (see Table 7-1). Please note that in a physics world, we should strive to use the variables *phy_position_x* instead of *x* and *phy_position_y* instead of *y*. If plain x and y don't work in your project(s), try replacing them with the aforementioned physics-based variables.

CHAPTER 7 PHYSICS IN GAMEMAKER

Table 7-1. *The four basic functions for creating movement in physics-based objects in GameMaker*

physics_apply_impulse(xpos, ypos, ximpulse, yimpulse)	Applies an instantaneous impulse to a physics object.
physics_apply_angular_impulse(amount)	Applies an instantaneous rotational impulse. Good for explosion/hit reactions, pinball game mechanics, and falling debris.
physics_apply_force(xpos, ypos, xforce, yforce)	Applies a continuous force to a physics-enabled object. For a constant force, you need to call it every step/frame (e.g., in the Step event).
physics_apply_torque(amount)	Applies a continuous rotational force. Best used for gears, windmills, winches, and cranks.

The functions physics_apply_impulse and physics_apply_force in Table 7-1 actually work on vectors defined by two sets of coordinates. These physics actions are calculated from the distance of an initial position and a set of destination coordinates (see Figure 7-2).

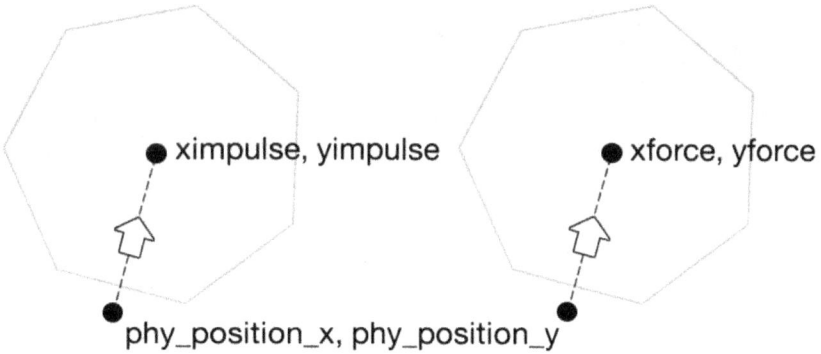

Figure 7-2. *A visualization of physics_apply_impulse and physics_apply_force in GML*

CHAPTER 7   PHYSICS IN GAMEMAKER

The calculations for the aforementioned functions are done in units resembling newtons.[5] To be more accurate, GameMaker uses a scaled physics simulation inspired by real-world units.

A Simple Physics Demonstration

A project file called *Simple Physics* has been prepared to demonstrate the basics of GameMaker's physics system. In it, you drive a car using WASD controls. You are able to push physics-enabled objects around. Should these objects collide with sensor objects, marked as green areas, they will vanish (see Figure 7-3).

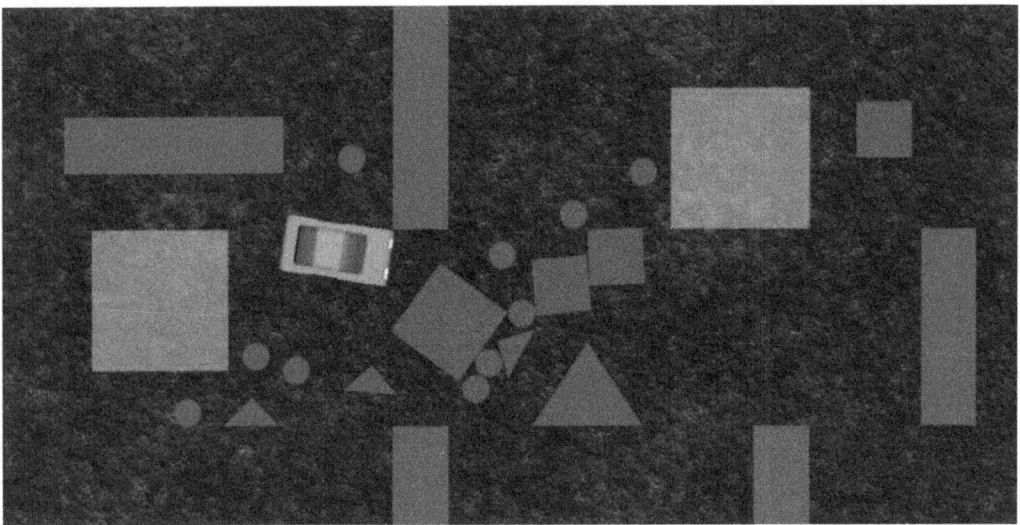

Figure 7-3. *A close-up from Simple Physics showing the automobile, the gray static physics objects (i.e., walls), the two green sensor objects, and the numerous types of movable physics objects*

Simple Physics demonstrates the following features:

- Movement using physics_apply_force and rotation using physics_apply_torque

- Physics object forward direction using lengthdir_x and lengthdir_y

---

[5] A *newton* is defined as the amount of net force required to accelerate a mass of one kilogram at a rate of one meter per second squared.

238

- Object scaling and collisions with sensor objects
- Object parenting

There is but one main actor in the project and it's called *obj_Car*. Let's examine its Step event next.

```
// STEP
// Movement inputs
var drive = keyboard_check(ord("W")) - keyboard_check(ord("S"));
var steer = keyboard_check(ord("A")) - keyboard_check(ord("D"));
// Get forward direction
var dir_x = lengthdir_x(2, -phy_rotation);
var dir_y = lengthdir_y(2, -phy_rotation);
// Apply movement force if moving/driving
if drive != 0 physics_apply_force(phy_position_x, phy_position_y, dir_x * drive * acceleration, dir_y * drive * acceleration);
// Apply steering if turning
if steer != 0 physics_apply_torque(-steer * phy_speed * 8000);
```

If W or S are pressed, a force is applied on obj_Car using physics_apply_force; the forward/backward placement of this force is calculated using lengthdir_x and lengthdir_y. These two functions gauge the rotational angle of obj_Car using the property *phy_rotation*. If we were to place a force directly on the center of the object, it would not move because it would not really be a vector anymore. The two-pixel (2) distance set in both lengthdir_x and lengthdir_y is therefore highly important here.

As for steering, obj_Car can rotate left and right with the turning rate being influenced by its speed. For this mechanic, we examine a property called *phy_speed*. The function physics_apply_torque is then leveraged to perform the movement.

Now, in Simple Physics, obj_Crate (a parent) has two children, namely, obj_Crate2 and obj_Crate3. There is also a single sensor object called obj_Sensorblock. When these crate objects are pushed over obj_Sensorblock, they disappear; your car remains unaffected.

Physics objects in GameMaker can be easily scaled in the IDE, and they will still detect collisions correctly. We can do this simply by grabbing the edges of these objects in the room editor. In our demonstration, we have both the rectangular and triangular objects scaled to different dimensions. From a cosmetic perspective, this works best with single colors or extremely simple sprites. More elaborate designs may look rather janky when scaled up this way.

Physics Properties in GML

All physics objects in GameMaker have several built in properties; *phy_rotation* used in our demonstration project is just one of them. Let's take a good look at the rest next.

- **phy_speed:** Returns the current speed of the physics-enabled instance. This property cannot be used to set speed.

- **phy_active:** When set to "true," an instance takes part in the physics simulation. When set to "false," it remains visible but does not take part in the proceedings.

- **phy_position_x/phy_position_y:** These are used to set or get the x and y positions of physics-based instances; should not be used for movement as this can cause instability. Use the previously mentioned dedicated functions instead.

- **phy_bullet:** If set to "true," GameMaker is advised it is dealing with fast-moving instances that need more robust collision detection. This is typically a good setting for most rapidly traveling projectiles.

- **phy_linear_velocity_x/phy_linear_velocity_y:** These variables are used to get or set the x and y components of an instance's linear velocity vector.

- **phy_linear_damping:** Used to get or set the linear damping of an instance.

- **phy_angular_damping:** Used to get or set the angular damping of an instance.

- **phy_rotation:** Used to get or set the angle of an instance's fixture in degrees.

- **phy_mass:** Retrieves the mass of the instance in Box2D's virtual kilograms; this value is automatically calculated based on the surface area of the assigned fixtures and their density. For example, you can examine an instance's phy_mass to discover how heavy it is and decide if a character will manage to push it around.

- **phy_com_x/phy_com_y:** Retrieves the centers of mass (defined in pixels) on the horizontal and vertical axis on an instance, respectively. These values are calculated automatically based on the density, inertia, and mass of each instance; there is a function for altering them at will which will be discussed later in the chapter.

- **phy_inertia:** Retrieves the inertia value of an instance, which refers to an entity's resistance to angular acceleration.

Happy Physics: A Demonstration in Three Rooms

The project file *Happy Physics* contains multiple demonstrations for GameMaker physics set in three different rooms. First, we have *Jam Capers* which features a plethora of physics shapes and a simulated jelly-like substance created using LiquidFun, the previously mentioned soft-body particle system. *Compromised Soccer* gives us three instances of a ragdoll in action, feverishly trying to kick a few spherical objects around while shifting about in simulated water. Finally, we have the most accurately titled *soft-body particle group demonstration with color mixing*. In it, we are shown the power of grouped soft-body particles in the form of a rectangle, circle, and a rather wobbly pyramid.

You can switch between these three presentations by hitting the left and right arrow keys.

The first room, Jam Capers, demonstrates the following features:

- Viscous soft-body particles created with LiquidFun
- Gravity and collisions
- Rotating static obstacles

The project has a spawner object, the sensibly called *obj_Spawner,* which is used to create instances of randomly chosen physics objects. These include a circular shape (obj_Ball), a rectangle, and two different convex shapes. The last three are all "children" of obj_Ball (see Figure 7-4) as enabled by the parent/child system of inheritance.

CHAPTER 7   PHYSICS IN GAMEMAKER

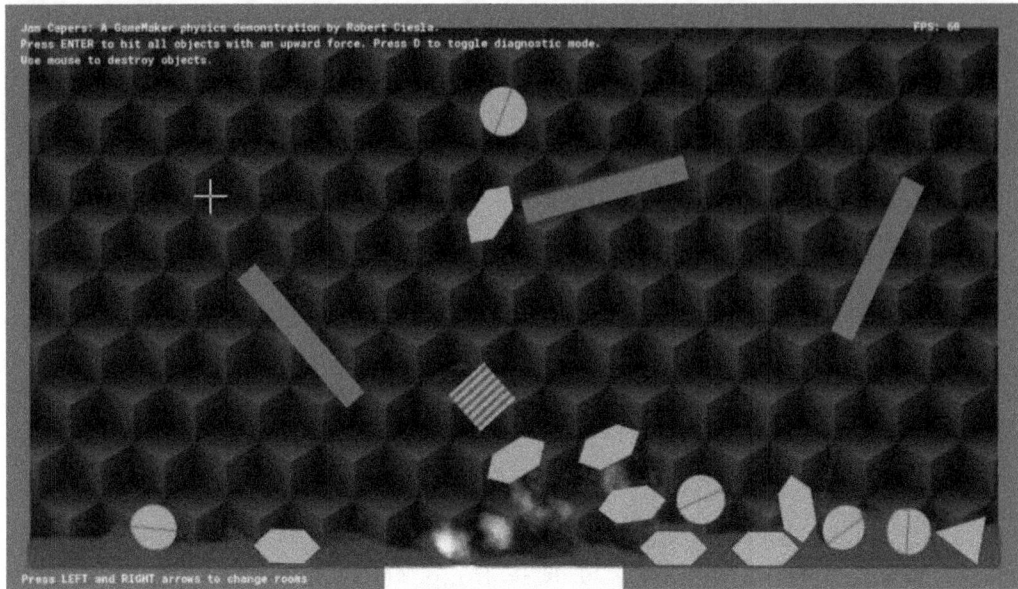

Figure 7-4. *A screenshot of Jam Capers*

A yellow block at the bottom of the screen, *obj_ObstacleSpecial,* is there to provide some upward spinning momentum for any shapes that come in contact with it. This is achieved using the function *physics_apply_impulse.* This effect can also be invoked by pressing the Enter key, but done this way you'll see it affect every moving shape in the room.

You'll notice two static rotating obstacles in the room; these are instances of *obj_ObstacleMoving.* They remain still by simply having their restitution set to zero inside the IDE.

Let us now take a peek at the very simple way LiquidFun is implemented in GameMaker. In Happy Physics, we spawn multiple of these soft-body particles at the beginning of each room. Let's take *obj_Jam* in Jam Capers for a closer look. This is its Create event:

```
// CREATE
physics_particle_set_radius(2);
physics_particle_set_max_count(10000);
// Flag instances as viscous i.e. sticky
flags = phy_particle_flag_viscous;
var xx=x, yy=y;
for(var i=0; i<physics_particle_get_max_count(); i++) {
```

```
physics_particle_create(flags, xx, yy, 0, 0, c_white, 1, 1);
xx++;
if xx>room_width { xx=0; yy+=50; }
}
```

First, we set the radius for the particle; this is a most crucial property. All soft-body particles in GameMaker are circular. Think of radius in this context as the size of a collision mask for these particles. The greater the radius, the more space each particle takes inside the simulation. The function *physics_particle_set_radius* typically works best with values between 1 and 4.

Next we set the maximum allowed number of particles with a function known as *physics_particle_set_max_count*. We opted for a fairly large number here as LiquidFun is quite capable without causing too much of a hit on performance. It can easily handle several thousand particles at once.

What follows is a definition of the particle type. These are stored here into a variable called *flags*. GameMaker's soft-body particles can be assigned with several types of qualities. The available options are discussed in Table 7-2.

Table 7-2. *The main types of soft-body particles in GameMaker also known as flag constants*

phy_particle_flag_water	Simulates the average liquid.
phy_particle_flag_tensile	Adds simulated surface tension into particles.
phy_particle_flag_viscous	Viscous particles tend to cling together more.
phy_particle_flag_zombie	Particles flagged as "zombies" simply self-destruct.
phy_particle_flag_elastic	Makes the particles slightly more bouncy.
phy_particle_flag_spring	Connects a particle with its nearest neighbor at the time of its spawning. Great for making gelatinous materials.
phy_particle_flag_powder	Gives particles a sand-like quality.
phy_particle_flag_colourmixing	Creates color mixes of two different types of particles. They must both have an alpha value lower than 1.0 for the effect to have a visible effect.
phy_particle_flag_wall	Creates an immobile, static type of particle.

Getting back to the Create event inside Jam Capers, a for loop is there to simultaneously spawn the maximum number of particles we previously defined. Like you may deduce, *physics_particle_create* is the function responsible for bringing about new soft-body particles.

For soft-body particles to actually appear on-screen, we need to draw them. For this task, we need a sprite. Luckily, there's a lovely 8×8 image resource called *spr_Water* inside the project. Next up, we have the following statement in the Draw event of obj_Jam:

```
// DRAW
physics_particle_draw_ext(flags, 1, spr_Water, 0, 1, 1, 0, c_purple, 0.2);
```

The above function, *physics_particle_draw_ext,* is actually an advanced approach as it offers far more flexibility than its common counterpart *physics_particle_draw* (see Table 7-3).

Table 7-3. *The parameters of physics_particle_draw_ext*

physics_particle_draw_ext(flags, category, sprite, subimage, xscale, yscale, angle, colour, alpha)			
flags	Flag constant(s).	yscale	Vertical scale of the particle. Enter 1 for original size. Will not change the size of the collision mask.
category	A user-defined category.	angle	Angle in degrees.
sprite	Name of sprite resource.	colour	Accepts GameMaker constants, e.g., c_purple, c_lime, etc.
subimage	The image_index of the sprite.	alpha	Opacity between 0.0 and 1.0.
xscale	Horizontal scale of the particle. Enter 1 for original size. Will not change the size of the collision mask.		

As for the more basic drawing function *physics_particle_draw,* it takes the following four parameters: flags, category, sprite resource, and subimage.

Compromised Soccer with Ragdolls

A *ragdoll* in a video game context is a simulation of a character's body when it kicks the bucket, gets knocked out, or is otherwise incapacitated. This has become a bit of a staple in both 2D and 3D games over the years. Ragdolls, like other more complicated physics components, consist of *joints* and *fixtures*. A fixture refers to the shape and physical properties of individual objects while joints constrain the motion of these objects based on specific properties.

Now, in *Compromised Soccer*, we have three instances of ragdolls created with GameMaker's physics system. Each character consists of 12 parts: the head, the torso, upper and lower arms, upper and lower legs, and feet. All of these are first created as separate instance types in our project (e.g., *obj_Body, obj_Head, obj_LeftFoot*, etc.) These objects contain very little apart from accurately defined collision masks (see Figure 7-5).

Figure 7-5. *The three merry ragdolls of Compromised Soccer in action*

The actual "blueprint" for our ragdoll is defined inside *obj_JointSystem*. It is here where we first spawn all of the 12 body parts of the ragdoll and then connect them together with *revolute joints*. We simply use *instance_create_layer*, a variation of instance_create_depth. You'll notice all of these instances are associated with variables for later. For example, this is how the torso and head are created inside the Create event of obj_JointSystem:

```
// Create torso
var **torso** = instance_create_layer(x, y+38, "Instances", obj_Body);

// Create head last
var **head** = instance_create_layer(x, y - 35, "Instances", obj_Head);
```

The coordinates and the sprites' origin points are very important here to get the optimal placement, and they would vary considerably between entities of different sizes. Now, there is a special function in GameMaker for creating ragdolls:

physics_joint_revolute_create: It is by using this function we can create a character where the parts stick together no matter what. Let's next examine all of the 11 parameters of this fine function in detail (see Table 7-4).

Table 7-4. The 11 parameters of physics_joint_revolute_create

physics_joint_revolute_create(inst1, inst2, anchor_x, anchor_y, ang_min, ang_max, ang_limit, max_motor_torque, motor_speed, motor, collide)

inst1	The instance to be connected with the one in inst2.
inst2	The instance to be connected with the one in inst1.
anchor_x	The x coordinate for the joint.
anchor_y	The y coordinate for the joint.
ang_min	The lower allowed limit for the joint angle.
ang_max	The higher allowed limit for the joint angle.
ang_limit	Set this parameter to "true" to limit the angle of the joint.
max_motor_torque	Sets the maximum motor torque used to reach the desired motor speed.
motor_speed	Set the motor's rotational speed.
motor	Set this parameter to "true" to activate motor.
collide	Set this parameter to "true" to enable collisions between inst1 and inst2 (i.e., the two components of the joint).

A motorized joint refers to a type of component that applies torque to spin the connected physics objects. Think swinging limbs in a ragdoll or propellers in an aircraft. In Compromised Soccer, we have no need for motorized joints for our characters, hence the "false" or zero (0) for this parameter.

Let's go back to the Create event of obj_JointSystem to see how the head is connected to the torso.

```
// Connect head to torso
head_ = physics_joint_revolute_create(torso, head, head.x, head.y, -20, 20,
true, 0, 0, 0, 0);
```

Since the head is not supposed to rotate much, we set the minimum angle at −20 degrees and a maximum of 20 degrees.

The occasional twitching and kicking of the ragdolls in Compromised Soccer is achieved by a periodic summoning of physics_apply_impulse in an Alarm event inside *obj_Body*.

Wobbly Pyramids with Particle Groups

Finally, we have the third room and a project called *soft-body particle group demonstration with color mixing*. What it demonstrates is particles in LiquidFun can be grouped to create larger shapes. In GameMaker, this is achieved using the functions *physics_particle_group_begin* and *physics_particle_group_end* (see Figure 7-6).

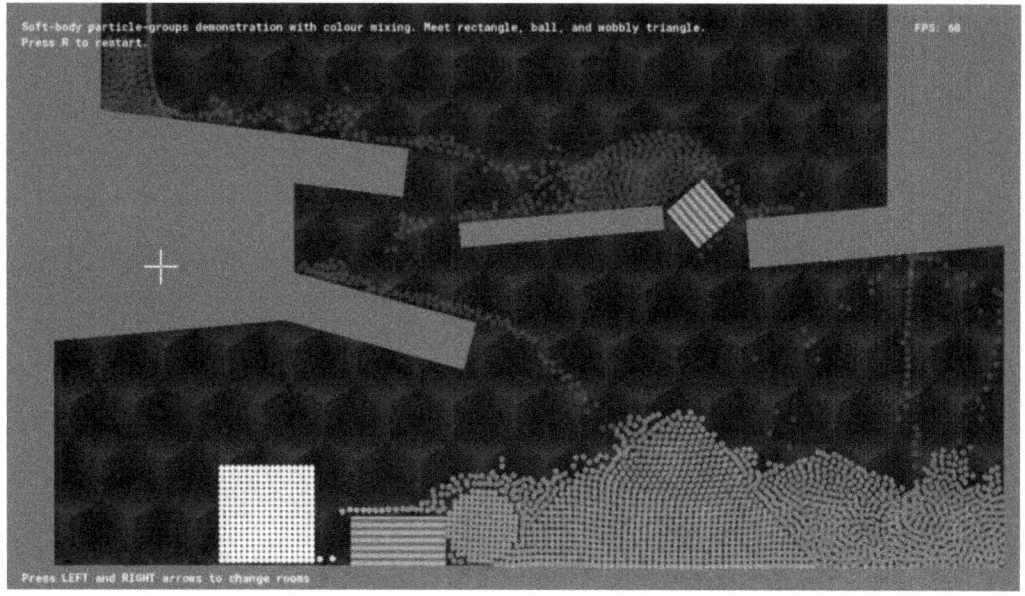

Figure 7-6. *A screenshot from soft-body particle group demonstration with color mixing*

In the project, the steps for creating grouped particles take place in the Create event of *obj_Grouped*. We have one group for each shape in the demo, namely, a ball, the famed wobbly pyramid, and a rectangle. Let's take a closer look at said Create event.

```
flags = phy_particle_flag_spring | phy_particle_flag_tensile| phy_particle_flag_colourmixing;
groupflags = phy_particle_group_flag_solid | phy_particle_group_flag_rigid;
groupflags2 = phy_particle_group_flag_solid;
```

First, we create the flag constants for the particles and store them into variable *flags*. There's an interesting type of definition in there, which enables color mixing. This refers to a rather fanciful effect where the different colors of the particles influence each other. Next we have two sets of group constants, stored into *groupflags* and *groupflags2*, respectively. The first set of constants are shared by our ball and rectangle. The second set is exclusively reserved for the pyramid; you probably notice it differs in only one respect. The definition for rigidity is not there, ergo the wobbly quality.

Now, this is how we define the first grouped entity, the ball:

```
// Define group 1: Ball
physics_particle_group_begin(flags, groupflags, x, y-100, 0, 0, 0, 0, c_blue, 1, 1, 2);
physics_particle_group_circle(50);
group1 = physics_particle_group_end(); // Store group ID as group1
```

Here we have the two previously mentioned functions in action. Let us examine the busier of these, i.e., physics_particle_group_begin (see Table 7-5).

Table 7-5. *The parameters in physics_particle_group_begin*

physics_particle_group_begin(flags, group_flags, x, y, angle, xv, yv, ang_velocity, col, alpha, strength, category)

flags	Flag constant(s).	yv	The initial vertical velocity.
group_flags	Group constant(s).	ang_velocity	The initial angular velocity.
x	The initial horizontal position of the particle group.	col	The base color for the particle group.
y	The initial vertical position of the particle group.	alpha	The group's opacity. Set between 0.0 and 1.0.
angle	The angle of the particle group in degrees.	strength	The cohesion strength between particles in the group. Set between 0.0 and 1.0.
xv	The initial horizontal velocity.	category	A user defined, arbitrary category.

Particle groups in GameMaker have only two possible flags (a.k.a. group constants): *phy_particle_group_flag_solid* and *phy_particle_group_flag_rigid*. The former makes the group impenetrable by outside particles while the latter defines the overall malleability of the group. A particle group not marked as rigid will be more jelly-like in its movements.

Getting back to the first collision group, the function *physics_particle_group_circle* is there to create a circular shape. The circle is centered at the x and y coordinates specified in physics_particle_group_begin.

Next we have the soft-body triangle. This is a polygonal shape consisting of three points, each defined using the function *physics_particle_group_add_point* which simply takes x and y coordinates as its only two parameters.

```
// Define group 2: Triangle
physics_particle_group_begin(flags, groupflags2, x, y, 0, 0, 0, 0, c_lime,
1, 1, 2);
physics_particle_group_polygon();
physics_particle_group_add_point(200, 200);
physics_particle_group_add_point(400, 400);
physics_particle_group_add_point(0, 400);
group2 = physics_particle_group_end(); // Store group ID
```

The triangular entity uses groupflags2 for its group constants, which lacks the flag *phy_particle_group_flag_rigid*. This offers us the previously mentioned jelly-like quality.

Finally, there's the dependable rectangle. This form is defined using the function *physics_particle_group_box*. It takes half the width and height of the rectangle-to-be as its parameters (e.g., a box set with 60, 60 will be approximately 120 × 120 pixels in size, depending on the size of individual particles).

```
// Define group 3: Rectangle
// This group shares group-flags with group 1
physics_particle_group_begin(flags, groupflags, x-400, y+300, 0, 0, 0, 0,
c_yellow, 1, 1, 2);
physics_particle_group_box(60, 60);
group3 = physics_particle_group_end(); // Store group ID
```

In *Room3*, we also have two instances of *obj_Faucet*. They are there to release some lovely LiquidFun-powered gunk into the demonstration. This is done in the Step event of said objects using *physics_particle_create*. The maximum soft-body particle count for this room is set at 4000 using the function *physics_particle_set_max_count*. It is most important we limit the number of soft-body particles to avoid potentially dramatic slowdowns in our projects.

Simple Fixtures: A Demonstration

We have another presentation of GameMaker's physics capabilities on deck, called *Simple Fixtures*. Now that we have explored revolute joints with the ragdolls in Compromised Soccer, it's time we try out a few more types of joints:

- Distance joints and their more flexible brethren, rope joints
- Welded joints
- Wheel joints
- Prismatic joints (i.e., fixed axis joints)

In *Simple Fixtures*, you once again commandeer a blue automobile from a top-down view and drive it around with standard WASD controls. Only this time a gray car is tied to your vehicle using a rope joint (see Figure 7-7).

CHAPTER 7   PHYSICS IN GAMEMAKER

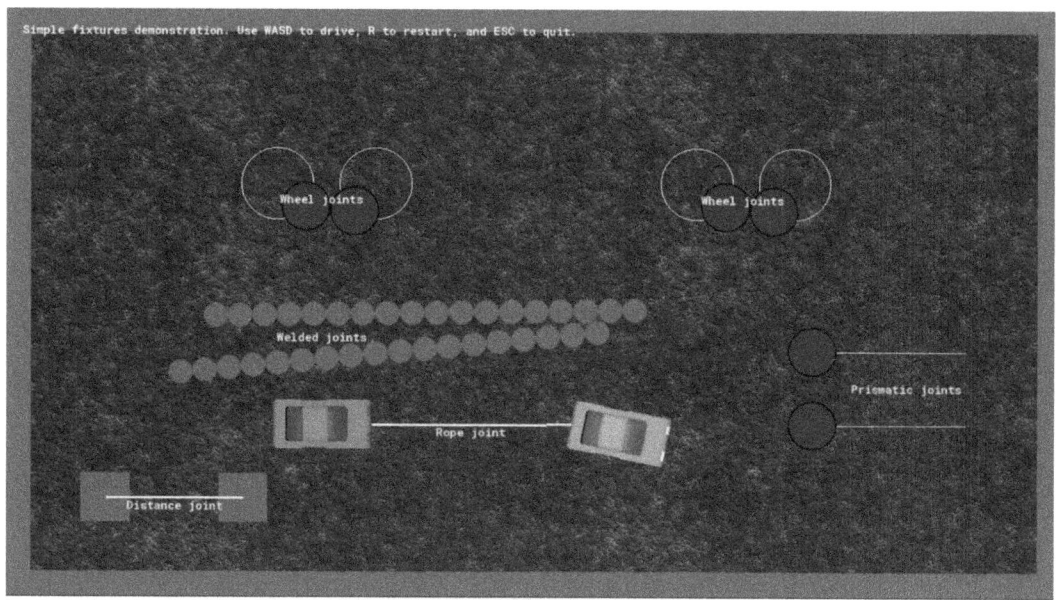

Figure 7-7. *A screenshot of Simple Fixtures*

A number of contraptions are also scattered in the room demonstrating other types of fixtures and joints. There are quite a few in this project, and we will get right into them next.

- **Distance joints** maintain a fixed distance between two anchor points on two objects, acting like a rigid connection. Objects connected this way can freely rotate around their anchor points.

- **Rope joints** create a flexible connection that goes slack if the objects are closer than their defined maximum length. The "roped" objects cannot ever exceed this length.

- **Weld joints** connect several physics objects so they move as a single unit. The end result is a flexible combination of objects with adjustable oscillation and damping.

- **Prismatic joints** let two physics objects move relative to each other along a single, fixed axis while preventing rotation or movement perpendicular[6] to that axis. These types of joints simulate telescoping motion, like a piston, a sliding door, or perhaps a simple drawer.

---

[6] Lines are called perpendicular if they intersect precisely at 90 degrees.

251

- **Wheel joints** combine a prismatic joint for linear motion and a revolute joint for rotation. They are typically used to simulate wheels attached to a vehicle chassis.

Musings on Distance Joints

A *distance joint* is the simplest type of physics-based connection in GameMaker. They are best suited for portraying rigid machinery, such as levers, cranks, and catapult arms. In Simple Fixtures, this technique is implemented using two objects, namely, *obj_Box* and *obj_Box2*. The Create event of the former is responsible for the joint and it looks like this:

```
// Create fixture for distance joint
var fixture = physics_fixture_create();
physics_fixture_set_box_shape(fixture, 32, 32);
// Create obj_Box2
var box2 = instance_create_layer(x + 180, y, "Instances", obj_Box2);
// Create the distance joint itself
physics_joint_distance_create(self, box2, x, y, box2.x, box2.y, true);
// Clean up
physics_fixture_delete(fixture);
```

First, a fixture is created with *physics_fixture_create*. This fixture is then given a box-like collision shape with the dimensions of 32×32 pixels (these are half-width and half-height, so the total size is 64×64 pixels which is the exact size of the object's sprite). An instance of *obj_Box2* is created 180 pixels right to *obj_Box* on a layer named "Instances." This instance is associated with the handle *box2*.

The distance joint itself is created next using the function *physics_joint_distance_create*. Finally, we have the function *physics_fixture_delete* which is there to purge any memory needed to store the fixture.

Let us now gaze upon the function for creating distance joints, *physics_joint_distance_create*. Compared to the other types of joints available in GameMaker, it has a refreshingly low number of parameters (see Table 7-6).

Table 7-6. *The seven parameters in physics_joint_distance_create*

physics_joint_distance_create(inst1, inst2, w_anchor1_x, w_anchor1_y, w_anchor2_x, w_anchor2_y, collide)

inst1	The first instance to connect with the joint	w_anchor2_x	The second x coordinate for the joint
inst2	The second instance to connect with the joint	w_anchor2_y	The second y coordinate for the joint
w_anchor1_x	The first x coordinate for the joint	collide	Set to "true" if the two instances can collide with each other
w_anchor1_y	The first y coordinate for the joint		

Reflecting on Rope Joints

Let us next peek under the hood of *obj_Car2* in Simple Fixtures. It is in the Create event of said object that we define a rather fetching rope joint which is tied to *obj_Car*, the entity controlled by the player.

```
rope = physics_fixture_create();
physics_fixture_set_circle_shape(rope, sprite_get_width(sprite_index) * 0.5);
physics_fixture_bind(rope, self);
physics_fixture_bind(rope, obj_Car);
physics_joint_rope_create(self, obj_Car, phy_position_x , phy_position_y, obj_Car.phy_position_x - 64, obj_Car.phy_position_y, 250, true);
physics_fixture_delete(rope);
```

The first statement creates a new fixture called *rope*. We then configure this fixture to have a circular shape with the radius of half the width of the sprite (of index 0, i.e., the first and only subimage in this sprite resource).

There are two handy functions in GML for fetching a sprite's dimensions: *sprite_get_width* and *sprite_get_height*. They return the respective original, untransformed dimensions of a sprite resource in pixels. Their only parameter is a sprite index.

The function *physics_fixture_bind* takes a fixture (which you are to create and associate with a shape) and attaches it to an object or instance. A wonderfully simple function, it takes only two parameters and we execute it twice, for *obj_Car2* (using the keyword *self*) and *obj_Car*, respectively. Then we have another busy function by the name of *physics_joint_rope_create,* which takes eight parameters (see Table 7-7).

Table 7-7. *The eight parameters in physics_joint_rope_create*

physics_joint_rope_create(inst1, inst2, w_anchor1_x, w_anchor1_y, w_anchor2_x, w_anchor2_y, maxlength, collide)

inst1	The first instance to connect with the joint	w_anchor2_x	The second x coordinate for the joint
inst2	The second instance to connect with the joint	w_anchor2_y	The second y coordinate for the joint
w_anchor1_x	The first x coordinate for the joint	maxlength	The maximum length of the joint in pixels
w_anchor1_y	The first y coordinate for the joint	collide	Set to "true" if the two instances can collide with each other

If all objects inside a room are defined as physics-enabled in the GameMaker IDE and their physics parameters are optimally defined, it is often not necessary to introduce *physics_fixture_bind* into the proceedings—at least in the case of smaller projects. For one, this is the case with the demonstration on distance joints in Simple Fixtures.

Meditations on Weld Joints

Let's next marvel at the very flexible entities known as *weld joints.* Forces applied to one "welded" object affect the entire joined structure. This technique is great for combining smaller objects into one large structure: think boss foes, vehicles, or bridges.

You'll notice joints in GameMaker are defined and used in a rather similar way. This is what the Create event of *obj_Weldjoints* looks like:

```
thingy = physics_fixture_create();
// Set fixture shape to circle
physics_fixture_set_circle_shape(thingy, 64);
var prev_thingy = noone; // Track previous shape for welding
```

Above, a variable called *prev_thingy* is initialized as *noone,* a value meaning "no object." Variable *prev_thingy* tracks the previously created object in order to connect it to the next one. Following this line, we have a nice little for loop because we are creating eighteen (18) welded instances of *obj_Crate2*. These objects will be spaced apart horizontally by 32 pixels.

The function *physics_fixture_bind* connects the circular fixture (thingy) to each crate, giving it the appropriate physics properties (i.e., circular shape, 64-pixel radius).

```
// Create 18 shapes in a row
for (var i = 0; i < 18; i++) {
    // Create new shape
    // We can use x and y because this spawner object is not physics-based
    var new_thingy = instance_create_layer(x + (32 * i), y, "Instances",
    obj_Crate2);
    physics_fixture_bind(thingy, new_thingy);
```

For every obj_Crate2 after the first (addressed with *i > 0*), a weld joint is created to connect the current object (new_thingy) to the previous one (prev_thingy), like this:

```
    // Weld to previous shape (except first one)
    if i > 0 {
        physics_joint_weld_create(prev_thingy, new_thingy,
        x + (32 * i) - 20, y, // Midpoint between shapes
        0, 10, 12, true);
    }
    prev_thingy = new_thingy; // Remember for next iteration
}
```

CHAPTER 7 PHYSICS IN GAMEMAKER

The current crate (new_thingy) is stored into prev_thingy for the next iteration, ensuring the next instance of obj_Crate2 connects to it. Finally, we remove the data structure no longer needed: out goes the fixture called thingy.

```
// Clean up the fixture
physics_fixture_delete(thingy);
```

Now, let us examine all of the eight parameters used with physics_joint_weld_create in some more detail (see Table 7-8).

Table 7-8. *The eight parameters in physics_joint_weld_create*

physics_joint_weld_create(inst1, inst2, anchor_x, anchor_y, ref_angle, freq_hz, damping_ratio, collide)			
inst1	The first instance to connect with the joint	ref_angle	The joint angle to maintain
inst2	The second instance to connect with the joint	freq_hz	The oscillation frequency for the joint (in hertz)
anchor_x	The x coordinate for the joint	damping_ratio	The damping ratio for the joint
anchor_y	The y coordinate for the joint	collide	Set to "true" if the two instances can collide with each other

The *reference angle* (ref_angle) defines the desired relative orientation between inst1 and inst2 in degrees. The *damping ratio* refers to a value that sets how much the joint resists bouncing when the objects move relative to each other. A large damping ratio creates a stiff and inflexible weld. The *oscillation frequency* (freq_hz) determines how "springy" the construct is. If a welded entity wobbles all over the screen, try decreasing the oscillation frequency. Lower values of, say, under 20 make it much less twitchy.

Ruminations on Wheel Joints

In Simple Fixtures, we have two instances of rotating wheel joints. Each wheel is created inside a respective *obj_WheelBase* and this is what their Create events look like:

```
var main = physics_fixture_create();
physics_fixture_set_circle_shape(main, 64);
var wheel = physics_fixture_create();
physics_fixture_set_circle_shape(wheel, 32);
// We can use x and y because this spawner object is not physics-based
wheel_inst1 = instance_create_layer(x+64, y + 100, "Instances", obj_Wheel);
wheel_inst2 = instance_create_layer(x-64, y + 100, "Instances", obj_Wheel);
physics_fixture_bind(main, self);
physics_fixture_bind(wheel, wheel_inst1);
physics_fixture_bind(wheel, wheel_inst2);
physics_joint_wheel_create(self, wheel_inst1, wheel_inst1.x+32, wheel_
inst1.y+32, 1, 1, true, 2000, 2, 1, 1, false);
physics_joint_wheel_create(self, wheel_inst2, wheel_inst2.x+32, wheel_
inst2.y+32, 1, 1, true, 1000, 2, 1, 1, false);
physics_fixture_delete(main);
physics_fixture_delete(wheel);
```

As a reminder, the function called *physics_fixture_bind* takes a fixture and attaches it to an object or instance. This gives the object physics properties so it can connect with other physics objects. Here *physics_fixture_bind* is used to assign circular fixtures to the main body (referenced as *self*) and two instances of object type *obj_Wheel* (i.e., *wheel_inst1* and *wheel_inst2*).

Now, the function *physics_joint_wheel_create* has a whopping 12 parameters, which will all be examined next (see Table 7-9).

Table 7-9. *The 12 parameters in physics_joint_wheel_create*

physics_joint_wheel_create(inst1, inst2, anchor_x, anchor_y, axis_x, axis_y, enableMotor, max_motor_torque, motor_speed, freq_hz, damping_ratio, collide)

inst1	The first instance to connect with the joint	enableMotor	Set to "true" to activate motor
inst2	The second instance to connect with the joint	max_motor_torque	Sets the maximum torque used to achieve the desired motor speed
anchor_x	The x coordinate where the joint is anchored	motor_speed	The rotational speed for the motor
anchor_y	The y coordinate where the joint is anchored	freq_hz	The oscillation frequency for the joint in hertz
axis_x	The x component of the wheel axis vector	damping_ratio	The damping ratio for the joint
axis_y	The y component of the wheel axis vector	collide	Set to "true" if the two instances can collide with each other

Prismatic Joints

Lastly, we have a pair of prismatic joints in our presentation. These are the types of joints with the most constraints. Below is the Create event of *obj_Prismatic,* which is responsible for setting up a prismatic joint in the program. You shall see two of these in action in Simple Fixtures.

```
var main = physics_fixture_create();
physics_fixture_set_circle_shape(main, 64);
var prismatic = physics_fixture_create();
physics_fixture_set_circle_shape(prismatic, 64);
other_id = instance_create_layer(x, y, "Instances", obj_Wheel);
physics_fixture_bind(main, self);
physics_fixture_bind(prismatic, other_id);
```

physics_joint_prismatic_create(self, other_id, x, y, -1, 0, 0, 200, true, 1000, 2400, 1, true);
physics_fixture_delete(main);
physics_fixture_delete(prismatic);

You'll once again notice the setup is rather similar to the other types of joints presented in this chapter. Table 7-10 presents the parameters of the function physics_joint_prismatic_create.

Table 7-10. The 13 parameters in physics_joint_prismatic_create

physics_joint_prismatic_create(inst1, inst2, w_anchor_x, w_anchor_y, w_axis_x, w_axis_x, lower_trans_limit, upper_trans_limit, limit, max_motor_force, motor_speed, motor, collide)

inst1	The first instance to connect with the joint	upper_trans_limit	The upper permitted limit for the joint movement
inst2	The second instance to connect with the joint	limit	Set to "true" to limit joint movements
w_anchor_x	The x coordinate where the joint is anchored	max_motor_force	Sets the maximum movement speed for the motor
w_anchor_y	The y coordinate where the joint is anchored	motor_speed	Set the motor speed
w_axis_x	The x component of the axis vector	motor	Set to "true" to enable motor
w_axis_y	The y component of the axis vector	collide	Set to "true" if the two instances can collide with each other
lower_trans_limit	The lower permitted limit for the joint movement		

Remember to adjust max_motor_force based on the weight of objects: objects with more density need more force.

CHAPTER 7 PHYSICS IN GAMEMAKER

Physics Space Combat: Frolicking with Galactic Worms

There's yet another exciting demonstration for this chapter. *Physics Space Combat* is there to show us the following features:

- Mouse-based controls liken to a typical real-time strategy (RTS) game, including a drag-to-select mechanism for player craft
- A handful of small enemy craft firing projectiles at the player's ships
- A single large enemy consisting of numerous welded joints (i.e., the galactic worm in question)
- A background layer with a two-tone deep blue gradient effect and some stars plotted with *draw_point*

In this presentation, you can select your fleet (consisting of six purple craft) by drawing a rectangle over them with the left mouse button. You can then send them to a destination point by clicking the right mouse button anywhere on the screen (see Figure 7-8).

Figure 7-8. *A screenshot of Physics Space Combat*

If manual targeting is off, your ships will periodically fire on the nearest hostile craft. If manual targeting is on, you can direct fire using your mouse cursor and tap the space bar to launch a barrage of projectiles. Manual targeting is toggled using the Enter key in the demonstration.

All ships and the worm in Physics Space Combat are regular physics-based objects. There are also two types of projectiles: *obj_Bullet* is for your craft and *obj_EnemyBullet* for the foes. These projectile classes are both set to "sensor" inside the GameMaker IDE. This makes the instances of these objects lack a physics-based presence in the room, but we can still detect their collisions using dedicated events. This approach is taken because in this context, projectiles do not need to spin and/or wobble and/or push other objects around.

On Targeting

Like previously mentioned, Physics Space Combat offers two modes of targeting: manual and automatic. A (global) Boolean variable called *global.mouse_targeting* is used to inspect the targeting mode status. If this variable is set to "true," the space bar can be used to send projectiles toward the mouse position (i.e., *mouse_x* and *mouse_y*). This functionality is found inside each instance of *obj_Ship*.

The variable *global.mouse_targeting* is toggled on and off inside *obj_Controller* in an event called *Key Up - Enter*. A "key up" event in GameMaker is triggered when a specific key is released; in this case, we are observing the status of the Enter key.

Spitting Bullets Using a Custom Script

We have a custom function in the project (found inside *GreatScripts*) called *FireBullet*. It is used to fire both friendly and unfriendly projectiles. It is issued with four parameters: *targetship, bullet, speed,* and *atmouse*. The last parameter will be given the previously discussed variable *global.mouse_targeting* in the case of using FireBullet with the player's craft.

Now, the first parameter, targetship, is used on the very first line inside Firebullet which is as follows:

```
var target = instance_nearest(phy_position_x, phy_position_y, targetship);
```

CHAPTER 7   PHYSICS IN GAMEMAKER

The very handy GameMaker function *instance_nearest* is there to probe a location defined by phy_position_x and phy_position_y for any instances specified in *targetship*. If one is found, it is stored inside variable *target*. If no instances are found, instance_nearest returns the value of *noone*. The script continues as follows:

```
var speed_magnitude=speed;
    if target != noone {
        // Create the projectile
        projectile = instance_create_layer(phy_position_x, phy_position_y,
        "Instances", bullet);
        // Set the target ship
        projectile.target = instance_nearest(phy_position_x, phy_
        position_y, targetship);
```

Next we take one of the function arguments, *speed*, and store it into *speed_magnitude*. If there is a target, we create a projectile using *instance_create_layer*, assigning it a handle simply called *projectile*. We then set a target for the aforementioned projectile using dot notation (i.e., *projectile.target*) once again summoning the function *instance_nearest*. The listing continues as follows with us examining the variable *atmouse*:

```
if !atmouse {
        // Calculate direction to the target ship
        var dir = point_direction(phy_position_x, phy_position_y, target.
        phy_position_x, target.phy_position_y);
        } else var dir = point_direction(phy_position_x, phy_position_y,
        mouse_x, mouse_y);
        // Set initial velocity toward the target ship
        with (projectile) {
        phy_linear_velocity_x = lengthdir_x(speed_magnitude, dir);
        phy_linear_velocity_y = lengthdir_y(speed_magnitude, dir);
        phy_rotation = dir;
        phy_bullet = true; // Set object's bullet-flag to true
        }
    }
}
```

In the above snippet, we first check if variable *atmouse* is set to false. If it is, we proceed with a code block. A familiar function *point_distance* is used to calculate the direction to the target ship; this value is stored into variable *dir*. Next we address all instances stored in *projectile* using the with keyword and give them some good old-fashioned linear velocity. We finish this code block off by switching on a Boolean by the name of *phy_bullet*. This property basically enables additional precision for fast-moving objects in the physics simulation.

Setting *phy_bullet* to "true" inside an object enables *continuous collision detection*. This setting improves precision but adds an additional computational drain and should thus only be used with fast-moving objects, such as projectiles.

We have two other custom functions in this project, namely, *prepare_stars* and *draw_stars*. These are used to create a static field of stars for the background and resemble what we did in *Space Heck* way back in the book except this time our stars are immobile.

Moving Ships in Space

Let us now take a gander at the space craft in the project and how their movements are created. This applies to both the player's craft of the type *obj_Ship* and all enemy craft (i.e., *obj_Enemy*). A slightly simplified version of this approach is embedded inside the *obj_WormPiece* as well. Basically, in Alarm event zero (0), a periodic force is applied to a craft toward the coordinates set with variables *target_x* and *target_y*. This is done every 15 steps/frames which in our project this translates to a quarter of a second. The maximum speed for a craft is limited to prevent overtly swift movements; this is gauged using the built-in variable *phy_speed*. Also, getting close to target_x and target_y results in a reduction of both horizontal and vertical velocities (adjusted with *phy_linear_velocity_x* and *phy_linear_velocity_y*, respectively).

CHAPTER 7 PHYSICS IN GAMEMAKER

On Selection Rectangles

Physics Space Combat features an object called *obj_Controller* which handles the project's GUI. For one, it offers a drag-to-select mechanism for the player's craft. When the left mouse button is pressed, a drawing flag is set to true, indicating the start of a selection rectangle. When the left mouse button is released, the drawing flag is set to false. This is all done in the Step event of obj_Controller, which looks like this:

```
if mouse_check_button_pressed(mb_left) {
    drawing = true;
    start_x = mouse_x; start_y = mouse_y;
}
if mouse_check_button_released(mb_left) drawing = false;
x = start_x; y = start_y;
if drawing {
    with(obj_Ship) {
        // Normalize rectangle bounds to handle any drag direction
        var x1 = min(other.x, mouse_x);
        var y1 = min(other.y, mouse_y);
        var x2 = max(other.x, mouse_x);
        var y2 = max(other.y, mouse_y);
        // Check if a friendly ship is inside the rectangle
        if x > x1 && x < x2 && y > y1 && y < y2 selected = true;
         else selected = false;
    }
}
```

Variables *x1* and *y1* are set to the top-left corner of the selection rectangle by taking the minimum of the starting point (other.x and other.y) and the current mouse position (*mouse_x* and *mouse_y*). Variables *x2* and *y2* are set to the bottom-right corner by taking the maximum value of the same coordinates. This ensures the rectangle is correctly defined regardless of the drag direction, whether it is executed left-to-right or right-to-left.

More Joints: Meet Gear and Pulley

Believe it or not, but there are two more funky types of joints left to discuss. One is the amazing *gear joint*. This is a special type of construct that connects two other preexisting joints (which are either revolute or prismatic) and makes them work together like gears inside a contraption. A gear joint doesn't directly connect objects like other types of joints do. Instead, it links them "remotely" and makes their movements match. The gear joint basically makes two joints communicate with each other.

The other type of joint discussed in this section is the *pulley joint*. Basically, this refers to a pair of connected objects sharing a virtual rope. This type of connection associates two instances via two anchor points set somewhere in the room. It also allows local anchor offsets for both instances to customize the connection point relative to their sprite origins. Pulley joints make great elevators, hanging platforms, and balance scales in games.

Gear and Pulley Joints: A Demonstration

Let us take a look the very last demonstration of physics in this chapter, the fittingly titled *Gear and Pulley Joints*. The left side of this project room presents us with a gear joint system, consisting of a round winch object (*obj_Cog*) and a platform (*obj_Platform*). Both of these objects are found inside the gear group of the asset browser. You can either operate the winch directly by pressing the keys A and Z or indirectly by either spawning spheroid[7] objects on the platform. You can also move said platform up and down by pressing the keys S and X (see Figure 7-9).

---

[7]A spheroid is a sphere-like form. Sometimes you just can't quite match a circular sprite's outline with an accurate physics collision shape in GameMaker—and thus a spheroid is born.

CHAPTER 7   PHYSICS IN GAMEMAKER

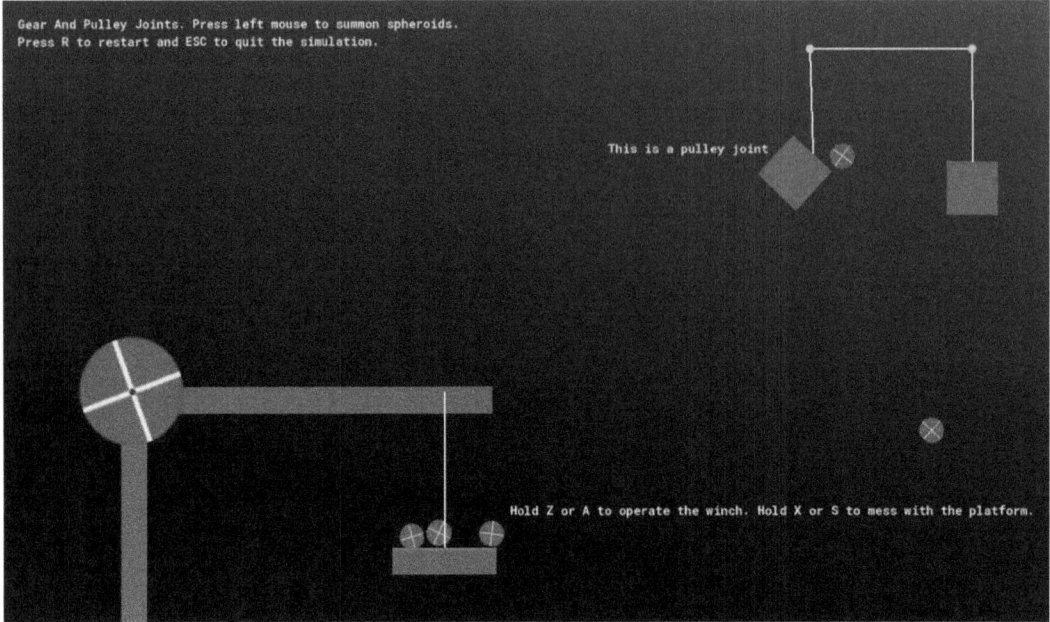

Figure 7-9. *A screenshot of Gear and Pulley Joints*

When using keyboard control on the winch, we are simply applying torque to it. This is a gear joint where the winch and the platform are connected. A force applied to one also has an effect on the other. The gear joint in this presentation uses the functions *physics_apply_torque* and *physics_apply_impulse* for its physics effects.

The right upper side of the project room features a *pulley joint.* In our demonstration, the two instances are made to collide with each other; this can be switched off.

Gear joints link existing joints (revolute or prismatic) for rotational coordination, while pulley joints directly connect instances with a rope-like system.

Now, the two instances of *obj_Box* are connected via a simulated rope visualized using *draw_line_width*. To see how this pulley system works, click left mouse button on top of the objects to spawn some spheroids—and watch them go to town.

Both of these contraptions are defined in their respective Create events inside *obj_GearStructure* and *obj_PulleyStructure*. The two functions to pay close attention to are *physics_joint_gear_create* and *physics_joint_pulley_create*. Let us take a look at the former first (see Table 7-11).

CHAPTER 7　PHYSICS IN GAMEMAKER

Table 7-11. The five parameters in physics_joint_gear_create

physics_joint_gear_create(inst1, inst2, joint1, joint2, ratio)			
inst1	The first instance to connect with the joint	joint2	A previously defined revolute or prismatic joint
inst2	The second instance to connect with the joint	ratio	Sets the velocity ratio between joint1 and joint2
joint1	A previously defined revolute joint		

The *physics_joint_gear_create* function links two joints, which can be revolute, prismatic, or one of each. Like you may remember, a prismatic joint enables linear sliding along a fixed axis. If both joints are prismatic, the gear joint synchronizes their linear movements. A revolute joint allows rotation around a point and if both joints are revolute the gear joint synchronizes their rotations, simulating mechanisms like interlocking gears. The ratio parameter controls the relative motion between the joints.

Finally, we have the lengthy function known as *physics_joint_pulley_create* with its 13 parameters to gawk at (see Table 7-12).

Table 7-12. The 13 parameters in physics_joint_pulley_create

physics_joint_pulley_create(inst1, inst2, w_anchor1_x, w_anchor1_y, w_anchor2_x, w_anchor2_y, l_anchor1_x, l_anchor1_y, l_anchor2_x, l_anchor2_y, ratio, collide)			
inst1	The first instance to connect with the joint	l_anchor1_x	The local x coordinate where joint 1 is anchored to the first instance
inst2	The second instance to connect with the joint	l_anchor1_y	The local y coordinate where joint 1 is anchored to the first instance
w_anchor1_x	The x coordinate for the first joint anchoring	l_anchor2_x	The local x coordinate where joint 2 is anchored to the second instance

(continued)

Table 7-12. (*continued*)

w_anchor1_y	The y coordinate for the first part of joint anchoring	l_anchor2_y	The local y coordinate where joint 2 is anchored to the second instance
w_anchor2_x	The x coordinate where the second part of the joint is anchored	ratio	Sets the velocity ratio between two instances
w_anchor2_y	The y coordinate where the second part of the joint is anchored	collide	Set to "true" if the two instances can collide with each other

As mentioned before, the pulley joint is anchored at two fixed points at the room coordinates set with *w_anchor1* and *w_anchor2*. These are in essence the pulleys over which the virtual rope passes. The joint connects to the sprite origin in each instance (i.e., the center of mass). However, you can override this arrangement by using the parameters *l_anchor1_x/y* and *l_anchor2_x/y*.

The ratio parameter in a pulley joint determines the relative movement between the two connected objects. A ratio of 1.0 will make the two instances move equal distances in their respective directions. A ratio set under 1.0 moves instance1 less than instance2 and a ratio set above 1.0 does the reverse.

Changing Mass and Inertia During the Gameloop

An excellent function by the name of *physics_mass_properties* is available to provide fine-tuning to your physics objects' mass, center of mass, and rotational inertia, should the need for this arise. The function takes four arguments:

```
physics_mass_properties(mass, local_center_x, local_center_y, inertia)
```

The first parameter redefines the mass of an object in Box2D's simulated kilograms. As previously mentioned, mass is automatically calculated in GameMaker based on an object's surface area and density. This typically works best. However, if you insist on taking a walk on the wild side, feel free to reconfigure this parameter.

Next in the function, we have two parameters for horizontal and vertical centers of mass, both of which take a number of pixels as input (e.g., settings of −8 and 0 would shift the center of mass to the left of the origin point by 8 pixels). Shifting the center of mass affects the instances' balance and rotation and can result in some dramatic instability.

Finally, we have the inertia value, which defines how resistant an instance is to changes to its rotational velocity; the higher this value, the higher its resistance.[8]

We can fool around selectively with these settings, too, and not change every parameter simultaneously. Let's say we want to set centers of mass ten pixels left and up and leave the other two parameters intact. This is how we would do it:

```
physics_mass_properties(phy_mass, -10, -10, phy_inertia);
```

And if we were to adjust mass and inertia and leave the centers of mass alone, we would do something like this:

```
physics_mass_properties(67, phy_com_x, phy_com_y, 400);
```

Adjusting Physics Precision

You can adjust the speed of the physics simulation using a handy function called *physics_world_update_speed(value)*. This function is mentioned for your reference. By default, this is set to the game speed (which is usually set at 60). You may wish to increase the update speed to potentially gain additional precision for the physics; this may or may not cause performance issues in busier rooms.

Good Practices in Physics-Based Projects

On occasion, you may experience strange behavior from your objects. When working in GameMaker physics, you should keep an eye on a number of factors at all times.

- Choose the simplest type of collision mask possible for your objects. Keep them as basic as you can; sometimes a box shape can work well enough even with a sprite with minor protrusions.

---

[8] The inertia value cannot be a negative number.

- Update your collision shapes inside the IDE as needed. They will not get automatically refreshed after you retouch your sprites. Use zoom to your advantage in the collision shape editor.

- A sprite's origin points matter especially when working with physics-based joints. Experiment with readjusting them in the sprite editor. Often the center spot of a sprite works best.

- Apply impulses only when necessary as they can be quite computationally costly for continuously running actions. Only use impulses for things like jumping characters and recoil.

- Objects made to move with GML properties like *phy_speed_x* make collisions with other types of physics objects highly unpredictable. You may see the error message "WARNING: Too many manifolds in collision" under these conditions, which means the physics system is getting overwhelmed. It's best to avoid this scenario whenever you can.

- Don't forget to leverage the function *physics_draw_debug* in your objects' Draw events to get a clear picture of your physics-based collision masks.

On Collision Categories and Parenting in Physics

While flexible, the GameMaker implementation of Box2D can have issues with resource management in larger projects. The system imposes a strict limit of 32 collision categories per room. Each unique object that can collide in the physics simulation consumes one of these collision categories. You may eventually come across the dreaded error message stating "Unable to assign a collision category for object" once all of these resources are exhausted.

It is always a good idea to group similar physics objects under a single parent and check for collisions with the parent instead of individual objects. For example, instead of managing ten different obstacle objects separately, assign them all to a single parent object and check for collisions with the parent. This reduces the number of required collision categories and can also make things run a lot smoother.

Collision Groups vs. Collision Categories

We briefly touched on *collision groups* at the beginning of this chapter. They are not to be confused with collision categories discussed in the previous section. As a refresher, collision groups are a user-defined mechanism to control physics-based collisions between specific groups of objects. We can assign objects into three main categories by simply labeling an object with a specific type of number.

- Objects set with positive group numbers always collide with objects assigned with the same number (e.g., group 2 objects only collide with other group 2 objects).

- Objects in the same negative collision group never collide with objects sharing the negative number, even if a Collision event is defined inside them. For example, let's say we have two objects belonging to group −5. They will ignore each other completely, allowing them to fully overlap.

- Objects in group zero (0) only collide with other objects if they have an explicitly defined Collision event inside them. This way you can control collisions through event logic rather than forcing them to happen either always or never.

Collision groups can be assigned both inside the GameMaker IDE as well as during the gameloop. For quick and easy assignments, we can simply navigate to the physics section of the object inspector and enter our collision group there.

For setting collision groups during the gameloop, there is a method called *physics_fixture_set_collision_group*. We can apply it to any physics objects dynamically created with GML. This shall be demonstrated in the next section.

The valid values for collision groups range from −32,768 to 32,767. It's best to stay in single digits with them if you can. Collision groups may cause a performance hit in your games if used too lavishly.

CHAPTER 7   PHYSICS IN GAMEMAKER

Ad Hoc Physics Objects

Being a topic already touched upon with all the joint structures, we can create new physics-based objects right inside the gameloop. This is perfectly feasible for more simple shapes, too. The project called *Ad Hoc Physics Objects* shows how we can create (joint-free) rectangular and a circular objects all with pure GML without creating any collision shapes in the IDE. The only prerequisite is having suitably shaped sprites available in the asset browser. *Ad Hoc Physics Objects* lets you plot circular, static objects with your mouse while rectangular objects keep spawning and falling down from the top of the screen. Pressing right mouse button on an object removes it (see Figure 7-10).

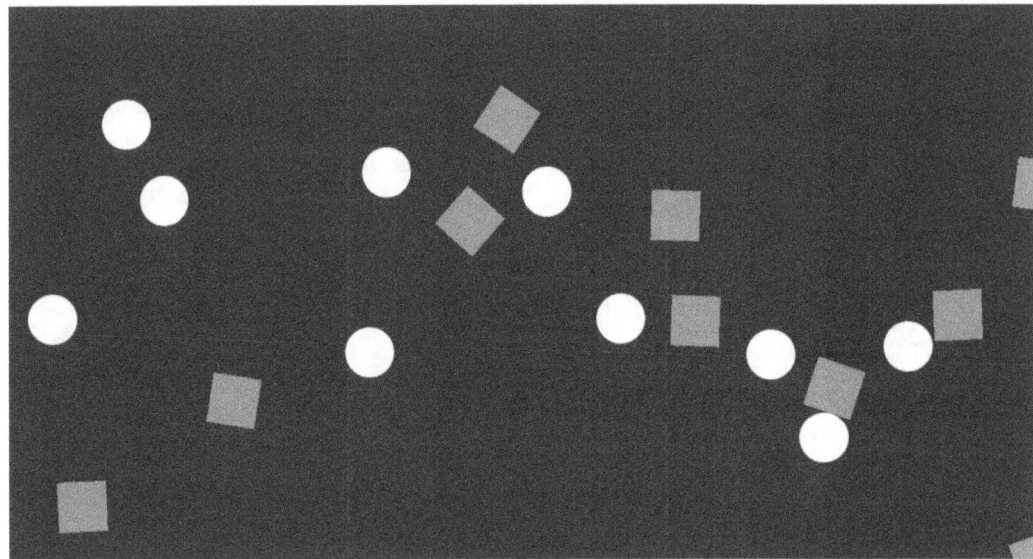

Figure 7-10. *A screenshot of Ad Hoc Physics Objects. The white spheres represent immobile objects*

Let's assume we have a 64×64 pixel square sprite and a similarly sized circle. First, we create a physics-based box in the Create event of *obj_AdHoc1* (not even the checkbox called *Uses Physics* needs to be ticked for it).

```
// CREATE
sprite_index = Sprite1; // Assign a sprite for this object
var happy_Box = physics_fixture_create();
physics_fixture_set_box_shape(happy_Box, sprite_width*0.5, sprite_height*0.5);
```

272

```
physics_fixture_set_collision_group(happy_Box, 1);
physics_fixture_set_density(happy_Box, 1.0); // Density
physics_fixture_set_restitution(happy_Box, 0.3); // Bounciness
physics_fixture_set_friction(happy_Box, 0.2); // Friction
physics_fixture_bind(happy_Box, self);
physics_fixture_delete(happy_Box);
```

And here's obj_AdHoc2, the immobile ball:

```
// CREATE
sprite_index = Sprite2; // Assign a sprite for this object
var happy_Ball = physics_fixture_create();
physics_fixture_set_circle_shape(happy_Ball, sprite_width*0.5);
physics_fixture_set_collision_group(happy_Ball, 1);
physics_fixture_set_density(happy_Ball, 0.0); // Set density
physics_fixture_set_restitution(happy_Ball, 0.2); // Bounciness
physics_fixture_bind(happy_Ball, self);
physics_fixture_delete(happy_Ball);
```

New instances of obj_AdHoc1 and obj_AdHoc2 will be spawned in the Alarm event inside obj_Controller every second and a half (i.e., 90 steps). The controller object also contains the important statement *physics_world_create(0.1)* in its Create event. Unless you use the checkbox labeled *Enable Physics* in the GameMaker IDE to turn a room into a physics world, the aforementioned function is needed for the ad hoc approach to work. The function takes one parameter, as in the *pixel-to-meter ratio*. This value determines how many pixels correspond to one meter in the physics world. A value of 0.1 means 1 meter equals 10 pixels in the simulation.

Without using the function *physics_fixture_set_collision_group*, a physics object will default to belonging to collision group zero, meaning it will only collide if it has Collision events. In addition, any potential IDE-based definitions of a collision shape will be overridden in the above implementations. Also notice the useful property called *sprite_width* which, when halved, works a treat for these purposes as long as the sprite's origin point is centered.

Fixture Manipulation

There are a fairly large number of parameters for us to adjust when it comes to dynamically created physics objects/fixtures. Table 7-13 details these properties, some of which were used in the previous project.

Table 7-13. *GameMaker fixture properties*

`physics_fixture_set_density(fix, value)`	Sets the density of an object. Values between 0.1 and 10.0 work best. Set to zero for immovable objects.
`physics_fixture_set_friction(fix, value)`	Sets the friction of an object. Values between 0.1 and 1.0 work best.
`physics_fixture_set_linear_damping(fix, value)`	Sets the linear damping of an object. Values between 0.1 and 5.0 work best. Set to zero for space-related escapades.
`physics_fixture_set_angular_damping(fix, value)`	Sets the angular damping of an object. Values between 0.1 and 5.0 work best.
`physics_fixture_set_restitution(fix, value)`	Sets the restitution of an object. Values between 0.2 and 0.5 work best. Going over 1.0 may cause bizarre actor behavior.
`physics_fixture_set_sensor(fix, true/false)`	Changes the object into a sensor, i.e., an object that experiences no physics effects in the simulation.
`physics_fixture_set_kinematic(fix, true/false)`	Makes the object kinematic, i.e., controllable by variables (e.g., phy_position_x and phy_position_y, etc.) Often used for moving platforms.
`physics_fixture_set_awake(fix, true/false)`	Toggles an object's state between active (awake) and inactive.

If you've created a physics-based object using the IDE, a physics fixture is automatically created and bound to the object. You can still change the physics parameters of these types of objects in real time. This involves accessing or replacing the fixture, updating its properties, and rebinding it to the object.

Mixing Regular and Physics-Based Objects

Regular and physics-enabled objects can coexist peacefully in your rooms—with some limitations. Most importantly, they cannot be readily be made to collide with each other as basic Collision events do not work under these scenarios. Regular objects can still detect physics objects around them using functions like *place_meeting*, but physics objects won't react to regular objects unless you manually apply physics-based responses within them.

Naturally, functions like *physics_apply_impulse* will have no effect on nonphysics-based objects. Setting horizontal and vertical speeds for regular objects inside a physics-based room (i.e., *hspeed* and *vspeed*) will also not have any effect. We must use basic coordinate-based movements (i.e., the manipulation of *x* and *y*) for regular objects inside physics-based rooms.

As demonstrated in the section "Simple Ad Hoc Physics Objects," we can turn plain objects Newtonian quite effortlessly.

Elements of a user interface are usually best kept strictly in the non-Newtonian realm, unless you specifically want them to react to the physics simulation. Invisible controller objects are best kept outside of it at all times.

In Closing

In this chapter, we discussed the basics of the GameMaker physics system, including the following topics:

The main physics settings for objects (e.g., density, restitution, and collision groups) and other related properties (e.g., phy_speed and phy_mass):

- Collision shapes (i.e., box, circle, and convex)
- Ragdolls using revolute joints (i.e., physics_joint_revolute_create)
- All varieties of GameMaker physics joints
- Soft-body particles with LiquidFun, including particle groups

The chapter to come will deal with topics such as real-time audio effects, sequences, and game controllers.

CHAPTER 8

Sequences, Audio Effects, and Gamepads

This chapter has three electrifying topics: sequences, real-time audio effects, and gamepad control. All of these elements can add value to your games considerably when implemented correctly. As was the case with previous chapters, we shall have some helpful demonstrations for all of the aforementioned topics as well.

Although sequences may seem daunting at first, once you master their basics they become a flexible and possibly an invaluable tool for adding pizzazz into your games. As always, you are encouraged to experiment with the provided GameMaker projects related to this chapter.

A Primer on Sequences

Most types of games benefit from having cutscenes. If these are prerendered video files, they are fairly easily implemented. However, if a cutscene takes places inside a game world using a game's assets, things may become cumbersome. Thankfully, instead of issuing several manually defined instances to manipulate other assets, a single *sequence* is often all you need. Sequences are a great way to create moments of solid presentation in GameMaker, in a way reminiscent of web technology popular in the early 2000s.[1]

Cutscenes aside, sequences can be used to create impressive menus and room transitions.

---

[1] For those in the know, sequences are basically a kind of *Adobe Flash* inside GameMaker.

CHAPTER 8　SEQUENCES, AUDIO EFFECTS, AND GAMEPADS

Let's now go through some basic concepts of GameMaker's sequences. Firstly, there is the *canvas* which is simply the area on the screen where we drag our assets onto and position them as we please. Next we have *keyframes,* a concept referred to simply as *keys* inside the sequence editor. Animations in a sequence are interpolated between these keyframes. Let's say we have a sprite placed at 100 pixels from the right (i.e., x = 100). To move it around inside a sequence, we would position the playhead in the dopesheet/timeline to however many frames ahead we want to and reposition the sprite at its final resting place. Let's say this is 300 pixels from the right; we would drag the sprite to this position in the canvas at the aforementioned playhead position. Finally, we would click on the plus sign found in the keyframe controls for this final position. This would create the movements for the sprite between the initial position/first keyframe and the last keyframe in the timeline (x=101, 102, 103 etc.); this is what interpolation means in this context.

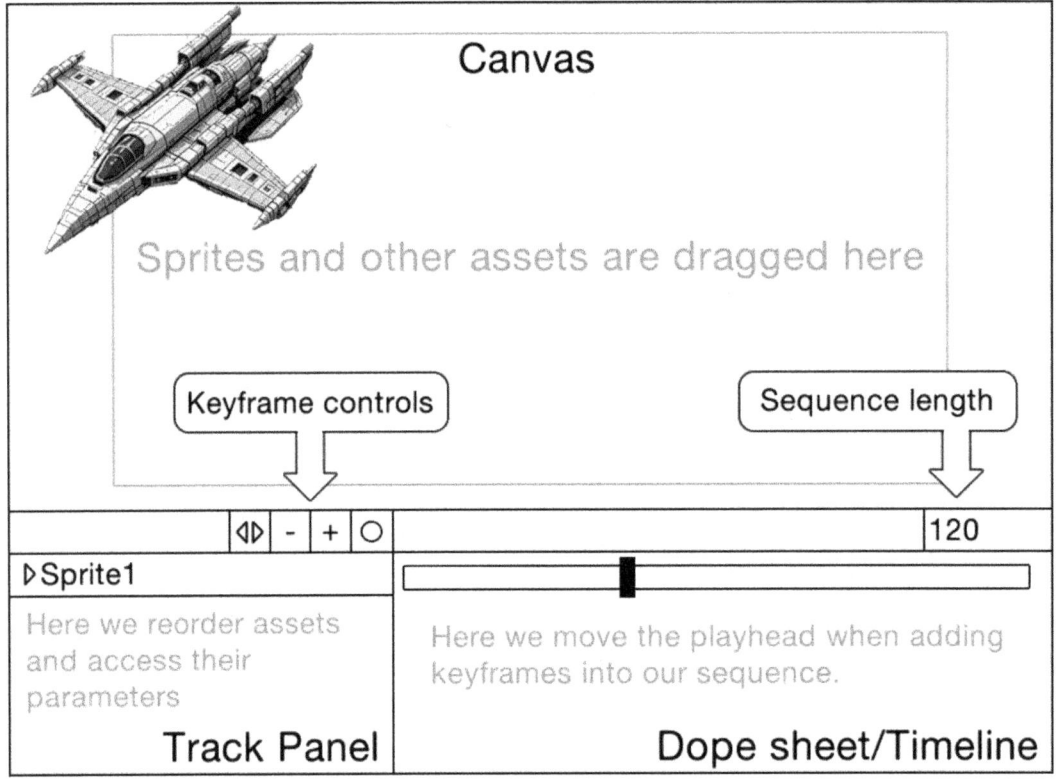

Figure 8-1. *A simplified view of the GameMaker sequence editor*

As evident from Figure 8-1, the keyframe controls are found above the track panel. The most heavily used buttons in your sequences will probably be the middle two with which you can respectively delete or add keyframes. The button with a circle (titled *automatically record changes*) toggles a workflow where any alterations on asset parameters (e.g., position, scale, or rotation) automatically result in a new keyframe. We get to change the length of our sequences at any point by entering it into the appropriately titled box *Sequence length* next to the playback controls.

Every asset dragged onto the canvas creates a new "track" in the sequence editor *track panel* found on the left side of the screen. This is used both for arranging asset depths and setting keyframes for specific asset properties. The variables to be adjusted in the track panel depend on which type of asset is in question. A simple sprite may only offer *position* while a string of text may have properties like *shadow offset* and *softness*.

To access specific asset variables in the track panel, we simply need to click on the little arrow icon in front of an asset's name.

We can animate assets with any of the parameters found in the track panel. Tracks can be grouped for better organization of your assets. A lock feature is there, too, to offer editing safety and comfort; this becomes an increasingly important feature the more complicated your sequences become.

Making a Very Simple Sequence

Making your first sequence in GameMaker is rather effortless. Just right-click on the asset browser on the right of the IDE and select Create ➤ Sequence. The main sequence view will now open. Drag any sprite from the asset browser onto the canvas (or create one if you have none available). This will set the starting position for your graphics asset in the sequence; it can be changed later. There will now be a set of keyframes underneath the canvas. By default, GameMaker assigns your sequence a modest 60 of them.

A setting called *automatically record changes* should be on by default, denoted by a little white ball. Move the playhead of the sequence to the very last frame, i.e., frame number 60. Now drag the sprite asset on to some other location on the canvas. With the aforementioned setting active, all of the animation will be created automatically for you and the sprite should graciously move between its starting and ending positions. You can preview the animation by clicking the triangular play icon beneath the canvas. See Figure 8-2 for a view from a simple sequence.

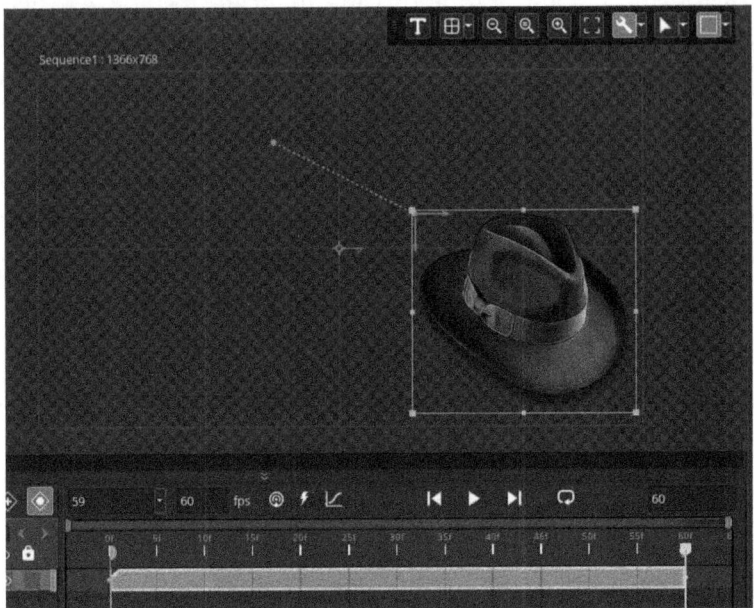

Figure 8-2. *A close-up of the last frame (i.e., frame 60 out of 60) in a simple GameMaker sequence featuring a moving fedora. Notice how the editor previews the motion path*

Broadcast Messages

A fetching icon vaguely reminiscent of an @ character sits above the sequence timeline. This is used to add a *broadcast message* into the proceedings. Any game actor/instance with an event called *Broadcast Message* (found in the event category of *Other*) can pick up such a message from a sequence. The aforementioned event can then be filled with whatever type of tasks we desire. Basically, a broadcast message is a type of signal to influence (potentially multiple) instances.

CHAPTER 8   SEQUENCES, AUDIO EFFECTS, AND GAMEPADS

Simple Sequences: A Demonstration with Penguins

Let us now take a gander at the first demonstration project for this chapter. *Simple Sequences* features the following techniques:

- Sequences with sprite movements and text tracks
- Sequence-based fade in/fade out room transitions
- Broadcast messages
- Basic sequence manipulation using GML
- Persistent objects

The project has the following three sequences: *Fade_transition, Grande_finale,* and *Penguin_sequence.* It also has the following three objects: *obj_Button, obj_Controller,* and *obj_FadeInOut.* The presentation is divided between two rooms (*Room1* and *Room2*). See Figure 8-3 for a screenshot of the project.

Figure 8-3. *A screenshot of Simple Sequences*

All of the sequences are 120 frames in length. The first one, Penguin_sequence, contains five assets: two tracks of text with SDF enabled (a feature discussed in previous chapters), two sprites, and a single object. This sequence provides a scrolling

CHAPTER 8   SEQUENCES, AUDIO EFFECTS, AND GAMEPADS

background graphic, a penguin sprite, and a few welcoming words. At frame 120 (i.e., the last frame of the sequence), a message is broadcast. This message is caught by obj_Controller in its dedicated event called Broadcast Message. Once said message is received, obj_Controller plays a little fanfare and sets a flag related to displaying some information to "true" (see Figure 8-4).

Text is added into a sequence by first clicking the T-shaped icon displayed inside the sequence editor labeled *Add a Text Track* and then clicking on the canvas.

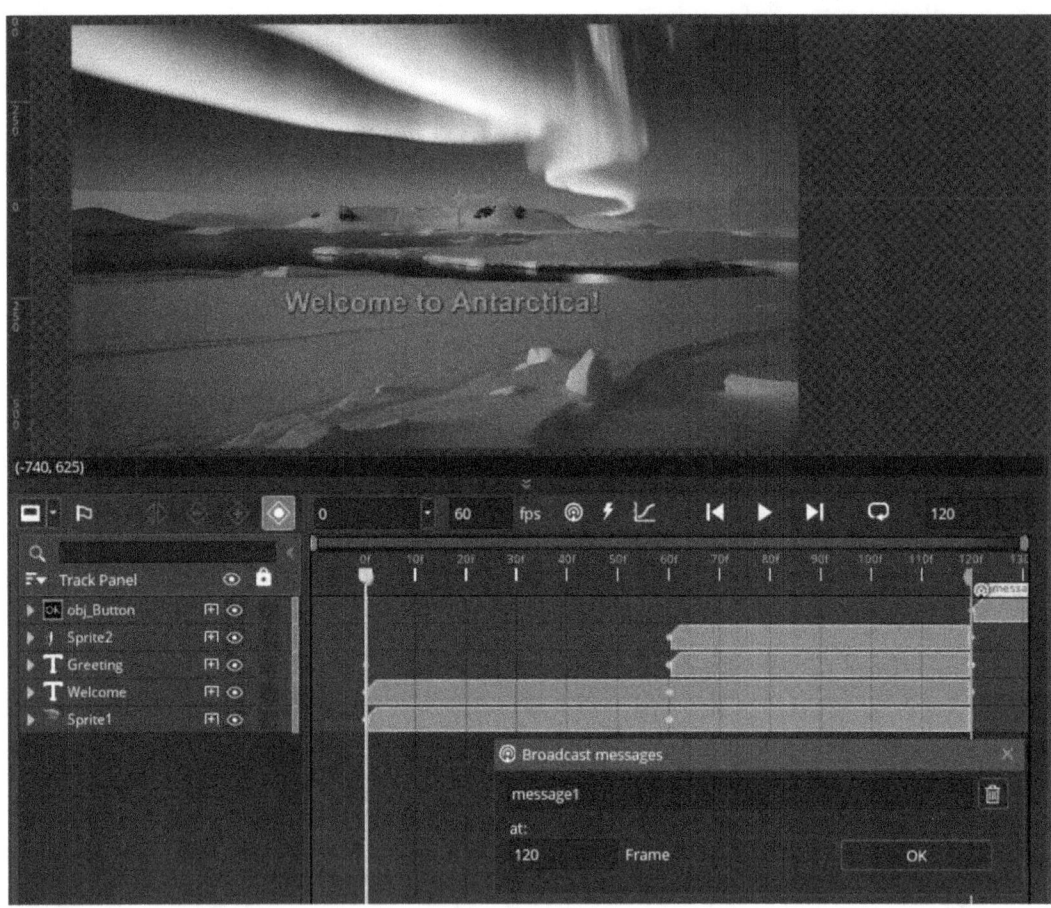

Figure 8-4. *The editor view for Penguin_sequence in the first room of Simple Sequences. The playhead rests on the first frame. Also visible is the window for the broadcast message (i.e., message1) inserted into the last frame of the sequence*

The second room consists of two more penguins making an appearance along with a text proclaiming "That's all folks." This text asset is animated using rotation and scaling accessed in the track panel.

The project at hand has some simple room transitions as well. Namely, it features a fade in/out for both of its rooms inside a sequence called *Fade_transition*. This is implemented by having a plain all-black sprite (spr_Fade) stretched to cover the entirety of the canvas and manipulating its alpha/opacity value. A related object, namely, *obj_FadeInOut*, leverages some GML to carry out the transitions.

Let us now take a look inside *obj_FadeInOut* to see how GML can be used with sequences. The following code represents the entirety of the aforementioned object and its two events:

```
// CREATE
sequence = layer_sequence_create("Instances", 0, 0, Fade_transition);
// Halve layer playback speed
layer_sequence_speedscale(sequence, 0.5);
// STEP
if layer_sequence_get_headpos(sequence) == 60 {
    layer_sequence_pause(sequence);
}
if layer_sequence_is_finished(sequence) {
    layer_sequence_destroy(sequence);
    if room!=Room2 room_goto_next(); else game_end();
}
```

The above two events contain several important functions for sequence manipulation in GML. First, we have *layer_sequence_create* which summons a new instance of a sequence and creates a handle for it. We follow this up with *layer_sequence_speedscale*, a function for basically altering a sequence's playback speed.

We can easily fetch the position of a sequence's playhead (i.e., the current frame) with the function known as *layer_sequence_get_headpos*. To pause a sequence, we have *layer_sequence_pause*. Please note that you cannot unpause a sequence with this function; to resume playback, you need to execute *layer_sequence_play*. Finally, we have *layer_sequence_is_finished*, which returns true if a sequence has run its course, and *layer_sequence_destroy* which removes a sequence instance from memory.

CHAPTER 8   SEQUENCES, AUDIO EFFECTS, AND GAMEPADS

The object *obj_Button* is there to await user input when a sequence is stopped. This occurs twice in Simple Sequences and only by clicking on this icon do we get to resume the proceedings. This is what the aforementioned object's only event (left pressed) looks like:

```
layer_sequence_play(obj_FadeInOut.sequence);
instance_destroy();
```

Above, we simply start the playback of a sequence (aptly named just plain *sequence*) defined inside another object, obj_FadeInOut, when the left mouse button is pressed on obj_Button. Sequences need not have global handles as we can use dot notation to access them.

Let us now recap some of these most useful functions (see Table 8-1).

Table 8-1. *The seven most pertinent GML functions for manipulating sequences*

handle = layer_sequence_create(layer, x, y, sequence_name)	Creates a sequence on a layer at the specified x and y coordinates. Stores this reference into "handle."
layer_sequence_get_headpos(handle)	Returns the current frame/position of the sequence playhead.
layer_sequence_is_finished(handle)	Returns "true" if a sequence has played all the way through.
layer_sequence_pause(handle)	Pauses the playback of a sequence.
layer_sequence_play(handle)	Starts/resumes the playback of a sequence.
layer_sequence_speedscale(handle, scale)	Sets playback speed scale for a sequence. A setting of 0.5 halves the frame rate.
layer_sequence_destroy(handle)	Deletes a sequence instance from memory.

More on Persistent Objects

The object obj_Controller in the above project is flagged as "persistent" in the GameMaker IDE. This means any instances of it will survive a change of rooms. They will be active until they are explicitly destroyed.

Ticking the checkbox in the IDE aside, objects can be marked as persistent dynamically with GML simply by typing in *persistent = true* inside an event.

CHAPTER 8 SEQUENCES, AUDIO EFFECTS, AND GAMEPADS

We can also use a function to control object persistence: *object_set_persistent*. It takes two parameters, namely, object index and a Boolean, as follows:

```
object_set_persistent(obj_Goober, true);
```

This function will make any instances spawned from the affected object persistent. If the destination room lacks a layer with the same name or depth as the one assigned to such an instance, a new layer will be created to accommodate this instance across room transitions. This new layer will have the same name as the original layer.

Menu Moments: A Demonstration

Let us next explore a simple menu system implemented using a sequence which leverages a technique called *moments*. Menu Moments presents us an animated menu of four buttons, a game logo (with complementary copyright information), and a spinning AI-generated image of a leaping goober. See Figure 8-5 for the sequence editor view of this demonstration.

Figure 8-5. *The sequence editor view of the last frame of Menu Moments*

CHAPTER 8   SEQUENCES, AUDIO EFFECTS, AND GAMEPADS

A *moment* in GameMaker parlance refers to a specific frame in a sequence's timeline which is made to execute a custom function. Moments are added by clicking on the icon of a lightning bolt in the sequence editor. Once you do this, a window opens in the IDE, and you are to enter a name for your function. If one with the entered name does not exist, you can click on the plus icon in this window to create it. Once this is done, you are taken to a script file which is to contain the GML associated with the function and others like it.

Moments cannot take parameters. They are intended to work as fairly simple functions that can still leverage the flexibility of GML on a keyframe basis in sequences.

Now, the main (and only) sequence in the demonstration, *Curious_Sequence,* is added in the room creation code as follows:

```
var happy_sequence = layer_sequence_create("Assets_1", 0, 0, Curious_Sequence);
layer_sequence_speedscale(happy_sequence, 0.5);
```

Menu Moments has only one type of object, namely, *obj_Button,* which represents a basic user interface element for us to click on. Each instance of this object is to have a variable called *message* inside. The default value for this variable is set to "Nothing."

The project has a total of six moments, five of which are dedicated to playing sound effects. The project has three different functions for these moments, all of which are stored in the same script file inside the project. The first of these moments, called *AssignButtonMessages,* is the most complex of the three and it looks like this:

```
function AssignButtonMessages() {
    // Create an empty array and a variable (i) for iteration
    var buttons = []; var i = 0;
    // Store all instance IDs of obj_Button into the array
    with(obj_Button) {
        buttons[i] = id; i++;
    }
    array_sort(buttons, function(a, b) { return a.y - b.y; });
    if array_length(buttons) >= 3 {
        buttons[0].message = "Start Game";
        buttons[1].message = "Options";
```

```
        buttons[2].message = "Restart";
        buttons[3].message = "Exit";
    }
}
```

The above moment, triggered in the first frame of the project's sequence, issues four instances of obj_Button some labels. We do this by iterating through the active instance IDs of these object instances and storing them into an array simply called *buttons;* this is once again executed using the most useful keyword called *with*. The labels presented here replace the default contents of variable *message* set in each instance.

Now, a sorting of the above array's values is done with the statement *function(a, b) { return a.y - b.y; }*. This is a so-called *inline function,* meaning one that is defined inside the "action." With it, we operate on two values, namely, the vertical position (i.e., y) of values a and b. This approach sorts buttons in ascending order by their y value. Without sorting, the statement *with (obj_Button)* might set our instances in an unpredictable order; we want to have the message labels in the same order as we issue them in function AssignButtonMessages.

Real-Time Audio Effects

So far in the book, we have covered both basic audio functions and positional audio in GameMaker. It is time we explore the even more advanced possibilities the software has to offer. It's time to learn about real-time audio effects.

For us to harness the flexibility and power of dynamic audio effects, we need to have an *audio bus*. This is an element used to group and control multiple audio emitters together. It basically acts like a mixer, letting you apply effects or adjust volume or panning for all sounds passing through it.

Real-time audio effects use *audio emitters*, a topic we previously discussed in the context of positional audio. With dynamic audio, we need to have an emitter, too, which is then routed into an aforementioned audio bus.

An **audio bus** is a way to organize your game audio assets. For example, you could have different buses for music, sound effects, and background ambience. GameMaker has one audio bus by default, referred to as the *main audio bus*.

CHAPTER 8   SEQUENCES, AUDIO EFFECTS, AND GAMEPADS

Now, you can connect an audio emitter to an audio bus using the function *audio_emitter_bus()*. Any sound played by that emitter goes through the assigned bus. You can connect multiple emitters to the same bus to process their sounds together with specific types of effects.

The function known as *audio_bus_create()* creates a new audio bus, like this:

```
// CREATE
regular_bus = audio_bus_create(); soundfx_bus = audio_bus_create();
```

We could then add the following statements to a listing to play two different types of audio through the buses we just created:

```
regular_emitter = audio_emitter_create();
soundfx_emitter = audio_emitter_create();
// Route regular emitter to regular bus
audio_emitter_bus(regular_emitter, regular_bus);
// Route soundfx emitter to soundfx bus
audio_emitter_bus(soundfx_emitter, soundfx_bus);
// Add reverb-effect to sound fx bus
soundfx_bus.effects[0] = audio_effect_create(AudioEffectType.Reverb1, { size: 0.9, mix: 0.6 });
// Start playing looped uneffected audio on regular_emitter
audio_play_sound_on(regular_emitter, Sound1, true, 1);
alarm[0]=160;
// ALARM 0
// Play the same audio file through the effect-bus
audio_play_sound_on(soundfx_emitter, Sound1, false, 1);
alarm[0]=160;
// CLEANUP
audio_emitter_free(regular_emitter); audio_emitter_free(soundfx_emitter);
```

Even if you create a custom bus with audio_bus_create(), its audio output is still routed into the GameMaker's main audio bus, which is the final/master channel for all sounds in a game.

CHAPTER 8   SEQUENCES, AUDIO EFFECTS, AND GAMEPADS

The previous listing is actually a part of a demonstration called *Audio Effects,* more accurately it is found on its second room (i.e., Room2). Let us look at this project and its primary demonstration in detail next.

Audio Effects: A Presentation

A project file by the simple name of *Audio Effects* demonstrates seven real-time audio treatments found inside GameMaker's formidable sonic arsenal. They are as follows:

- **Reverb:** A smooth echo effect great for creating many types of ambience. Think caverns, auditoriums, or cramped water closets.

- **Delay:** Provides gradually disappearing distinct echoes. On shorter time settings (e.g., <40 ms) can be used as a "thickener" of sound.

- **Low-pass filter:** Dampens frequencies above a set point. Makes sounds more muffled/masked.

- **Bitcrusher:** Reduces the fidelity of sounds. Used for creating things like faulty phone reception or damaged robots.

- **High-pass filter:** Dampens frequencies below a set point. Used to remove bass and for simulations of tinny speakers.

- **Tremolo:** Injects sounds with rapid alterations of volume for a "choppy" effect.

- **Peak EQ:** An equalizer for boosting or cutting a specific part of the frequency spectrum.

The demonstration allows you to switch any of the above effects on and off to hear them in action. This is done with the keys 1 through 7 on your keyboard. Pressing the space bar will toggle between the two different demonstrations in the project, set up in *Room1* and *Room2*, respectively. See Figure 8-6 for a screenshot of Room1.

CHAPTER 8 SEQUENCES, AUDIO EFFECTS, AND GAMEPADS

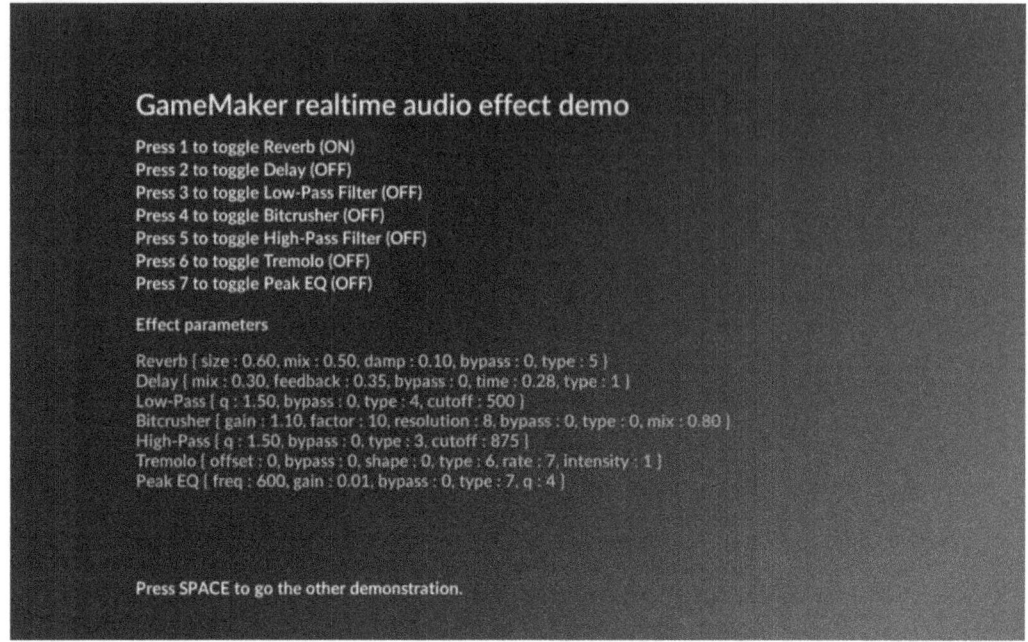

Figure 8-6. The first room in audio effects, a demonstration

The first demonstration in Room1 displays the various parameters issued to the effects. You'll notice their sets of parameters vary considerably. Let us next go through these parameters in detail. Each audio effect has its parameters stored in a struct (e.g., AudioEffectType.Reverb1), a data structure discussed previously in the book.

AudioEffectType.Reverb1

- **Bypass:** If set to "true," the effect is switched off.

- **Size:** The size of the space. Set between 0.0 and 1.0. Overtly large reverb sizes can introduce quite a bit of sonic clutter and are best avoided.

- **Damp:** The intensity of high-frequency dampening. Set between 0.0 and 1.0. Lower damping values typically result in brighter and longer reverbs, making the virtual space sound less occupied.

- **Mix:** The proportion of the original/reverberated signal. Set between 0.0 and 1.0. A value of 0.0 gives 100% of the original signal; a value of 1.0 gives 100% of the reverberated signal.

AudioEffectType.Delay

- **Bypass:** If set to "true," the effect is switched off.
- **Time:** The length of the delay in seconds.
- **Feedback:** The proportion of the delayed signal which is fed back into the delay line. Range: 0.0–1.0.
- **Mix:** The ratio of the original/delayed signal in the output. A value of 0.0 gives 100% of the original signal; a value of 1.0 gives 100% the delayed signal.

AudioEffectType.LPF2

The low-pass filter:

- **Bypass:** If set to "true," the effect is switched off.
- **Cutoff:** The cutoff frequency of the filter in hertz. Frequencies above the cutoff will be reduced.
- **Q:** The quality/bandwidth factor, set between 0.0 and 100.0. Indicates how peaked in gain the frequency is around the cutoff. The greater the value, the greater the peak.

AudioEffectType.HPF2

The high-pass filter:

- **Bypass:** If set to "true," the effect is switched off.

- **Cutoff:** The cutoff frequency of the filter in hertz. Frequencies below the cutoff will be reduced.

- **Q:** The quality/bandwidth factor, set between 0.0 and 100.0. Indicates how peaked in gain the frequency is around the cutoff. The greater the value, the greater the peak.

AudioEffectType.Bitcrusher

Creates a "lo-fi" sound reminiscent of old or failing electronic devices. It works by reducing the bit depth and/or sample rate of the audio.

- **Bypass:** If set to "true," the effect is switched off.

- **Gain:** The input gain going into the effect. Hard distortion begins at a value of 1.0

- **Factor:** The factor by which the original signal is downsampled. Range: 0.0–100.0.

- **Resolution:** The bit depth at which the signal is resampled. Range: 1.0 to 16.0.

- **Mix:** The proportion of the original/distorted signal in the output. Range: 0.0–1.0.

AudioEffectType.Tremolo

Alters up the audio level periodically for a "choppy" sound. Uses a *low-frequency oscillator (LFO)* element for this, which come in different waveforms (or "shapes") including sine, square, and triangle.

- **Bypass:** If set to "true," the effect is switched off.

- **Rate:** The frequency/speed of the LFO modulating the gain, set between 0.0 and 20.0 Hz.

- **Intensity:** Sets the intensity of the volume drop. Set between 0.0 and 1.0.

CHAPTER 8 SEQUENCES, AUDIO EFFECTS, AND GAMEPADS

- **Offset:** The proportion of a waveform's period that the right-hand channel's LFO should be offset by when comparing to the left-hand channel. Ranges between 0.0 and 1.0.

- **Shape:** The waveform shape that the LFO should output.

AudioEffectType.PeakEQ

A frequency equalizer:

- **Bypass:** If set to "true," the effect is switched off.

- **Freq:** The central frequency set between 20 and 20000.

- **Q:** The quality/bandwidth factor. The greater the q, the narrower the range of frequencies to be boosted/cut around the central frequency. Range: 1.0 to 100.0.

- **Gain:** The amount of gain at the central frequency. Range: 0.0 to infinity. Values below 1.0 (e.g., 0.5 or 0.1) represent negative gain, i.e., cutting.

Mixing Digital Audio

Red Book Audio, dating back to the mighty compact disc from 1982, is still the gold standard for digital audio. This format uses a 44.1 kHz (i.e., kilohertz) sampling rate and 16-bit resolution. It covers the human hearing range and has a decent signal-to-noise ratio. A sampling rate refers to the number a sound is sampled per second. In the case of Red Book, it is a solid 44100. Resolution in this context refers to dynamic range: 16-bit audio offers 65536 possible amplitude levels for audio signals. This is plenty for most purposes, including video games. Simulated lower resolution audio (e.g., 8-bits or even less) is sometimes still used for a more retro vibe and for special effects.

Basic Red Book 16-bit audio has 96 decibels (dB) of dynamic range. This is visualized in a typical digital audio workstation's level meter as a bar going from −96 dB (the quietest level) up to 0 dB, above which digital distortion begins to appear.

The human hearing range is between 20 Hz and 20000 Hz (i.e., 20 kHz). This is typically also the range where all our digital audio is delivered in. Our ears are most sensitive between 1000 and 4000 Hz at the so-called mid-frequencies where human speech is produced. The sensitivity to higher frequencies, i.e., above 16 kHz, decreases with age. Many (even young) adults don't perceive frequencies above 16 kHz at all. Low frequencies below 40 Hz are often felt more than heard, provided a speaker setup is even capable of reproducing them.

A well-balanced audio file has no major peaks anywhere along the frequency spectrum for its intended purpose and it does not exhibit digital distortion. Audio mixing is basically a surgical process where unnecessary frequencies are removed and what constitutes unnecessary depends on the context. Explosions tend to have lots of low-frequency rumble below 150 Hz, but this would not work well for human speech. Conversely, a primarily high-frequency sound like a computer beep does not generally need any information below 150 Hz. Unnecessary frequencies left in an audio file may muddy the proceedings later on when several instances of them are played back simultaneously. Boosting frequencies is rarely necessary. It's usually better to cut the frequencies we don't need to emphasize those that we do.

Before importing audio into GameMaker, make sure your source material is at least adequately mixed with no major peaks or valleys at any point of the frequency spectrum. Again, digital distortion should be avoided at all costs and it is unfixable. This phenomenon occurs when the audio signal exceeds the maximum amplitude of digital audio (i.e., 0 decibels).

There are several excellent *digital audio workstations (DAWs)* available for free, such as *Oceanaudio* and *Audacity*. Make sure to experiment mixing your game audio on them. An equalizer (EQ) should always be your primary tool. Please note that every act of manipulation in any DAW tends to degrade the fidelity of a sound file very slightly. Applying EQ (or any other effect) dozens of times on a single file may result in rather unnatural audio, especially when it comes to speech. Also make sure you never "drown" your audio in effects such as reverb. At least in the case of more ambitious projects, it's best to keep your game audio as dry as you can in the mixing stage and instead apply ambience in real time using GML.

When mixing your audio inside a digital audio workstation, make sure you use uncompressed audio formats at that stage, such as WAV or AIFF. Let GameMaker handle the conversion to MP3 or OGG.

We are also not limited to the built-in effects each DAW offers us. Many so-called plugin effects are available, too, often for free.[2] It's worth keeping in mind all effects, including EQs, have a "flavor" to them. Some work better for specific types of material than others.

On Digital Dynamics and Compressors

There is one often overlooked but extremely important sound-related topic left: video game audio dynamics. For a game to be enjoyable, the volume of its audio assets needs to be finely balanced. This should take place both on the level of individual audio elements as well as the entire runtime mix, whenever possible. These can be hefty tasks, but luckily there is a class of tools that automate some of these processes.

Compression[3] is one effect the modern consumer really can't avoid experiencing daily; it's applied in pretty much all of our digital audio. A *compressor* is used to control the dynamics of audio. They come in hardware and software-based varieties. Thankfully, one is included with GameMaker, too, and it can be summoned in real time. A compressor is there to even out the volume levels in any type of audio; it reduces sudden peaks and makes the overtly quiet parts louder. It can also be used in more creative applications for specific effects, especially in the realm of music production.

The two most important parameters for any type of compressor are *threshold* and *ratio*. The former represents the volume level at which the compressor kicks into action. The latter decides how much volume is reduced when a signal reaches the aforementioned threshold. A ratio of, say, 4:1 is a moderately powerful form of compression in which every four decibels (dB) of input signal that exceeds the threshold results in a one (1) dB increase of the output signal. This reduces louder passages considerably. A ratio of 1:1 would mean no compression is to be applied at all. As for a ratio of ∞:1 this will effectively stop the signal going above the threshold altogether; a compressor with this setting is actually referred to as a *limiter*. This type of dynamics control is used to boost audio material to its absolute highest volume without causing digital distortion (see Figure 8-7).

---

[2] *Analog Obsession, Voxengo,* and *TDR* offer several excellent free plug-in effects for all major digital audio workstations (to name just three manufacturers).

[3] Dynamics compression is not to be confused with audio file compression (e.g., the MP3 format) although both of these technologies are rather ubiquitous as of the 1990s.

CHAPTER 8   SEQUENCES, AUDIO EFFECTS, AND GAMEPADS

Audio signals are sometimes routed through historical hardware compressors at a 1:1 ratio just for the unique sound (or indeed the "flavor") a unit produces.

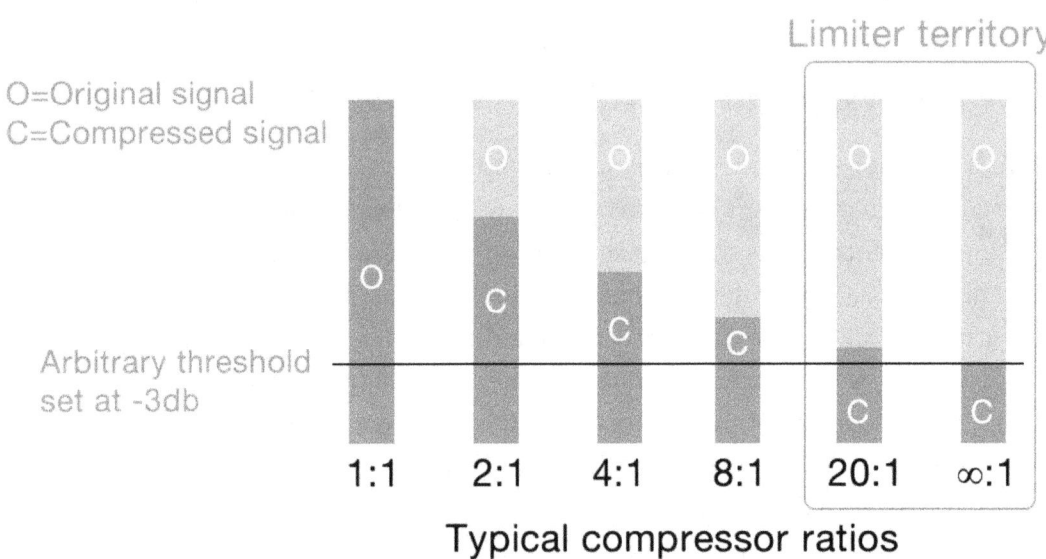

Figure 8-7. *A visualization of some popular ratios for audio compression*

Let us next discuss the parameters found in the struct representing GameMaker's take on compression.

AudioEffectType.Compressor

A tool for controlling dynamics:

- **Bypass:** If set to "true," the effect is switched off.

- **Ingain:** The volume gain applied to the input signal. Range: between 0 and infinity.

- **Threshold:** The amplitude level above which the compressor will activate. Range: between 0.001 and 1.

- **Ratio:** Determines how much gain reduction the compressor applies when the signal passes a threshold level. Range: between 1 and infinity.

- **Attack:** The responsiveness, in seconds, of the compressor when compressing audio going above the threshold. Range: 0.001 to 0.1.

- **Sustain:** The responsiveness (in seconds) of the compressor when stopping compressing audio below the threshold. Range: 0.01 to 1.

- **Outgain:** The gain amount applied to the output signal. This is used to compensate for the overall reduction of volume caused by the compression process. Range: 0 to infinity.

A compressor on an audio bus with the right settings may offer clarity and extra "punch" into your games' audio. Although not absolutely necessary, this effect is well worth experimenting with, especially in busier projects. If you choose to implement it, making compression a feature players can toggle on and off at will, too, may be a superior idea.

Even the finest of compressors can't fix digital distortion. Any digital audio exceeding 0 dB in volume is best rerecorded or discarded.

Dialing in a fast attack value (<10 ms) means a compressor will reduce volume more quickly after the signal exceeds the specified threshold. This is useful for preventing digital distortion both during recording or mixing as the signal will simply not have enough time to reach overtly high volumes. However, in some cases, a low attack will result in a sound being pushed back in the mix too aggressively effectively muting it. This often occurs with typically bass-heavy sounds, such as explosions. It all depends on the material at hand. A slow attack value (>10 ms) acts in a smooth way and is often a more "safe" choice for things like explosions and gunfire.

A compressor's release setting is a parameter for controlling how quickly the volume reduction returns to zero. At low compression ratios, fast release times (<100 ms) sound most natural. However, with higher compression ratios, fast release settings can give audio an excessively aggressive feel; compression with quick release times may lead to undesirable "pumping" effects. Slow release settings of up to a second or two work best for material which benefits from transparent volume control (e.g., background ambience and environmental sounds).

We shall now move away from topics related to digital audio to discuss another important matter: gamepads.

CHAPTER 8 SEQUENCES, AUDIO EFFECTS, AND GAMEPADS

Gamepads in GameMaker

We are not limited to keyboard and/or mouse controls for our games. A total of 12 gamepads can be configured for use with GameMaker. Microsoft Windows supports both older *DirectInput* and modern *Xinput* controllers used by Xbox consoles. In GameMaker, Xinput gamepads are assigned into slots between 0 and 3 while the rest (i.e., 4 to 11) are reserved for DirectInput devices. To an extent, gamepad compatibility in GameMaker also depends on how it is implemented by the hardware manufacturer; although a rare scenario, some controllers just might not work in this context.

Most computers running macOS do not support Xinput devices out of the box and need a third-party driver. Even then, support for such controllers may be fickle and require quite a bit of configuring. You may find older PlayStation 3 and Xbox 360 controllers are best supported on macOS (as DirectInput devices).

As for gamepad support on Linux (Ubuntu), GameMaker requires you to install additional libraries (i.e., *jstest-gtk* and *joystick*). GameMaker offers solid gamepad support for all of its supported consoles (i.e., PS4/PS5/Switch/Xbox). Gamepads are supported in HTML5 games in most major browsers; only Apple's Safari might have issues with them.

The Three Pillars of GameMaker Gamepads

The game controller support provided by GameMaker can be roughly split into three components. First, we need to define a data structure to store gamepad IDs into. A basic array is enough for this purpose. Then we leverage a special event called *Async System* to detect any connected devices. Finally, we summon specific GML functions to actually read controller/gamepad data. See Figure 8-8 for a rundown of this process.

CHAPTER 8   SEQUENCES, AUDIO EFFECTS, AND GAMEPADS

Gamepad Data Structure E.g. a global array which stores the status (found/not found) for all of the 12 gamepad-slots.	Create-event of obj_Controller
Async - System A special event inside any object where we detect gamepads.	obj_Controller
GML Functions Specific functions for reading gamepad-input e.g. gamepad_button_check_pressed etc.	Step-events of obj_Player1, obj_Player2 etc.

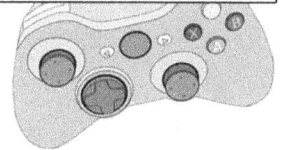

Figure 8-8. *The three main components for gamepads in GameMaker and their typically associated objects*

The aforementioned approach to gamepads will be fully leveraged in our next project.

Twin Stick Fun with Gamepads

We are next going to take a look at another demonstration. *Twin Stick Fun with Gamepads* is a simple starting point for two types of top-down twin stick games. It also shows us how to detect and use multiple gamepads in GameMaker (see Figure 8-9).

CHAPTER 8   SEQUENCES, AUDIO EFFECTS, AND GAMEPADS

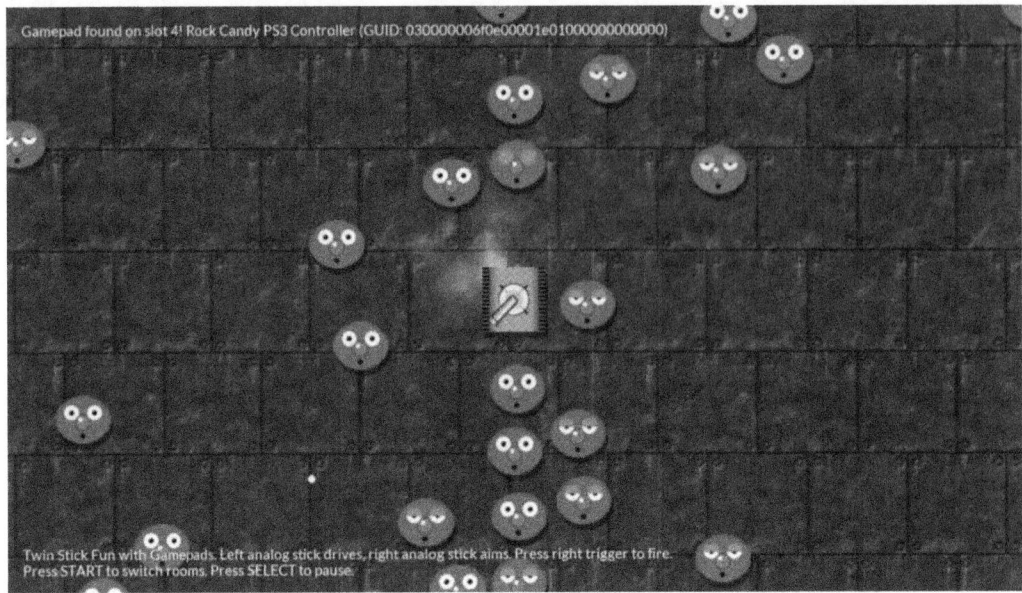

Figure 8-9. *A screenshot of the first room (i.e., Room1) in Twin Stick Fun with Gamepads*

The project demonstrates the following techniques:

- Scanning a system for gamepads using an asynchronous event
- Analog stick movement and aiming
- Pausing a game with the select button
- Controller rumble/vibration
- Retrieval of gamepad globally unique identifier (GUID) and description
- Using multiple gamepads (implemented in the second room, i.e., Room2)

Most modern gamepads have two analog sticks on top of them. In the first room of this prototype, the player drives a tank using the left analog stick in a gamepad and aims the turret with the other one. Pressing the right trigger button will send projectiles at the direction of the turret also introducing a dramatic rumble into your gamepad. Multiple green-faced hostiles spawn into the battlefield for your blasting pleasure.

Detecting Gamepads in Async System

In our project an object called *obj_Controller* features an important event known as *Async System*. This is one of GameMaker's so-called asynchronous events, which essentially run in the background simultaneously with the rest of your game. These events execute their statements until their requested tasks are completed. Async System, like its name hints at, is a so-called system-level event often used for detecting gamepads. This event uses a DS map called *async_load* to retrieve information. A DS map is a type of data structure discussed previously in the book; you may remember these are referred to as "key and value pairs." The keys in this context are *event_type* and *pad_index*. In our example, their values are stored into variables *event* and *pad* respectively for later access. Now, let us take a peek at the aforementioned asynchronous event in our prototype next, found inside obj_Controller:

```
// ASYNC - SYSTEM
var event = async_load[? "event_type"];
var pad = async_load[? "pad_index"];

if event == "gamepad discovered" {
   global.gamepads[pad] = true; // Store connected gamepad in array
   gamepad_set_axis_deadzone(pad, 0.3); // Set dead zone
   gamepad_set_button_threshold(pad, 0.1); // Set trigger threshold
   // Play sound on connection
   audio_play_sound(Sound1, 1, false);
} else if event == "gamepad lost" {
   global.gamepads[pad] = false; // Mark slot as no pad found
}
```

When the Async System event is triggered by a gamepad connecting or disconnecting, the previously mentioned DS map *async_load* will be populated by the following key/value pairs:

- **event_type:** The type of event described by one of the following strings:
  - **"gamepad discovered":** A gamepad has been connected.
  - **"gamepad lost":** A gamepad has been disconnected.

- **pad_index:** The index of the gamepad (0–11) that was connected or disconnected.

In the above example, we used a global array called *global.gamepads* to store the status of the player's game controllers; this is represented by a Boolean (i.e., *true* for pad found or *false* if pad not found) in each array value. A sound effect is played whenever a gamepad is detected.

The aforementioned array is defined in the Create event of obj_Controller in the following fashion:

```
// CREATE
// Create an array for all 12 potentially connected gamepads (slots 0-11)
global.gamepads = array_create(12, false);
```

The Async System event will not trigger unless you have at least one gamepad-related function (e.g., *gamepad_button_check*) set up somewhere inside your game.

On Analog Input and Vibration

A "dead zone" for analog sticks is a value between 0.0 and 1.0 which will define the point at which the game detects the stick as having moved; a dead zone of 0.5 means no movement is registered until the stick has been pushed at least halfway in some direction. This is an attribute well worth experimenting with. A dead zone of zero (0) is usually far too sensitive for most purposes. A similar function by the name of *gamepad_set_button_threshold is* used to control the sensitivity of the triggers buttons.

Controller vibration is also a feature implementable in GML. It takes one function to enable said feature, namely, *gamepad_set_vibration,* and a system of switching it off when vibration is no longer needed. In Twin Stick Fun, we use an alarm in the same object the vibration is executed in (i.e., *obj_Player*) to disable vibration at a slightly later point. The function takes two parameters, namely, the intensity of the effect for a controller's left and right motors, respectively. These are issued in the range of 0.0 to 1.0 for each.

GML for Gamepads

It does not take that many functions to leverage gamepads in GameMaker. The project at hand demonstrates the seven core functions for gamepads featured in Table 8-2.

Table 8-2. *The seven basic functions for working with gamepads in GML*

gamepad_is_connected(slot)	Returns "true" if a gamepad is connected at the specified slot.
gamepad_get_device_count()	Either returns the number of gamepads connected or the number of available slots; this will depend on the platform.
gamepad_set_axis_deadzone(index, value)	Sets the "dead zone" of the joystick axis.
gamepad_set_button_threshold(index, value)	Sets the threshold setting of the analog buttons.
gamepad_button_check_pressed(index, button)	Reads single presses of specific gamepad buttons.
gamepad_axis_value(index, value)	Gets the value of the different axes of an analog controller.
gamepad_set_vibration(index, left, right)	Sets the amount of vibration for the left and right controller motors between 0.0 and 1.0.

For detecting a single press of a button, your go-to function is *gamepad_button_check_pressed*. For a continuous press of a button, you would use *gamepad_button_check*. Let's next take a look at the button constants associated with these functions (see Table 8-3).

CHAPTER 8   SEQUENCES, AUDIO EFFECTS, AND GAMEPADS

Table 8-3. Gamepad button constants in GameMaker

gp_face1	A on an Xbox controller	gp_shoulderl	Left shoulder button
gp_face2	B on an Xbox controller	gp_shoulderlb	Left trigger button
gp_face3	X on an Xbox controller	gp_shoulderr	Right shoulder button
gp_face4	Y on an Xbox controller	gp_shoulderrb	Right trigger button
gp_padu	D-pad up	gp_padr	D-pad right
gp_padd	D-pad down	gp_padl	D-pad left
gp_select	Select button	gp_start	Start button

The two analog sticks found in most modern gamepads offer many possibilities. Luckily, we can leverage them to their fullest potential inside GameMaker (see Table 8-4).

Table 8-4. The six main analog stick constants. All of them are accessed using gamepad_axis_value apart from gp_stickl and gp_stickr

gp_axislh	Left stick horizontal axis	gp_stickl	The left stick pressed in (as a button)
gp_axislv	Left stick vertical axis	gp_stickr	The right stick pressed in (as a button)
gp_axisrh	Right stick horizontal axis		
gp_axisrv	Right stick vertical axis		

Let's visualize a typical modern game controller and how the previously discussed constants relate to it (see Figure 8-10).

CHAPTER 8 SEQUENCES, AUDIO EFFECTS, AND GAMEPADS

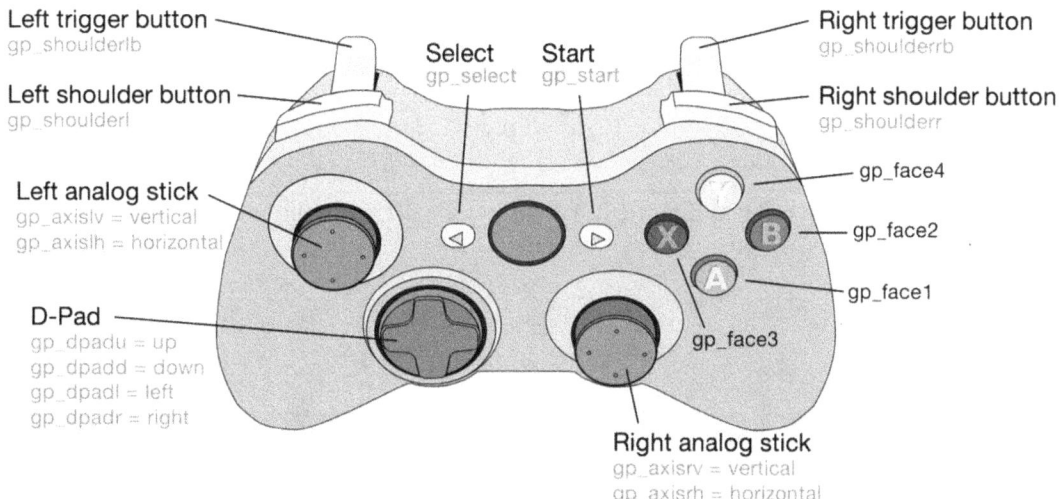

Figure 8-10. *A typical gaming controller with the associated GameMaker gamepad constants*

Pausing Games with Select

Pressing the select button on a controller in the first room of Twin Stick Fun summons an object by the name of *obj_Pause*. This is implemented using a plain *gamepad_button_check_pressed* in conjunction with the constant *gp_select*. In the object's Create event, we deactivate all on-screen instances, apart from the object itself, using *instance_deactivate_all*. Issuing this function a "true" makes it work as described. Finally obj_Pause's Draw GUI event is used to draw a gray rectangle to cover the paused game's proceedings.

Retrieving a GUID and Controller Description

We can fetch both the *globally unique identifier (GUID)* and a description of our connected gamepads in GameMaker with the following two functions: *gamepad_get_guid* and *gamepad_get_description*. In Twin Stick Fun, these two are summoned inside the Draw GUI event of obj_Controller (placed inside Room1).

A GUID is used to uniquely identify game controllers from the large pool of devices being manufactured; it is basically a string of numbers of varying lengths. In this context, it can be a useful tool to differentiate between plugged-in Xbox and PS-type gamepads. You can then use this information to create custom input mappings for the different types of controllers.

CHAPTER 8 SEQUENCES, AUDIO EFFECTS, AND GAMEPADS

The function *gamepad_get_description* returns a more human-friendly description of the connected gamepads, which can provide a useful way of displaying basic controller information in your games' menus.

Gamepad-related GUID and descriptions may vary dramatically across different platforms.

Implementing Local Co-Op with Gamepads

The second room (i.e., Room2) in Twin Stick Fun is dedicated to demonstrating the detection and leveraging of multiple gamepads. This room has five types of objects: *obj_Controller2*, *obj_Participant*, *obj_Projectile*, and *obj_Obstacle* with its children (i.e., obj_Obstacle_1, obj_Obstacle_2, and obj_Obstacle_3). This part of the project detects up to four gamepads. Each player, represented by an instance of obj_Participant, responds to the left analog controller in each respective gamepad for movement. Pressing the right trigger will make a character spawn an instance of obj_Projectile. Both participants collide with obj_Obstacle and its children using the familiar function *place_meeting* discussed in depth previously in the book. The projectiles use an IDE-based collision event to gauge impacts with the obstacles. See Figure 8-11 for a screenshot of Room2.

CHAPTER 8 SEQUENCES, AUDIO EFFECTS, AND GAMEPADS

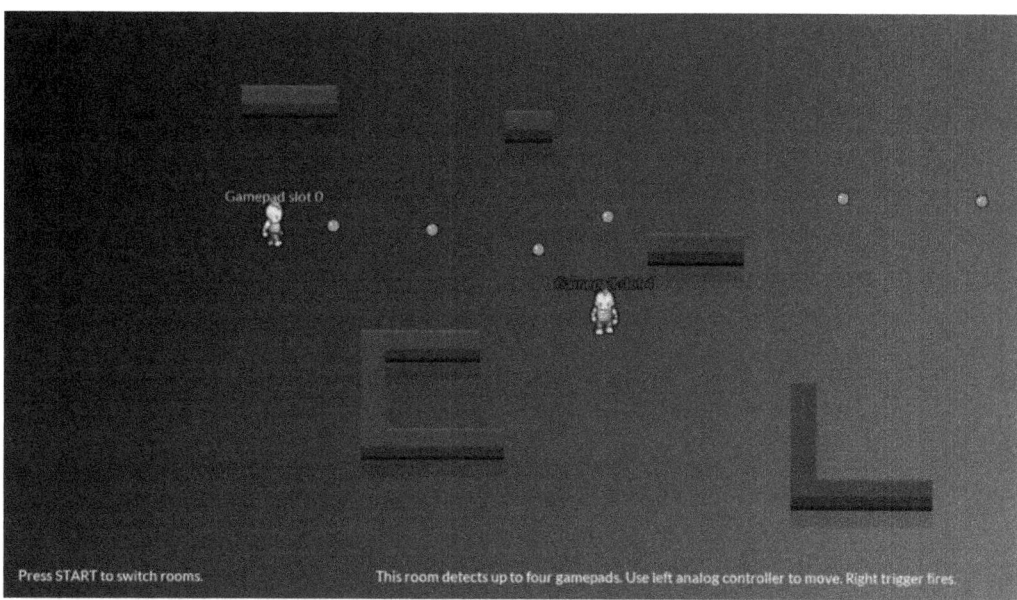

Figure 8-11. *A screenshot of the second room in Twin Stick Fun with Gamepads*

When a gamepad is connected, a new instance of *obj_Participant* is spawned at a position calculated based on the gamepad slot (i.e., slot 0 is x=100, slot 1 is x=220, slot 2 is x=340, etc.) These instances are stored in an array called *participant_instance*, indexed by the gamepad slot variable (i.e., pad). Each gamepad is then associated with a specific participant object.

The statement *text_color = make_color_rgb(100 + i * 50, 255 - i * 50, 200)* inside the Step event of *obj_Controller2* sets a unique color for a participant's text asset based on the contents of variable *i*. The variable *text_color* is defined inside obj_Participant. It defaults to white (i.e., *c_white*) but we can and do set it externally.

Staying in Room2, we use a variable called *my_pad* to transfer information between obj_Controller2 and instances of obj_Participant.

Next we shall examine the Step event of obj_Controller2, inside of which we control many a parameter for instances of obj_Participant:

```
// STEP
// Count active gamepads and store this value into variable active_count
var active_count = 0;
for (var i = 0; i < 11; i++) {
    if gamepad_active[i] active_count++;
}
```

307

CHAPTER 8   SEQUENCES, AUDIO EFFECTS, AND GAMEPADS

```
// Check for disconnected gamepads (scan all 12 slots)
for (var i = 0; i < 11; i++) {
      // A gamepad is disconnected (! = not)
      if gamepad_active[i] && !gamepad_is_connected(i) {
gamepad_active[i] = false; // Mark slot as inactive
// Check if participant exists
if instance_exists(participant_instance[i]) {
instance_destroy(participant_instance[i]); // Destroy participant instance
      participant_instance[i] = noone; // Clear instance reference
      audio_play_sound(Sound4,1,false); // Play a sound
        }
   }
}
```

As previously discussed, GameMaker supports up to 12 simultaneous gamepads populated in slots 0–11. Even though this demonstration is designed to only support up to four, all of these slots need to be scanned.

```
// Check for connected gamepads (scan all 12 slots)
for (var i = 0; i < 11; i++) {
   if gamepad_is_connected(i) && !gamepad_active[i] && active_count < 4 {
      gamepad_active[i] = true;
      active_count++; // Increment active count
      participant_instance[i] = instance_create_layer(100 + i * 120, 100,
      "Instances", obj_Participant);
      // Adjust two variables for a specific instance of obj_Participant
      with (participant_instance[i]) {
      my_pad = i;
      text_color = make_color_rgb(100 + i * 50, 255 - i * 50, 200);
      }
    }
    // Check for start button on active gamepads only
    if gamepad_active[i] && gamepad_button_check_pressed(i, gp_start)
    game_restart();
}
// Iterate through the four potential participants
```

```
for (var i = 0; i < 11; i++) {
    if gamepad_active[i] && instance_exists(participant_instance[i]) {
        // Store left analog stick input into h_axis and v_axis
        var h_axis = gamepad_axis_value(i, gp_axislh);
        var v_axis = gamepad_axis_value(i, gp_axislv);
```

The last code block of this event directly accesses all instances of obj_Participant. Here we apply movement to these instances, of which there will be as many as you have supported gamepads connected into your system (up to four in this case). We also process collisions with all instances of obj_Obstacle here.

```
// Address all instances of obj_Participant using keyword "with"
with (participant_instance[i]) {
    // Move participant/player with h_axis and v_axis
    // as long as instance is not colliding with obj_Obstacle
    if !place_meeting(x + h_axis * 5, y, obj_Obstacle) x += h_axis * 5;
    if !place_meeting(x , y+ v_axis * 5, obj_Obstacle) y += v_axis * 5;
```

Next we have the code for firing projectiles. A variable called *proj_dir* is used for storing the direction of these projectiles. It is fed the output from the function point_direction, which in turn is issued with the horizontal and vertical axes of a gamepad's analog stick.

```
    // Fire projectile with left trigger
    if gamepad_button_check_pressed(my_pad, gp_shoulderrb) {
    var proj_dir = 0;
    if h_axis != 0 || v_axis != 0 { // Moving: use analog stick direction
    proj_dir = point_direction(0, 0, h_axis, v_axis);
    } else { // Not moving: use sprite direction
                if sprite_index == spr_Right proj_dir = 0;
                else if sprite_index == spr_Left proj_dir = 180;
                else if sprite_index == spr_Down proj_dir = 90;
                else if sprite_index == spr_Up proj_dir = 270;
            }
```

At this point, we summon the projectiles using instance_create_layer. Each projectile is given a handle (i.e., "proj") which lets us manipulate their properties using dot notation.

```
var proj = instance_create_layer(x, y, "Instances", obj_Projectile);
proj.direction = proj_dir+choose(-random(5),0,random(5));
proj.speed = choose(12,11); // Set projectile speed to 11 or 12
proj.owner_pad = my_pad; // Store the firing participant's gamepad index
            }

if h_axis != 0 || v_axis != 0 { // If either axis value is not zero..
            image_speed = 0.8; // Animate sprite at 80% speed
            // Change sprite index based on axis i.e. movement direction
            if h_axis > 0 sprite_index = spr_Right;
            if h_axis < 0 sprite_index = spr_Left;
            if v_axis > 0 sprite_index = spr_Down;
            if v_axis < 0 sprite_index = spr_Up;
            } else image_speed = 0; // Halt sprite animation when not moving
        }
    }
}
```

Let us now peek inside the deceptively simple obj_Projectile. It has only one event: a collision with obj_Participant. A launching speed does not need to be defined inside it due to the previously described approach of using instance handles and dot notation.

```
// COLLISION with obj_Participant
// Ensure not colliding with the firing participant
if other.my_pad != owner_pad {
    instance_destroy();
}
```

The statement *other.my_pad != owner_pad* makes sure a projectile only collides with instances of obj_Participant that do not represent whoever fired the projectile.

In Closing

In this chapter, we discussed these powerful features of GameMaker:

- The basic workflow for sequences and their core functions (e.g., layer_sequence_create, layer_sequence_pause, and layer_sequence_is_finished)

- Messages and moments in sequences
- GameMaker's real-time audio effects (reverb, delay, bitcrusher, etc.)
- The basics of digital audio mixing and dynamics
- The implementation of gamepads inside GameMaker using an asynchronous system event

In the chapter to come, we shall learn how to deploy our projects for all of the available platforms in GameMaker, including Windows and Android.

CHAPTER 9

Debugging and Sharing Your Game

This chapter is about deployment for platforms supported by GameMaker as we learn how to create executable packages ready for distribution. We will also examine problem-solving in the field of game development, also known as debugging.

When we are ready to distribute a game we need a final deliverable. This refers to a file, or a set of files, that your potential customers are to receive. These deliverables come in different forms depending on the platform you are deploying for.

As discussed previously in the book, there are two ways of running/deploying GameMaker games: by using a *virtual machine (VM)* or using the *compiler (YYC)*. The former is slower, but the latter takes a bit more of configuration to get working. When delivering games in their final form for distribution, you should always opt for the compiled approach.

Now, we access our deployment platforms by clicking the bullseye icon (labeled "Targets") in the top right corner of the GameMaker IDE (see Figure 9-1).

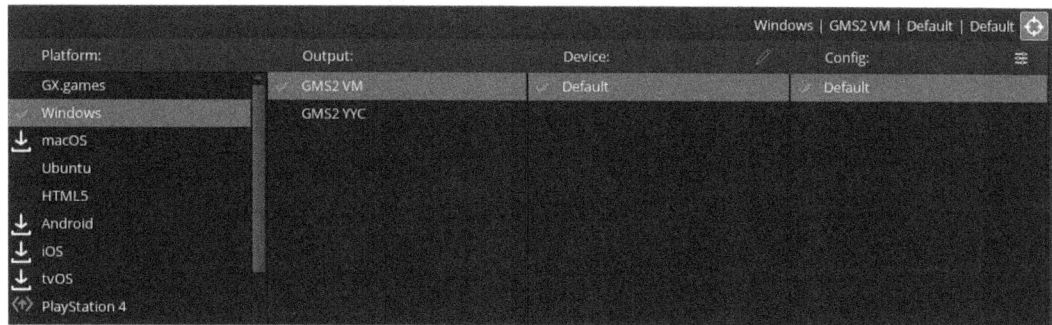

Figure 9-1. *The target selection window in GameMaker*

You can see all of your available platforms on the left side of the window that opens. In Figure 9-1, we have selected Windows and GameMaker's virtual machine (again, that's the slower running option best suited for testing, not deployment).

Keeping It Clean

The asset cache can over time grow into a hefty pile of corrupted resource files. It's therefore a good idea to completely clean the GameMaker asset cache before deployment. Clearing the cache ensures that GameMaker uses the most recent versions of your audiovisual resources.

As mentioned back in the first chapter of this book, there's a button for this in the IDE. You clean the asset cache by clicking the dustpan icon next to the stop icon or by pressing Control+F7 (see Figure 9-2).

Figure 9-2. The icon for cleaning the asset cache in GameMaker

The Opera GX Browser (GX.games)

GX.games is an online gaming platform developed by Opera, integrated with the Opera GX browser (as discussed in the very first chapter of this book) and GameMaker. Deploying for this ecosystem is a simple way to make your games playable online. Despite running inside a browser, GX.games can handle even some of the more technically demanding 2D games.

To deploy for Opera GX, we shall need to go through the following steps:

- Register an Opera account at https://auth.opera.com if you do not have one.

- Sign into your Opera account inside GameMaker by clicking the profile icon on the top right corner of the interface (see Figure 9-3).

CHAPTER 9   DEBUGGING AND SHARING YOUR GAME

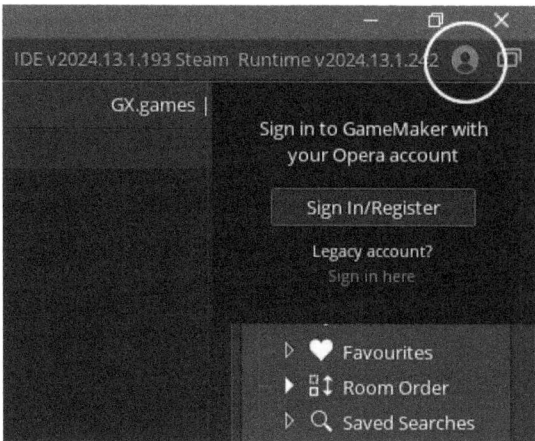

Figure 9-3.   The icon for signing into your Opera account

- Now click on the previously mentioned target icon in the upper right corner of the GameMaker IDE and select GX.games as the platform (see Figure 9-1).

- Click Create Executable found in the top row of the GameMaker IDE (see Figure 9-4).

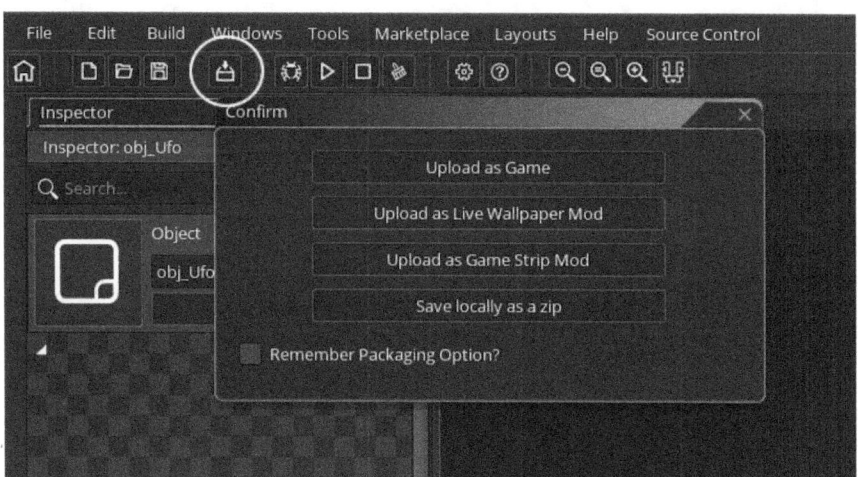

Figure 9-4.   The icon labeled Create Executable and the ensuing window

- Select Upload as Game to enter your game into GX.games.

315

All platforms have numerous options for us to tinker with. In the case of GX.games, the option window looks like this.

Building for Windows

Microsoft's venerable operating system is probably the most popular choice for publishing games made with GameMaker. It is also perhaps the easiest of the available platforms to deploy for. Basically, we create either a zipped (compressed) package of all of your game's assets or a single executable installer (see Figure 9-5).

Figure 9-5. *The icon labeled Create Executable and its options for Windows games*

The options are as follows:

- **Package as installer:** Creates a standard (x64) Windows-compatible executable installer file.

- **Package as zip:** Compresses your games files into a single zip file for the x64 Windows ecosystem.

- **Package as installer for Arm64:** Creates an executable installer for the Arm64 architecture. This is for versions of Windows that run on Arm-based hardware.

- **Package as zip for Arm64:** Compresses your games files into a single zip file for the Arm64 architecture.

CHAPTER 9 DEBUGGING AND SHARING YOUR GAME

Now, x64 is the standard architecture for Intel and AMD processors while Arm64 represents a newer processor paradigm. While x64 is computationally very efficient, it is also more power-hungry compared to Arm64. The latter is becoming an increasingly popular approach for many laptops and other portable devices.

GameMaker will only deliver games for 64-bit versions of Windows.

Setting Up Visual Studio for Windows and YYC

As always, you should build finished versions of your game with YYC instead of VM. For this, some additional downloads and/or setting up for Windows are needed. Namely, you should have Microsoft's completely free Visual Studio Community 2022 on your PC. It is available here:

https://visualstudio.microsoft.com/vs/community

When you run the installer, you will be presented with an interface used for getting Visual Studio Community 2022 up and running. When presented with Workloads, click *Desktop development with C++*. Install the software and restart your computer.

We must now direct GameMaker to the directory location of the framework we just installed. Start GameMaker and open **File ➤ Preferences.** Locate the section labeled *Platform Settings* and finally the *Windows* section (see Figure 9-6).

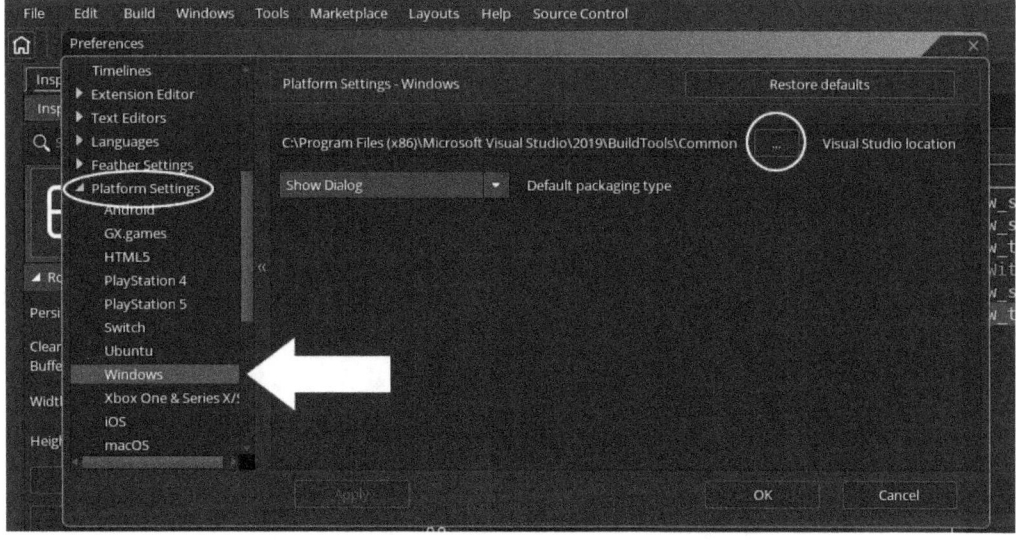

Figure 9-6. *The GameMaker Preferences window with active platform settings*

CHAPTER 9 DEBUGGING AND SHARING YOUR GAME

The default location path for Visual Studio looks something like this on Windows 10:

- C:\Program Files\Microsoft Visual Studio\2022\Community\Common7\Tools\VsDevCmd.bat

Clicking the icon with three dots (as highlighted in Figure 9-5) will open a window for locating the framework. You need to first find the directory that has the file VsDevCmd.bat inside it and then click Open. Doing this will let GameMaker leverage Visual Studio for highly optimized YYC output. You only need to do this once; GameMaker will remember the location for all of your different Windows projects.

Creating executables with YYC is a much slower process compared to VM, but well worth the wait prior to releasing your game to the public. Most more complicated games tend to run much better if compiled with YYC.

Building for Linux

GameMaker's (as of June 2025) experimental Linux IDE only supports Ubuntu 24 and 22. A separate Windows PC is required for creating games for Windows and any consoles. Also, to deploy for the Apple ecosystem (i.e., macOS, iOS, and tvOS) from a Linux PC, a separate Mac is needed.

This section will describe the process of deploying for Linux when you are on a Windows PC. It is recommended you have Linux on a separate physical computer when deploying your GameMaker projects. However, you *can* use Ubuntu[1] running on a virtual machine[2] inside your Windows PC; this is not officially supported. A virtual machine is a software-based installation of an operating system running inside your main operating system.

Once you have a Ubuntu installation ready, you will need to install the required development libraries and tools. This process was discussed in-depth in the first chapter of the book.

---

[1] You can download Ubuntu at https://ubuntu.com/download/desktop.
[2] An example of a free virtual machine for this purpose is Oracle's *VirtualBox* which is available for both Windows and macOS at https://www.virtualbox.org/.

CHAPTER 9   DEBUGGING AND SHARING YOUR GAME

We must now open the target selection icon in the top right corner of the GameMaker IDE as shown in Figure 9-7.

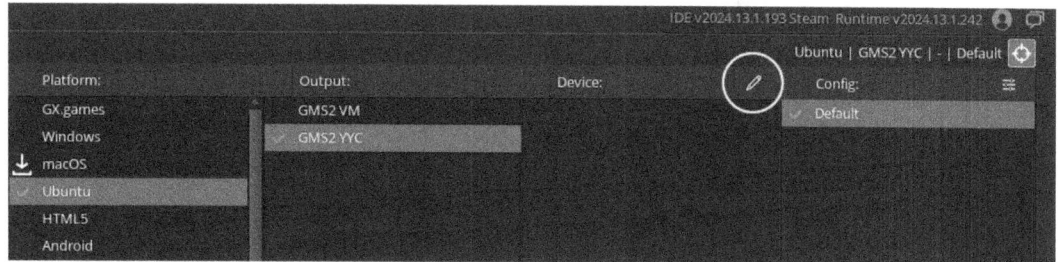

Figure 9-7. *The target selection window in GameMaker with Ubuntu Linux being selected*

Click the pencil icon labeled *Device Editor*. This will open a new window shown in Figure 9-8.

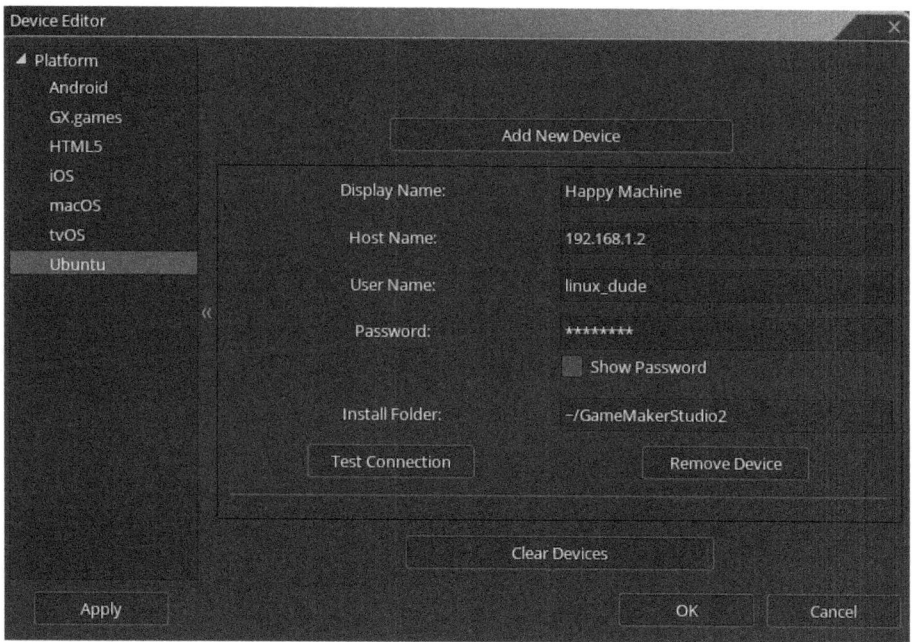

Figure 9-8. *The Device Editor window in GameMaker*

- **Display Name** denotes a name that you can give to your Linux PC or virtual machine.

- **Host Name** is the IP address or device name of the Ubuntu system that is to host the game (the IP is a usually something in the style of "192.168.1.2"). To get the this address of a Ubuntu system, you simply have to go to that device's Settings menu and click the Network icon.

- **User Name** and **Password** are for the Ubuntu user account that will be used for creating your game.

- **Install Folder** is the location for the necessary components required to run your game.

After entering this information, click on *Test Connection* to see if your workstation is able to reach the Linux PC. If your configuration settings are functioning, you can now build games on your Windows PC and have them run on the Linux system.

Building for macOS

The basic workflow for using GameMaker from a Mac is more or less identical to the Windows version. However, for testing your games in VM, you need to install the Mono framework, which is available for free here:

https://www.mono-project.com/download/stable

Now, deployment for Apple devices from a Windows PC can be an arduous but rewarding experience. First of all, you absolutely need a physical Mac to go along your Windows PC; using a virtual machine (as per with Linux) is not recommended and might violate Apple's terms.

You also need an Apple developer account, which can be created here:

https://account.apple.com/account

A free Apple account allows testing with a *Mac Development Certificate* but restricts distribution. A paid account ($99/year) is required for *Developer ID* and Mac App Store distribution.

You must have *Xcode* installed on your system as well. This is Apple's free software development framework, and it is available here:

https://developer.apple.com/xcode

CHAPTER 9 DEBUGGING AND SHARING YOUR GAME

You now need to link your developer account with Xcode. This takes the following steps:

- Navigate to Xcode ➤ Preferences.
- At the top-left side of the window, click the *Accounts* button.
- In the lower left corner, click the *Add* button (+).
- Choose *Apple ID* from the ensuing pop-up menu. Enter your Apple Developer ID and password. Click *Sign In*.

The various related certificates should be then retrieved. Select the Apple ID you just added. On the right of the window, click *Team Name* and then the button *Show Details*.

At this point, make sure you have an Ethernet cable connected between your Windows PC and the Mac. Using Wi-Fi for connecting these devices may prove problematic. Alternatively, if you have a router device, you can plug-in Ethernet cables from both computers into that to create a connection.

Next we shall permit remote login and file sharing between your main PC and its Apple Mac counterpart. Open *System Preferences on your Mac* and click *Sharing*.

- Tick the *Remote Login* checkbox then the *File Sharing* checkbox. In file sharing, click *Options*.
- Select *Share files and folders using SMB,* which is short for *Server Message Block,* a type of client-server communication protocol.
- Select the checkbox next to the user account that will be used to share files with Windows. Enter the password for that user and click *OK*. Also click *Done*.

Open *Network preferences* (at *View* ➤ *Network*) and select your active connection. Then click *Advanced*.

- Click the WINS tab, then enter the workgroup name used by your Windows computer; they typically use either "WORKGROUP" or "MSHOME."
- Click *OK and Apply*.

   If you don't know the workgroup name, open *Control Panel* ➤ *System and Security* ➤ *System* on the Windows computer.

321

Back to Mac

We next need to configure some settings inside GameMaker back on your Windows PC.

- Go to File ➤ Preferences ➤ Platform Settings ➤ macOS.

- Enter your Default team identifier. If you need to double check your team ID, sign in to developer.apple.com and browse to the section called Membership details.

- Set up the Mac as a build target in Device Editor. This step is similar to Linux deployment. Click the target icon in the top right part of the GameMaker IDE. Choose macOS as the deployment platform. Click the pen icon to open the Device Editor, click Add New Device, and enter the details for your Mac.

When compiling with YYC, GameMaker sends the project to Xcode, where you must select the appropriate certificate and provisioning profile under *Signing & Capabilities*. For plain old VM builds, GameMaker handles signing automatically using the certificates configured in Xcode.

Sometimes you need to type the following string into the Terminal app in macOS to get Xcode to play ball with GameMaker (press Enter after typing):

Sudo xcode-select -s /Applications/Xcode.app/Contents/Developer

This sets the active developer directory for Xcode command-line tools using a command called *sudo* (or "superuser do"). You need to enter your administrator password after issuing this command.

Again, when deploying for the Apple ecosystem, prepare to enjoy a lot of configuration, a bunch of digital certificates, and stern restrictions. However, you do not need a top-of-the line Apple device for use with GameMaker. A second-hand Mac Mini (often available for less than $300) is a perfectly fine computer when deploying your games for Apple devices.

Building for iOS (iPhone and iPad)

To deploy GameMaker games for iOS, you first need to take care of the steps in the previous section up to the heading titled "Back to Mac." Most importantly, make sure your development PC has Xcode fully running and you have secured yourself an Apple developer account.

> As of iOS 16, you need to enable a setting called *Developer Mode* in your iOS device(s) when working with GameMaker. This should be available at **Settings ➤ Privacy And Security** in your iPhone/iPad.

Now, connect your iPhone into your development Mac with a data cable. You should see a window with the message "Trust this Mac?". Tap on Yes or Trust.

Click the target icon in the top right corner of the GameMaker IDE. Then locate the pen icon and click on it. In the window that opens, click *Detect Devices*. This will populate the Device Manager with all the available iOS devices found by Xcode on the Mac.

Once devices are detected, they appear in a list where you can optionally rename their display names. Note that renaming only affects how devices are shown in Target Manager and does not alter any settings within Xcode.

Troubleshooting Undetected Devices

If no devices are detected but the connection test to the development Mac succeeds, the issue may be that Xcode hasn't been recently opened on your Mac. This sometimes prevents Xcode from preparing its device list for GameMaker. To resolve this, follow these steps:

1. Open Xcode on your Mac.
2. Just wait a few moments.
3. Attempt device detection again in GameMaker.

If a physically connected device still isn't detected:

1. In Xcode, navigate to Window > Devices.
2. Verify the device appears in the list. If it doesn't, check the physical connection to the Mac.
3. Look for a spinning circle icon next to the device. If present, Xcode is still processing the device's contents. Wait for this to complete before retrying detection in GameMaker.

CHAPTER 9   DEBUGGING AND SHARING YOUR GAME

Both physical and simulated devices from Xcode will be detected and listed. Please note the latter may exhibit vastly different performance characteristics compared to their physical counterparts.

Make sure to launch the simulator from Device Manager before starting the app building process to avoid lengthy delays. Long app-building delays can sometimes cause issues, particularly on older Macs with less system memory (RAM) installed.

Always test your games on physical iOS devices when preparing the final deliverables.

Building for Browsers (HTML5)

After the sometimes tricky process of deploying for Apple devices, let us take a look at the refreshingly simple way to export your games for browsers in JavaScript form. There are but a couple of steps to this. First, we use the now-familiar target icon to select HTML5 as the output platform. Then we click on the also familiar pen icon to enter the device editor, which in this case is all about browsers (see Figure 9-9).

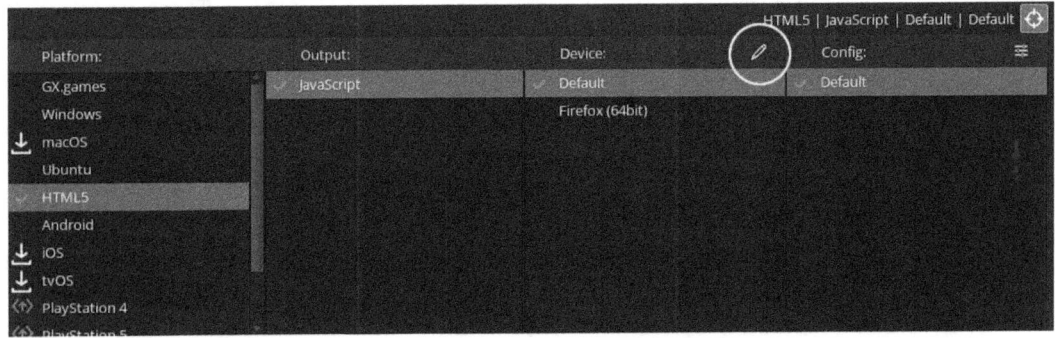

Figure 9-9. *The target selection window in GameMaker with HTML5 being selected*

Figure 9-10 depicts the device editor for HTML5. It is here where you choose the browser you want to preview your game on. The button labeled Detect Browsers usually functions well, but in case it doesn't, you can manually add new browsers.

324

CHAPTER 9   DEBUGGING AND SHARING YOUR GAME

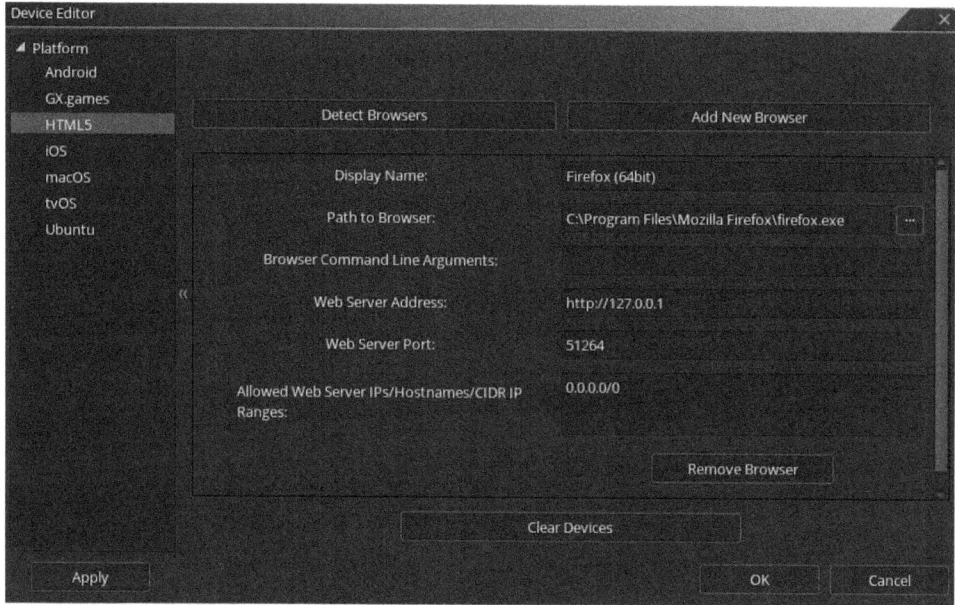

Figure 9-10. *The Device Editor window for HTML5*

A *port* in the context of networks is a way for a computer to know which program it should forward data to when it arrives from a network. They are a kind of an identifier; different programs/services can be assigned with a different and unique port. For example, port number 80 is reserved for the http protocol, which governs data transfer between the internet and its clients (i.e., browsers).

In GameMaker, the option titled *Web Server Port* is usually best left at its default of 51264; a different value might be needed in case your operating system has reserved that particular port for some other purpose.

Network ports span a range between 1 and 65536. Port zero (0) is never used.

The option *Web Server Address* usually works just fine at its default setting, which should only be changed if you encounter problems. This default setting (i.e., http://127.0.0.1) is a so-called loopback IP address, also referred to as "localhost." It is commonly used by devices to communicate with themselves when testing.

When clicking the icon for *Create Executable* for HTML5 deployment, you are given two options:

CHAPTER 9 DEBUGGING AND SHARING YOUR GAME

- **Package as loose files**: Deploys the game as uncompressed files into a folder of your choosing. You must then upload these files to an online hosting service.

- **Package as zip**: Deploys the project as a single compressed zip file.

Running a deployed HTML5 project locally (i.e., from your computer) will usually result in the game not working properly. Browser games made with GameMaker are intended to be run online.

Let us take a look at some of the settings for HTML5 found in Preferences ➤ Platform Settings ➤ HTML5.

- **Obfuscate:** When this setting is enabled, the HTML5 runner code will be obfuscated even in debug mode. This makes it harder for someone to alter the code when running the game. This setting only applies to debug mode in the HTML5 export.

- **Pretty print:** *Pretty printing* refers to a cosmetic practice of formatting code so that it is easier to read by humans. This setting will have no effect on performance.

- **Remove unused functions:** When checked, GameMaker's compiler will remove any functions that are not being used in your game. This process typically reduces the size of the final JavaScript file, possibly improving performance.

- **Enable debug rename:** When enabled, variable and function names in the JavaScript code are renamed even in debug mode. This makes the code harder to reverse engineer when inspected in a browser's developer tools, while still allowing debugging.

- **Enable conditional compilation:** When enabled this feature removes unnecessary code intended for other platforms (e.g., Windows) from the final JavaScript output, often reducing file size and improving performance.

CHAPTER 9   DEBUGGING AND SHARING YOUR GAME

- **Keep JSDoc:** JSDoc refers to a markup language used to add documentation directly within JavaScript code. This makes the code more readable and better documented. It can be helpful when debugging, especially if you're inspecting the JavaScript output in a browser's developer tools.

- **Verbose:** When enabled, GameMaker produces detailed logs in the browser's console (accessible via browser developer tools). These logs include additional information about the game. This feature is only useful for debugging purposes.

Popular sites for hosting browser games include GameJolt and Kongregate.

Building for Android

Before we get to deploy GameMaker projects for Android, we need *Android Studio*, the free app development framework from Google:

https://developer.android.com/studio

Download the software from the link above and install it. Fire it up and you should see the screen shown in Figure 9-11.

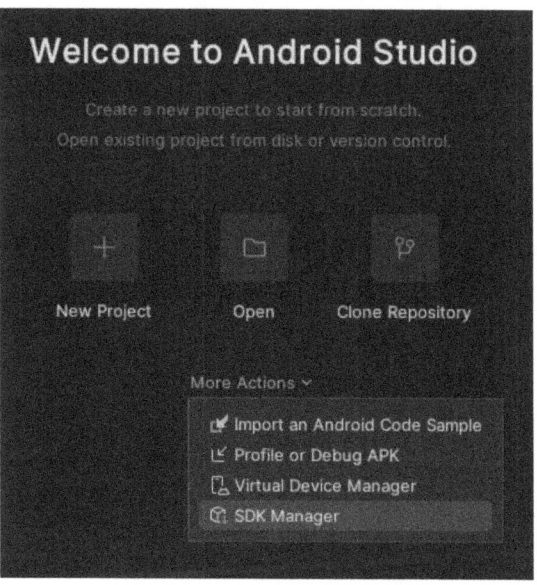

Figure 9-11. *The starting screen in Android Studio*

CHAPTER 9   DEBUGGING AND SHARING YOUR GAME

Click *More Actions* and select *SDK Manager*. Navigate to *SDK Tools* and click the checkbox next to *NDK (Side by side)*. An icon will appear (see Figure 9-12). Click on it to download the tool.

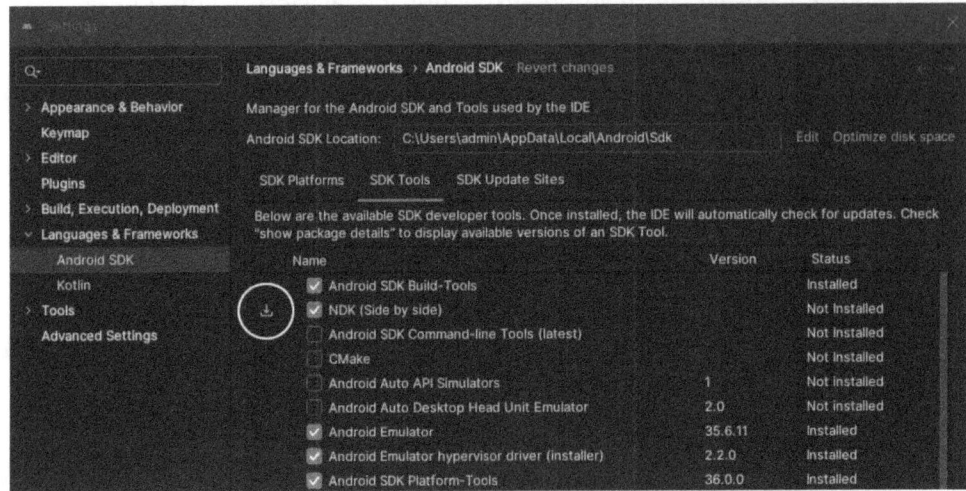

Figure 9-12. *The screen for downloading NDK in Android Studio*

The Android NDK refers to a *native development kit,* which lets you use the YYC compiler within the Android ecosystem. Next we are going to setup this platform inside GameMaker.

Android's tools may automatically download and install additional software packages during builds in GameMaker. This is normal and you should let these installations to proceed if prompted.

Navigate to *Preferences* ➤ *Platform Preferences* ➤ *Android*. We are going to set the file paths to Android Studio's various components (see Figure 9-13).

CHAPTER 9   DEBUGGING AND SHARING YOUR GAME

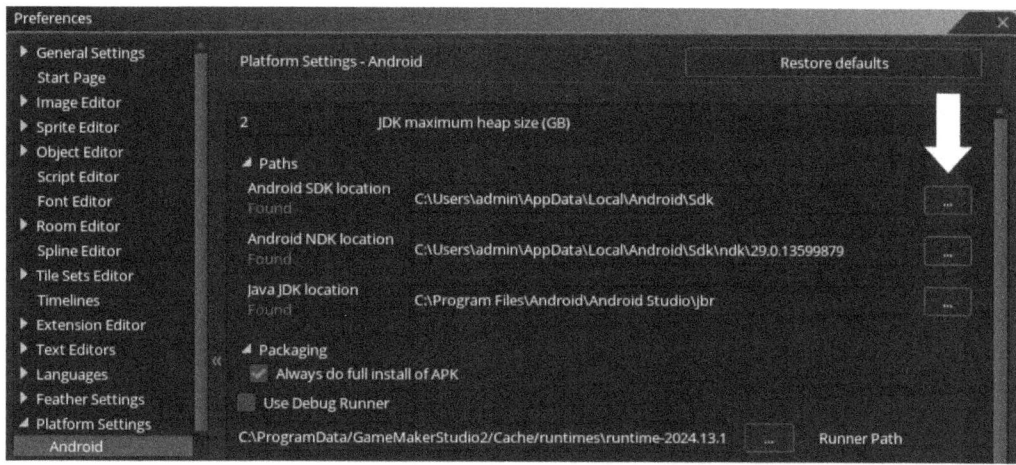

Figure 9-13. *A partial view of the platform preferences for Android in GameMaker*

There's three important file locations for us to work with.

- **Android SDK location:** On Windows, this defaults to C:\Users\<username>\AppData\Local\Android\Sdk.

- **Android NDK location:** This is in the previous location's subfolder named *ndk* denoted by its version number (e.g., C:\Users\<username>\AppData\Local\Android\Sdk\ndk\29.0.13599879).

- **Java JDK location:** On Windows, this defaults to C:\Program Files\Android\Android Studio\jbr.

We now need to generate a *keystore file*. This is done in the same window where we set the aforementioned file locations. This is a file that will be used to code-sign your Android apps. You are to issue the following information before you can click *Generate Keystore* and save this file somewhere on your computer:

- **Common name:** Your full name.

- **Password:** The password you want to use for the keystore file. This must be *at least* six characters long.

- **Alias:** This is the name of the "user" for this keystore and can differ from common name.

329

- **Alias password:** This needs to be the same password as the previous one.

- **Organizational unit:** The department of the company that you are in (e.g., Marketing).

- **Organization:** The name of your game studio (e.g., "Super Jolly Games").

- **Location:** The name of the city where you are located.

- **Country:** A two letter "ISO-code of your country of residence (e.g., FI for Finland, KM for Comoros, etc.).

In order for GameMaker to detect your device, it must be connected to the PC or Mac using a USB cable. The device must also have *Developer Mode* and *USB debugging* enabled.

Developer Mode is disabled by default. It needs to be switched on from the Android phone. The menu location of this setting varies between different devices. For example, on *Samsung Galaxy* phones, it is found in *About phone > Software Information.* Once you find the location of the Developer Options screen, you can enable USB debugging from the same menu.

Connecting an Android Phone to Windows

Connect your Android device to your PC using a USB data cable; some cables are only used for charging and won't function for data transfer. The device drivers should get installed automatically at this stage if need be.

Now, you can test your phone drivers are operational using the following methods:

- If you have already set up a PATH variable to point to the *Android Debug Bridge (ADB)* directly, then simply hit Windows Key and R to open a new Run window and type *cmd*. Hit Enter and type *adb devices* and hit Enter again.

- Go to your Android install folder. Locate the "platform-tools folder inside it (e.g., C:\Users\<username>\AppData\Local\Android\Sdk\platform-tools) and then hold down the Shift key. Right-click in some empty space and choose "Open a command window here." Now type *adb devices* and hit Enter to see a list of connected devices.

GameMaker should now be able to auto-detect the device in the Device Manager window. If Windows does not recognize your device at all at this stage, you might have to manually install your Android device's required drivers.

Also, in case you have a Google device, you need to install the *Google USB Driver*. This can either be done from Android Studio. See Figure 9-11 again and scroll further down on this view. Alternatively, you can use the following link:

https://developer.android.com/studio/run/win-usb

Connecting an Android Phone to macOS

First off, download and install the free *Android File Transfer* app from the following link:

https://android.p2hp.com/filetransfer/index.html

Once this app is installed on your Mac, follow these steps:

- Open *Android File Transfer*.
- Unlock your Android device.
- Connect your device to your computer with a USB data cable.
- On your device, tap the "USB for…" notification.
- Select Transfer files.
- Wait for an Android File Transfer window to open on your Mac.

GameMaker should now be able to detect your device. Every time you connect it to the Mac from now on, the Android File Transfer app will open automatically.

Wrapping Up Android Shenanigans

We finally get to the last stage of Android deployment. Click the target icon in the upper ride side of GameMaker's IDE. Select Android as the platform. Then click the familiar pencil icon to access the *Android Device Manager*. It is from there we can detect connected Android devices.

Again, for GameMaker to detect your phone/device, the following conditions need to be met:

- The device must be plugged into the PC or Mac using a USB data cable.

- Both Developer Mode and USB debugging must be enabled on the device.

- On Mac, you will also need to have the Android File Transfer app installed.

Next we configure some more settings. Navigate to *Game Options* ➤ *Android* in the GameMaker IDE. It is usually a solid idea to make sure the *Build Settings* (found in a section called *General*) reflect the most up-to-date version of the API.

The section called *Architecture* contains three checkboxes, which reflect the types of devices your game is to support. The default setting of *Arm64* is usually the best choice as it represents the most modern type of Android device.

The *Graphics* section of Android preferences includes these two pertinent settings:

- **Screen color depth**: Using a setting of 16 bits can improve game performance but may cause jagged, visible gradients in colors (i.e., banding). For smoother color gradients and often better overall visuals, you can opt for 24 bits, but this setting may slightly impact performance.

- **Device support:** Sets whether your project is to support only devices that have a dedicated GPU or all devices. If your game has any advanced drawing functions like alpha blending/opacity and surfaces, it's best to choose the option *Only support Android devices with a GPU* as older devices may not run your game very well.

After all the setting up is done, you click the button labeled *Create Executable*. This will result in an apk file, which is short for *Android Package Kit*.

Deploying for PS4, PS5, and Nintendo Switch

Most beginners will not be engaging in the more costly and complicated process of developing for modern consoles. This section is not about the technical details of deployment for these systems, rather it is intended as an overview for these proceedings.

The process of developing and publishing GameMaker games for modern consoles requires quite a lot of administrative work—and indeed coinage. Firstly, you need approval as a registered developer with Sony, Microsoft, or Nintendo. It is only after you become an approved developer when you gain access to the manufacturers' software development kits (SDKs). This can be a difficult endeavor. Deploying GameMaker games to PlayStation 4 (PS4), PlayStation 5 (PS5), Xbox, and Nintendo Switch also requires the fairly expensive *GameMaker Enterprise* subscription.[3]

For PS4 and PS5, you can register as a partner using this link:

`https://partners.playstation.net`

Consumer PS5 consoles cannot be used for development. A PS5 developer kit is required for testing and debugging your game. Sony offers a PS5 *Development Hardware Loan Program,* providing complimentary development and testing kits to approved developers in regions like the United States, Canada, Europe, UK, Australia, New Zealand, and parts of Asia. These kits mimic PS5 hardware and let you thoroughly test performance, graphics, and DualSense controllers, among others.

Creating an executable for PlayStation consoles in GameMaker results in a pkg file.

Now, for Nintendo Switch, you must register here:

`https://developer.nintendo.com`

Approval grants access to the *Nintendo Developer Portal,* where you can order dev kits, download SDKs, and access documentation. After registering, you must contact *Nintendo Regional offices* (developers@nintendo.eu for Europe or Australia or thirdpartypublisher@noa.nintendo.com for the United States or elsewhere). This is where you get to pitch your project and seek authorization to become a Nintendo Switch developer.

`https://developer.nintendo.com/group/development/getting-started/g1kr9vj6/middleware/gamemaker-studio2`

Targeting Nintendo in GameMaker and creating an executable results in an nsp file, which is short for *Nintendo Submission Package.*

---

[3] As of July 2025, GameMaker's Enterprise license costs €679.99 per annum.

Deploying for Xbox One and Series X/S

For Xbox development in GameMaker, you need an ID@Xbox account, available here:

https://developer.microsoft.com/en-GB/games/publish/program-selection

Once approved, you need to make a *Secure GDK Middleware Request* at this address:

https://developer.microsoft.com/en-us/games/support/request-gdkx-middleware

As long as you have a GameMaker Account associated with the same email address you have registered with as an Xbox developer, Microsoft will apply the relevant licensing to that account.

If you do not have a GameMaker account associated with the same email address you have registered as an Xbox developer, Microsoft will ask you to create a GameMaker Account.

Clicking the Create Executable button in the GameMaker IDE generates a msixcv file[4] which represents the installer for your Xbox game.

You can use an older version of GameMaker (such as 2022.3.0.625) with the UWP[5] export module still in it if you insist on running Xbox games locally. Enable developer mode on your Xbox and transfer the UWP build over to your console to test your game. This works only on the individual Xbox in use and not for distribution.

A Primer on Debugging in GameMaker

A *bug* is a problem in a computer program. The term *debugging* refers to the process of removing these problems. Untamed bugs can cause the following types of issues:

- **Sluggish performance:** A game may work otherwise well but starts to run exceptionally slowly at some point, which may stem from problems like uncontrolled spawning of too many object instances.

- **Crashing:** A game crashes completely, perhaps throwing an error message in GameMaker (e.g., "undefined variable").

---

[4] MSIXVC is short for Microsoft Installer for Xbox Virtual Console.
[5] UWP, as discussed in Chapter 1, stands for *Universal Windows Platform*. This technology has been phased out from GameMaker.

- **Odd behaviors:** Game actors act strangely and not in the way the developer intended, e.g., enemies walk through walls or the player gets stuck in them.

- **Cosmetic issues:** Visual problems like strangely animated sprites and misaligned text.

GameMaker offers plenty of advanced tools to handle glitches in the code. Before we get into them, let us discuss some common precautions and good practices to reduce issues before they get the chance to emerge.

Use *instance_exists* or *instance_number*. The former function is there to detect whether an instance exists in a room and the latter returns the count of specific instances. Let's say you are accessing a variable inside an instance of *obj_Player* using the dot notation from some other object like this:

```
// This is being done outside of obj_Player from, say, obj_Controller
obj_Player.health -= 5;
```

Should an instance of obj_Player exist in a room, all will be well. However, if said instance is not there, the provided statement would crash your game. Obviously, nonexistent instances cannot be accessed. Now, let us modify obj_Controller like this:

```
if instance_exists(obj_Player) obj_Player.health -= 5;
```

This will put a safeguard in place and variables inside obj_Player will only be altered should an instance of this object exist; the game will run smoothly whether an instance of obj_Player is in a room or not. Alternatively, you could also do this for the same result:

```
if instance_number(obj_Player)>0 obj_Player.health -= 5;
```

Always limit the number of instances with instance_number. When you are spawning instances into a room using, say, GameMaker's Alarm system, make sure you set a hard upper limit using instance_number. This technique looks like this:

```
// This is the alarm zero -event of, say, obj_Controller
if instance_number(obj_Wasp)<100 instance_create_depth(0, 0, 0, obj_Wasp);
```

Above, we allow a maximum of one hundred instances of *obj_Wasp* spawn into a room. Not using this technique can quickly bring a device on its knees as the instances keep coming in endlessly. It can also be used to control the difficulty level of your games by not introducing a massive number of enemies into the arenas of battle.

Use the Outside Room event. A bullet or missile can't do much if it manages to escape a room. Even if they are not visible on-screen, they are still soaking up system resources. To remove such instances, use the Outside Room event (click *Add Event* ➤ *Other* ➤ *Outside Room* inside the object inspector) and add a simple *instance_destroy* into it.

Keep your ears peeled for *audio_is_playing*. This function is a valuable tool for preventing excessive triggering of audio. If you experience distorted or cacophonous sound in your games, a likely culprit is the overuse of audio_play_sound. For example, if you want to have a single theme song play continuously across all of your game's rooms, you would only want to trigger it once in the title screen. This scenario requires you to leverage audio_is_playing in the following manner:

```
if !audio_is_playing(Friday) audio_play_sound(Friday,1,true);
```

This reads as follows: play an audio resource called *Friday* (on repeat) but only if it is not already playing. Notice the use of the not operator (i.e., !). Naturally, this technique can be used for any type of audio resource as well during gameplay.

Use array_length for your array work whenever feasible. Going out of bounds with arrays is a common mistake for beginning indies. The following listing would result in a crash, because there are only three elements in this array and not five like the for loop might have you believe:

```
// This will return "Variable Index [3] out of range [3]"
var my_array = [1, 2, 4];
for (var i = 0; i < 4; i++)
{ show_message(my_array[i]); }
```

The corrected version looks as follows:

```
var my_array = [1, 2, 4];
for (var i = 0; i < array_length(my_array); i++)
{ show_message(my_array[i]); }
```

Pay attention to variable scope. This factor determines how variables are accessed, directly impacting code behavior and performance. As discussed in previous chapters, GML offers three levels of variable scope:

- **Local:** Variables declared with keyword *var* (e.g., var happiness = 100) are temporary and only exist within the event or script they are defined in. They use less memory (RAM) than other types of variables.

- **Instance:** Variables without var defined in an object's events (e.g., happiness = 100) work only inside specific instances of that object. These variables are freed from memory when an instance is destroyed.

- **Global:** Variables declared with keyword *global* (e.g., *global.happiness*) can be accessed from any event inside any object. They are also available to all scripts and *Creation Code* segments inside rooms.

Local variables are destroyed after an event or script that uses them ends. Use these types of variables for internal iteration and other temporary calculations that don't need to persist. The most common example of a local variable is the for loop and its classic "i" (e.g., *for(var i=0; i ..)*, etc.).

Instance variables are general-purpose tools for keeping track of an instance's life cycle. Like you probably know at this point, there are many built-in instance variables such as *x* and *y* for coordinates and *image_alpha* for transparency (in the case of instances that have sprites assigned to them). Please be aware that instance variables inside objects marked as "Persistent" retain values across rooms; this may or may not cause unpredictable behavior.

Global variables should not be used with more complicated data structures (e.g., ds_lists or ds_maps) in large quantities to avoid stressing a device's resources. They are best used for gauging game-wide states like audiovisual settings and whether a game is paused or not. Also, having multiple objects modify the same global variables can cause issues as your games get more complex.

Use descriptive names for all of your variables, e.g., *player_name* or *enemy_type*. Surrealism has its place, but not in this context.

Always destroy unneeded data structures. Keep those *Game End* and *Room End* events close, using functions like *ds_list_destroy* and *part_system_destroy* whenever applicable. This will help optimize your game and potentially reduce instability.

Align your text with care. When leveraging a Draw event (e.g., draw GUI), be aware that every string of text in it is influenced by preceding drawing functions such as *draw_set_color* and *draw_set_halign*. This can become very apparent when drawing strings on far sides of the screen. Make sure to align your text appropriately especially when using dynamic string elements (i.e., strings of varying lengths such as names).

```
draw_set_halign(fa_left); name="Mr Goober Doobie Woobie";
draw_text(20, 100, "Hello " + name);
// With this line the text to follow never overflows the screen
draw_set_halign(fa_right);
draw_text(940, 100, "Hello " + name);
```

Mind your depths and visibility. If you hear sounds and experience other actions from objects that are seemingly invisible, it's possible they are running at the wrong levels of depth. Remember, in GameMaker, object depths range between −16000 (the closest to the screen) and 16000 (the very bottom). Also, confirm that your objects' visible checkbox is ticked in the IDE.

Use inheritance in bigger projects. For cutting down development time, you can't beat inheritance. As previously discussed in the book, this technique lets you create parent objects with specific behaviors (e.g., movement and collisions) that are passed on to their "children." These child objects can then represent different variations of fundamentally the same kind of object. Think different types of foes, bonus items, or projectiles. This can greatly aid in the organization of your objects.

Use event descriptions to better organize your code. When you add a new event into an object, GameMaker populates its top two lines with the following:

```
/// @description Insert description here
// You can write your code in this editor
```

You can safely delete the second line but make sure you edit the first one to describe what your event is about. It is unhelpful to have, say, 12 Alarm events inside an object with no way of knowing what awaits inside them. So let's say you do indeed have an Alarm event that plays a silly sound effect every two seconds. Put this into the first line of the event:

```
/// @description Play silly sound effect
```

Doing this for all of the special events (i.e., alarms, user events, perhaps keyboard input, etc.) will ensure you will develop more efficiently, not constantly clicking on events to see what they are doing.

CHAPTER 9   DEBUGGING AND SHARING YOUR GAME

Confirm your game not working is not due to objects missing from a room. This happens. Remember to actually drag objects into rooms from the asset browser.

Deactivate instances whenever possible. The fewer active instances you have in a room, the smoother the proceedings will usually be. Under some scenarios, it's best to deactivate as many instances as you can without impacting gameplay. One such scenario is when you have games that use the camera system to follow an object.

To demonstrate this technique, a project by the name of *Instance Optimization* has been prepared for you. The project spawns 2300 rectangular instances of *obj_Thingy* and features a camera following a pair of cherries around. The room is 1920 × 1080 in size, and the main viewport comes in quaint 640 × 360. All instances of obj_Thingy not present in viewport zero (0) will be deactivated (see Figure 9-14).

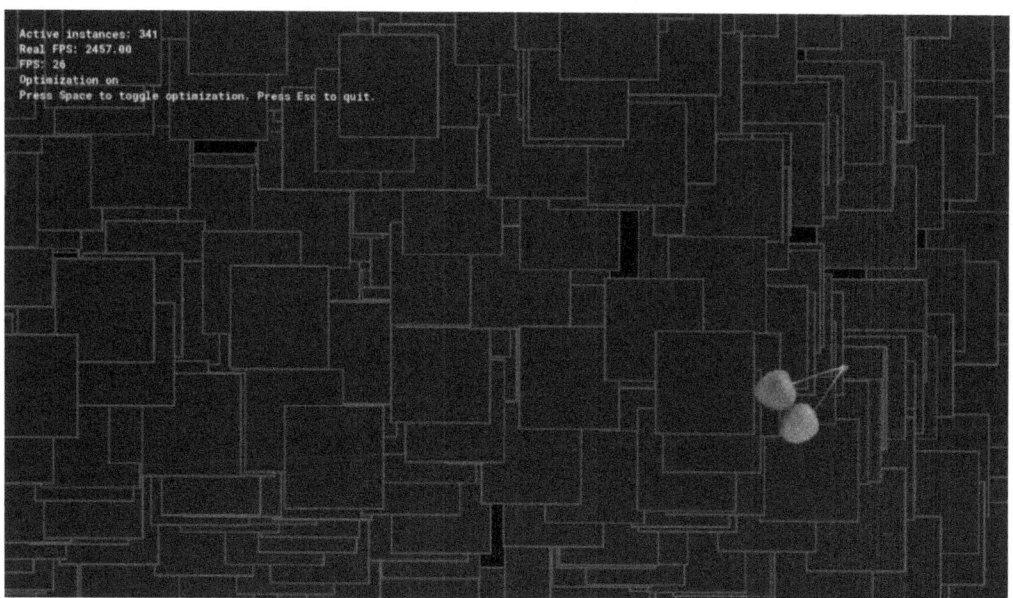

Figure 9-14. *A screenshot of Instance Optimization*

This project is available for download at the file repository for this book here:

https://github.com/Apress/Next-Generation-Gamemaking

The Step event of *obj_Controller* in this demonstration shows how we deactivate instances outside of the currently active view and reactivate them as they enter it. First, a Boolean variable called *is_optimized* is used to gauge if the optimization has been switched on or not. In this example, this variable is toggled using the space bar in a separate event. Now, let us gaze upon the Step event:

```
// STEP
// Deactivate all instances of obj_Thingy
if is_optimized { instance_deactivate_object(obj_Thingy);

// Get properties for camera 0 (set up in the IDE)
var view_x = camera_get_view_x(view_camera[0]);
var view_y = camera_get_view_y(view_camera[0]);
var view_width = camera_get_view_width(view_camera[0]);
var view_height = camera_get_view_height(view_camera[0]);

// Reactivate instances of obj_Thingy inside camera view 0
instance_activate_region(view_x, view_y, view_width, view_height, true);
} else instance_activate_all();
```

The above event has two functions you should become familiar with: *instance_deactivate_object* and *instance_activate_region*. The latter takes four camera parameters and a Boolean for either "inside" or "outside." In this example, this is set to inside with a "true." If set to "false," the function will deactivate instances outside of a specified region.

The demonstration displays two variables: *fps* and *fps_real*. Let us discuss the difference between them which gets often confused. The latter is the number of CPU steps that GameMaker completes rendering in a second. Real_fps is a continuous approximation calculated based on the time (in milli- or microseconds) between steps. It is typically a lot larger than fps, which refers to the amount of steps GameMaker is set to ideally complete per second, usually set to 60. If fps_real gets less than fps, your game will begin to show signs of slowdown.

On a mid-tier video card,[6] this presentation should give you about 2200 real fps when the optimizations are enabled and way less than 1900 when they are not.

As previously mentioned, the viewport size in this demonstration is 640 × 360. If we were to halve this to 320 × 180, you will see a major jump up in real_fps (when optimization is turned on). The smaller the viewport, the greater the amount of inactive instances. This results in even better rendering performance when it comes to real_fps using this method of optimization.

Locate things anywhere using Search and Replace. You can find specific variables, functions, and other statements stored anywhere inside your project with this great feature. This is something that becomes increasingly important as your projects grow in

---

[6] This refers to cards like the AMD RX6600 or an Nvidia 3060.

size. You can access this feature by navigating to *Edit* ▶ *Search & Replace* or by pressing Shift + Ctrl + F. Not only can you locate code this way, but you can also replace parts of it as needed (see Figure 9-15).

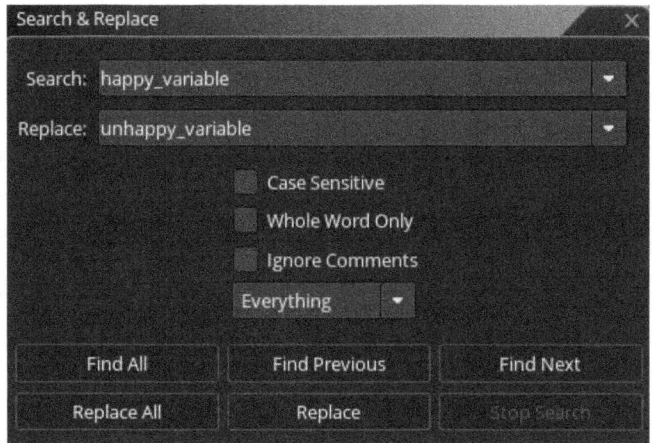

Figure 9-15. The Search & Replace window in GameMaker

GameMaker Debugger Basics

GameMaker has a dedicated tool for highlighting your games' potential issues. The mighty *Debugger* is activated by clicking the bug icon in the toolbar next to the play button (or by pressing F6). Your game will then execute with GameMaker's debugging features enabled.

For beginners, perhaps the most important feature of the debugger is the *profiler*. This tool shows you some important metrics about your game, including the number of calls being made for different actions/functions inside specific events. An unusually large number of calls indicates optimization is in order for that particular segment of your project. You activate the profiler by starting your game in debugging mode and navigating to the section called *Others* and clicking *Start Profiling* (see Figure 9-16).

CHAPTER 9   DEBUGGING AND SHARING YOUR GAME

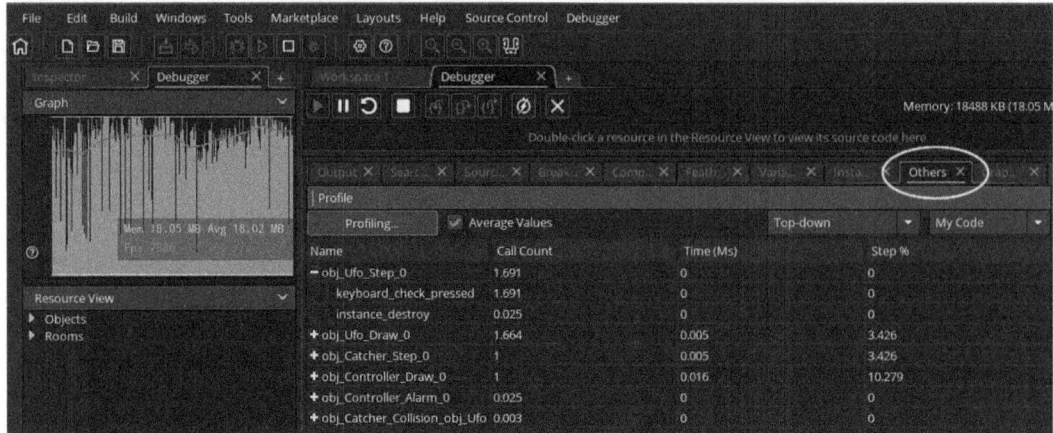

Figure 9-16. A view of the GameMaker profiler in action

The profiler presents data in the following four columns:

- **Name:** The event, script, or function being profiled. Double-clicking a name opens its code in the Source window. Clicking the column header sorts names alphabetically.

- **Calls:** Displays the total (or average) number of times a script, function, or event has been executed since profiling started. Large numbers in this column may warrant optimizations on the affected resource.

- **Time:** Shows total or average execution time. This helps you see which parts of your game are taking the most time to process, so you can fix the problematic code causing the lagging.

- **Step %:** Shows how much time a specific event, script, or function takes up within one game step. Even normal drawing operations tend to be heavy on the system. But if other types of scripts or functions show a high Step %, it means they need to be optimized.

Keeping an Eye on RAM and FPS

The section labeled *graph* in the debugger (also visible in Figure 9-16) displays how much system memory (RAM) is being used and a game's average (and current) frames per second (FPS). Basically, graph shows how your game's performance changes over time. Pairing the average PC with a fairly simple GameMaker game should get you an fps value of a couple thousand at least. Remember: an fps of a mere 60 is considered acceptable.

Dramatic drops in fps and increased memory use indicate issues. Graph is most useful for exposing problematic patterns in your games stemming from poorly optimized scripts or perhaps an excess of instances in a room.

Watching Your Variables

With the debugger, you can lend a close eye to specific variables. You do this by navigating to the tab titled *Variables* and clicking *Add new watch* (see Figure 9-17).

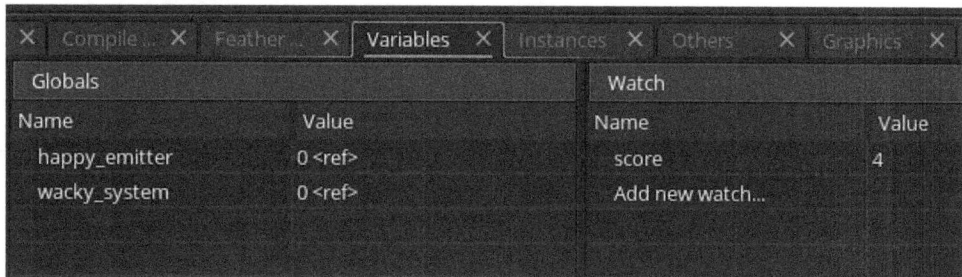

Figure 9-17. The Variables window in the GameMaker debugger where a variable called "score" is under close scrutiny

This is a great way to get to the root of some problems, such as a score counter (or gold, or health, etc.) not changing when it's intended to. You can also watch several variables at once to solve more complex issues.

CHAPTER 9   DEBUGGING AND SHARING YOUR GAME

Breakpoints

Breakpoints in GameMaker's debugger pause the flow of your game at specific points. They let you check what's happening in your game when it comes to variables and other elements at exact moments of your choosing. Breakpoints are added by first navigating to the object event of your choice and the exact line of GML you wish to pause your game at. You can then either right-click on the line and choose *Toggle Breakpoint* or simply press F9 (see Figure 9-18).

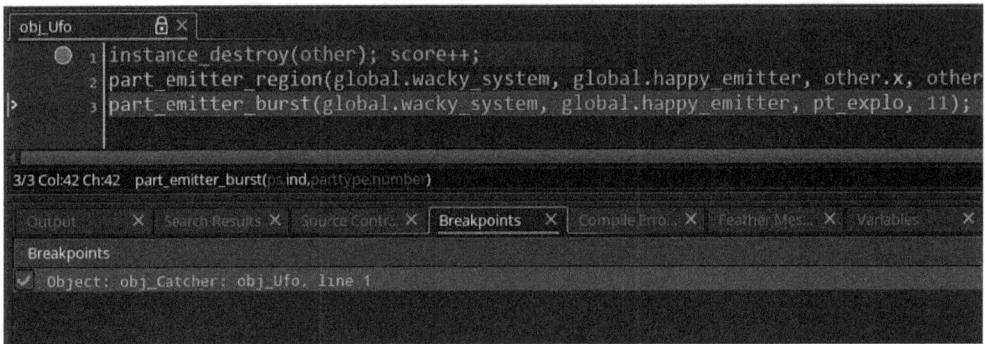

Figure 9-18. *A Collision event between obj_Catcher and obj_Ufo inside the former. A breakpoint has been set on the first line of this event as denoted by a red sphere*

When using this feature, start with a single breakpoint in a specific spot where a problem seems to persist. Combine this approach with the Variables window to monitor your variables when the game is paused. Disable breakpoints (right-click to toggle breakpoint or press F9) when you're done to avoid unnecessary pauses. Setting too many breakpoints at once can make debugging needlessly complicated.

When attempting to debug, please remember to start your game using the bug icon or by pressing F6. Otherwise, the debugging features do not work.

Implementing Touch-Screen Controls

Before we end this chapter, we shall tackle a most important topic: how touch-screen controls are implemented in GameMaker. These consist of specific events found inside the IDE under the group labeled *Gesture*. They are further grouped in two varieties: local (affecting specific objects) and global (affecting the entire screen). See Table 9-1 for some of the most commonly used gestures.

CHAPTER 9 DEBUGGING AND SHARING YOUR GAME

Table 9-1. *Some commonly used events when implementing controls for mobile games in GameMaker*

Gesture > Global > Tap	Detect a tap anywhere on the screen.
Gesture > Global > Double Tap	Detect a double tap anywhere on the screen.
Gesture > Tap	Detect a tap on a specific object.
Gesture > Double Tap	Detect a double tap on a specific object.
Gesture > Drag Start	Triggered when a player taps an object and maintains pressure.
Gesture > Dragging	Triggered for every step that the drag position changes above a default minimum threshold of 0.1 inches.
Gesture > Drag End	Triggered when the user releases the touch, but only if a Drag Start event has been previously triggered.

Again, gestures are added just like any other events in the GameMaker IDE (see Figure 9-19).

Figure 9-19. *Gesture events in the GameMaker IDE*

345

CHAPTER 9   DEBUGGING AND SHARING YOUR GAME

GameMaker gestures use a DS map by the name of *event_data* to store gesture-related properties. See Table 9-2 for some pertinent variables found inside event_data.

Table 9-2. *Some important elements of the event_data DS map used with gestures*

Element	Description	Example syntax
posX	The horizontal position of the touch/tap.	happyX = event_data[? "**posX**"];
posY	The vertical position of the touch/tap.	happyY = event_data[? "**posY**"];
isflick	Returns a "1" (true) if the end of the drag is detected as a flick. Only used in the Drag End event.	Flicked = event_data[? "**isflick**"];
diffX	The horizontal difference between the position of the current touch and the position of the last touch in a gesture.	flickX = event_data[? "**diffX**"];
diffY	The vertical difference between the position of the current touch and the position of the last touch in a gesture.	flickY = event_data[? "**diffY**"];

If you deploy a mobile project as a desktop title later on, be aware that Gesture events can also be triggered by mouse actions. Clicks of the left mouse button simulate taps. You can also perform flicks and dragging behaviors with the mouse.

Now, let's say we have an object called *obj_MobileTomato*. To make it teleport to a position set by a tap on a touch-screen, all we need is the following code in a single Global Tap event:

```
// Global Tap
// Define variables for fetching tap position x and y
var touch_x = event_data[? "posX"];
var touch_y = event_data[? "posY"];

// Move the object to the touch position
x = touch_x;
y = touch_y;
```

GameMaker's Double Tap events detect rapid, successive taps/clicks typically within a very short time window.

Let us next take a peek at how to implement dragging behavior with Gesture events. This refers to a player pressing down on an object, moving it around while still applying pressure, and finally letting go of the screen (or left mouse button). We can do all this by using four events, namely, Create, Drag Start, Dragging, and Drag End:

```
// Create
is_dragging = false; // Create a variable to track dragging-status

// Drag Start
is_dragging = true;

// Dragging
if is_dragging {
    x = mouse_x;
    y = mouse_y;
}

// Drag End
is_dragging = false;
```

Gesture events aside, mobile games are made with GameMaker the exact same way as desktop projects. Mobile games, too, can use the physics system (as discussed in Chapter 7) and all the other great features of the software.

In Closing

In this chapter, we discussed the following topics:

- Deployment for Windows, Linux, the Apple ecosystem, and others
- Setting up GameMaker for YYC output
- The main features of GameMaker's debugging framework, including breakpoints

CHAPTER 9 DEBUGGING AND SHARING YOUR GAME

- Game optimization techniques
- The implementation of basic touch-screen controls

The final chapter contains more merrymaking in the form of additional techniques for many of the topics featured so far in this book. We shall also explore a most jolly genre of games: the platformer.

CHAPTER 10

Assorted Superior Techniques

The final chapter of the book will expand on a number of topics mentioned so far and also introduce brand-new techniques. We will take a thorough look at blend modes, surfaces, and the many lesser known object events of GameMaker. As always, a number of downloadable projects will be served to demonstrate these techniques.

Before we get down to business with these topics, we shall tackle a most delightful genre of games: the beloved platformer.

Platformer Prototype

One immensely popular type of game is indeed the platformer. Think classic 2D franchises like *Super Mario Bros, Sonic the Hedgehog,* and more recently games like *Cuphead.* To demonstrate how this genre of games can be approached with GameMaker, we have *Platformer Prototype.* This project has the following features:

- Character walking and jumping mechanics
- Collisions with the environment, including moving platforms and foes
- A basic foe (*obj_MovingFoe*) that does not get stuck, falls down with simulated gravity, and changes direction upon horizontal collision with the environment
- Enemy generator objects, teleportation, and coin collecting
- The ability to bounce on top of enemies to destroy them

CHAPTER 10 ASSORTED SUPERIOR TECHNIQUES

- A basic camera setup created within the GameMaker IDE that follows the player
- A health bar for the player

All of the projects mentioned in this chapter are available from the following link:

https://github.com/Apress/Next-Generation-Gamemaking

Now, Platformer Prototype is intended to give you a starting point for making platformers of your own; its resources are intentionally sparse (see Figure 10-1).

Figure 10-1. *A screenshot of Platformer Prototype. Even when surrounded with dastardly foes, our protagonist maintains a stern, but wise gaze.*

You are advised to use your growing knowledge of games making to implement additional features. These might include some of the following:

- First aid kits (for which a starting point is included in the project file)
- Character death and game over
- A selection of connected levels in separate rooms (think functions like *room_goto* or *room_goto_next*)
- A more varied set of foes
- Title screens, sound effects, and custom particle effects

CHAPTER 10   ASSORTED SUPERIOR TECHNIQUES

Let us next go through some of the object events found in Platform Prototype. We'll begin with the object representing the player.

obj_Player

By the time we peek into its Step event, obj_Player is the most complicated one in the project. However, its Create event is fairly basic as we simply define some pertinent properties like this:

```
// CREATE
hsp = 0; // Horizontal speed holding variable
vsp = 0; // Vertical speed holding variable
move_speed = 4; // Movement speed
jump_speed = -10; // Jump speed
grav = 0.5; // Gravity
health_points = 100; // Player health
window_set_cursor(cr_none); // Disable mouse cursor
```

Adjustments to these properties will have an immediate effect on the game's proceedings, especially when it comes to the variables *move_speed* and *jump_speed*. The duo of *hsp* and *vsp* are temporary holding variables for horizontal and vertical velocity, respectively; their values are calculated and applied during the gameloop.

The Step Event of obj_Player

This rather busy event contains most of the mechanics of this prototype. Let us go through it block by block. First, we have the keyboard controls. These are implemented using the function *keyboard_check* for horizontal movement and *keyboard_check_pressed* for jumping.

```
// STEP
// Get right/left input
var move = keyboard_check(ord("D")) - keyboard_check(ord("A"));
hsp = move * move_speed; // Set base horizontal speed
// Jumping
```

CHAPTER 10　ASSORTED SUPERIOR TECHNIQUES

```
if keyboard_check_pressed(vk_space) && (place_meeting(x, y + 1, obj_
platform) || place_meeting(x, y + 1, obj_MovingPlatform)) {
// A sound effect might be most suitable here..
    vsp = jump_speed; // Jump if on any platform
}
```

A jump is only allowed to execute if the player is standing on a static or moving obstacle, as gauged by the function *place_meeting*. Otherwise, some strange mid-flight aerobatics might take place and ruin the mechanic completely.

Next we have a more simple section for changing sprites under specific conditions. The player only has two sprite resources: *spr_Player* with its four frames of animation and *spr_Jump* with its one. When the player's horizontal speed reaches zero, we display only the first frame of spr_Player. When there's more horizontal velocity, we animate the four frames at 40% speed. In addition, whenever a player is jumping (as gauged by their vertical speed), we switch sprites to spr_Jump. Also, in this section, we apply gravity on the player.

```
// Sprite handling
if hsp == 0 { // Gauge horizontal speed
    image_index = 0; // Idle sprite
} else {
    image_speed = 0.4; // Animate at 40% speed when moving
}
if vsp < 0 { // Gauge vertical speed
    sprite_index = spr_Jump; // Jump sprite
} else {
    sprite_index = spr_Player; // Default sprite
}
vsp += grav; // Apply gravity to vertical speed
```

What follows are a number of collision checks. The first one of these tracks if the player is standing on a moving platform in order to make the player ride on it. A great function by the name of *instance_place* (to be discussed later) is used for fetching properties from any instances of *obj_MovingPlatform* colliding with the player.

```
// Check if obj_Player is on top of a moving platform
var platform = instance_place(x, y + 8, obj_MovingPlatform);
```

CHAPTER 10 ASSORTED SUPERIOR TECHNIQUES

```
if platform != noone && vsp >= 0 { // Only apply if falling or stationary
    if x > platform.bbox_left + 2 && x < platform.bbox_right - 2 {
        x += platform.hspeed; // Move with platform
    }
}
```

The two properties named *bbox_left* and *bbox_right* refer to *bounding boxes*. These are read-only variables that return the position of the left and right hand bounding boxes for an instance, as defined by its sprite. In the above snippet, we make sure that the object is within these horizontal bounds of the platform with a small margin of two (2) pixels on either side.

Next we have three somewhat similar collision checks.

```
// Horizontal collision with static platforms
if place_meeting(x + hsp, y, obj_platform) {
    while !place_meeting(x + sign(hsp), y, obj_platform) {
        x += sign(hsp);
    }
    hsp = 0;
}
// Vertical collision with static platforms
if place_meeting(x, y + vsp, obj_platform) {
    while !place_meeting(x, y + sign(vsp), obj_platform) {
        y += sign(vsp);
    }
    vsp = 0;
}
// Vertical collision with moving platform
if place_meeting(x, y + vsp, obj_MovingPlatform) {
    while !place_meeting(x, y + sign(vsp), obj_MovingPlatform) {
        y += sign(vsp);
    }
    vsp = 0;
}
```

CHAPTER 10   ASSORTED SUPERIOR TECHNIQUES

You may have noticed a function called *sign* in the above segment. It is used to determine whether a given number is positive, negative, or zero. For example, the statement *sign(hsp)*[1] returns 1 if you're moving right, −1 if moving left, and 0 if stationary.

If a collision is detected (using place_meeting), *obj_Player* is moved one pixel at a time toward the platform in the direction of movement until it is right next to the platform but never overlapping it. This is done using a while loop which ensures *obj_Player* stops just before the collision would occur. This prevents it from getting stuck inside the platform and ensures pixel-perfect collision detection.

Now, obj_Player's Step event continues with the incrementation of x with hsp and y with vsp to create horizontal and vertical movement, respectively.

```
// Apply hsp and vsp to x and y to move player
x += hsp;
y += vsp;
// Horizontal enemy/hazard zone collision
if place_meeting(x, y, obj_Hazard) health_points--; // Lose health
// Check if player is on top of a foe (i.e. the jump attack)
var foe = instance_place(x, y + 12, obj_MovingFoe);
// Confirm player is above foe's top edge
if foe != noone && vsp >= 0 && y <= foe.bbox_top + 4 {
    foe.Health--; // Reduce enemy health
    vsp = jump_speed * 0.8; // Jump with 80% strength when on top
    // Maybe make a better hit-effect?
    effect_create_above(ef_ring, foe.x, foe.y, 1, c_yellow);
    // Also add a sound effect?
}
```

The previous segment of code introduces the attack mechanic familiar from many classic platformers. We leverage instance_place again, this time to gauge when the player is on top of a foe (i.e., an instance of obj_MovingFoe). If this is indeed the case, we make

---

[1] Like you probably remember, *hsp* is a custom variable which is used for horizontal movement in this demonstration. Its vertical counterpart is called *vsp*.

the player jump/bounce; the foe's life variable is also reduced by one unit. Variable *Health* is defined in the Create event of *obj_MovingFoe* and is set to three (3) by default. This means an instance of obj_MovingFoe takes three successful jump attacks to destroy.

A jumping attack does no harm to the player. Only horizontal contact with foes does and this mechanic is implemented with the following line: *if place_meeting(x, y, obj_Hazard) health_points--*. A simple place_meeting is all that takes.

On instance_place

A function called *instance_place* offers more thorough collision mechanics compared to *place_free* and *place_meeting*. Unlike those two, instance_place can be used to access some specific properties inside a specific instance of an object. The duo of *place_free* and *place_meeting* can merely return a Boolean in regard to collisions (i.e., true or false). Also, unlike *place_free*, instance_place is not limited to solid objects. It works with any specified object type.

Implementing instance_place basically needs three steps. First, we need to assign it with a (temporary) variable. This variable is then compared against the keyword *noone* (as in "no one") which in this context represents a scenario where no collisions occur with the instances in question. Thirdly, we get to manipulate the variables inside specific instances or trigger events inside them. The formula for using instance_place is as follows:

```
var something_neat = instance_place(x, y, obj_Something); // Step 1
if something_neat != noone { // Step 2
// If a collision with obj_Something occurs i.e. if something is NOT noone
// Step 3
something_neat.happiness++; // Perform an action for this "something"
}
```

Making Levels for Platformers

The map in Platform Prototype was plotted inside the room editor with the standard 32 × 32 grid switched on (see Figure 10-2).

CHAPTER 10   ASSORTED SUPERIOR TECHNIQUES

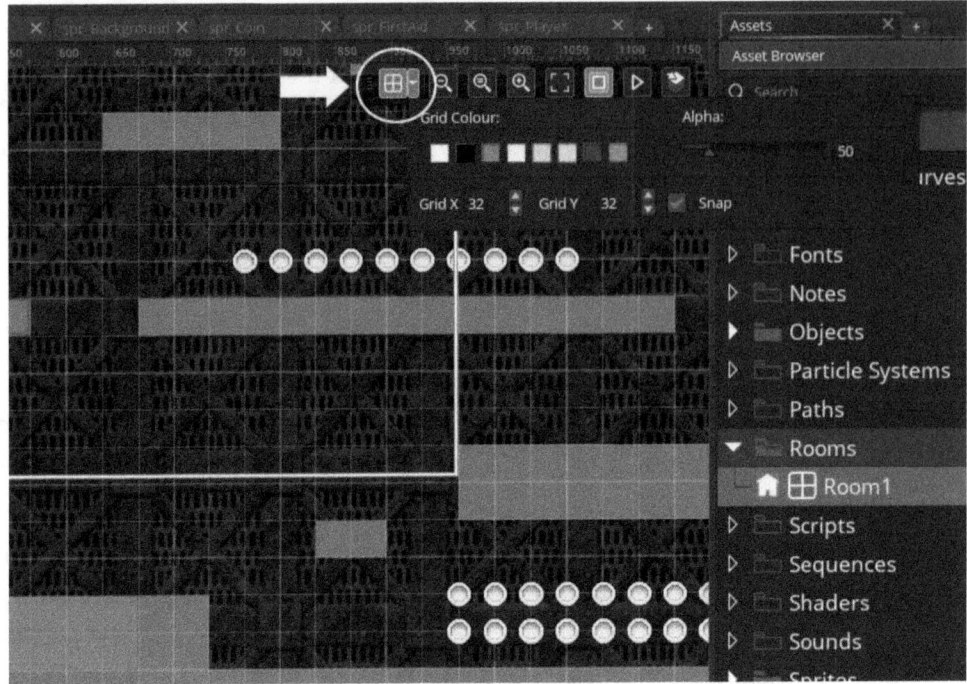

Figure 10-2. The grid controls in the GameMaker room editor

Dragging instances of obj_Platform into the room editor from the asset browser is a simple enough task; you can also resize them vertically or horizontally to create longer and wider blocks. To resize instances in the room editor, you move the mouse cursor to the edge of an instance until it turns into a variety of arrow icons. You can then simply click and drag the object to resize it.

GameMaker Blend Modes

Basically, *blend modes* are ways to manipulate the red, green, blue, and alpha (RGBA) components of visual assets using a source and a destination. They draw things blended with whatever else is already drawn beforehand. By default, GameMaker draws everything using a blend mode called *bm_normal*. This simply reproduces a visual asset on-screen the way it is stored. Other basic blend modes include *bm_add, bm_max,* and *bm_subtract* which will be discussed next.

- **bm_add** combines source and destination colors in an "additive" manner. Visuals drawn in this blend mode are often bright and high in contrast. They are often used for dramatic effects like lights, sci-fi projectiles, or holographic projections.

- **bm_max** takes the maximum value of source and destination components. It can amplify color intensity in overlapping regions, such as when used for particle-based explosions and other such effects. In sprites, it can introduce useful degrees of transparency, turning a solid-looking object less opaque.

- **bm_subtract** removes the source pixel's RGBA values from the destination pixel's values. This mode is typically used for shadows and only works well when drawing on top of something that has clearly visible colors.

See Table 10-1 for the equations in play for calculating the final output of each blend mode.

Table 10-1. GameMaker's blend mode formulas

bm_normal	Result = (Source * SourceAlpha) + (Destination * (1 - SourceAlpha))
bm_add	Result = (Source * SourceAlpha) + Destination
bm_max	Result = max(Source, Destination)[2]
bm_subtract	Result = Destination - (Source * SourceAlpha)

Using Blend Modes in GML

A blend mode is activated in GameMaker using the function *gpu_set_blendmode*. If you were to use, say, additive drawing, you would type in *gpu_set_blendmode(bm_additive)* into a Draw event.

---

[2] The function *max* applied to each individual colour channel (i.e., RGBA), simply takes the greater value between the source pixel's channel and the destination pixel's channel.

We can use blend modes on any visual element. The simplest way to use one would be something like the following when drawing a sprite:

```
// DRAW
gpu_set_blendmode(bm_additive);
draw_self();
gpu_set_blendmode(bm_normal);
```

When you are finished drawing in a special blend mode, please remember to switch back to **bm_normal** or your game will probably end up looking a tad too psychedelic.

Wacky Blend Modes

A project has been prepared for you to see GameMaker's basic blend modes in action. There are two rooms in *Wacky Blend Modes*. The first room in this presentation demonstrates four blend modes over two different backgrounds. You can move shapes and sprites around with your mouse. Use the mouse buttons to cycle the colours of the circles[3] used with bm_subtract and bm_max. Pressing the Space key changes the backdrop and the Enter key switches rooms (see Figure 10-3).

---

[3] With most blend modes, the color of the shape being drawn (e.g., circle, rectangle, line) is of utmost importance for the end result.

CHAPTER 10 ASSORTED SUPERIOR TECHNIQUES

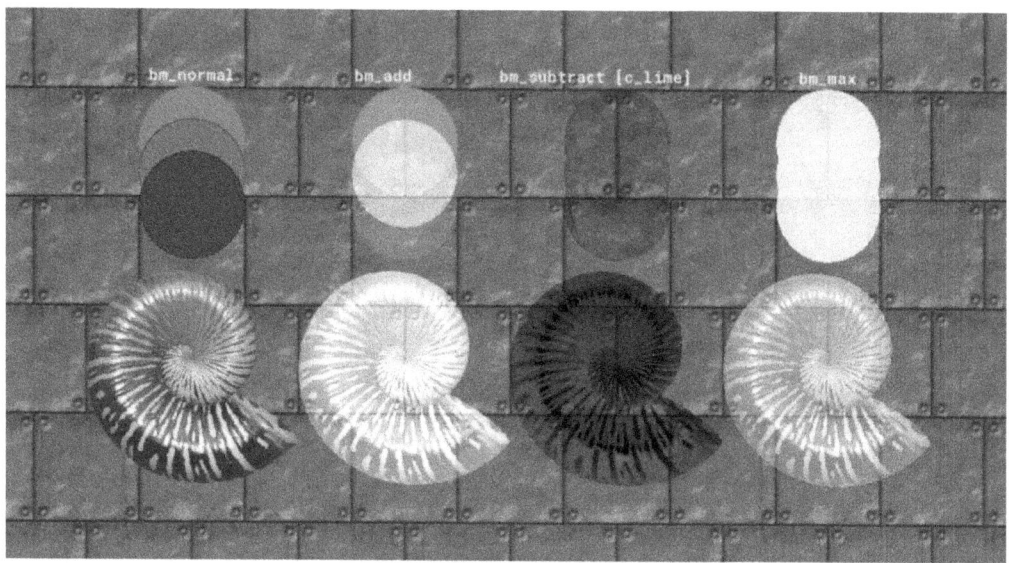

Figure 10-3. *A screenshot of Wacky Blend Modes with its assortment of circles and seashells*

Two More Fascinating Blend Modes

The blend modes in GameMaker do not stop at the four previously mentioned. We also have *bm_reverse_subtract* and *bm_min*. The second room of Wacky Blend Modes introduces these to us in the form of a mouse controlled section of the screen (see Figure 10-4).

CHAPTER 10 ASSORTED SUPERIOR TECHNIQUES

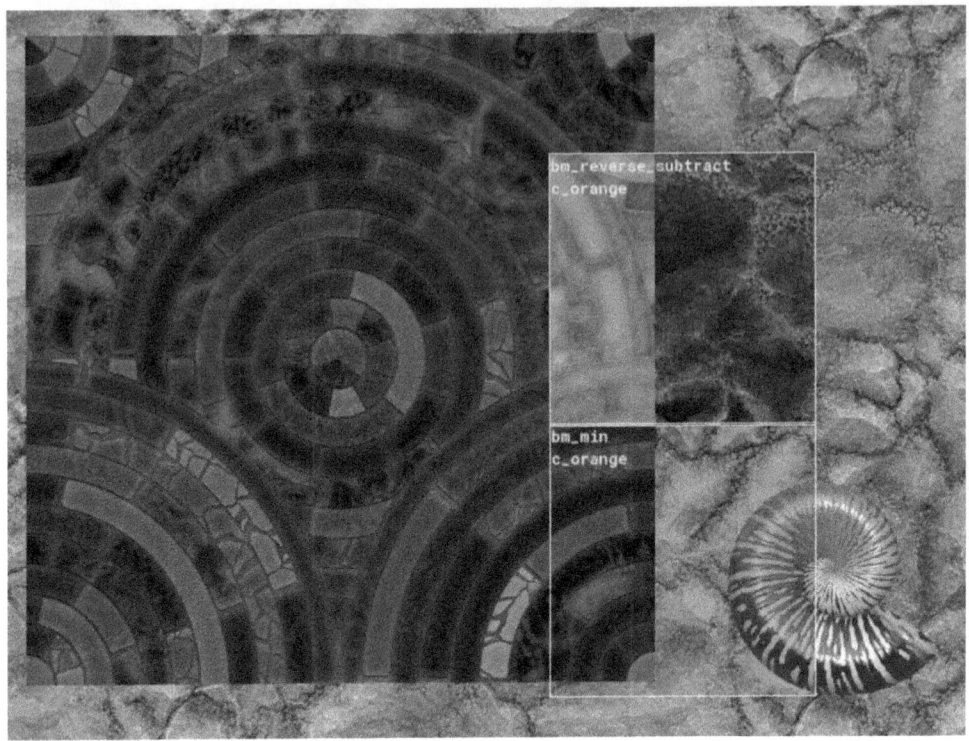

Figure 10-4. *The second room of Wacky Blend Modes*

Basically, bm_min will make things darker. If you draw a darker color over a lighter one, the dimmer color will persist for those channels (i.e., red, green, blue).

The rather quirky blend mode called bm_reverse_subtract has its uses. Using it can result in startling and visually complex results when applied to particles, for one. It can also provide a glitchy look which may be appropriate for some scenarios. This blend mode will also alter the look of most types of in-game terrain in interesting ways (see Table 10-2).

Table 10-2. *More GameMaker's blend mode formulas*

bm_min	Result = min(Source, Destination)
bm_reverse_subtract	Result = max(0, Source - Destination)

Optimizing Blend Modes

As mentioned previously in the book, blend modes are best used sparingly. Your games experience a minor slowdown every time you change a blend mode. However, these can add up quickly for some major issues. The best way to optimize blend modes is to group them in an effective way to reduce drawing calls. Let us explore the wrong and right way to do this with Table 10-3.

Table 10-3. An example of grouping blend modes

Wrong	Right (grouped)

gpu_set_blendmode(**bm_add**);
draw_text(20, 20, "Hello!");
gpu_set_blendmode(**bm_normal**);
draw_text(20, 40, "Greetings!");
gpu_set_blendmode(**bm_add**);
draw_text(20, 60, "Good evening!");
gpu_set_blendmode(**bm_normal**);
draw_text(20, 80, "Hi!");
	gpu_set_blendmode(**bm_add**);
	draw_text(20, 20, "Hello!");
	draw_text(20, 60, "Good evening!");
	gpu_set_blendmode(**bm_normal**);
	draw_text(20, 40, "Greetings!");
	draw_text(20, 80, "Hi!");

Use gpu_set_blendmode as infrequently as you can. Often the cosmetics it can bring may not be worth the computational costs. To err on the side of caution, limit your use of blend modes for presentation outside of the gameloop and have them enhance things like title screens.

We shall now move on to the next topic: GameMaker's amazing surfaces. A *surface* (as mentioned in Chapter 3) is a texture in video memory which is not displayed on-screen until you're ready to make it happen. Surfaces allow you to composite graphics before displaying them.

Surface Tomfoolery

Let us jump into the action and observe a project called *Surface Tomfoolery,* which demonstrates the following techniques:

- Creating two different surfaces with surface_create
- Drawing said surfaces with surface_draw and surface_draw_ext

CHAPTER 10   ASSORTED SUPERIOR TECHNIQUES

- Using blend modes with surfaces
- Removing surfaces from memory when no longer needed with surface_free

The program displays the sprite of a seashell (i.e., *Sprite1*) and overlays it with two different surfaces. One of these (i.e., surf_one) represents an orange glow while the other (i.e., surf_two) is a simple line of text repeated thrice on top of the other visuals on-screen. You can press Space to toggle surf_one on and off. Pressing Escape will quit (see Figure 10-5).

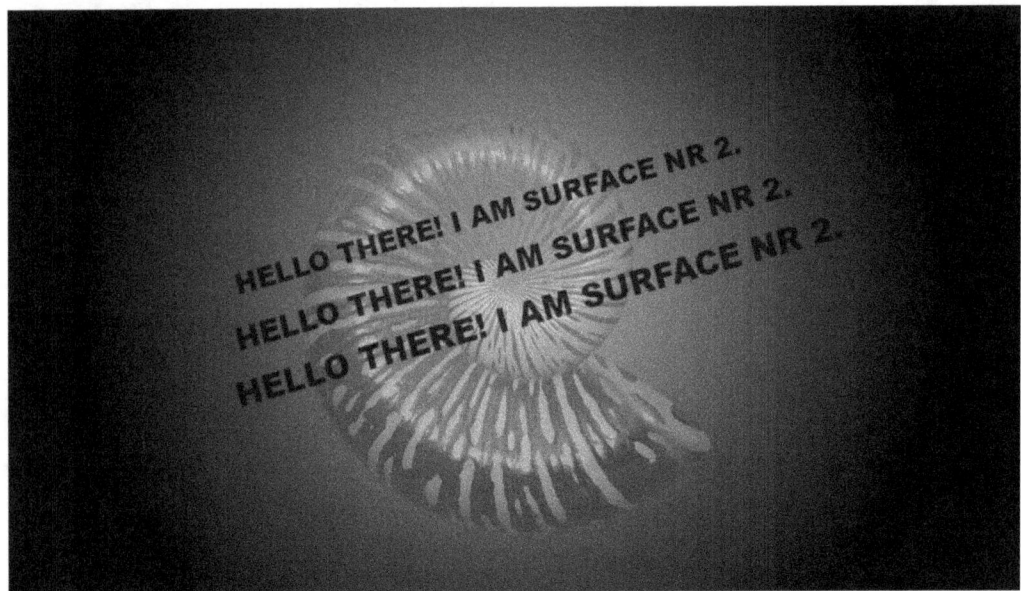

Figure 10-5. *A screenshot of Surface Tomfoolery. The first surface is the glow around the clamshell. The second surface, displayed three times, contains a brief informative message.*

Now, Figure 10-6 is there to represent the general four-stage workflow for surfaces in GameMaker and is worth taking a look at.

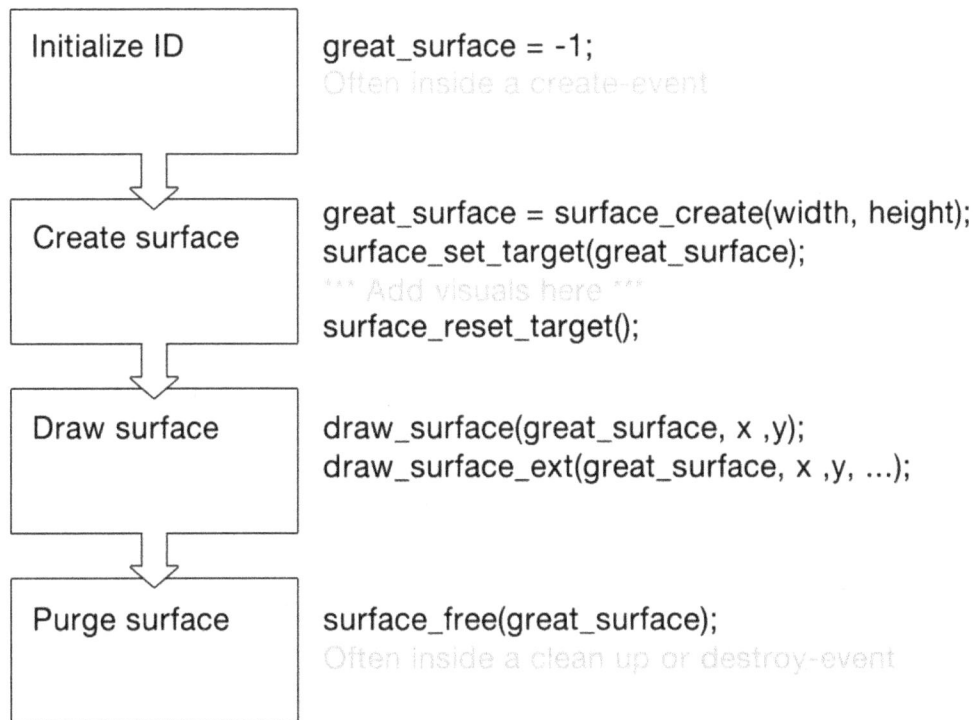

Figure 10-6. *The surface workflow in GameMaker*

Surface Tomfoolery has a single room with one object, which we shall examine next.

obj_SurfaceController

The two surfaces in the project, i.e., *surf_one* and *surf_two*, are composited in the Create event of obj_SurfaceController. Thus begins the Create event of the aforementioned object:

```
// CREATE
surf_one = -1; surf_two = -1; // Initialize surface IDs
surface_on = true; // Custom variable for displaying surface one
```

These are very important statements. We must first define empty IDs for the two surfaces to come (surf_one and surf_two) or there will be errors during runtime. Moving on we shall create the first surface and composite things on it without drawing anything on the screen right away. A number of functions related to surfaces will be unveiled.

```
// Check if surface exists, create if needed
if !surface_exists(surf_one) surf_one = surface_create(room_width, room_
height);
// Set surf_one as render target
surface_set_target(surf_one);
// Switch to additive blending
gpu_set_blendmode(bm_add);
// Draw a glowing circle
draw_circle_colour(x, y, 500, c_orange, c_black, false);
// Gradient from orange to black
// Switch to normal blending
gpu_set_blendmode(bm_normal);
// Draw a sprite
draw_sprite_ext(Sprite1, 0, x, y, 1, 1, 0, c_white, 0.3);
// Reset render target
surface_reset_target();
```

When creating a surface, we should always use surface_exist to check whether it has been already defined or not; this is just a good practice. The function used to actually create a surface, i.e., surface_create, has parameters for width and height in pixels.

To begin adding visuals to a surface, we issue a function by the name of surface_set_target. At this point, we draw the sprites and primitive shapes we want in our surface. When we are done adding visuals to it, we run a function called surface_reset_target. These two functions constitute a code block that basically sandwiches your visual assets. In Surface Tomfoolery, blend modes are summoned, too, which surfaces are perfectly capable of utilizing.

We next create the second, much more simple surface like this:

```
// CREATE SURFACE 2
// Check if surface exists, create if needed
if !surface_exists(surf_two) surf_two = surface_create(605, 85);
// Set surf_two as render target
surface_set_target(surf_two);
draw_set_font(Font1); draw_text(0, 0, "HELLO THERE! I AM SURFACE NR 2.");
surface_reset_target();
```

CHAPTER 10 ASSORTED SUPERIOR TECHNIQUES

As you can tell, this surface (i.e., surf_two) contains just a simple string of text.

Drawing Surfaces

Let us next observe how we can display our carefully prepared surfaces on the screen. In our demonstration, this is done inside the Draw event of obj_SurfaceController.

```
// DRAW
// Draw background sprite
draw_sprite(Sprite1, 0, x, y);
// Draw first surface if surface_on equals "true"
if surface_on draw_surface(surf_one, 0, 0);
// Draw second surface multiple times
// Draw it in black with slightly reduced opacity, enlarged gradually &
rotated by 15 degrees
for(var i=0; i<3; i++) {
draw_surface_ext(surf_two, 350, 60*i+330, 1+i*0.1,1+i*0.1,15,c_black,0.8);
}
```

The Draw event above displays the two surfaces using two different functions. First, we have the basic *draw_surface*. It takes a surface ID and xy coordinates as its only three parameters. This function is perfectly adequate for basic surface work.

The second surface in our demonstration uses a far more complicated function called *draw_surface_ext*. See Table 10-4 for a rundown on all of its parameters.

365

Table 10-4. *The eight parameters of the function draw_surface_ext*

draw_surface_ext(id, x, y, xscale, yscale, rot, col, alpha)	
surface ID	A previously arbitrarily defined surface identifier. In Surface Tomfoolery, this is *surf_two* which in this context refers to the second surface in the demonstration.
x	The horizontal position of the surface in pixels.
y	The vertical position of the surface in pixels.
x scale	The horizontal scale of the surface. A one (1) refers to the default scale.
y scale	The vertical scale of the surface. A one (1) refers to the default scale.
rotation	A degree of rotation for the surface.
color	A blending color for the surface. This parameter accepts GameMaker color constants like c_lime, c_red, etc. A value of c_white displays the surface in its original, uncolorized form.
alpha	The opacity of the surface to be displayed. A value of one (1) makes it fully visible. To make a surface half-transparent use a value of 0.5.

The same surface can be drawn on-screen several times and in different sizes and colors if we so desire. In our demonstration, we used a for loop to achieve some of this. The iterator variable "i" was fed into draw_surface_ext to change the scale of the surface being drawn during each iteration of the loop. You can naturally use more simple approaches in your surface workflow as well.

Using **draw_surface** or **draw_surface_ext** does not modify a surface in any way and it remains exactly as originally defined.

Tiled Backgrounds with Surfaces

Surfaces offer us a great way to make simple on-demand tiled visuals. Let's say we have defined a surface called *metallic_backdrop*. Let's assume this happens to be a representation of a metallic tile created using a sprite of a rather compact size. By adding the following single statement into an object's Draw event, we get a nice infinite horizontally and vertically tiled metallic background:

```
draw_surface_tiled(metallic_backdrop, 0, 0);
```

This function takes surface id, x, and y as its only parameters.

Secrets of the Application Surface

As mentioned way back in Chapter 3, the *application surface* is like the final canvas for displaying graphics in games made with GameMaker. It is automatically managed by the software by default and works fine most of the time. However, it can be manually disabled in order to unleash full manual control when it comes to screen scaling and special visual effects. Also, some more archaic hardware may struggle working with the application surface. You can use the following function to toggle it on and off:

```
// Set to "true" to enable and "false" to disable
application_surface_enable(true);
```

To check if the application surface is enabled, you can use a function called *application_surface_is_enabled* which returns "true" if it is and "false" if it is not. The following snippet does this check and toggles the application surface on or off depending on its state.

```
if application_surface_is_enabled()
{
    application_surface_enable(false);
}
else {
    application_surface_enable(true);
}
```

There's a function to enable or disable the automatic drawing of the (enabled) application surface, too, called *application_surface_draw_enable*. Please be aware that if you switch off the automatic drawing process and draw the application surface manually, you may experience issues with the alpha components of your games' visuals. To minimize this, you can turn off alpha blending using another function called *gpu_set_blendenable*.

```
application_surface_draw_enable(false); // Disable automatic drawing
gpu_set_blendenable(false); // Disable alpha blending
draw_surface(application_surface, 0, 0); // Draw application surface
gpu_set_blendenable(true); // Enable alpha blending
```

CHAPTER 10 ASSORTED SUPERIOR TECHNIQUES

More on GameMaker's Drawing Pipeline

Having only been previously mentioned in passing, this is a good spot to examine GameMaker's sequence of Draw events in more detail. The application surface has a lot to do with them, too.

1. **Predraw:** The application surface is created in this event (if it doesn't exist) and its render target is set. This is a suitable event for adjusting blend modes or for drawing something on the blank space underneath and next to views (if a camera system is in use).

2. **Draw begin:** Will let you draw things before/underneath whatever is drawn in the main Draw event. You can use draw begin to set up drawing-related properties, too, like color and opacity/alpha.

3. **Draw:** The main event for drawing all of your main sprites and/or primitive shapes; usually, you only need to use this one for most of your game actors.

4. **Draw end:** Draws things after the main Draw event. The application surface render target is also reset in this event.

5. **Postdraw:** The application surface is drawn to the display buffer by default here. Again, you can switch this off using *application_surface_draw_enable*. This is a useful event for adding effects on top of the object such as overlays, additional sprites, or postprocessing effects.

6. **Draw GUI begin**: This is the event for placing background elements for your GUI, such as primitive shapes (e.g., rectangles).

7. **Draw GUI:** Main GUI elements like text and icons go here.

8. **Draw GUI end:** In case you want to draw something on top of the other two GUI events, you can use this event.

CHAPTER 10 ASSORTED SUPERIOR TECHNIQUES

The Application Surface and GML

The application surface can be addressed in GML using the aptly named constant *application_surface*. Any surface-related function works with this constant. For one, we can resize this surface using *surface_resize* like this:

```
surface_resize(application_surface, 1280, 720); // 1280 x 720 pixels
```

The next statement resizes the application surface to the width and height of viewport zero (0):

```
surface_resize(application_surface, view_wport[0], view_hport[0]);
```

> The application surface should not be resized every frame (i.e., inside Draw events) as this is quite computationally intense.

The width and height of any surface, including the application surface, can be retrieved using the functions *surface_get_width* and *surface_get_height*.

If you ever want to display the dimensions of the current application surface, you can do something like this:

```
draw_text(20, 20, string(surface_get_width(application_surface)) + " x "
+ string(surface_get_height(application_surface)));
```

The Application Surface and Your GUI

There's a function called *display_set_gui_size* when you want a consistent GUI resolution (as created in the draw GUI event) across different display sizes or application surface resolutions. It affects how the GUI layer is scaled and displayed relative to the application surface. Let's say you wanted the game (i.e., what the application surface presents) at a full HD resolution and the GUI at plain HD resolution. You would simply add the following statements in an object's Create event:

```
surface_resize(application_surface, 1920, 1080); // Game at 1920x1080
display_set_gui_size(1280, 720); // GUI resolution at 1280x720
```

CHAPTER 10   ASSORTED SUPERIOR TECHNIQUES

Resizing Your Surfaces

Sometimes you need to resize your surfaces and for that we have a function called *surface_resize*. It takes three parameters: surface ID, width, and length. This function neither crops nor stretches a surface, but rather recreates it with the same ID. The surface will be initialized as blank and all the visuals need to be redrawn into it. The functions surface_resize and surface_create may seem similar since both can be used to define a surface. However, both have their unique uses. For one, other parts of your project may reference a specific surface ID. Recreating a surface by first destroying a surface (using surface_free) and recreating it with surface_create might disturb GameMaker's drawing pipeline. This can potentially cause crashes during runtime. Despite the somewhat clumsy workflow, resizing with surface_resize is optimized for scenarios where a surface ID is already defined and offers a touch of extra stability.

The application surface, too, is happy to work with **surface_resize**. Actually, the process of resizing this surface is far less complicated as GameMaker will automatically update its contents.

Taking Screenshots with Surfaces

Sometimes you want to be able to take in-game screenshots. This is easily done with a jolly function by the name of *surface_save* and feeding it some delicious application_surface. The function takes just two parameters: the surface ID and a filename.

```
surface_save(application_surface, "happy_screen.png");
```

The function saves an image of a game's proceedings in the png format. These screenshots will be saved into the following locations:

- **Windows:** C:\Users\<Username>\AppData\Local\<GameName>
- **macOS:** ~/Library/Application Support/<GameName>
- **Linux:** ~/.local/share/<GameName>

Surfaces Summarized

Although not absolutely necessary for games, the correct use of GameMaker's surfaces can add a smidgen of class to any project. For one, we can create complicated, dynamically crafted scenes onto a surface with minimal processing overhead. In some cases, we can decrease the computational costs of having hundreds of static object instances and display them as a single surface instead.

Please remember that if a game window loses focus or is minimized (such as Alt+Tabbing to a different application on Windows) a surface might actually vanish. They are stored in graphics memory[4] which makes them susceptible to being overwritten by other graphics data. For this reason, you should always use the fail-safe function *surface_exists* before drawing your surfaces on-screen. Also, if you need to summon surface_resize during runtime keep in mind you need to recreate the surface's visuals as this function erases them prior to resizing the surface.

The *application surface* is the final canvas for displaying graphics. It is automatically managed by GameMaker by default and works fine most of the time. Some developers may want to switch to manual control of the application surface for specific purposes; thankfully GameMaker allows for this, too.

Let us next recap the GML associated with this topic. You will find some of the most important surface-related functions in Table 10-5.

Table 10-5. *Ten prominent functions for surface manipulation in GML*

surface_exists(id)	draw_surface(id, x, y)
surface_create(id, width, length)	draw_surface_ext(id, x, y, xscale, yscale, angle, colour, alpha)
surface_set_target(id)	draw_surface_tiled(id, x, y)
surface_reset_target()	surface_free(id)
surface_resize(id, width, length)	surface_save(id, filename)

---

[4] Graphics memory is found on your GPU/video card, or in the case of integrated video cards, shared with system RAM. As of 2025, most GPUs have 8 gigabytes or more of video memory.

CHAPTER 10   ASSORTED SUPERIOR TECHNIQUES

We shall now leave surfaces behind and start covering the many object events not yet discussed in this book.

On User Events

GameMaker's *User Events* consist of 16 custom events that you can define and trigger manually with your code. They are found by navigating to *Add Event* ➤ *Other* ➤ *User Events*. While not mandatory, using these events can make recurrent tasks easy to get carried out. They are triggered from inside other events (e.g., step) using the function *event_user*. For example, the following statement triggers user event number one:

event_user(0);

GameMaker's 16 user events are numbered between 0 and 15.

Let's see a slightly more elaborate example of user events:

```
// STEP
if keyboard_check_pressed(vk_space) { // when space-key is pressed..
    event_user(0); // Call user event 0 i.e. the first event
    event_user(1); // Call second user event (1) as well
}
// USER EVENT 0
hspeed *= 2; // Double the object's horizontal speed
audio_play_sound(Booster,1,false); // Play a sound effect
// USER EVENT 1
global.fuel--; // Manipulate some variables
damage += 3;
```

User events may come in handy when you need to execute specific, often repeating actions during particular moments. This can range from playing sound effects to having an object perform some acrobatics called from within its other events (e.g., step or collision). Also, if multiple objects need to engage in similar behavior, you can define user events in a parent object and have its children inherit these events.

At best user events can cut down development time here and there. Be aware that you cannot directly draw anything from inside user events: functions like draw_text won't work inside of them.

Step Begin vs. Step vs. End Step

Let us now address the trio of Step events. Most of the time, the plain Step event is enough even for moderately complicated games. The other two still have their uses. Step begin can be used to influence an object's position or other properties before movement is applied. The end Step event can be used to prevent a player's movement through obstacles after movement; it lets you react to the results of the plain Step event's logic. If you experience strange collision behavior when working with place_meeting and other such functions, try setting your clamping/limiting into the end Step event. Drawing visuals in GameMaker is resumed right after this event.

Using all three Step events might look something like this:

```
// STEP BEGIN
// Reset movement speed
horizontal_speed = 0; vertical_speed = 0;
// STEP
// Update movement based on input
horizontal_speed = keyboard_check(ord("D")) - keyboard_check(ord("D")) * 4;
vertical_speed = keyboard_check(ord("S")) - keyboard_check(ord("W")) * 4;
x += horizontal_speed; y += vertical_speed;
// END STEP
// Limit x and y inside the room
x = clamp(x, 0, room_width);
y = clamp(y, 0, room_height);
```

Outside View and Intersect View

There are two categories of view-related events to be found in *Add Event* ➤ *Other* ➤ *Views*. While intersect boundary and outside view are quite a similar group of events, they offer enough of a difference to justify their separate existence. These events rely on

CHAPTER 10   ASSORTED SUPERIOR TECHNIQUES

a viewport and camera system being enabled in a room (set up via the room editor in the IDE or typed in using GML). If no views are active, these events won't function properly. Each category supports eight events numbered from zero to seven.

- **Outside view:** These events are triggered when an instance's bounding box as defined by its sprite moves completely outside the edges of a specified view.

- **Intersect boundary:** These events are triggered when an instance's sprite crosses/intersects the edge of a specified view, but the instance has not fully left it. If such an instance has no sprite, then its x or y position will be used instead.

Intersect boundary can be used to detect when an object is about to leave a view but is still partially visible. For one, you can force an object to stay inside a specific view using this category of events. Or you could detect when some type of object is about to enter a view from the outside, such as a hostile hoodlum, and implement other appropriate behaviors.

A typical use case for the outside view events is simply destroying projectiles (e.g., bullets or missiles) as they leave the active view. Just adding a function like instance_destroy into these events will accomplish this. You can also achieve a wraparound mechanic easily by repositioning objects on the opposite side of a view after they are done crossing it (think a simple space shooter with asteroids). This way you don't need to constantly destroy and spawn instances.

Animation Events

There is yet another trio of events we shall discuss: animation end, animation update, and animation event. The first one of these deals with the subimages found in your sprites as gauged with the property called image_index. The other two are for advanced developers and will not be discussed in detail.

- **Animation end:** This event is triggered when an object's sprite reaches its last subimage. You might use this to remove an explosion object that ran its course. Alternatively, you can use this event to change sprite animations smoothly on-the-fly, letting each complete its run without abrupt interruptions.

- **Animation update and animation event:** These events are only used with *skeletal animation functions*[5] which are out of the scope of this book.

Path Ended

We discussed paths extensively in Chapter 6. Path ended is a handy event right there in the IDE for object instances that have been set on a movement path. Like its name suggests, it is triggered when a traveling instance has simply reached its path's end.

But now we shall move away from events and enjoy another demonstration, this time on how to save and load game settings.

Saving and Loading Settings

A project called *Saving and Loading* is here (see Figure 10-7) to show you how to save and load some arbitrary game settings. It is time we put some functions introduced in the previous chapter to use in this context, too. After all, repetitio est mater studiorum.

---

[5] GameMaker supports *Spine,* a type of skeletal animation framework created by *Esoteric Software.* A trial version of this product is available for free at https://esotericsoftware.com/spine-download

CHAPTER 10 ASSORTED SUPERIOR TECHNIQUES

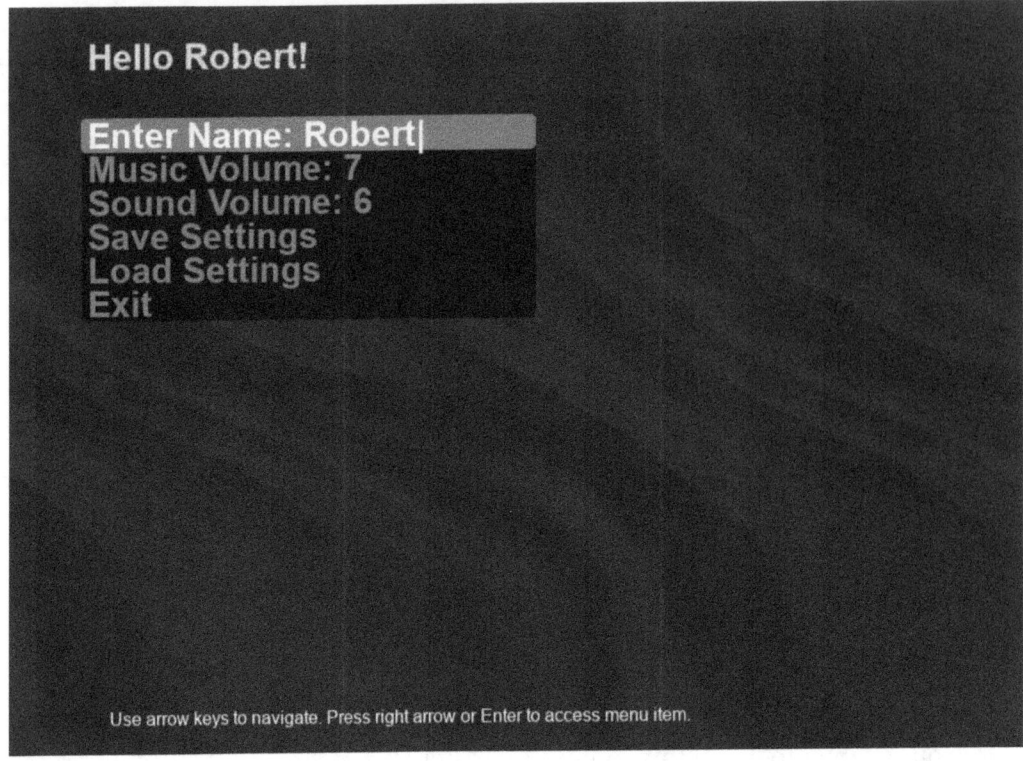

Figure 10-7. *A screenshot from Saving and Loading*

This demonstration has one object, *obj_Controller*, inside one room. It shows the following:

- How to manipulate variables using a traditional menu system with a switch-case–based design under the hood

- Clamping values, receiving a full string of keyboard input, and the wonders of the modulo operator

- Saving real numbers and strings into a text file and loading them

- A relaxing, smoothly scrolling background layer set up from the IDE

- Making custom functions inside objects and executing them ad hoc

While this example deals with audio settings, no audio will actually be produced. Feel free to add this on your own. You should use functions like audio_is_playing, audio_sound_gain, and audio_play_sound. You can feed the two variables *music_volume* and *sound_volume* to the appropriate functions. Import audio files, loop the music, and have the user interface provide audio(visual) feedback when the gamer navigates the menu.

Let us examine the Create event of obj_Controller, shall we? It begins with some simple enough definitions for a six-item array and several variables.

```
// CREATE
menu_items = ["Enter Name", "Music Volume", "Sound Volume", "Save
Settings", "Load Settings", "Exit"];
menu_index = 0; music_volume = 0; sound_volume = 0; your_name = "";
entering_name = false;
max_items = array_length(menu_items);
settings_file = "settings.txt";
```

Here variable *max_items* is used to store the length of the *menu_items* array. In this example, the length of said array is used in numerous events; therefore, it makes sense to store it in a single variable (instead of summoning array_length time after time).

We next have our first custom function called *save_happy_settings*. There we have four important functions for opening, manipulating, and closing files (first discussed all the way back in Chapter 2).

```
function save_happy_settings() { // Create a custom function for writing
our settings
var file = file_text_open_write(settings_file);
    file_text_write_string(file, your_name + "\n"); // Save name
    file_text_write_real(file, music_volume);
    file_text_write_real(file, sound_volume);
    file_text_close(file);
}
```

The function for loading settings also contains a *file_exists* to make sure a file is actually there before we try to access it. Without this check, GameMaker would return an error.

```
// Create a function for reading our settings
function load_happy_settings() {
if file_exists(settings_file) {
    var file = file_text_open_read(settings_file); // Open file
    your_name = file_text_read_string(file); // Read string
```

```
        music_volume = file_text_read_real(file); // Read number
        sound_volume = file_text_read_real(file); // Read number
        file_text_close(file); // Close file
            }
    }
}
load_happy_settings(); // Execute the function
```

The functions *file_text_read_string* and *file_text_read_real* are there to access strings of text and numeric data, respectively. The player's name obviously belongs to the former category of data.

The menu itself is drawn inside a draw GUI event. An enchanting half-transparent rounded black rectangle created using *draw_roundrect* surrounds it.

```
// DRAW GUI
// Create transparent background
draw_set_color(c_black); draw_set_alpha(0.5);
draw_roundrect(94, 102, 512, 283, false); draw_set_alpha(1);

draw_set_color(c_aqua); draw_set_font(Font1);
draw_text(100, 30, "Hello " + your_name + "!");
var y_pos = 100;
for (var i = 0; i < max_items; i++) {
    draw_set_color(c_gray);
    if i == menu_index draw_roundrect_ext(93, (y_pos + i * 30)+2, 512, (y_
    pos + i * 30)+33, 10, 10, false);
```

We used a formidable for loop to display the menu in which the temporary variable *i* refers to each item (e.g., 0 for "Enter Name" and "1 for Music Volume," etc.) The active menu item is highlighted with a lovely rounded rectangle drawn underneath the text with *draw_roundrect_ext*.

```
    var text = menu_items[i];
    // First menu item
    if i == 0 text += ": " + (entering_name ? your_name + "|" : your_name);
    if i == 1 text += ": " + string(music_volume); // Second menu item
    if i == 2 text += ": " + string(sound_volume); // Third menu item
if i != menu_index draw_set_color(c_gray); else draw_set_color(c_white);
    draw_text(100, y_pos + i * 30, text);
```

```
}
draw_set_font(Font2); draw_set_color(c_white);
draw_text(120, 630, "Use arrow keys to navigate. Press right arrow or Enter
to access menu item.");
```

As for the Step event in obj_Controller, we have the code for detecting keystrokes and using the switch case technique to operate the menu. The modulo operator (%) returns the remainder after division, making the index wraparound to 0 if it reaches or exceeds *max_items*.

```
// STEP
// Execute next code block as long as entering_name is not "true"
if !entering_name {
if keyboard_check_pressed(vk_down) {
    menu_index = (menu_index + 1) % max_items;
}
if keyboard_check_pressed(vk_up) {
    menu_index = (menu_index - 1 + max_items) % max_items;
}
```

Next we use clamp to limit the range of two variables, i.e., music_volume and sound_volume.

```
if keyboard_check_pressed(vk_left) {
    switch (menu_index) {
        case 1: // Reduce music volume
            music_volume = clamp(music_volume - 1, 0, 10);
            break;
        case 2: // Reduce sound effect volume
            sound_volume = clamp(sound_volume - 1, 0, 10);
            break;
    }
}
if keyboard_check_pressed(vk_right) {
    switch (menu_index) {
        case 1: // Increase music volume
            music_volume = clamp(music_volume + 1, 0, 10);
```

```
            break;
        case 2: // Increase sound effect Volume
            sound_volume = clamp(sound_volume + 1, 0, 10);
            break;
    }
}
```

We then have the two custom functions, *save_happy_settings* and *load_happy_settings*, as defined in the object's Create event. This approach makes things a lot easier to read; experiment with making your own custom functions whenever feasible.

```
if keyboard_check_pressed(vk_enter) {
    switch (menu_index) {
        case 0:
            entering_name=true;
            break;
        case 3: // Save settings
                    save_happy_settings();
                break;
        case 4: // Load settings
            load_happy_settings();
                break;
        case 5: // Exit program
                game_end();
                    break;
    }
}
```

Finally, we arrive at the else statement for the code block dealing with the variable *entering_name*. We summon the handy function *keyboard_string* (as discussed earlier in the book) to store a maximum of ten letters for a player's name inside variable *your_name*. The letter limiting is achieved by observing the output from a function called *string_length*.

```
} else { // Code block for when entering_name IS "true"
    // Name input mode
    your_name = keyboard_string;
```

```
    if string_length(your_name) > 10 {
   // Limit name length to ten characters
   your_name = string_copy(your_name, 1, 10);
      keyboard_string = your_name;
   }
   if keyboard_check_pressed(vk_enter) {
       entering_name = false; // Exit name input mode
   }
}
```

On Vector Graphics in GameMaker

As previously mentioned in the book, there are two main types of images: raster-based and vectors. The former is what is created inside GameMaker or imported from sources like Adobe Photoshop. Consisting of individually plotted pixels, raster-based graphics don't always rotate well and magnifying them can make these types of visuals quite blocky or mushy. Vectors, on the other hand, scale and rotate beautifully, maintaining their sharpness and shape most of the time.

GameMaker supports the SVG format which is short for *scalable vector graphics*.[6] These assets are added into projects simply by dragging them into the GameMaker asset browser. When you do this, you get a window asking if you want to import a vector sprite as a vector. By clicking Yes, the image is added into your game in a the SVG format. Otherwise, it is translated into a raster-based sprite image.

Vector files can serve as wonderful background graphics or game logos. Their nature makes them pretty much infinitely scalable, should the need arise. You can leverage vector art in GameMaker simply by creating an asset layer in the IDE and dragging a vector image onto it. By using the dynamic resize and rotation controls of the IDE, the artwork can be adjusted to suit your needs; these are activated by placing the mouse cursor on the very edges of an image. You can also assign vector files into your game objects just as you would do with raster-based pixel graphics using the property *sprite_index*.

---

[6] The SVG specification is an open standard developed by the World Wide Web Consortium (W3C) since 1999. SVG files are created with specialized software such as *Adobe Illustrator* and *Inkscape*.

CHAPTER 10   ASSORTED SUPERIOR TECHNIQUES

One of the better providers of vector art is *SVG Repo*, found at `www.svgrepo.com`. Their files can be used for free even in commercial settings.

With an SVG file open in the sprite editor, you also have some new controls to contend with, namely, *Precision* and *Canvas frame settings*. The former sets the accuracy of the vectors being drawn while the latter offers three types of image previews (see Figure 10-8).

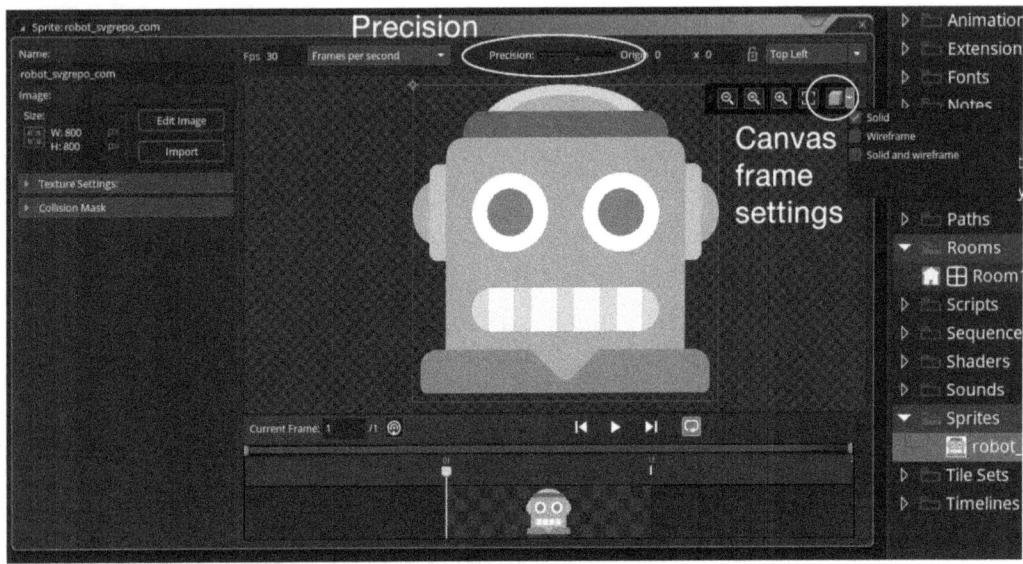

Figure 10-8. *An SVG file of a charming robot inside the GameMaker sprite editor with the Precision control and Canvas frame settings highlighted*

There are these three options for Canvas frame settings: *Solid, Wireframe,* and *Solid and wireframe.* You can best examine the level of accuracy of your vector file by switching on the wireframe mode which displays the vector's outlines. As a result of their wondrous scalability, more complicated vector graphics can be quite heavy on a device. That's why GameMaker has the Precision control for your SVG files; a vector file with a lower precision is easier on the system and can help with slowdown.

There are three special functions for working with SVG in GML. First off, we have *draw_enable_svg_aa*. This is used to set the antialiasing/edge smoothing for your svg files. The strength of this technique is adjusted with a function called *draw_set_svg_aa_level*. Finally, we can retrieve the strength of the antialiasing with *draw_get_svg_aa_level*. The following snippet demonstrates these functions:

CHAPTER 10   ASSORTED SUPERIOR TECHNIQUES

```
sprite_index=robot_svgrepo_com; // Assign a vector-file into sprite_index
draw_enable_svg_aa(true); // Switch anti-aliasing (AA) on
draw_set_svg_aa_level(0.5); // Set AA level to 50%
jolly_aa = draw_get_svg_aa_level(); // Store AA level into jolly_aa
```

Vectors describe things using magnitude (or amount) *and* direction. They have a multitude of uses in mathematics and computer science. Physics concepts like acceleration and force are vectors. Basic quantities that have a magnitude but lack a direction are called **scalars**. Examples of scalars include mass, speed, and volume.

Flash and SWF in GameMaker

SVGs aside, GameMaker has basic support for SWF files as well. These represent the output from *Adobe Flash,* a now retired vector-based technology very popular until 2010 or so. Flash animations were often paired with snippets of *Actionscript,* a proprietary scripting language. Animations using that technique will not usually work when imported into GameMaker. Also some visual glitches may appear in the case of more complex Flash animations.

If you have some SWF-based animations on standby and want to give them a whirl in GameMaker, you have a handful of functions to play with. See Table 10-6 for a rundown of these functions, which also summarizes the GML for SVG files.

Table 10-6. The GML for SWF and SVG file manipulation

SWF (Flash)	SVG
draw_enable_swf_aa	draw_enable_svg_aa
draw_set_swf_aa_level	draw_set_svg_aa_level
draw_get_swf_aa_level	draw_get_svg_aa_level

383

CHAPTER 10   ASSORTED SUPERIOR TECHNIQUES

The stronger the antialiasing for your vector graphics, the more of a hit there usually is on a system. Also, having the precision control in the IDE set too high for your vectors may cause slowdowns.

Checkpoints with Buffers

Let us tackle one great feature that is rather effortless to implement in GameMaker: *game checkpoints*. These can be created using a system of *buffers*. In programming, a buffer is a reserved temporary space within the system memory (RAM) used to store small amounts of data. Buffers are used for sequential short-term storage like receiving network data or indeed for storing a checkpoint in your game. They only persist as long as a game is running (and as long as they have not been intentionally destroyed).

There are four main types of memory buffers in GameMaker: fixed, grow, wrap, and fast (see Table 10-7).

Table 10-7. *The four types of buffers in GameMaker*

Fixed	Buffer is of fixed/constant size.
Grow	Buffer grows in size whenever necessary. This is the safest type of buffer.
Wrap	Whenever this buffer-type gets full it starts to overwrite the data stored at its beginning.
Fast	Offers slightly faster data processing. Most likely to crash your game.

For the purposes of a checkpoint, the best choice is a grow buffer. Now, implementing this technique is rather simple. Let's assume we have an object for this context, we'll call it *obj_Savestate*. This is what its Create event contains:

```
// CREATE
Buffer1 = buffer_create(1024, buffer_grow, 1);
is_saved = false;
```

First, we give the buffer an arbitrary name. Here we went for *Buffer1*. This is paired with a function by the name of *buffer_create*. It takes three parameters: buffer size in bytes,[7] buffer method, and byte alignment. The last parameter usually works well enough with a value of one (1).[8] So in our example, we make a buffer that consists of 1024 bytes, starting the buffer size with an educated guess (the grow method will actually resize it as needed). The buffer will be aligned to one byte. The Boolean variable *is_saved* is there simply to gauge later whether a buffer has been created or not.

Next we shall have an event for saving the game state. Let us use the event *Key Press - S* in the following fashion:

```
// KEY PRESS - S
is_saved = true;
buffer_seek(Buffer1, buffer_seek_start, 0);
game_save_buffer(Buffer1);
```

First, we set the Boolean (i.e., is_saved) to true. Two functions are then summoned. They are *buffer_seek* and *game_save_buffer*. The former sets the "playhead" of the buffer to a specific position; if it is not used, the buffer would continue writing at wherever said playhead was left. In this context (i.e., creating a single checkpoint), it would only increase the buffer's size unnecessarily, so we do a kind of a rewinding operation with *buffer_seek_start*.

We then need an event for loading the game state. Let's go with *Key Press - L* like this:

```
// KEY PRESS - L
if is_saved {
    buffer_seek(Buffer1, buffer_seek_start, 0);
    game_load_buffer(Buffer1);
}
```

---

[7] A bit is the smallest unit of digital information, represented by either a one or a zero. A byte consists of 8 bits.

[8] Byte alignment in GameMaker's buffers can be executed at 1, 2, 4, or 8 bytes. Settings other than 1 are often not needed and are mostly used by more experienced developers keen on maximizing their games' optimization.

CHAPTER 10   ASSORTED SUPERIOR TECHNIQUES

In this event, we first use the Boolean to see if a checkpoint has been saved. We then rewind the buffer using buffer_seek once more. Next there is a succinct function for loading the game state called *game_load_buffer*. Finally, in order to prevent memory leaks, we need to destroy our buffer after it's no longer needed. We can simply put the following statement into a room end or clean up event:

buffer_delete(Buffer1);

And this is how we can create and load checkpoints in GameMaker.

Checkpoints don't have to be implemented using keyboard controls. They can be summoned in, say, the collision event of some invisible object with which the player makes contact.

Free Audiovisual Resources for Your Games

Creating audiovisuals for your games can be daunting especially if you are a one-person team. Thankfully, there are a number of online repositories for free and reasonably priced graphics and other resources. Some of these are listed below. If you are making a commercial game, make sure the assets you plan to use are copyright-free (i.e., in the public domain or attached to a suitable *Creative Commons* license) or grant you a full commercial license after payment. Please be aware that "royalty-free" does not automatically mean "free to use however you want"; always read the licenses carefully.

- **Open Game Art** (opengameart.org)
- **Freesound.org**
- **ZapSplat. Free audio resources** (https://www.zapsplat.com)
- **We Love Indies audio resources** (https://www.weloveindies.com/en/join)
- **Kenney.nl assets** (https://kenney.nl/assets)
- **Craftpix.net** (https://craftpix.net/freebies)
- **itch.io game assets, both audio and graphics** (https://itch.io/game-assets)

- **Game Art 2D** (https://www.gameart2d.com)

- **Sprite Lib**: A free, popular, and exceptional collection of 2D sprites (https://www.widgetworx.com/projects/sl.html)

- **Game-icons.net**: Free icons in both PNG and SVG formats

- **Soundimage.org**: Music, sound effects, and texture images from Eric Matyas

- **Incompetech.com**: Royalty-free music from the legendary Kevin MacLeod

Importing Sprite Sheets

When looking for graphics for your games, you will come across many fetching *sprite sheets*. These are basically sprites with their animations presented in a single graphics file. This is a most handy way to deliver engaging animated visuals. Let us now revisit GameMaker's mighty sprite editor to take a look at how sprite sheets are leveraged.

You can take the following steps:

1. Import the sprite sheet resource by dragging the file into the asset browser from your explorer/Finder window.

2. Double-click on the resource.

3. In the next window, click *Edit Image*.

4. Select *Image ▶ Convert to Frames* from the upper file menu. This will open a view for editing animation frame settings. Adjust the parameters, the most important being frame width, frame height, number of frames, and frames per row. Click *Convert* after you are done. You should now have an animated sprite.

Alternatively, you can do the following:

1. Make an empty sprite resource by right clicking on the asset browser and selecting *Create ▶ Sprite*.

2. Click *Edit image*.

CHAPTER 10   ASSORTED SUPERIOR TECHNIQUES

3. Select *Image* ▶ *Import Strip Image* from the upper file menu and navigate to the location of the sprite sheet on your computer.

4. On the window that opens, adjust the parameters (frame width, etc.) according to the dimensions and layout of the sheet.

Frame width and height refer to the sprite's basic dimensions, and they are usually stated by the sprite sheet's creator(s). For the total number of frames and frames per row, we may need to use our deductive abilities on occasion (see Figure 10-9).

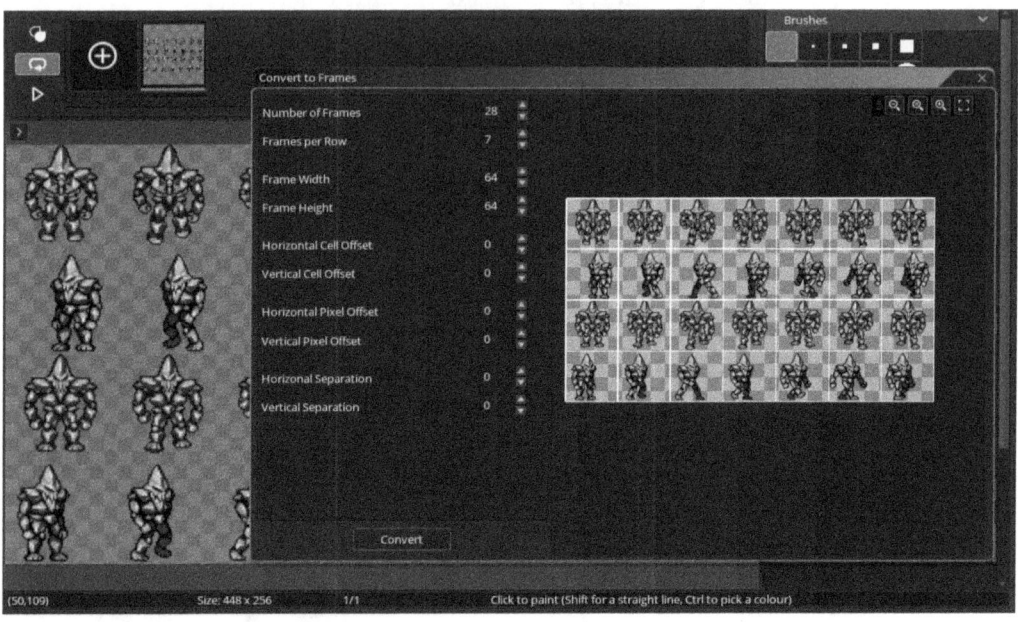

Figure 10-9. *The main tool for converting a sprite sheet into individual animation frames*

In Figure 10-9, we have a nice sprite sheet for a formidable golem.[9] The sprite is 64 × 64 pixels in size and the sheet offers us a total of 28 frames of animation across four rows. The settings for this particular sprite sheet are therefore as follows:

---

[9] The golem was created by Stephen "Redshrike" Challener with William Thompson contributing. It is found on OpenGameArt.org (`https://opengameart.org/content/lpc-golem`)

CHAPTER 10 ASSORTED SUPERIOR TECHNIQUES

- Number of frames: 28, frames per row: 7, frame width: 64, and frame height: 64

There are six more parameters in the frame conversion window which may come in handy at some point.

- **Horizontal and vertical cell offset:** Lets you skip a row and/or column of frames/cells

- **Horizontal and vertical pixel offset:** Offsets all frames by specific pixel amounts

- **Horizontal and vertical separation:** Separates the frames by a specific amount of pixels.

More on Texture Group Settings

You may remember the concept of texture groups as discussed in Chapter 3. As a reminder, texture groups are a way to optimize your games' graphics. For example, sprites only found on specific game levels/maps can be put on the same texture page to reduce texture swapping. A texture swap is a necessary evil best avoided whenever we can. Well-organized texture groups reduce the frequency of these incidents which usually slowdown a game considerably. A texture swap is best executed at the beginning or end of each level and not during gameplay.

We shall now examine the advanced settings of texture groups. You can access them from the GameMaker IDE by navigating to *Tools > Texture Groups*. See Figure 10-10 for the related window.

CHAPTER 10   ASSORTED SUPERIOR TECHNIQUES

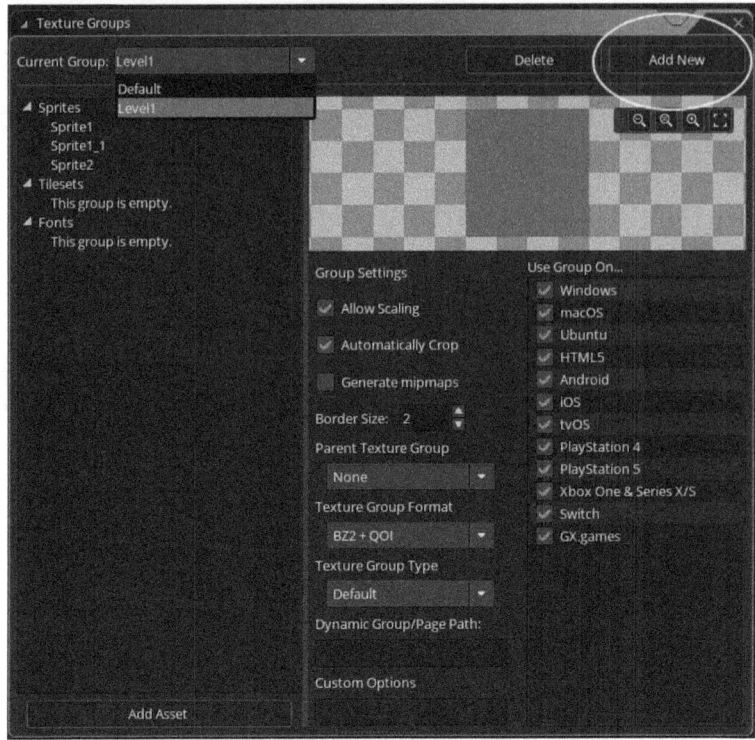

Figure 10-10.   The window for texture groups and settings inside the GameMaker IDE. The button for adding new texture groups is highlighted.

- **Allow scaling:** Disabling this option will force GameMaker to never scale a texture group. Enabling it will scale the textures if necessary to comply with platform-specific limits. Not allowing scaling may produce slightly sharper visuals, although the difference in quality is often negligible.

- **Automatically crop:** Ticking this box will remove any alpha/transparency around the edges of a texture group. Not enabling this feature preserves the original asset layout but may waste texture page space and lead to larger texture pages. Sometimes this can lead to more frequent texture swaps.

- **Generate mipmaps:** Enabling this option will generate your textures in multiple resolutions. This is typically only needed for 3D projects. Some more intense 2D camera work might also benefit from this option.

- **Border size:** Adds some padding pixels around sprites to prevent texture bleeding or strange artifacts at sprite edges. The default setting of two pixels usually works fine.

- **Parent texture group:** All visual assets assigned to child groups are placed on a texture page of a parent texture group as long as the parent group is included on a target platform.

- **Texture group format:** Sets the texture compression method.

    - **BZ2 + QOI:** This setting refers to a technique where the textures are compressed with both *bzip2*, a time-honored compression algorithm, and *Quite OK Image Format (QOI)*, a newer algorithm. This usually works well, but can add to the loading time of games running on lower-end devices; it represents a generally solid option for most projects.

    - **QOI:** This setting uses pure Quite OK Image Format for texture compression. Makes the resulting textures slightly larger in file size, but sometimes with a boost in (loading) performance.

    - **PNG:** Textures can be stored as PNG-compressed files with this setting. The approach works well across all platforms (Windows, HTML5, Android etc.) The files will not be as small as with BZ2 and/or QOI. The use of system memory (RAM) tends to be bigger with the PNG setting, too.

    - **Custom:** This setting allows you to specify nonstandard texture compression algorithms that aren't listed in the default options. Used mostly by experienced developers.

- **Texture group type:** This setting lets you choose between default/regular and dynamic texture groups. Dynamic texture groups are not loaded when the game starts. They are loaded when required (i.e., when visuals from it is drawn) or when they are accessed manually.

- **Use group on:** This setting decides which export platform receives a particular custom texture group. The default texture group is automatically used with all platforms and does not offer any boxes to untick.

CHAPTER 10   ASSORTED SUPERIOR TECHNIQUES

We shall next discuss dynamic texture groups in more detail.

Default vs. Dynamic Texture Groups

Dynamic texture groups let you to create and manage textures manually using GML. For most beginners, it will not be necessary to use this technique. However, dynamic texture groups are quite useful for more complicated projects when you need to maximally optimize performance. They can be leveraged by using these four functions:

- **texturegroup_load:** Loads a dynamic texture group from your storage/disk into main memory (RAM). Offers a Boolean parameter for "prefetching," which refers to moving the prepared graphics onto the video card (GPU).

- **texturegroup_unload:** Unloads a dynamic texture group from memory back to storage/disk.

- **texturegroup_set_mode:** Has three main uses: sets implicit (default) or explicit loading, offers a debugging mode, and lets you set a default/placeholder sprite which is displayed when the main texture has not been loaded yet. Implicit in this context refers to automatic loading of dynamic texture groups whenever GameMaker detects a need for specific visuals. Explicit loading refers to manual GML-based access of textures.

- **texturegroup_get_status:** Returns one of four status messages.

Remember, dynamic texture groups are created using the previously mentioned settings panel in the IDE by simply designating specific groups as "Dynamic" instead of "Default."

Now, the previously discussed functions can be used a little something like this:

```
// Set explicit mode to true, debug mode to false, and a default sprite
texturegroup_set_mode(true, false, spr_Jollysprite);
// Find out status for Level_1_Graphics
var status = texturegroup_get_status("Level_1_Graphics");
```

```
if status == texturegroup_status_unloaded // If status is "unloaded"..
{
    texturegroup_load("Level_1_Graphics", true); // ..Load texture group
}
```

The status messages for texturegroup_get_status are listed in Table 10-8.

Table 10-8. *The status messages for texturegroup_get_status*

texturegroup_status_unloaded	The texture group is still on disk and not yet loaded.
texturegroup_status_loading	The texture group is currently being loaded.
texturegroup_status_loaded	The texture group has been loaded into memory (RAM).
texturegroup_status_fetched	The texture group has been loaded and fetched into VRAM (video ram) and is ready to rock.

Let us recap the core GML associated with dynamic textures, shall we? (See Table 10-9.)

Table 10-9. *The four core functions for working with dynamic textures*

texturegroup_load(group, prefetch);	Loads a dynamic texture group. Accepts true or false for prefetching.
texturegroup_get_status(group);	Returns one of four status messages as displayed in Table 10-8
texturegroup_set_mode(mode, debug, sprite);	Sets implicit (default) or explicit loading mode, debug, and placeholder sprite.
texturegroup_unload(group);	Unloads a dynamic texture group from memory (RAM).

CHAPTER 10   ASSORTED SUPERIOR TECHNIQUES

Basic Video Playback in GameMaker

The playback of video files in GameMaker is supported. However, they must be in a compatible *file container format* like MP4 or AVI. A lot also depends on the *video codecs* being used. A video codec (coder/decoder) is a piece of *software that compresses and decompresses digital video*. Common codecs include H.264, VP9, and AV1. Each offers different types of output as it pertains to frame rate, resolution, and quality.

Whether a video will display on a device depends largely on which codecs are installed on the system in use. Not all end users have every codec. A generally safe bet is an MP4 file encoded in H.264. Also, you may run into copyright issues if you distribute your game with video encoded using proprietary codecs. Make sure you understand the license for the codec(s) used in your game's video files.

Now, to add a video file into a project, simply drag one from your file explorer/Finder window onto the GameMaker asset browser. You will get a window with the message "Would you like to add these files as Included Files?" Respond with resounding *Yes* to include the video file in your project. After this, you simply need an object with the following events to enjoy basic video playback in your game:

```
// CREATE
video_open("video.mp4"); // Load video file
video_enable_loop(true); // Make video loop. Set to "false" for non-looping playback
video_set_volume(1.0); // Set video volume to full (range: 0.0 - 1.0)

// DRAW
var video_data = video_draw();
var status = video_data[0]; // Video status is stored in the video_data array's first item (0)
var video_status = video_get_status();

// A status of 0 means we're ready for playback, a -1 would mean something is wrong
if status == 0 && video_status == video_status_playing
{
    // The video itself will be routed into the second item (1) in the video_data array
```

```
        draw_surface(video_data[1], 0, 0); // Draw video surface at the top
        left of the screen
}
// ROOM END
video_close();
```

All "included files" will be stored in a directory for your project called *datafiles* accessible with file explorer on Windows or a Finder window on macOS. The main takeaways from the previous snippet are the functions *video_open, video_close,* and *video_draw.* The array *video_data* is also of paramount importance when working with video files in GameMaker.

On AI Assets

The correct use of artificial intelligence can be beneficial to game developers. Especially one-person teams can benefit from the procedural generation of assets this technology can provide. However, in its current form, in 2025, AI cannot readily replace talented audiovisual artists. The term "ai slop" has indeed emerged to describe the look and feel of AI-generated material. Although powerful at crunching data, even portraying realistic human fingers can be a bit of a hurdle for our resolute generators. AI artwork usable inside GameMaker is limited mostly to presentational purposes. Generators capable of game actor sprites have not arrived en masse yet. It is often a hit and miss affair (see Figure 10-11).

CHAPTER 10   ASSORTED SUPERIOR TECHNIQUES

Figure 10-11.   The output from perchance.org/ai-pixel-art-generator with the prompt "four sprites of a 64 × 64 pixel space ship, top down, spritesheet, GameMaker"

While a generic AI art generator may struggle with game-ready assets, a number of more specialized generators are on their way. As of 2025, leading the charge is *Pixel Lab AI* (`https://pixellab.ai`) that offers mostly usable animated sprites. Some tweaking of these assets is still needed inside GameMaker's sprite editor (see Figure 10-12).

CHAPTER 10 ASSORTED SUPERIOR TECHNIQUES

Figure 10-12. *The output from pixellab.ai with the prompt "full-body view of a neckbeard"*

Pixelvibe by *Rosebud AI* (https://lab.rosebud.ai/ai-game-assets) is a another strong platform that can provide you with many types of visual assets (see Figure 10-13).

Figure 10-13. *The output from Pixelvibe with the prompt "full-body view of a neckbeard"*

CHAPTER 10   ASSORTED SUPERIOR TECHNIQUES

Quite a bit of controversy surrounds AI and artwork generated with it is not spared from criticism. Video game artists do and should take pride in their skills. AI-generated resources can be seen to devalue human artistry. The full range of emotional expression is rarely found in AI-generated work. It can be argued at least an excessive amount of AI artwork can cheapen a game somewhat. Also, the training data for many AI models is gathered from publicly available platforms like *DeviantArt* and *ArtStation* without the authors' consent. Some game distribution platforms, including *Steam*[10] and *itch.io*, have begun requesting information from developers regarding AI-generated assets in their products.

You are better off either drawing your own sprites or leveraging the available (free) online resources, some of which are of very high quality. Let humans triumph. However, AI art can be used as decent placeholder content in the early stages of your games.

As for audio assets, it is surprisingly easy to generate fairly natural sounding mediocre pop songs with AI in 2025 (and some fine background ambience). This remains a somewhat questionable approach in regard to the previously mentioned ethical implications. In addition the technical quality of free AI songs is often slightly subpar compared to professionally produced material. Paid AI services naturally offer more options for your audio mixing with usually an improved sound quality.

Usable sound effects are well within the reach of AI technology, too. Much of the same criticism levied on other types of assets applies in this context. As is the case with visuals, AI-generated sound effects tend to be a tad rough around the edges. You rarely get ready-to-use material from such a generator and a manual mixing stage is warranted. Issues such as excessive silent parts and overemphasized (bass) frequencies are common. Never use AI-generated sound effects without looking for and if necessary addressing these problems first. As always, make sure the audio material is converted into a lossless format such as WAV before engaging in mixing. Most assets from established professional sound libraries tend to "fit right in" your games better as they have been properly mixed.

---

[10] Valve Software states that "under the Steam Distribution Agreement, you promise Valve that your game will not include illegal or infringing content, and that your game will be consistent with your marketing materials" in an AI-related news item from January 2024.(`https://store.steampowered.com/news/group/4145017/view/3862463747997849618`).

Here are some AI-based audio services for your experimentation that you can access with a free Google and/or Facebook account:

- **Elevenlabs.io**: Offers both music and sound effects creation.
- **Suno.com**: A higher-end AI music generator. Has faced some legal issues[11] due to its training data practices.
- **Udio.com**: Provides music with decently imitated human voices.
- **sfxengine.com**: A service dedicated to sound effects.

In Closing

In this chapter, we discussed these powerful features of GameMaker:

- Platformer mechanics as demonstrated by Platformer Prototype
- The six basic GameMaker blend modes
- How to create, draw, and manipulate surfaces
- The application surface and how to work with it
- The trio of Step events, user events, and others
- How to save and load game settings
- The basics of 2D vector-based graphics in GameMaker
- Using buffers to store and retrieve checkpoints
- Advanced texture group settings, including dynamic texture groups

---

[11] Timbaland Shows Support For Music AI Creation Tool Suno Despite It Being Sued By Major Labels For Copyright Infringement (https://tech.yahoo.com/articles/timbaland-shows-support-music-ai-162105567.html?guccounter=1) for yahoo!tech by Samantha Dorisca (March 28, 2025).

CHAPTER 10   ASSORTED SUPERIOR TECHNIQUES

Making Games in a Putamen Nucis

The main takeaways from this book can be crystallized as follows:

- **The five basic building blocks of GameMaker games are rooms, objects, variables, sprites (visual assets), and audio files.**

- **Variables are data structures used to gauge object and game status:** They come in different types (Boolean, string, numeric, etc.) and can be arbitrarily named (e.g., cheese_cost, music_volume, game_paused, etc.). They come in three scopes: local (e.g., var i), instance, and global. Try to keep the number of variables to a minimum for the sake of efficiency and brevity.

- **GameMaker's objects are blueprints for instances and support inheritance:** Objects can be configured to have parent-child relationships, which transfer the "parental" properties on to "child" objects. The latter can also have additional events and properties of their own.

- **Put the right functions in the right object events:** If a function does not need to be executed every single step/frame, keep it out of the Step events. Use GameMaker's alarm system whenever you can. Do not perform any (heavy) calculations in the Draw events.

- **Always optimize your games for lower-end hardware:** Not everyone is willing or able to invest in state-of-the-art gaming devices. Watch out for overhead from blend modes and an excess number of on-screen instances. Surfaces can be a powerful ally. Destroy data structures (e.g., ds_maps, ds_lists, surfaces, etc.) as soon as they are no longer needed.

- **Control a game's difficulty level to keep things challenging but never overbearing.** This is a factor best judged by someone else than the developer(s).

- **Keep your user interfaces intuitive and display helpful information whenever necessary.** Do not leave gamers guessing how to play your game.

- **Learn to enjoy the incredible power and flexibility Box2D offers you:** Using physics can sometimes transform even a humdrum 2D game into an enchanting romp. Consider investing a considerable amount of time into GameMaker's physics system after you've become comfortable with GML's basic syntax and logic.

- **Organize your projects well:** Always name and group your assets logically inside the GameMaker IDE. For one, this makes projects easier to revisit in the future. Add comments on at least your more complicated statements and functions. Delete unneeded resources (both sprites and audio) to avoid storage bloat before releasing a game.

- **Treat game audio as seriously as game visuals:** Only use the finest music and sound effects in your games. Keep those sounds clean, punchy, and professional. Make sure the audio never degenerates into digital distortion. Use real-time effects whenever feasible (including some compression as discussed in Chapter 8). Unless you are a professional voice actor, do not record your own dialogue.

- **Maintain a good "feel" in your games:** Being a somewhat intangible quality, the feel of a game is nonetheless present or not present in every single title. For 2D games, it can be argued to consist of properties like game actors' momentum, attention to visual detail, proper collisions, and eye candy (e.g., particles and high-quality explosions). Physics-based games can often provide this good feel right out of the gate.

- **There are no pointless projects:** Even if a game remains an unfinished prototype on your computer, it represents a learning experience. Not all projects need to see a release date to benefit you as a developer.

CHAPTER 10   ASSORTED SUPERIOR TECHNIQUES

Afterword

At this point, you probably feel more confident about your abilities working with GameMaker. You are familiar with variables, arrays, and many of the core functions this excellent piece of software provides. You can put objects on-screen and have them do interesting things. You might even be able to discuss different looping methods all day long.

Both GameMaker and 2D games have a bright future. For developers, limitations sometimes create the greatest freedom. The way forward now is to create systems which impose technical restraints and challenge developers in novel ways. Despite the millions of video games released since the 1970s, innovation has not been depleted; it sometimes just seems that way.

After completely life-like audiovisual representations are fully achieved in video games (at around the release of PlayStation 7 or 8), simulation fatigue will probably set in. This can greatly reduce the revenue of most big game companies, which will dwindle as less gamers are interested in products embracing the realistic aesthetic. If the industry is to thrive, it has to provide innovation and make eccentric stylistic choices. Instead of open worlds, there will be small, static mazes. Instead of ray tracing, there may be more games with eight colors on-screen—or less.

We might also want to start questioning the value of graphic violence in video games. Nintendo's series of *Mario* games feature rotund plumbers jumping on strange creatures. *Tetris* by Alexey Pajitnov is a testament to the genius of blocks. Satoshi Tajiri's *Pokemon* offers a world of fantastical beings at war with each other presented in a family-friendly manner. Three of the most successful video game franchises in the history of this planet feature zero realistic violence.

There are very few things on this planet more frustrating than game development. Your F5 key will probably wear out at some point and keeping track of time might become rather difficult. But once you attain a level where you start to make games (or just prototypes) comfortably, the associated problem-solving becomes something you cannot let go of easily (the author was smitten by GameMaker back in 2011 and has never looked back).

Becoming fully comfortable with GameMaker, a real staple of 2D game development, is a major undertaking. Start small and optimize often. Things will start falling into place little by little as you spend more time with the software. Hopefully, this book nudged you in the right direction.

> *I learned not to worry so much about the outcome, but to concentrate on the step I was on and to try to do it as perfectly as I could when I was doing it.*
>
> —Steve Wozniak (1950–), cofounder of Apple Computers

Index

A

Ad Hoc Physics Objects, 272–273
Adobe Flash, 383
Ahead-of-Time (AOT), 23
AI, *see* Artificial intelligence (AI)
Ai slop, 395
Alarm-tied action, 85
Android, 328
    connect to macOS, 331
    connect to Windows, 330, 331
    developer mode, 330
    file locations, 329
    keystore file, 329
    platform preferences, 328, 329
    settings, 331, 332
    shenanigans, 332
Android Studio, 327, 328, 331
Angles
    degrees, 198, 199
    radians, 198, 199
Animations, 178
Animations Library, 178
AOT, *see* Ahead-of-Time (AOT)
Application surface, 367
    application_surface_draw_
        enabled(), 367
    application_surface_is_enabled(), 367
    GML, 369
    gpu_set_blendenable, 367
    graphics, 371
    GUI, 369
array_sort, 45

Artificial intelligence (AI), 395
    artwork, 398
    audio assets, 398
    audio services, 399
    generators, 395, 396
    Pixelvibe, 397, 398
    sound effects, 398
    training data, 398
    and Video game artists, 398
Asset-level volume/gain, 125
A-star (A*), 207, 212, 223, 225
    final-cost (F), 224
    grid-based pathfinding algorithm, 223
    ground-cost (G), 224
    heuristic-cost (H), 224
    mp_grid, 224
    Wobbly Legs, 224, 225
Audio assets, 126
Audio bus, 287
audio_channel_num, 130
Audio compression, 295, 296
Audio effects, 289
    AudioEffectType.Bitcrusher, 292
    AudioEffectType.Compressor, 296, 297
    AudioEffectType.Delay, 291
    AudioEffectType.HPF2, 292
    AudioEffectType.LPF2, 291
    AudioEffectType.PeakEQ, 293
    AudioEffectType.Reverb1, 290
    AudioEffectType.Tremolo, 292, 293
    demonstration, 289, 290
    presentation, 289

INDEX

audio_emitter_free, 212
Audio emitters, 207, 212
audio_falloff_set_model, 209
Audio file
    audio_play_sound, 127–130
    master volume and audio
        configuration, 130, 131
    OGG format, 124, 126
    pause audio, 129, 130
    pitch, 131
    Sound Group Mixer, 125
    sound instances, 129
    target options, 124, 126
        (*see also* Audio target options)
    volume/gain, 125
    WAV, WMA, MP3 and OGG
        formats, 123
Audio hardware, 122
audio_is_playing, 127, 336
audio_listener_
    orientation, 208, 209
audio_master_gain, 130
audio_pause_all, 129
Audio pipeline, 121
audio_play_sound, 127–130
Audio resource, 122, 123
audio_sound_gain, 127
audio_sound_get_pitch, 131
audio_sound_pitch, 131
audio_stop_all(), 127
audio_stop_sound(resource), 127
audio_system_is_available, 131
audio_system_is_initialised, 131
Audio target options, 124
    bitrate, 125
    output, 124
    quality, 125
    sample rate, 125
Audiovisual assets, 8
Audiovisuals resources, 386, 387
Auto-tiling, 179, 180

B

Bitmasking, 179
Blend modes, 356
    bm_add, 357
    bm_max, 357
    bm_min, 359, 360
    bm_normal, 356
    bm_reverse_
        subtract, 359, 360
    bm_subtract, 357
    formulas, 357, 360
    GML, 357
    gpu_set_blendmode, 361
    grouping, 361
    Wacky Blend Modes, 358, 359
Boolean variable, 115
Box2D, 231, 232, 234, 270
Box2D Lite, 231
Breakpoints, 344
brick_layer, 171, 172
Broadcast message, 280, 282
Buffers
    buffer_create, 385
    buffer_seek_start, 385
    Create event, 384
    definition, 384
    game_load_buffer, 386
    is_saved, 385
    Key Press event, 385
    playhead, 385
    types, 384
    uses, 384
Bug, 334

C

Cameras, 163, 164
    feisty_cam, 172
    viewports, 164
Camera system, 163
Clear Display Buffer, 19
Code Editor 2, 10
Collision, 109
Collision avoidance, 212
Collision groups, 235, 249, 271
Collision masks, 182, 195–197, 199
Collision mechanisms, 194
Comic Sans, 93
Compression, 295
Compressor, 295

D

DAWs, *see* Digital audio workstations (DAWs)
Debugger, 341, 342
Debugging, 313, 334
Degrees, 198, 199
Developer Mode, 323
Digital audio, 293–295
Digital audio workstations (DAWs), 294
Digital devices, 21
Digital dynamics, 295
Digital revolution, 1
Distance joints, 250–252, 254
Doppler effect, 209, 211
DnD environment, 103, 104
Drag-and-Drop (DnD) approach, 10, 109, 119
Drawing-related functions, 83
draw_path, 229, 230
draw_self, 115
draw_set_alpha(), 78, 117
draw_sprite, 102
DS grids, 49, 50
ds_list_find_value, 185
DS maps, 52
DS priority queue, 59
DS priority queues, 60
Dynamic audio effects, 287
Dynamics compression, 295

E

Effect layers
    functions, 174
    in GML, 175
    single-layer mode, 176
    use, 174
    visual effects, 174
Effect type, 174
Enumeration, 32
Events
    animation events, 374, 375
    Create event, 377
    Draw events, 368
    Path ended, 375
    Step event, 339, 373, 379
    User events, 372, 373
    View events, 373, 374
Exploding, 115

F

Feather, 11
feisty_cam, 172
FIFO, *see* First-in first-out (FIFO) data structure
Firebullet, 261
Fire particles, 143

INDEX

First-in first-out (FIFO) data structure, 57
Flag constants, 243, 248
Flags, 243, 248
Floor function, 35
Forces, GameMaker's physics
    angular impulse, 236
    force, 236
    impulse, 236
    torque, 236
FPS, *see* Frames per second (FPS)
Frames per second (FPS), 343
fx_set_single_layer, 176

G

gallant cursor_sprite, 187
Game checkpoints, 384
Game End, 152, 155
Gameloop, 12, 268, 271, 272
GameMaker, 1, 2, 23
    asset categories, 12
    assets, 15
    cleaning icon, 314
    concept, 18
    DnD, 10
    download, 4
    events, 14, 15
    Feather, 11
    functional video game, 12
    games, 313
    game templates, 7
    gestures, 346
    GML, 10
    grid controls, 356
    IDE, 8, 9
    intuitive and slick user interface, 20
    layers, 19
    Linux, 5, 320
    objects, 13, 14
    parameters, 15, 16
    requirements, 5
    Room Manager, 18
    room system, 18
    software ecosystems, 3
    target selection window, 313
    tiers, 3
    variables window, 343
    version, 1, 2
GameMaker fixture properties, 274
GameMaker IDE, *see* Integrated Development Environment (IDE)
GameMaker Language (GML), 1, 10, 25, 27, 126
    application surface, 369
    attribute, 45
    basic camera-related functions, 166, 167
    basic functions for manipulate audio, 127, 128
    blend modes, 357
    break keyword, 36
    clearing effects, 177
    code blocks, 53
    code commenting, 32
    collisions, 194–197
    common constants for keyboard input functions, 132, 133
    comparison operators, 30
    components, 27
    compound operators, 29
    conditional logic, 30
    constants, 32
    create event for obj_Zoomcam, 172, 173
    data structure, 51
    data structures, 48

INDEX

data types, 27
do/until loop, 35
DS grids, 48, 49, 51
DS map, 52
DS queues, 57–59
DS stacks, 56, 57
dynamic layers, 170, 171
effect layers, 175
elements, 66
enumeration, 32
file operation functions, 55
file operations, 53
functions, 284
gamepads, 303, 304
game_restart and *game_end*, 39
hierarchies
    DS lists, 51
inheritance, 41
item_names, 45
JSON data, 53
keyboard functions, 133
layer properties, 170, 171
lengthdir_x and lengthdir_y, 197, 198
for loop, 36
loops, 33
macros, 32
math functions, 37
modulo operator, 37
motion planning functions, 213, 214
objects, 65
obj_Turnip, 41
obj_Vegetable, 41
obj_Zoomcam, 171, 172
OOP, 43
path properties, 216, 217
path-related functions, 222, 223
pause-related audio functions, 129, 130
point method, 32

programming languages, 28
queues, 58
random numbers, 34
remapping keys, 135
repeat loop, 34
retrieve effects parameters, 176
segments, 34
set up camera, 166, 167
sharing methods, 63
static variables, 29
string conditional, 31
struct instantiation, 63
structs, 61, 63–65
SWF and SVG file
    manipulation, 383
switch case, 38
3D array, 47
3D audio system, 207
tileset management, 180, 181
typing in names, 134
values for path_endaction, 217
variables, 27, 31
variable scope, 40
visual functions, 66
visualization, particle
    pipeline, 161
volume-related audio functions,
    130, 131
while loop, 33
ZoomDemo, 171
GameMaker scripts, 94
GameMaker's physics, 250, *see* Physics
GameMakersurface workflow, 362, 363
GameMaker visual functions
    alpha value, 78
    asset browser, 68
    blend modes, 78
    collision mask, 101

INDEX

GameMaker visual functions (*cont.*)
   depth value, 76
   documentation, 97, 98
   drawing pipeline, 117
   image editor, 69, 70
   image formats, 71
   infinity, 100
   numeric value, 101
   operations, 77
   orthographic camera, 77
   PNGs, 71
   prototype, 105
   script/function, 98
   sprite editor, 68
   sprite layers, 70
   surface, 75, 76
   2D game development, 67
Gamemaking, 3
Gamepads, 298
   analog input, 302
   analog sticks, 304
   Async System, 301, 302
   button constants, 303, 304
   collision, 310
   components, 298, 299
   demonstration, 308
   functions, 303
   game controller, 304, 305
   gamepad_get_description, 306
   GUID, 305
   instance_create_layer, 309
   Linux, 298
   objects, 306
   obj_Obstacle, 306, 309
   obj_Participant, 306, 307, 309
   obj_Projectile, 306, 310
   pausing games, 305
   place_meeting, 306
   point_direction, 309
   text_color, 307
   Twin Stick Fun with Gamepads, 299, 300
   vibration, 302
   Xinput, 298
Game prototypes, 119
Gear joint, 265–267
Globally unique identifier (GUID), 305
global.mask_list, 184
global.mouse_targeting, 261
global.our_grid, 225, 226
Global variables, 40
Global video game industry, 2
GML, *see* GameMaker Language (GML)
GML Paths, 220
   clear_arrows, 220, 221
   make_happy_path, 220, 221
   obj_Arrow, 222
   path_add_point, 220
   path_rotate, 220, 221
   random_range, 221
Graphics memory, 371
GUI, 369
GUID, *see* Globally unique identifier (GUID)
GX.games, 314, 315

H

happy_direction, 190, 192
happy_tile_collision, 186, 187
Health variable, 29
HTML5
   Create Executable, 325
   device editor window, 324, 325

settings, 326, 327
target selection window, 324

I

IDE, *see* Integrated Development Environment (IDE)
image_angle, 191, 196, 198
Immersive_Audio_Demo, 209, 210
Inheritance-based hierarchies
    1D arrays, 44
    generic character, 42
    obj_Enemy, 42
    obj_StaticEntity, 42
instance_create_depth, 112
instance_deactivate_all, 193
Instance IDs, 184
instance_number, 114
instance_place function
    bounding boxes, 353
    collision mechanics, 355
    formula, 355
    implementation, 355
    obj_MovingFoe, 354
    obj_MovingPlatform, 352
    properties, 355
Integrated Development Environment (IDE)
    assets, 8
    layers added, 168, 169
    paths, 215
    room editor, 8
    settings for views, 164, 165
    toolbar, 8
    views, 165–167
    workspace, 8
Invisible objects, 182–184
io_clear, 136
iOS, 322, 323

J

JavaScript Object Notation (JSON), 53
JollyLayer, 185, 187
JollyTilemaps, 181, 182
JSON, *see* JavaScript Object Notation (JSON)

K

Keyboard buffer, 132
keyboard_check_direct, 133
keyboard_check_pressed, 132, 351
keyboard_clear, 135, 136
Keyboard control
    keyboard buffer, 132
    keyboard check, 132, 133
    keyboard_clear, 135, 136
    keyboard_set_map, 134
    keyboard_unset_map, 135
    Ord function, 133
    typing in names, 134
keyboard_set_map, 134
keyboard_string, 134
keyboard_unset_map, 135
Kinematic objects, 236

L

Last-in-first-out (LIFO), 56
Layer creation screen, 20
Layers, 20
lengthdir_x, 197, 198
lengthdir_y, 197, 198

INDEX

LIFO, *see* Last-in-first-out (LIFO)
Linux, 318–320
Linux version, 5
LiquidFun, 232, 241–243, 247, 250
Live zooming, 171
Loops, 33
Lossy format, 71

M

Machine language, 22
macOS, 298, 320–322
make_colour_rgb, 117
Moments, 285, 286
Motion planning, 212
    A*, 212
    collision avoidance, 212
    functions, 213, 214
    lower value, 214
    maxrot values, 214
    mp_linear_step, 213
    mp_linear_step_
        object, 213, 214
    mp_potential_settings, 213
    mp_potential_step, 213, 214
    Pathfinding, 212
    rotstep values, 214
    set onspot, 214
Motorized joints, 246
mouse_check_button, 187
mp_grid_add_instances, 226
mp_grid_draw, 229
mp_grid_path, 226
mp_linear_step, 213
mp_linear_step_object, 213, 214
mp_potential_step, 213, 214
mp_potential_step_object, 214
Multidimensional array, 46

N

NaN, *see* Not a number (NaN)
Newton's laws of motion, 232
    Box2D physics system, 232
    first law, 233
    second law, 233
    third law, 233
    universal gravitation, 233
Nintendo Switch, 333
Not a number (NaN), 99

O

obj_Arrow, 221, 222
obj_Bonus, 201
obj_Bullet features, 113, 155
obj_Car, 239, 253, 254
obj_Catcher, 150, 151
obj_Controller, 152, 184, 185, 187,
        224–226, 261, 264, 273
    Create event, 377
    Step event, 339, 379
Object-oriented language, 43
Object-oriented programming
        (OOP), 42, 43
object_set_persistent function, 285
obj_EmitterDoppler, 209
obj_EmitterMoving, 209
obj_Enemy, 154
obj_Fiend, 224–229
obj_Invisible, 183–185
obj_JointSystem, 245, 247
obj_Kiwi, 218
obj_Orbiter, 218, 219
obj_Platform, 356
obj_Player, 112, 154, 166, 182,
        190–193, 197

INDEX

collision checks, 353, 354
keyboard_check function, 351, 352
movements, 354
obj_MovingFoe, 355
place_meeting function, 352
properties, 351
obj_Robot, 199–201
obj_Sensorblock, 239
obj_Slower, 194
obj_Spawner, 241
obj_Starfield, 116, 117
obj_SurfaceController, 364
    Create event, 363
    Draw event, 365
obj_Teleporter, 200
obj_UAP, 183, 185–187
obj_Ufo, 150, 151
obj_Weldjoints, 255
obj_Zoomcam, 171, 172
OGG format, 124
    lossy/compressed file format, 124
    nonlossy/uncompressed audio, 124
    streamed type of sound, 124
Ogg Vorbis, 124
OOP, *see* Object-oriented programming (OOP)
Opcodes, 23
Opera, 2
Optimization, 21
Orbiter Paths, 218, 219
    functions, 219
    path_flip, 219
    path_get_length, 219
    path_get_name, 219
    path_mirror, 219
    path_shift, 219

P

Parent-child relationships, 41, 400
part_emitter_burst, 146
part_emitter_destroy, 156, 161, 162
part_emitter_exists, 157
part_emitter_region, 145
Partial game visuals, 73
Particle Collision Demo, 149
Particle_Fun, 143
Particles, 136
    collision demo, 149
    create new particles, 145
    create new shapes, 142
    definitions, 139
    emitters, 139
    emitters and types of regions, 145, 146
    fire particles, 143
    IDE particle system, 159
    memory management, 155–157
    obj_Bullet, 155
    obj_Catcher, 150, 151
    obj_Controller, 150
    obj_Enemy, 154
    obj_Player, 154
    obj_Ufo, 151
    on-screen, 157
    part_emitter_burst, 146
    particle definition functions, 140
    particle streams, 147
    particle system, 139
    part_particles_count, 157
    part_particles_create, 148
    part_type_size, 141
    shape-related definitions, 140, 141
    simple effects, 137
    simple GML visual effect types, 137
    simple particles, 137

INDEX

Particles (*cont.*)
   size_min, 141
   speed_wiggle, 142
   sprite-based collisions, 148
   stop and hide, 158
   unmanaged particle systems, 139
   wobbly pyramids with particle groups, 247–250
Particles recap, 160, 161
Particle streams, 147
part_particles_clear, 157
part_particles_count, 157
part_particles_create, 148
part_particles_create_colour, 148
Part_system_automatic_draw, 158
part_system_automatic_update, 158
part_system_clear, 157
part_system_create(), 145
part_system_depth, 143
part_system_destroy, 156, 161
part_system_drawit, 158
part_type_color2, 151
part_type_create, 148, 156
part_type_destroy, 156
part_type_shape, 141, 151
path_add, 216
path_add_point, 216
path_endaction, 216, 217
Pathfinding, 212
path_index, 216, 217
Paths, 215, 216, 220
   common path functions, 222, 223
   and drawing grids, 229, 230
   dynamic paths, 216, 217
   in IDE-based editor, 215
   main properties, 217
   our_path, 216
   path_add_point and path_set_kind, 217
   path editor, 216
   path_endaction, 216, 217
   path_index, 216, 217
   path-related parameters, 219
   path_speed, 216
   path_start, 216, 222, 226
   Shift Path, 216
   See also GML Paths
path_set_kind, 217, 221
path_speed, 216
path_start, 216, 222, 226
Persistent objects, 284
phy_particle_group_flag_rigid, 249, 250
phy_particle_group_flag_solid, 249
Physics, 275
   Ad Hoc Physics Objects, 272
   change mass and inertia, 268, 269
   collision categories and parenting, 270
   collision groups *vs.* categories, 271
   Compromised Soccer with ragdolls, 245–247
   distance joint, 252
   FireBullet, 261–263
   gear and pulley joints, 265
   gear joint, 265–267
   good practices in projects, 269, 270
   Happy Physics, project file, 241–244
   obj_Ship, 263
   prismatic joints, 258, 259
   pulley joint, 265, 266, 268
   rope joint, 253, 254
   selection rectangle, 264
   Simple Fixtures, 250–252
   simple physics demonstration, 238–240
   weld joints, 254–256

wheel joints, 256, 257
physics_apply_force, 237–239
physics_apply_impulse, 237, 242, 247, 266, 275
physics_apply_torque, 239, 266
Physics-based objects, 232, 233, 237, 261, 272, 274
Physics engine, 231
    Box2D, 231, 232, 234, 270
    forces (*see* Forces, GameMaker's physics)
    Newton's laws of motion, 232, 233
    object settings
        angular damping, 235
        collision events, 235
        convex and concave shapes, 234
        density, 235
        kinematic, 236
        linear damping, 235
        masks, 234
        restitution, 235
        sensor, 235
        start awake, 236
    rigid-body physics simulation, 231
    soft-body physics, 231
physics_fixture_bind, 254, 255, 257
physics_fixture_create, 252
physics_fixture_delete, 252
physics_fixture_set_collision_group, 271, 273
physics_joint_distance_create, 252, 253
physics_joint_gear_create, 266, 267
physics_joint_prismatic_create, 259
physics_joint_pulley_create, 266, 267
physics_joint_revolute_create, 246
physics_joint_rope_create, 254
physics_joint_weld_create, 256
physics_joint_wheel_create, 257, 258

physics_mass_properties, 268
Physics objects, built in properties, 240
    phy_active, 240
    phy_angular_damping, 240
    phy_bullet, 240
    phy_com_x/phy_com_y, 241
    phy_inertia, 241
    phy_linear_damping, 240
    phy_linear_velocity_x/phy_linear_velocity_y, 240
    phy_mass, 240
    phy_rotation, 240
physics_particle_create, 244, 250
physics_particle_draw, 244
physics_particle_draw_ext, 244
physics_particle_group_add_point, 249
physics_particle_group_begin, 247–249
physics_particle_group_box, 250
physics_particle_group_end, 247
physics_particle_set_max_count, 243, 250
physics_particle_set_radius, 243
Physics Space Combat, 260, 261, 264
physics_world_update_speed(value), 269
Pitch, 126, 128, 131
place_free, 182, 194, 195, 199, 200
place_meeting, 194, 195
Platformer Prototype
    features, 349, 350
    grid controls, 355
    screenshot, 350
PlayStation 4 (PS4), 333
PlayStation 4 (PS5), 333
PNG, *see* Portable Network Graphics (PNG)

INDEX

PNOG, 105, 107–109
Port, 325
Portable Network Graphics (PNG), 71
Precautions and good practices, reduce issues
    array_length, 336
    audio_is_playing, 336
    data structures, deletion, 337
    depth/visibility, 338
    event descriptions, 338
    functions, 340
    inheritance, 338
    instance_exists/instance_number, 335
    instance_number, 335
    instance optimization, 339
    Outside Room event, 336
    search and replace, 340, 341
    Step event, 339
    text alignment, 338
    variables, 336, 337, 340
    viewport size, 340
prev_thingy, 255, 256
Primitive, 79
    alarm, 84
    circle and ellipse, 82
    clamp, 81
    color presets, 80
    draw_roundrect_colour_ext, 81
    draw_set_color, 79
    draw_set_halign, 91
    outlined in Table, 81
    rectangle, 80
    triangle, 86, 87
    vertex formats, 87
    visuals elements, 79
Programming abstraction, 22
Pulley joint, 265, 266, 268
Pythagorean theorem, 95

Q

QOI, *see* Quite OK Image Format (QOI)
Quite OK Image Format (QOI), 391

R

RAM, 343
Raster formats, 72
Real-time audio effects, 287, 288
Rigid-body physics simulation, 231

S

Saving and Loading project
    audio functions, 376
    custom functions, 380
    draw_roundrect, 378
    draw_roundrect_ext, 378
    file_exists, 377
    file_text_read_real, 378
    file_text_read_string, 378
    keyboard_string, 380
    max_items, 377, 379
    music_volume/sound_volume, 379, 380
    obj_Controller, 376, 377, 379
    save_happy_settings, 377
    screenshot, 375, 376
    string_length, 380
Scripts, 95
SDF, *see* Signed distance field (SDF)
SDKs, *see* Software development kits (SDKs)
Sensor, 235
Sequences, 277
    aforementioned object, 283
    animations, 278
    broadcast message, 280, 282

INDEX

canvas, 278
Curious_Sequence, 286
events, 283
GML functions, 284
keyframe controls, 278, 279
menu moments, 285
    AssignButtonMessages, 286, 287
    buttons, 287
    inline function, 287
    obj_Button, 286
obj_Button, 284
obj_FadeInOut, 284
Penguin_sequence, 281, 282
playhead, 283
properties, 279
room transitions, 283
simple_sequence, 281
simple sequence, 279, 280
simplified view, 278
track panel, 279
Signed distance field (SDF), 92
silly_zoom_direction, 173
Simple Fixtures, 250–254, 256, 258
Simple Physics, 238
Single-layer mode, 176
Soft-body particles, 241–244, 250
Software development kits (SDKs), 23, 333
Sound Group Mixer, 125
Space Heck, 110
SpaceHeck02, 152
Spawning robots, 200, 201
Spheroid, 265, 266
Sprite editor, 68, 396
Sprite-related attributes, 103
Sprite sheets, 387–389
spr_Player, 352
Structs, 61–62
superior_scripts, 189, 191

Surfaces
    crafted scenes, 371
    creation, 364
    draw_surface, 365, 366
    draw_surface_ext, 365, 366
    functions, 363, 364, 371
    graphics memory, 371
    metallic_backdrop, 366
    screenshots, 370
    surface_exists, 371
    surface_resize, 370, 371
    surf_one, 363
    surf_two, 363
Surface Tomfoolery, 361–364
Switch case demonstration, 38

T

Tank Merriment, 187, 188
    bonus items, 201
    collision masks, 195–197, 199
    Combat, 189
    create event, obj_Player1, 190–192
    duplicate obj_Player1, 193
    features, 187, 188
    function gburst, 190
    function pburst, 190
    health rating, 189
    layers, 203
    lengthdir_x and lengthdir_y, 197, 198
    objects, 199
    obj_Slower, 194
    particle fences, 201, 202
    pause game with GML, 193, 194
    robots in a Maze, 199, 200
    shells, 189
    spawning robots, 200, 201
    superior_scripts, 189, 191

INDEX

Tank Merriment (*cont.*)
    two-player video game, 188
    views and cameras, 202, 203
    WASD control method, 188
Texture filtering, 103
Texture groups
    default *vs.* dynamic, 392, 393
    setting, 389, 390
        allow scaling, 390
        automatically crop, 390
        border size, 391
        format, 391
        mipmaps, 390
        parent texture group, 391
        type, 391
        Use group on, 391
    texture swap, 389
    window, 389, 390
Texture group window, 74
Texture swap, 74
    dimensions, 75
    optimization, 75
    presentation, 75
3D audio, 122, 124, 207
    vs. 2D audio, 122
3D audio system
    audio_emitter_create, 208
    audio_emitter_falloff, 208
    audio_emitter_position, 208
    audio_falloff_set_model, 209
    audio_listener_orientation, 208, 209
    audio_listener_position, 208
    audio_play_sound_on, 209
    Doppler effect, 209, 211
    functions, 207
    Immersive_Audio_Demo, 209
    immersive audio demo with spatial sound sources, 211
    obj_DopplerEmitter, 211
    obj_Emitter, 209
    obj_EmitterDoppler, 209
    obj_EmitterMoving, 209
    tinder_emitter, 208
    volume attenuation models, 210
3D GML arrays, 47
16-tile auto-tiling, 179
47-tile auto-tiling, 179
Tile-based animations, 178
TilemapCollisions, 183–186, 204
tilemap_get_at_pixel, 182, 183, 185
Tilemaps, 167, 182
    collisions with tilemap_get_at_pixel, 182
    TilemapCollisions, 183, 184
Tilesets, 19, 177, 204
    auto-tiling, 179, 180
    basic process, 177, 178
    happy_tile_collision, 186, 187
    integrate collisions with invisible objects, 182
    JollyTilemaps, 181, 182
    layers, 183
    management, 180, 181
    obj_UAP, 186, 187
    Tile Animation, 178
    and tile layers, 177, 178
    TilemapCollisions project, 183, 184
    visual resource, 177
tinder_emitter, 208, 212
Touch-screen controls, 344, 346, 347
Troubleshooting, undetected devices, 323, 324
2D audio *vs.* 3D audio, 122
2D audio system, 207

U

Universal gravitation, 233
Universal Windows Platform (UWP), 3
Untamed bugs, 334, 335
UWP, *see* Universal Windows Platform (UWP)

V

Valve Software, 398
Variable scope, 40, 336
Vector graphics, 381, 382, 384
Vector images, 72
Vertex-based primitives, 87, 88
Vertical text alignment, 91
Video playback, 394, 395
Viewports, 163, 164
Visual assets, 73
Visual Studio
　Windows, 317
　YYC, 317, 318

W

WASD control method, 188

W3C, *see* World Wide Web Consortium (W3C)
Web Server Address, 325
Web Server Port, 325
Wheel joints, 252, 256, 257
While loop, 33, 34
Windows, 1, 132, 160, 316–318
Windows ecosystem, 3
World Wide Web Consortium (W3C), 381

X

Xbox games, 334
Xcode, 323

Y

YoYo Compiler, 23
YoYo Games, 2, 4

Z

ZoomDemo, 171, 172

GPSR Compliance

The European Union's (EU) General Product Safety Regulation (GPSR) is a set of rules that requires consumer products to be safe and our obligations to ensure this.

If you have any concerns about our products, you can contact us on

ProductSafety@springernature.com

In case Publisher is established outside the EU, the EU authorized representative is:

Springer Nature Customer Service Center GmbH
Europaplatz 3
69115 Heidelberg, Germany